DARK HORSE NUMBER ONES

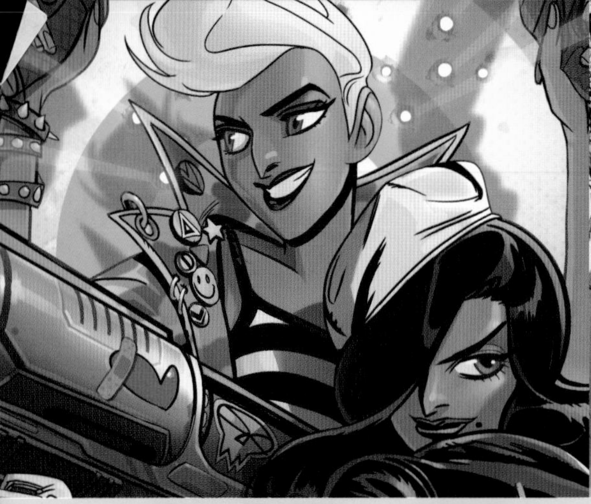

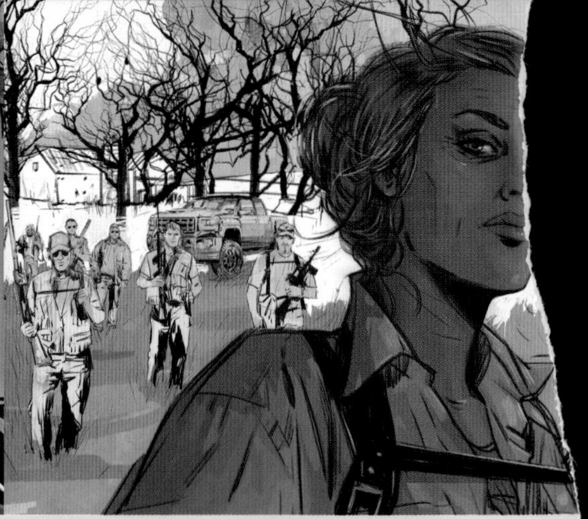

DARK HORSE NUMBER ONES

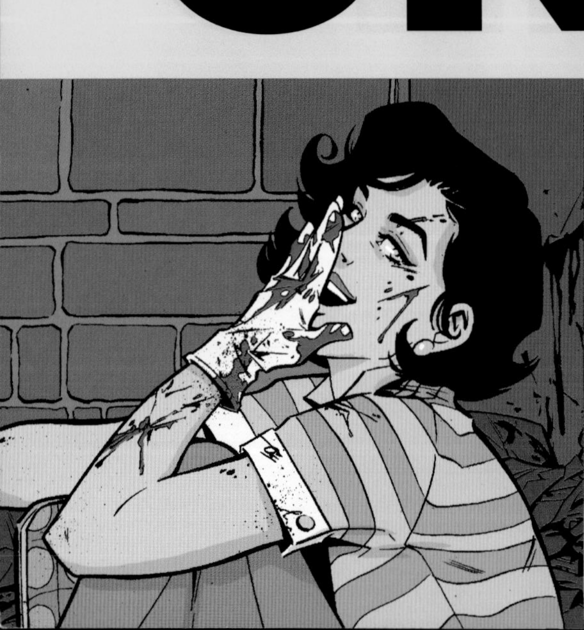

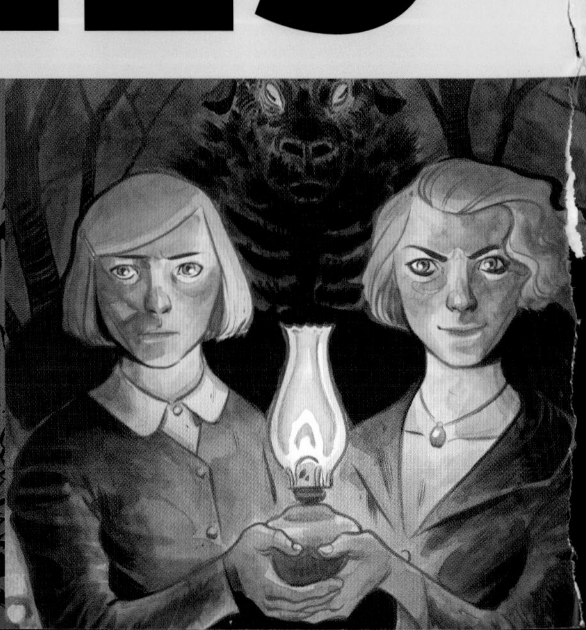

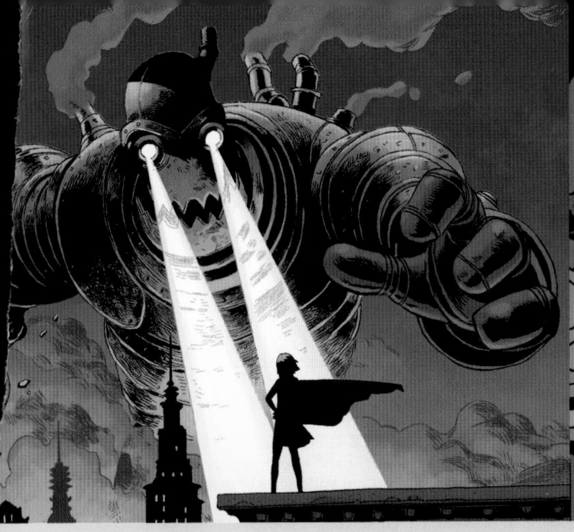
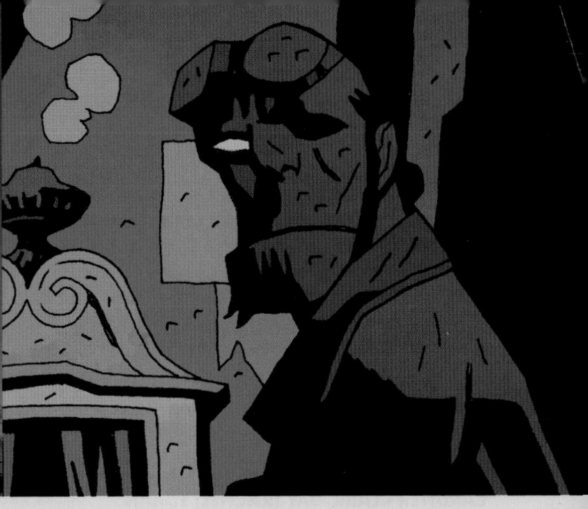

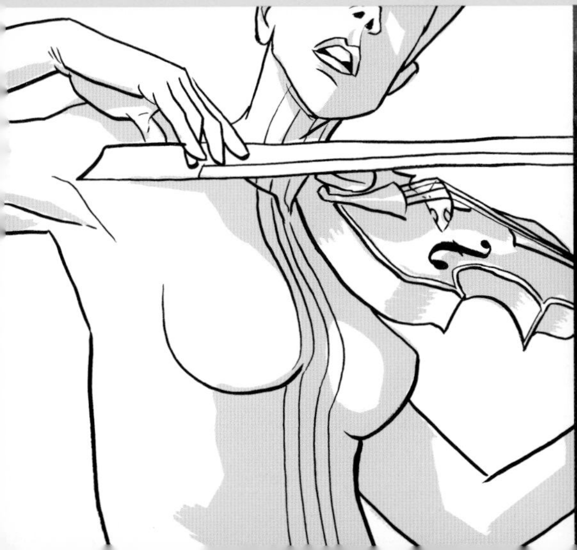
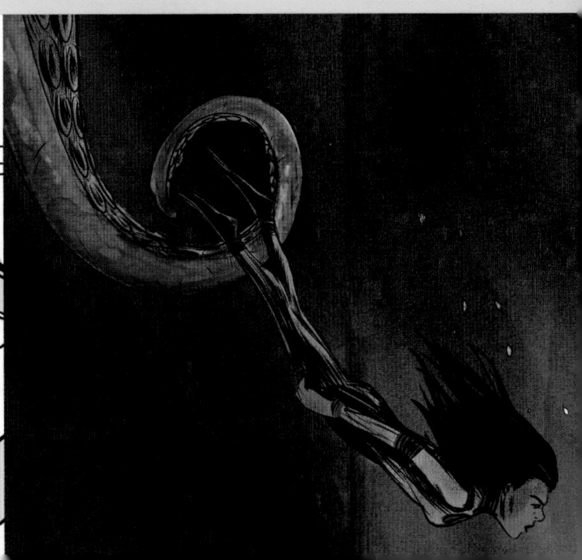

MIKE RICHARDSON
PRESIDENT AND PUBLISHER

**SCOTT ALLIE, DANIEL CHABON,
SPENCER CUSHING, BRENDAN WRIGHT**
ORIGINAL SERIES EDITORS

**KEVIN BURKHALTER, DANIEL CHABON,
CARDNER CLARK, JAY (RACHEL) EDIDIN,
SIERRA HAHN, JEMIAH JEFFERSON,
SHANTEL LaROCQUE, IAN TUCKER**
ORIGINAL SERIES ASSISTANT EDITORS

**DANIEL CHABON,
HANNAH MEANS-SHANNON**
COLLECTED EDITION EDITORS

JIMMY PRESLER
COLLECTION DESIGNER

MELISSA MARTIN
DIGITAL ART TECHNICIAN

NEIL HANKERSON
EXECUTIVE VICE PRESIDENT

TOM WEDDLE
CHIEF FINANCIAL OFFICER

RANDY STRADLEY
VICE PRESIDENT OF PUBLISHING

MATT PARKINSON
VICE PRESIDENT OF MARKETING

DAVID SCROGGY
VICE PRESIDENT OF PRODUCT DEVELOPMENT

DALE LaFOUNTAIN
VICE PRESIDENT OF INFORMATION TECHNOLOGY

CARA NIECE
VICE PRESIDENT OF PRODUCTION AND SCHEDULING

NICK McWHORTER
VICE PRESIDENT OF MEDIA LICENSING

MARK BERNARDI
VICE PRESIDENT OF DIGITAL AND BOOK TRADE SALES

KEN LIZZI
GENERAL COUNSEL

DAVE MARSHALL
EDITOR IN CHIEF

DAVEY ESTRADA
EDITORIAL DIRECTOR

SCOTT ALLIE
EXECUTIVE SENIOR EDITOR

CHRIS WARNER
SENIOR BOOKS EDITOR

CARY GRAZZINI
DIRECTOR OF SPECIALTY PROJECTS

LIA RIBACCHI
ART DIRECTOR

VANESSA TODD
DIRECTOR OF PRINT PURCHASING

MATT DRYER
DIRECTOR OF DIGITAL ART AND PREPRESS

SARAH ROBERTSON
DIRECTOR OF PRODUCT SALES

MICHAEL GOMBOS
DIRECTOR OF INTERNATIONAL PUBLISHING AND LICENSING

This volume collects issue #1 of *The Umbrella Academy: Apocalypse Suite*, originally published in 2007; issue #1 of *Lady Killer*, originally published in 2015; issue #1 of *Black Hammer*, originally published in 2016; issue #1 of *Dept. H*, originally published in 2016; issue #1 of *Briggs Land*, originally published in 2016; issue #1 of *Bounty*, originally published in 2016; issue #1 of *Harrow County*, originally published in 2015; and issue #1 of *Hellboy in Hell*, originally published in 2012; all from Dark Horse Comics.

Published by Dark Horse Books
A division of Dark Horse Comics, Inc.
10956 SE Main Street
Milwaukie, OR 97222

DarkHorse.com

International Licensing: 503-905-2377

To find a comics shop in your area,
call the Comic Shop Locator Service toll-free at 1-888-266-4226.

Library of Congress Cataloging-in-Publication Data

Names: Way, Gerard, author. | Bá, Gabriel, illustrator. | Jones, Joëlle, author, illustrator. | Rich, Jamie S., author. | Lemire, Jeff, author. | Ormston, Dean, illustrator. | Kindt, Matt, author, illustrator. | Wood, Brian, 1972- author. | Chater, Mack, illustrator. | Wiebe, Kurtis J., 1979- author. | Lee, Mindy, illustrator. | Bunn, Cullen, author. | Crook, Tyler, illustrator. | Mignola, Michael, author, illustrator.
Title: Dark Horse number ones 2017 / [Gerard Way, Gabriel Bá, Joëlle Jones, Jamie S. Rich, Jeff Lemire, Dean Ormston, Matt Kindt, Brian Wood, Mack Chater, Kurtis Wiebe, Mindy Lee, Cullen Bunn, Tyler Crook, Mike Mignola, and thirteen others].
Description: First edition. | Milwaukie, OR : Dark Horse Books, 2017. | "This volume collects issue #1 of The Umbrella Academy: Apocalypse Suite, originally published in 2007; issue #1 of Lady Killer, originally published in 2015; issue #1 of Black Hammer, originally published in 2016; issue #1 of Dept. H., originally published in 2016; issue #1 of Briggs Land, originally published in 2016; issue #1 of Bounty, originally published in 2016; issue #1 of Harrow County, originally published in 2015; and issue #1 of Hellboy in Hell, originally published in 2012; all from Dark Horse Comics"
Identifiers: LCCN 2016036448 | ISBN 9781506702964 (paperback)
Subjects: LCSH: Comic books, strips, etc. | BISAC: COMICS & GRAPHIC NOVELS / Anthologies.
Classification: LCC PN6726 .D367 2017 | DDC 741.5/973–dc23
LC record available at https://lccn.loc.gov/2016036448

First edition: March 2017
ISBN 978-1-50670-296-4

10 9 8 7 6 5 4 3 2 1
Printed in China

WELCOME TO DARK HORSE'S *NUMBER ONES* FOR 2017, bringing you the first issues of eight creator-owned series that are shaping and defining the comics medium today. From the fan favorite *The Umbrella Academy* by Gerard Way and Gabriel Bá to *Hellboy in Hell*, which represents the culmination of over twenty years of creator-driven universe building from Mike Mignola, these stories continue to challenge expectations about what comics are capable of.

The strikingly original female-assassin-led series *Lady Killer* from Joëlle Jones and Jamie S. Rich, the dynamic depth of underwater murder mystery in Matt Kindt's *Dept. H,* and the haunting psychological explorations of defunct superheroes in Jeff Lemire and Dean Ormston's *Black Hammer* set up and then knock down genre barriers to engage readers. Cullen Bunn and Tyler Crook's *Harrow County* uses the lens of its storybook style to redefine horror comics, social drama turns explosive in *Briggs Land* from Brian Wood and Mack Chater, and stylish adventurers take a galactic stage in Kurtis Wiebe and Mindy Lee's *Bounty.*

There is no better way to illustrate the potential of comics than to let these creative teams loose on the page to pursue their passion for crafting an unparalleled experience for the reader. Follow them to exotic locations from the furthest star to the depths of hell, from small towns to research outposts, and take a sidelong glance at what could easily be the house next door.

This volume is the discovery zone for your next must-read series, with bingeable volumes available to take you further into the wild worlds of these stories brought to you straight from the minds and hands of top industry talent.

This is Dark Horse, where creators are Number One.

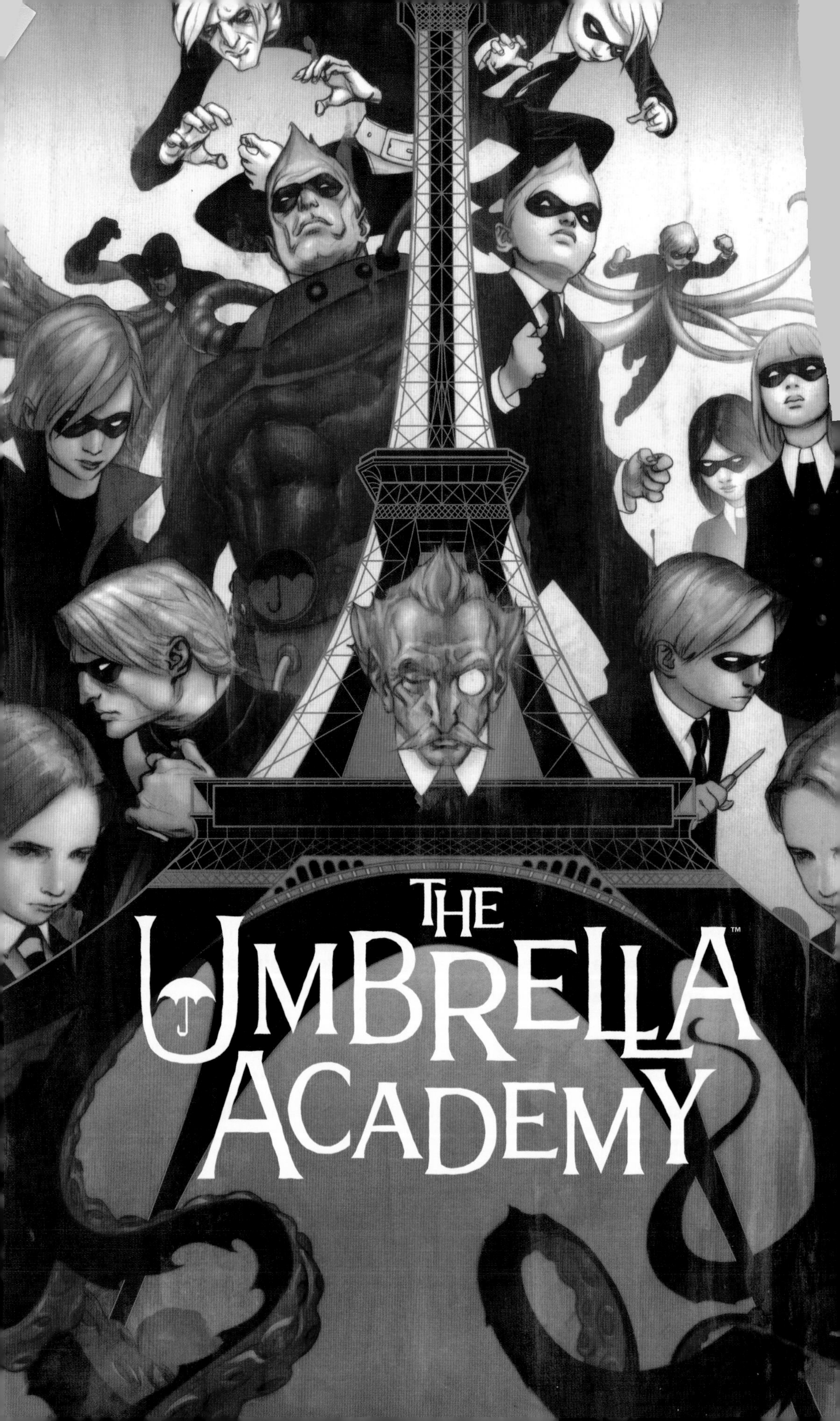
THE UMBRELLA ACADEMY™

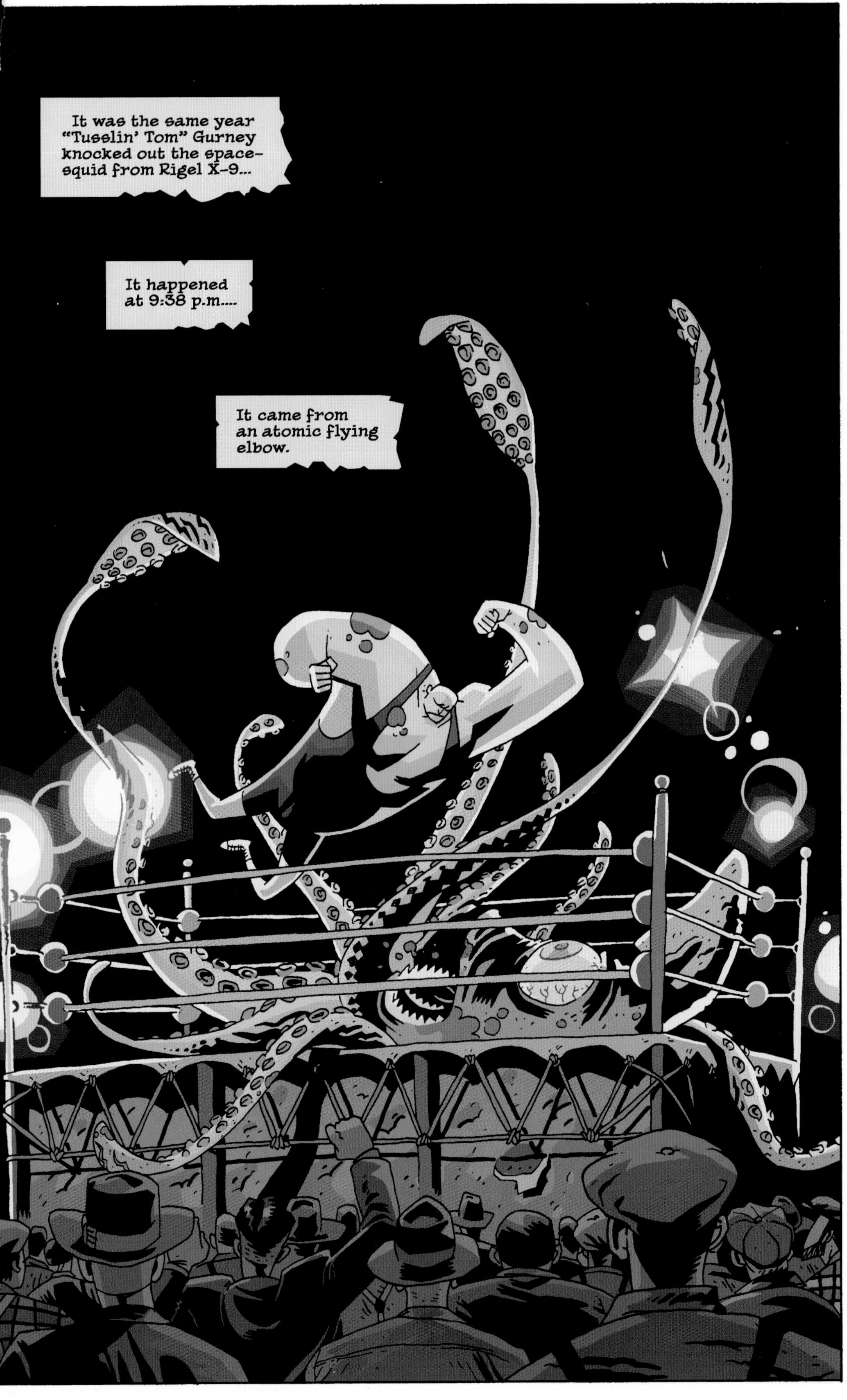
It was the same year "Tusslin' Tom" Gurney knocked out the space-squid from Rigel X-9...
It happened at 9:38 p.m....
It came from an atomic flying elbow.

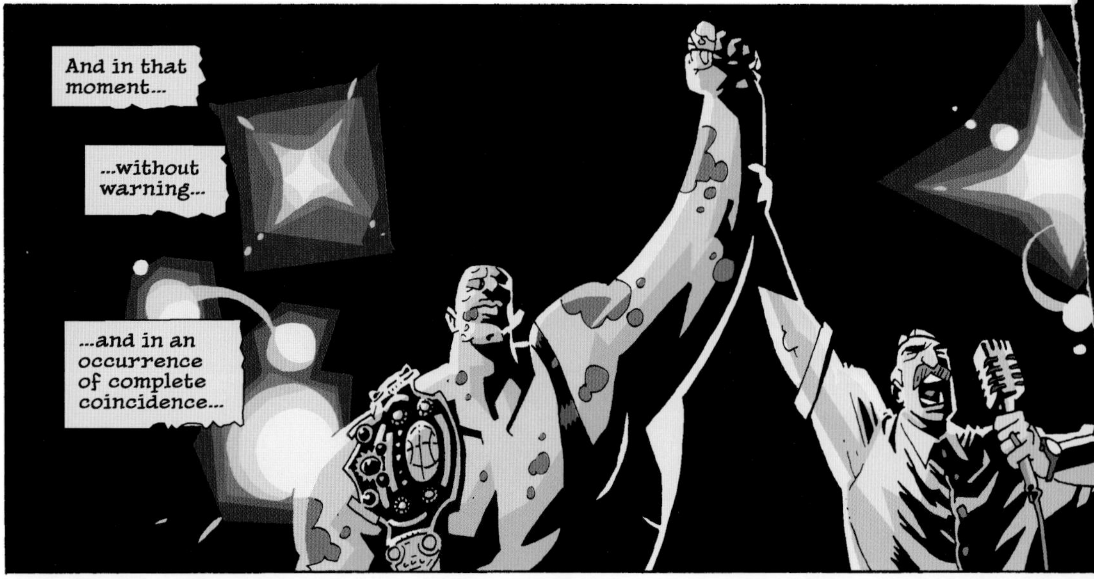
And in that moment...
...without warning...
...and in an occurrence of complete coincidence...

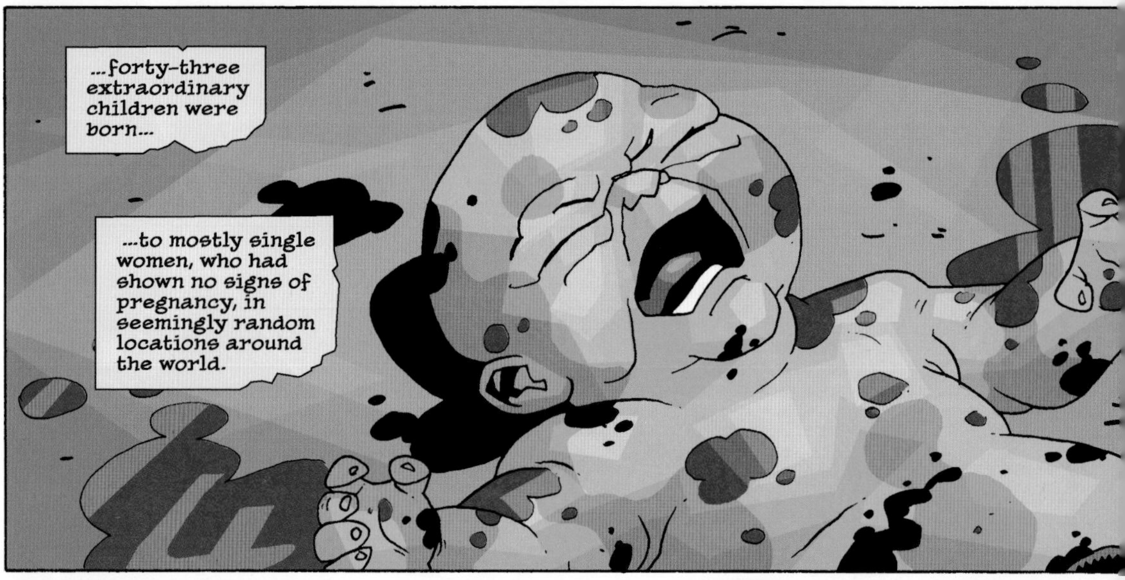
...forty-three extraordinary children were born...
...to mostly single women, who had shown no signs of pregnancy, in seemingly random locations around the world.

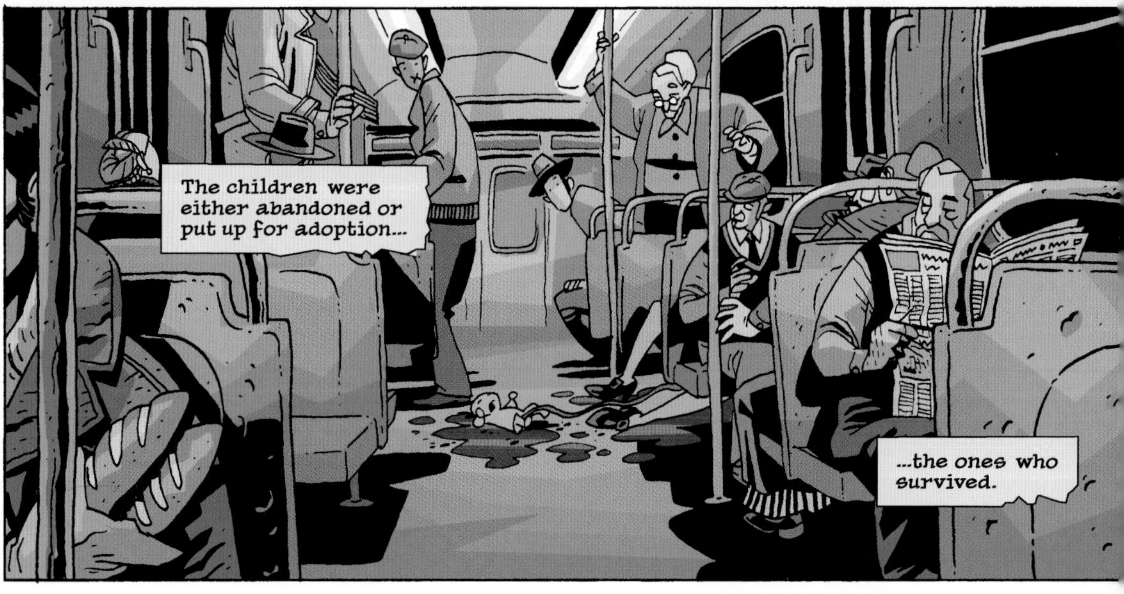
The children were either abandoned or put up for adoption...
...the ones who survived.

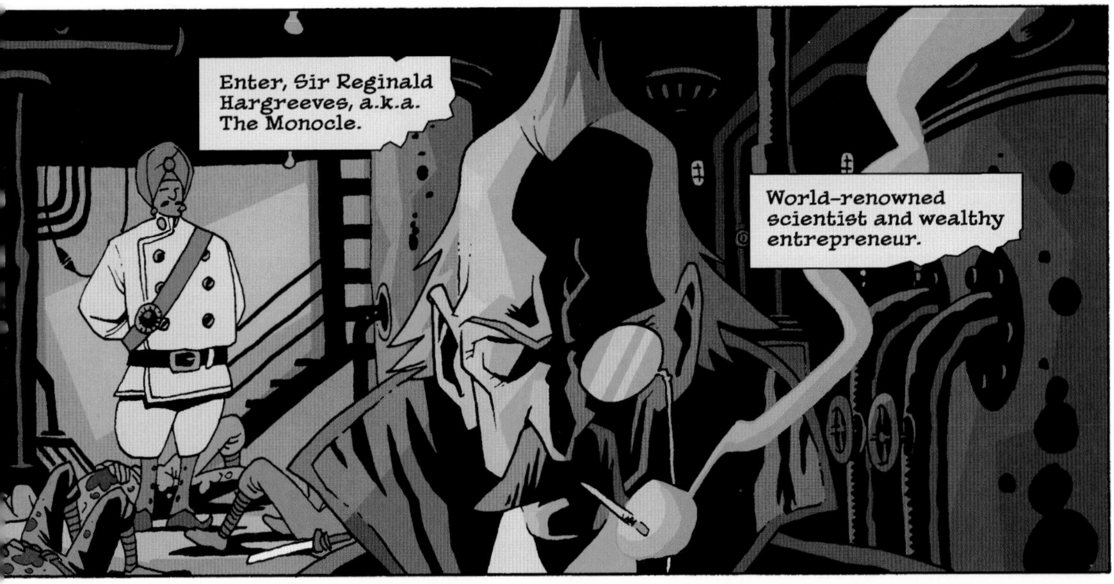
Enter, Sir Reginald Hargreeves, a.k.a. The Monocle.
World-renowned scientist and wealthy entrepreneur.

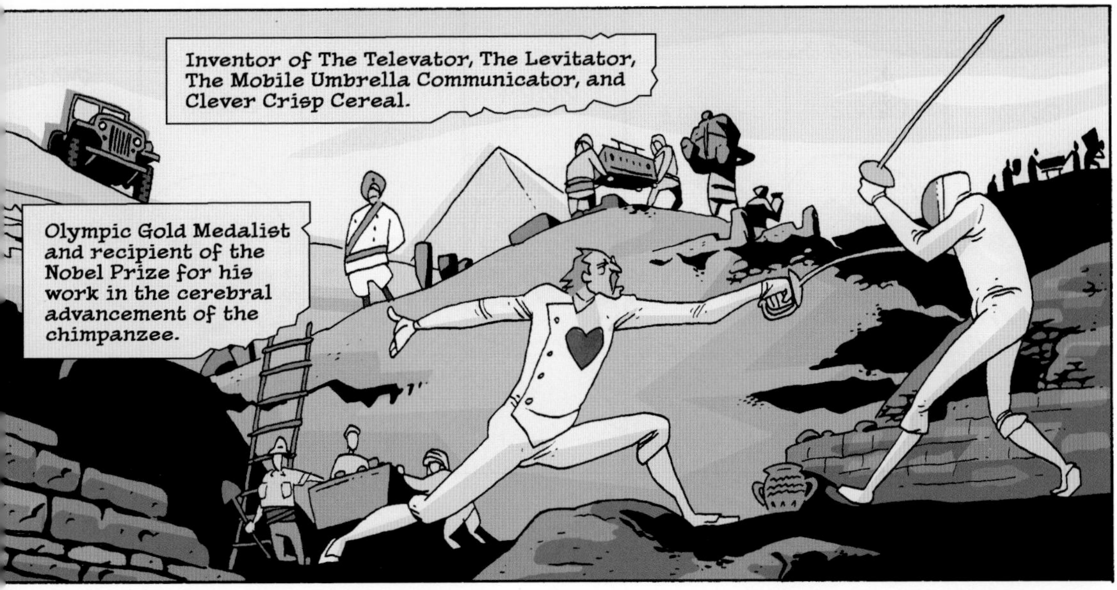
Inventor of The Televator, The Levitator, The Mobile Umbrella Communicator, and Clever Crisp Cereal.
Olympic Gold Medalist and recipient of the Nobel Prize for his work in the cerebral advancement of the chimpanzee.

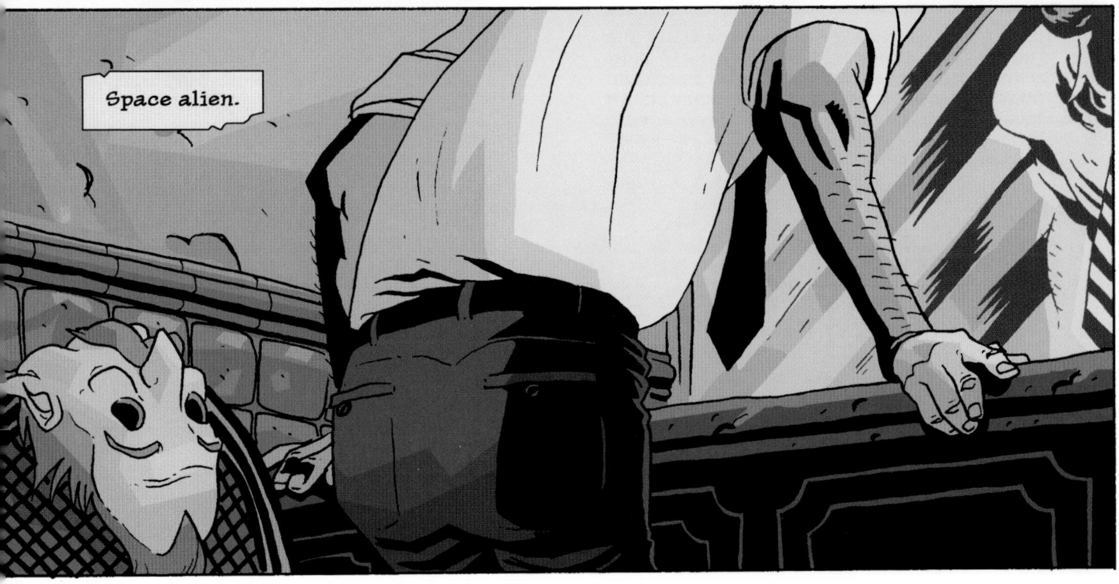
Space alien.

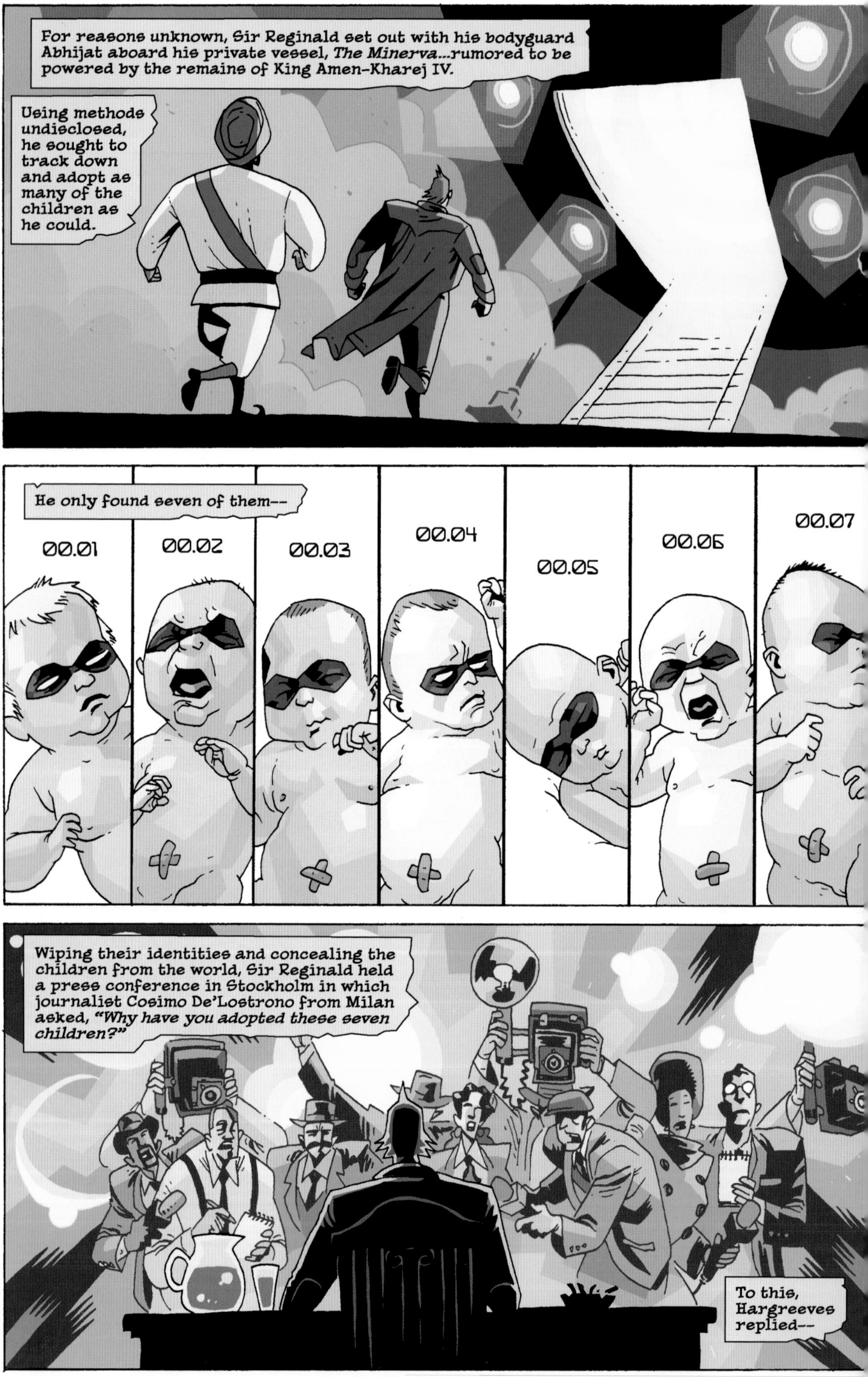
For reasons unknown, Sir Reginald set out with his bodyguard Abhijat aboard his private vessel, *The Minerva*...rumored to be powered by the remains of King Amen-Kharej IV.
Using methods undisclosed, he sought to track down and adopt as many of the children as he could.
He only found seven of them--
00.01
00.02
00.03
00.04
00.05
00.06
00.07
Wiping their identities and concealing the children from the world, Sir Reginald held a press conference in Stockholm in which journalist Cosimo De'Lostrono from Milan asked, *"Why have you adopted these seven children?"*
To this, Hargreeves replied--

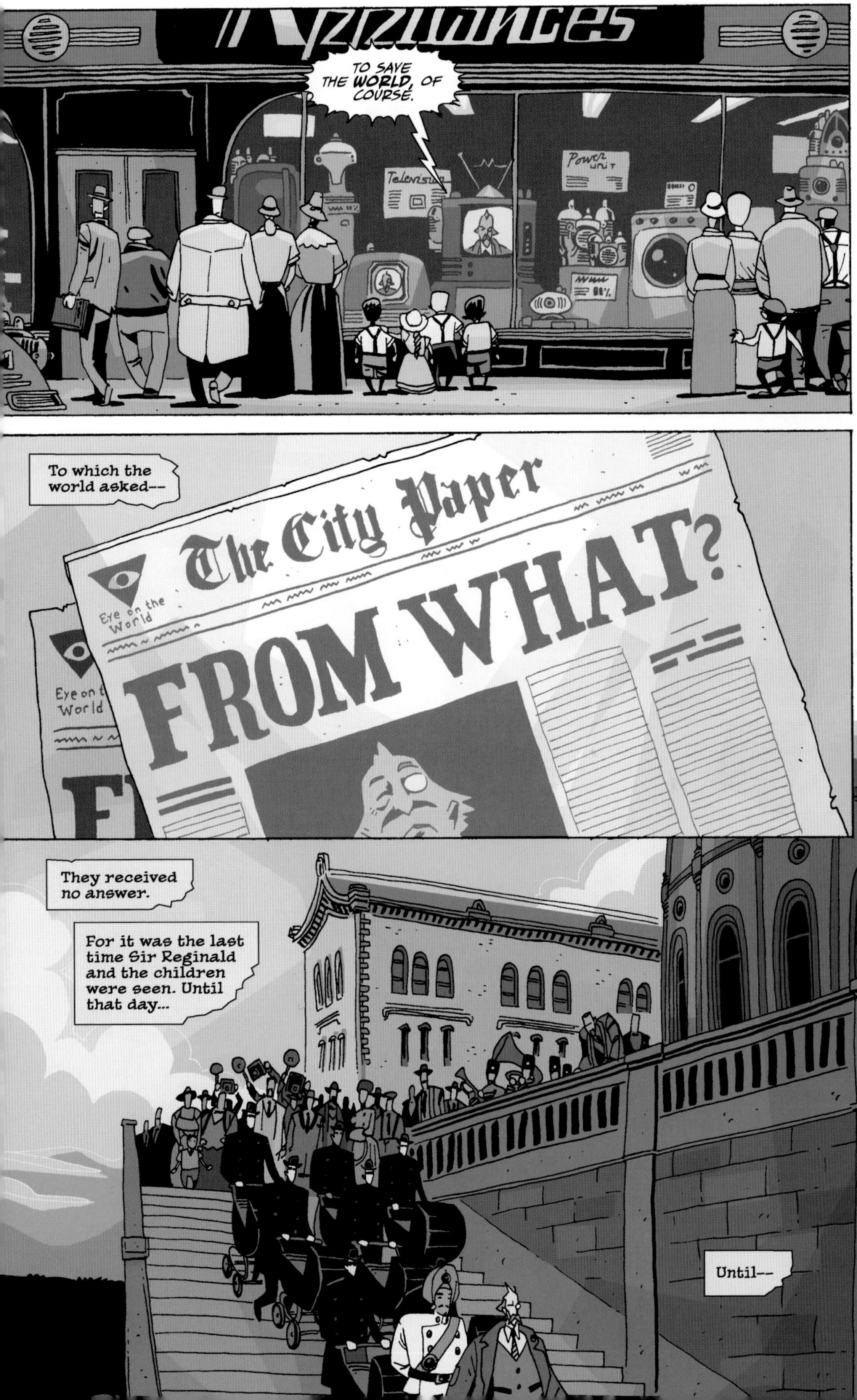
TO SAVE THE WORLD, OF COURSE.
Television
Power unit
To which the world asked--
The City Paper
Eye on the World
FROM WHAT?
They received no answer.
For it was the last time Sir Reginald and the children were seen. Until that day...
Until--

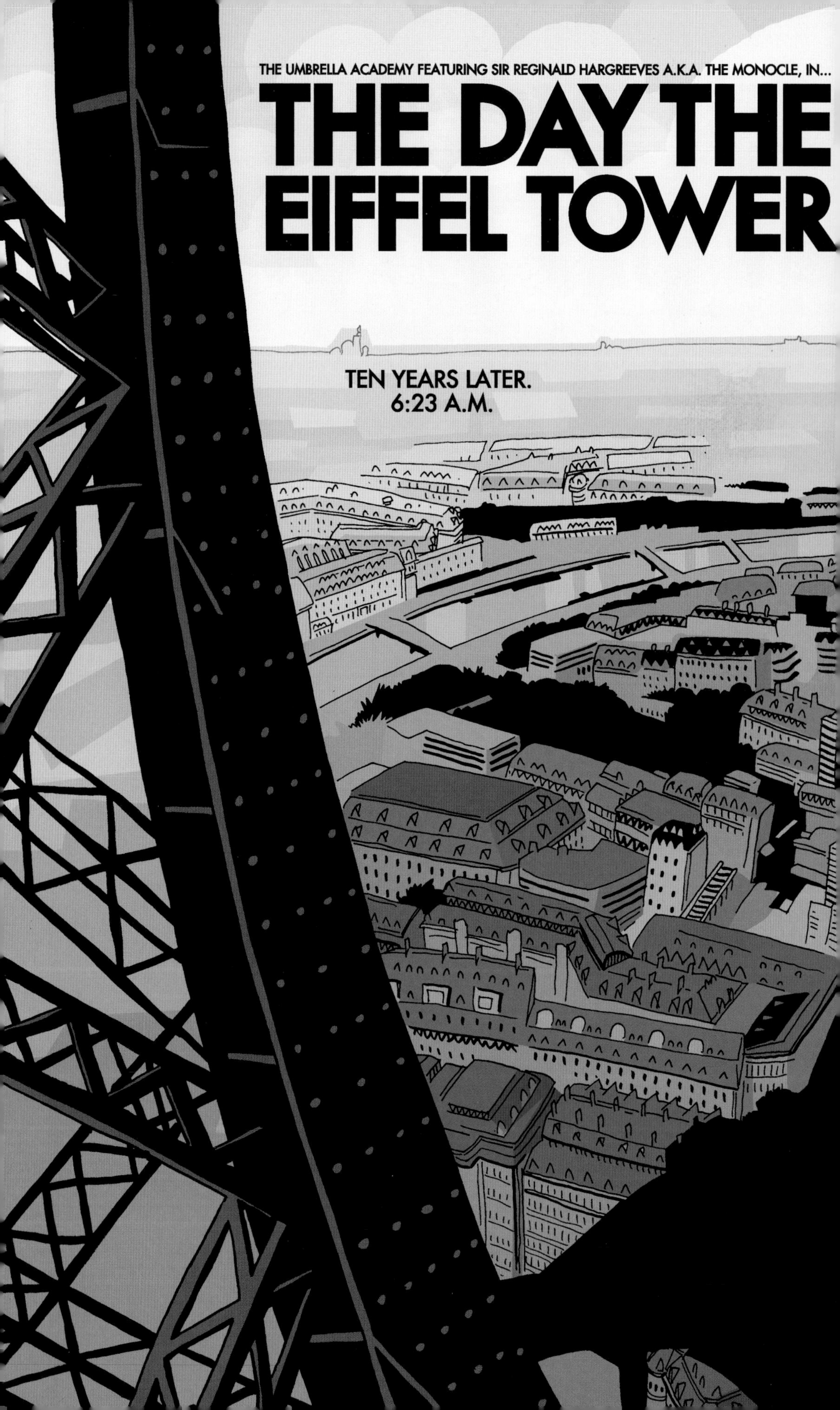
THE UMBRELLA ACADEMY FEATURING SIR REGINALD HARGREEVES A.K.A. THE MONOCLE, IN...
THE DAY THE EIFFEL TOWER
TEN YEARS LATER. 6:23 A.M.

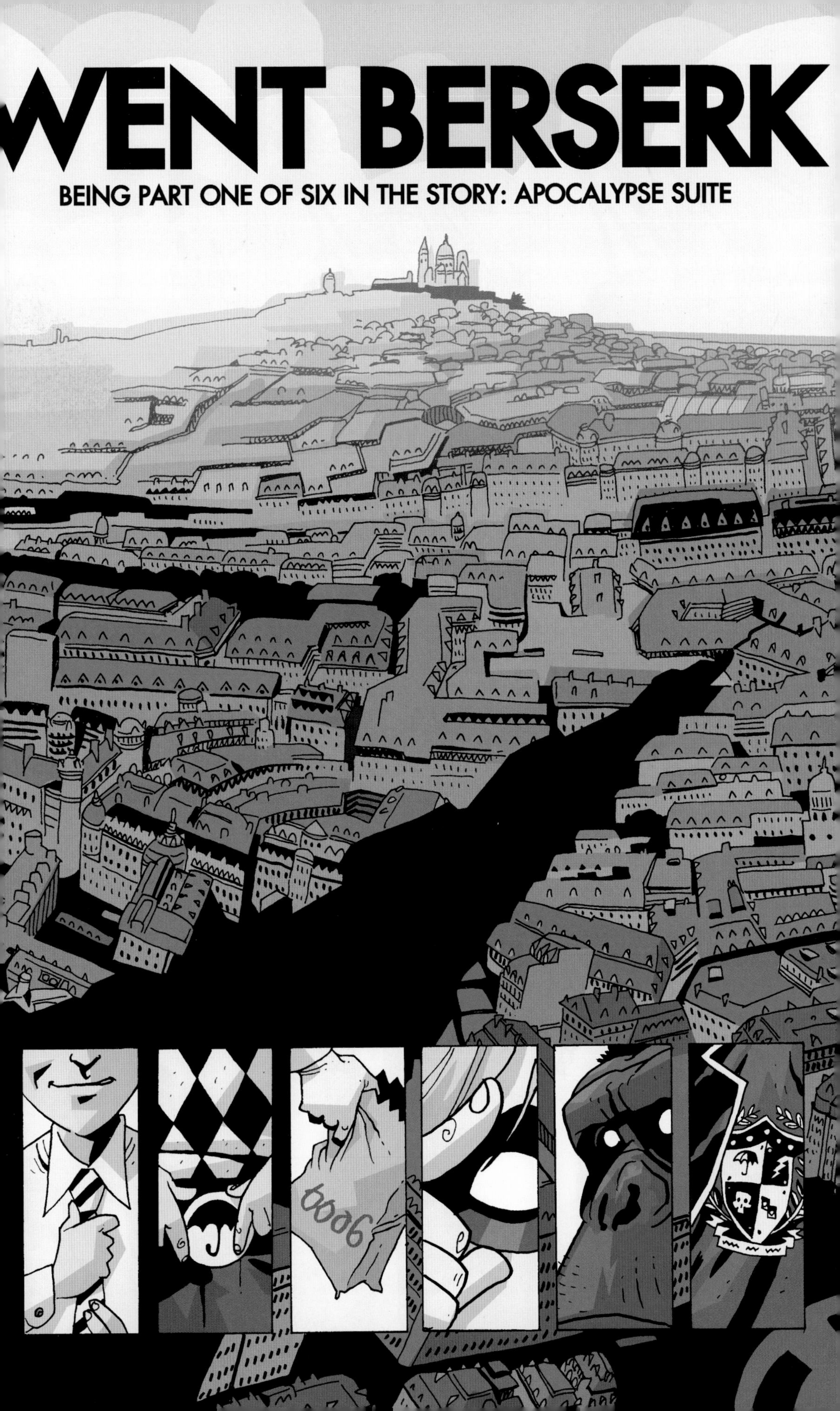
WENT BERSERK
BEING PART ONE OF SIX IN THE STORY: APOCALYPSE SUITE

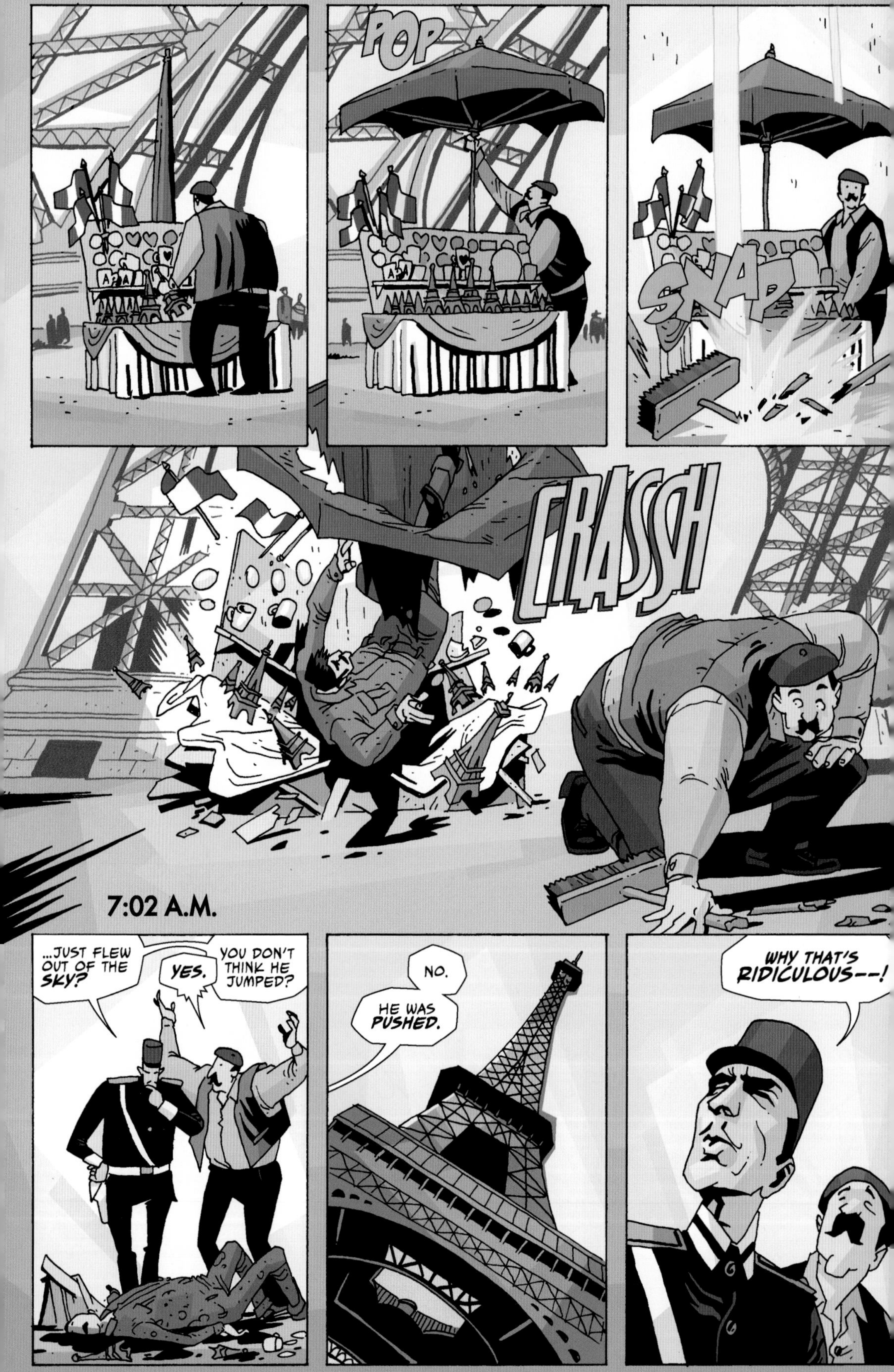
POP
SNAP
CRASSCH
7:02 A.M.
...JUST FLEW OUT OF THE SKY?
YES.
YOU DON'T THINK HE JUMPED?
NO.
HE WAS PUSHED.
WHY THAT'S RIDICULOUS--!

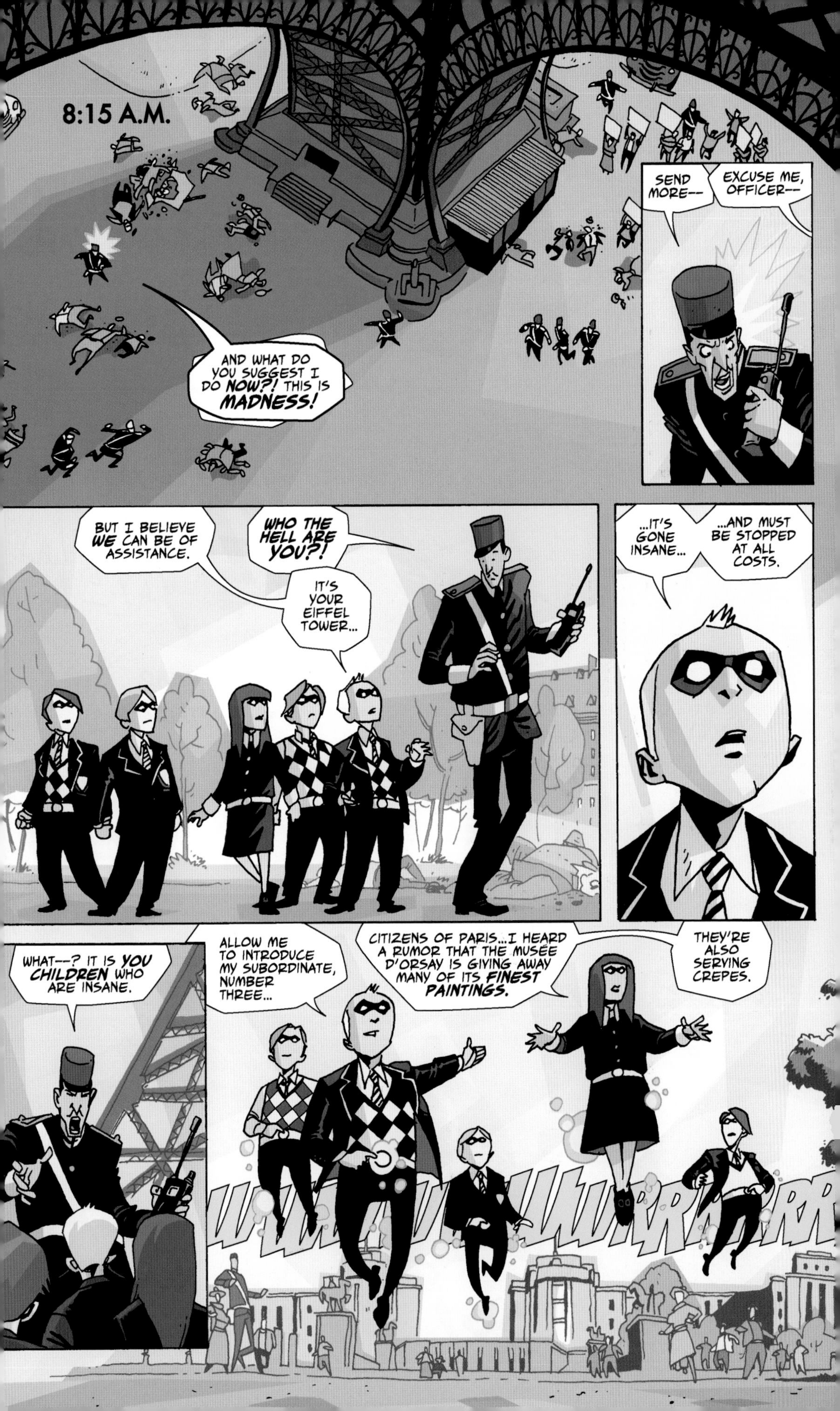
8:15 A.M.
AND WHAT DO YOU SUGGEST I DO NOW?! THIS IS MADNESS!
SEND MORE--
EXCUSE ME, OFFICER--
BUT I BELIEVE WE CAN BE OF ASSISTANCE.
WHO THE HELL ARE YOU?!
IT'S YOUR EIFFEL TOWER...
...IT'S GONE INSANE...
...AND MUST BE STOPPED AT ALL COSTS.
WHAT--? IT IS YOU CHILDREN WHO ARE INSANE.
ALLOW ME TO INTRODUCE MY SUBORDINATE, NUMBER THREE...
CITIZENS OF PARIS...I HEARD A RUMOR THAT THE MUSÉE D'ORSAY IS GIVING AWAY MANY OF ITS FINEST PAINTINGS.
THEY'RE ALSO SERVING CREPES.

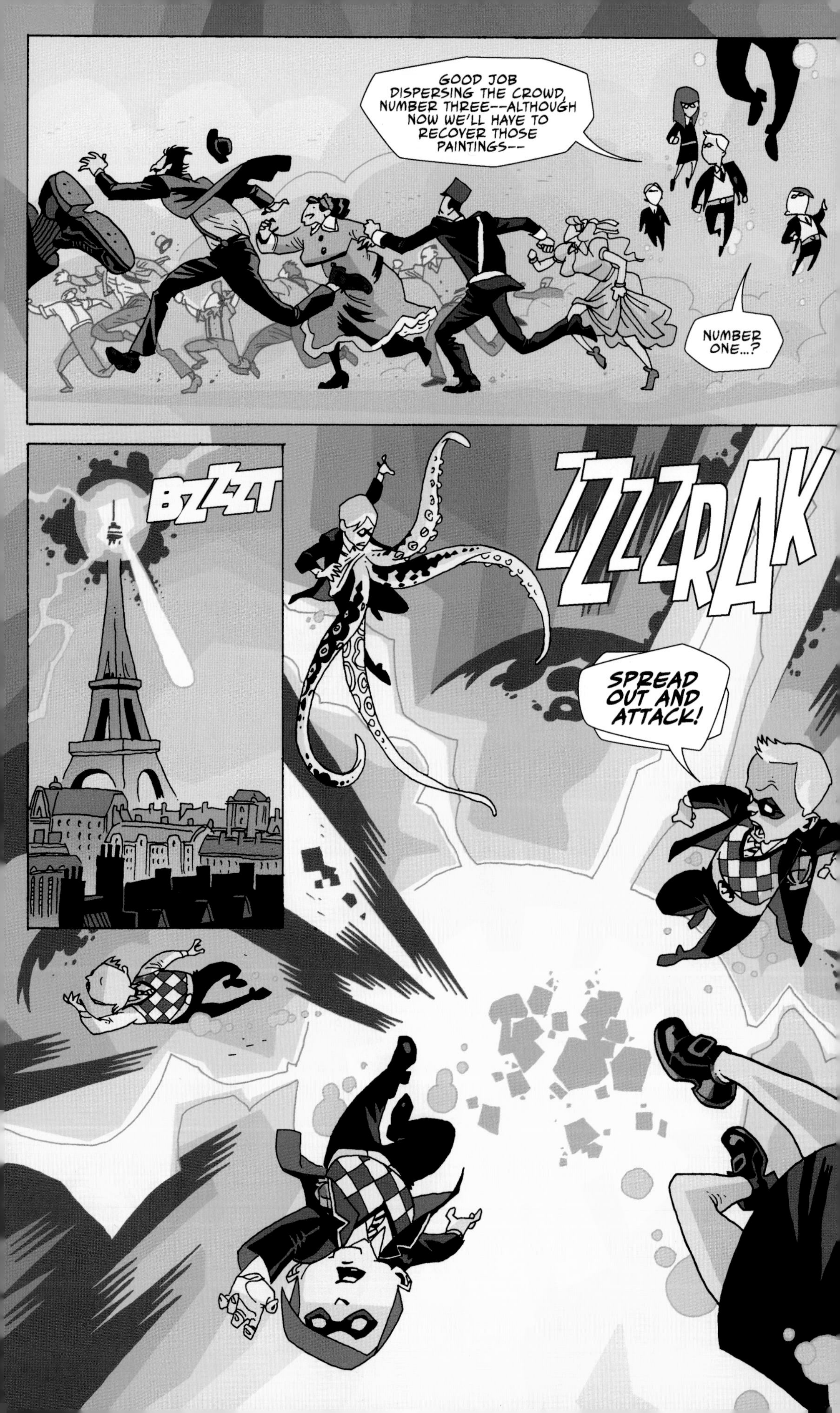
GOOD JOB DISPERSING THE CROWD, NUMBER THREE--ALTHOUGH NOW WE'LL HAVE TO RECOVER THOSE PAINTINGS--
NUMBER ONE...?
BZZZT
ZZZZRAK
SPREAD OUT AND ATTACK!

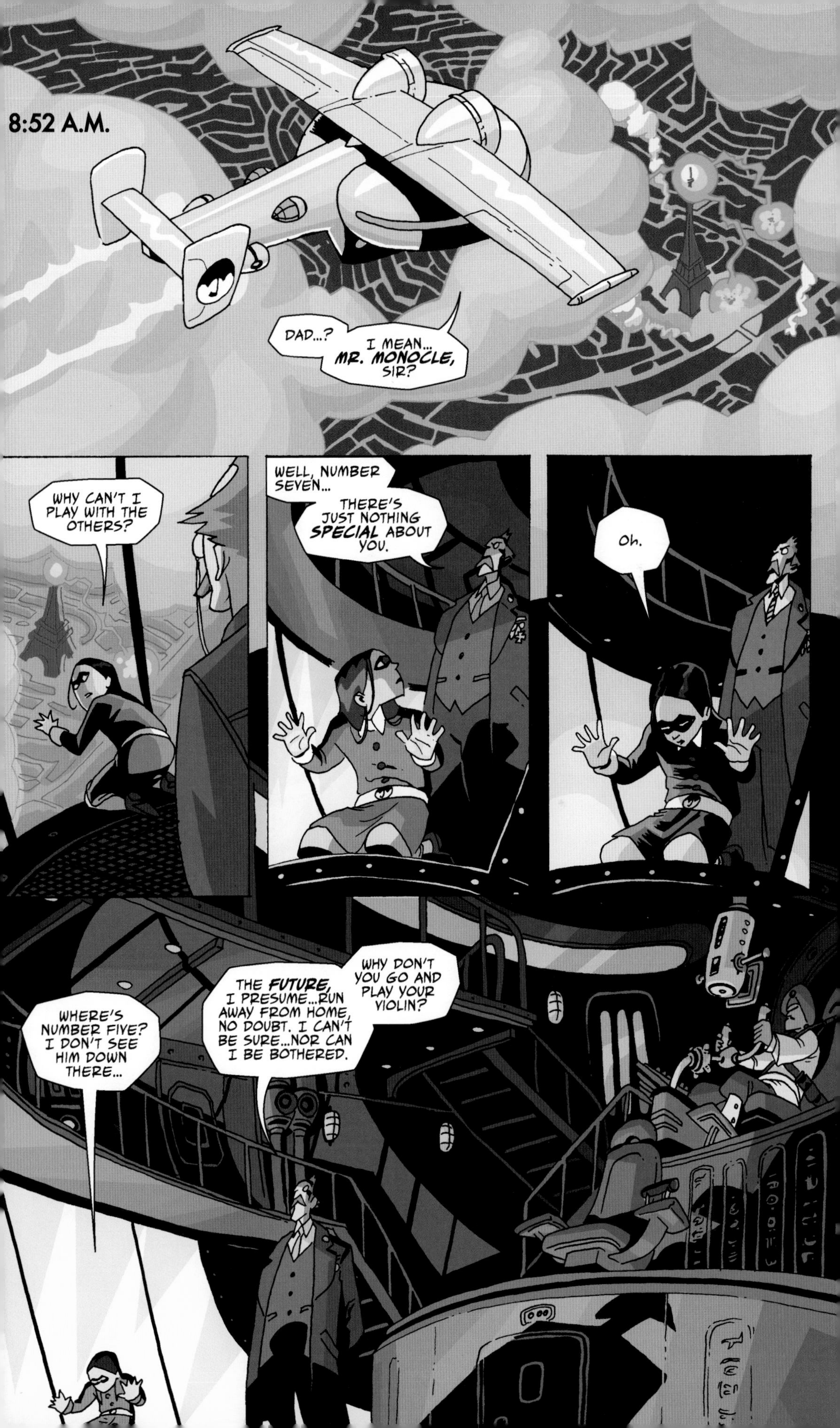
8:52 A.M.
DAD...?
I MEAN... MR. MONOCLE, SIR?
WHY CAN'T I PLAY WITH THE OTHERS?
WELL, NUMBER SEVEN...
THERE'S JUST NOTHING SPECIAL ABOUT YOU.
Oh.
WHERE'S NUMBER FIVE? I DON'T SEE HIM DOWN THERE...
THE FUTURE, I PRESUME...RUN AWAY FROM HOME, NO DOUBT. I CAN'T BE SURE...NOR CAN I BE BOTHERED.
WHY DON'T YOU GO AND PLAY YOUR VIOLIN?

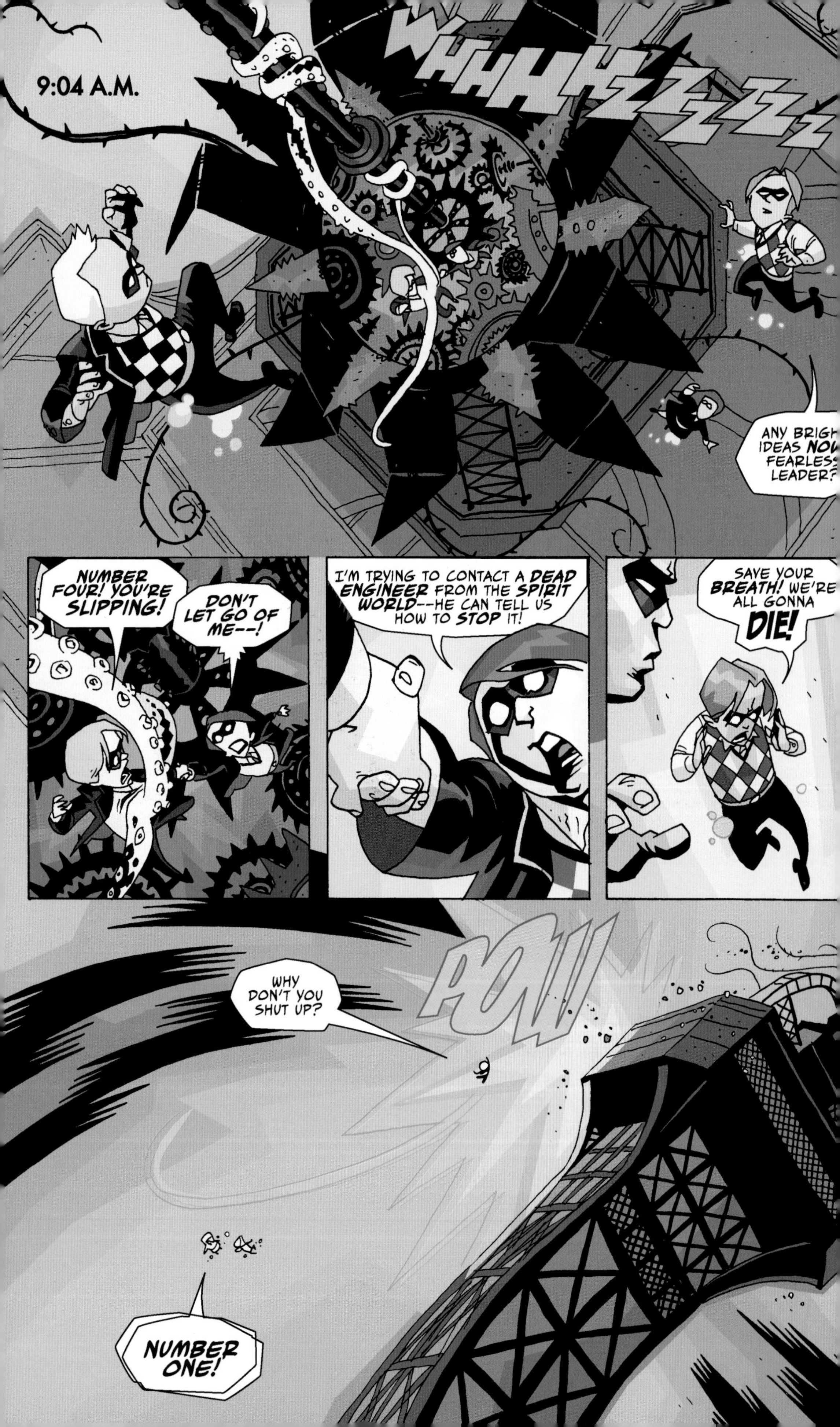
9:04 A.M.
WHHHHZZZZZZ
ANY BRIGH IDEAS NOW FEARLESS LEADER?
NUMBER FOUR! YOU'RE SLIPPING!
DON'T LET GO OF ME--!
I'M TRYING TO CONTACT A DEAD ENGINEER FROM THE SPIRIT WORLD--HE CAN TELL US HOW TO STOP IT!
SAVE YOUR BREATH! WE'RE ALL GONNA DIE!
POW
WHY DON'T YOU SHUT UP?
NUMBER ONE!

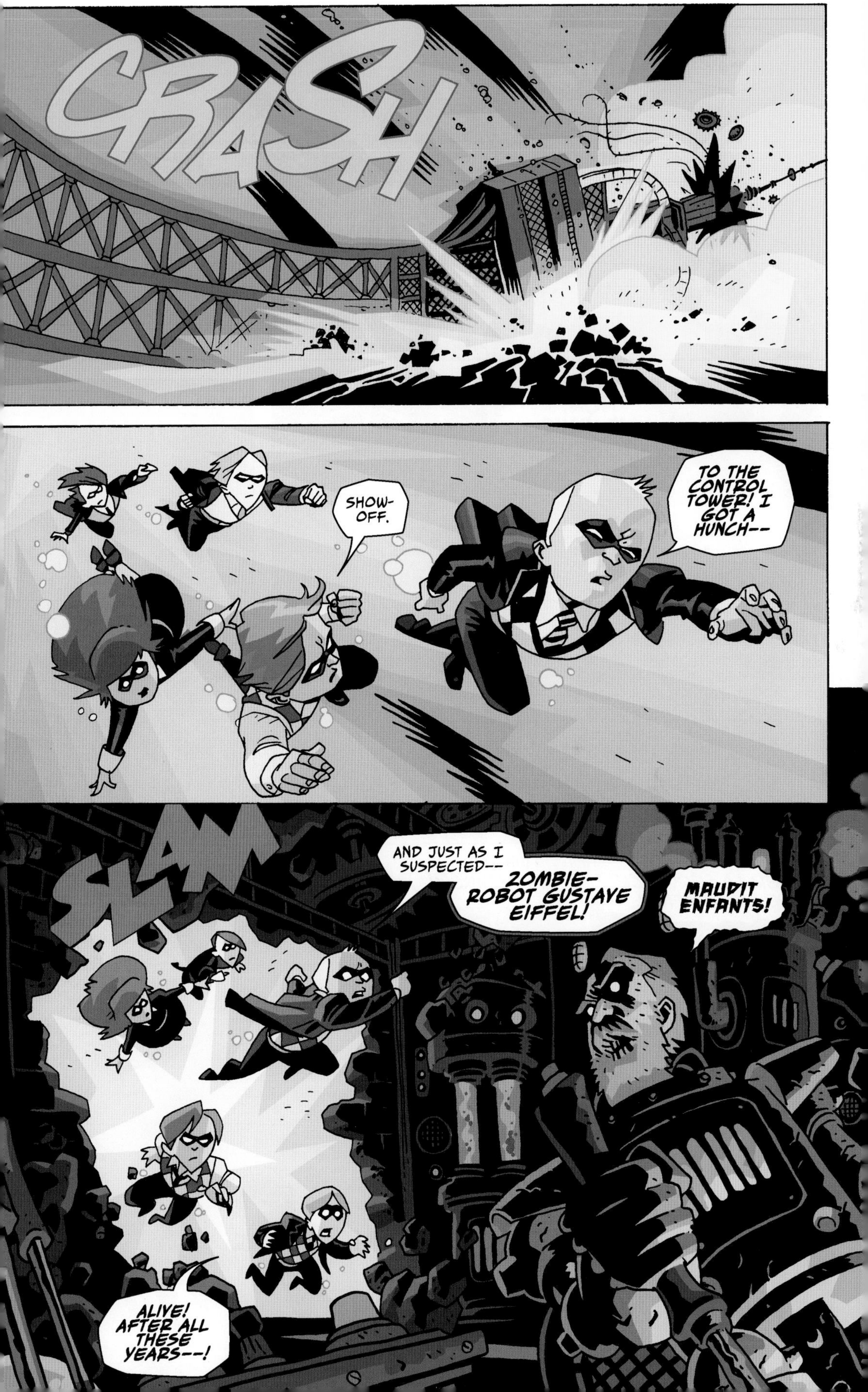
CRASH
SHOW-OFF.
TO THE CONTROL TOWER! I GOT A HUNCH--
SLAM
AND JUST AS I SUSPECTED--
ZOMBIE-ROBOT GUSTAVE EIFFEL!
MAUDIT ENFANTS!
ALIVE! AFTER ALL THESE YEARS--!

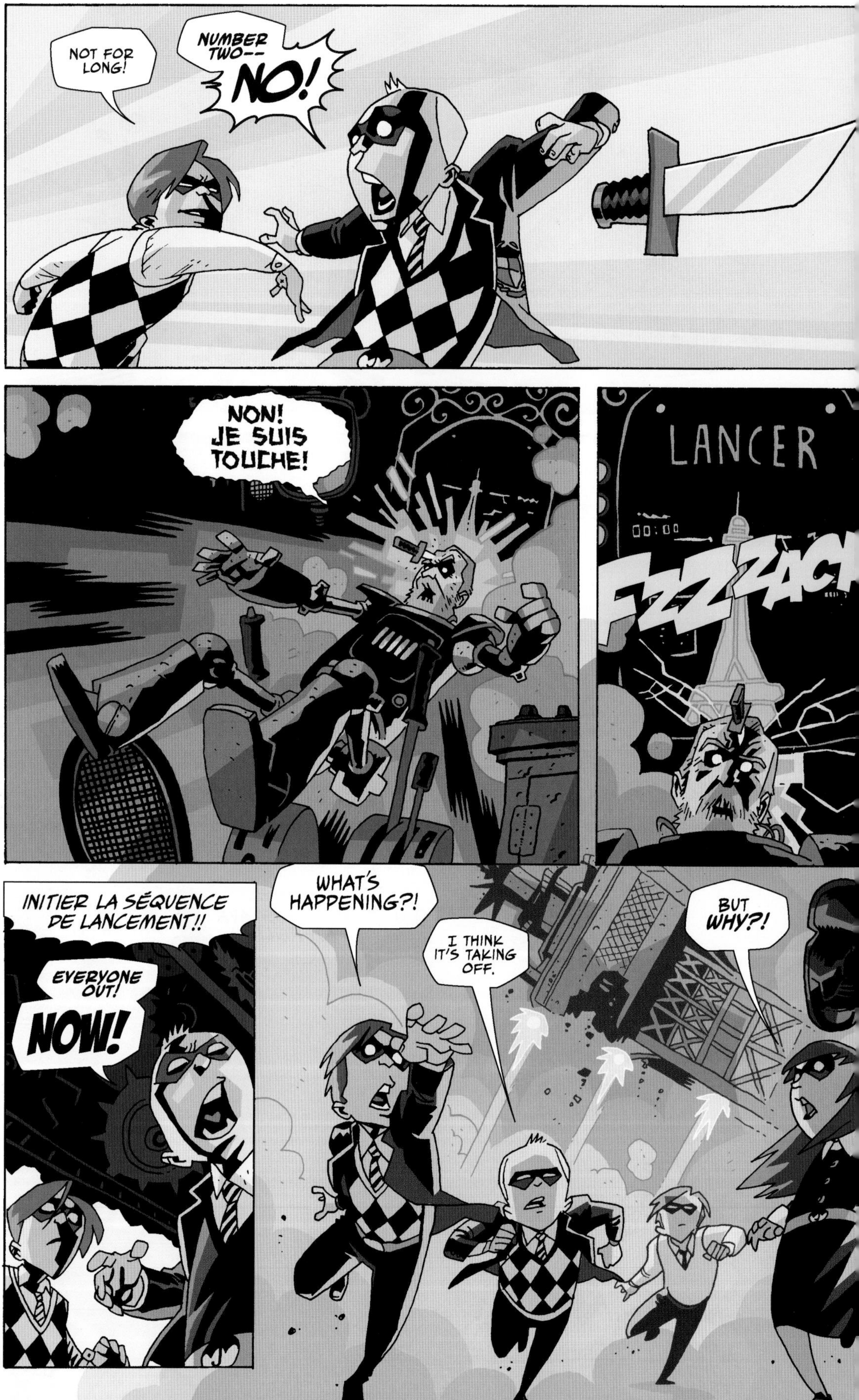
NOT FOR LONG!
NUMBER TWO-- NO!
NON! JE SUIS TOUCHE!
LANCER
00:00
FZZZACK
INITIER LA SÉQUENCE DE LANCEMENT!!
EVERYONE OUT! NOW!
WHAT'S HAPPENING?!
I THINK IT'S TAKING OFF.
BUT WHY?!

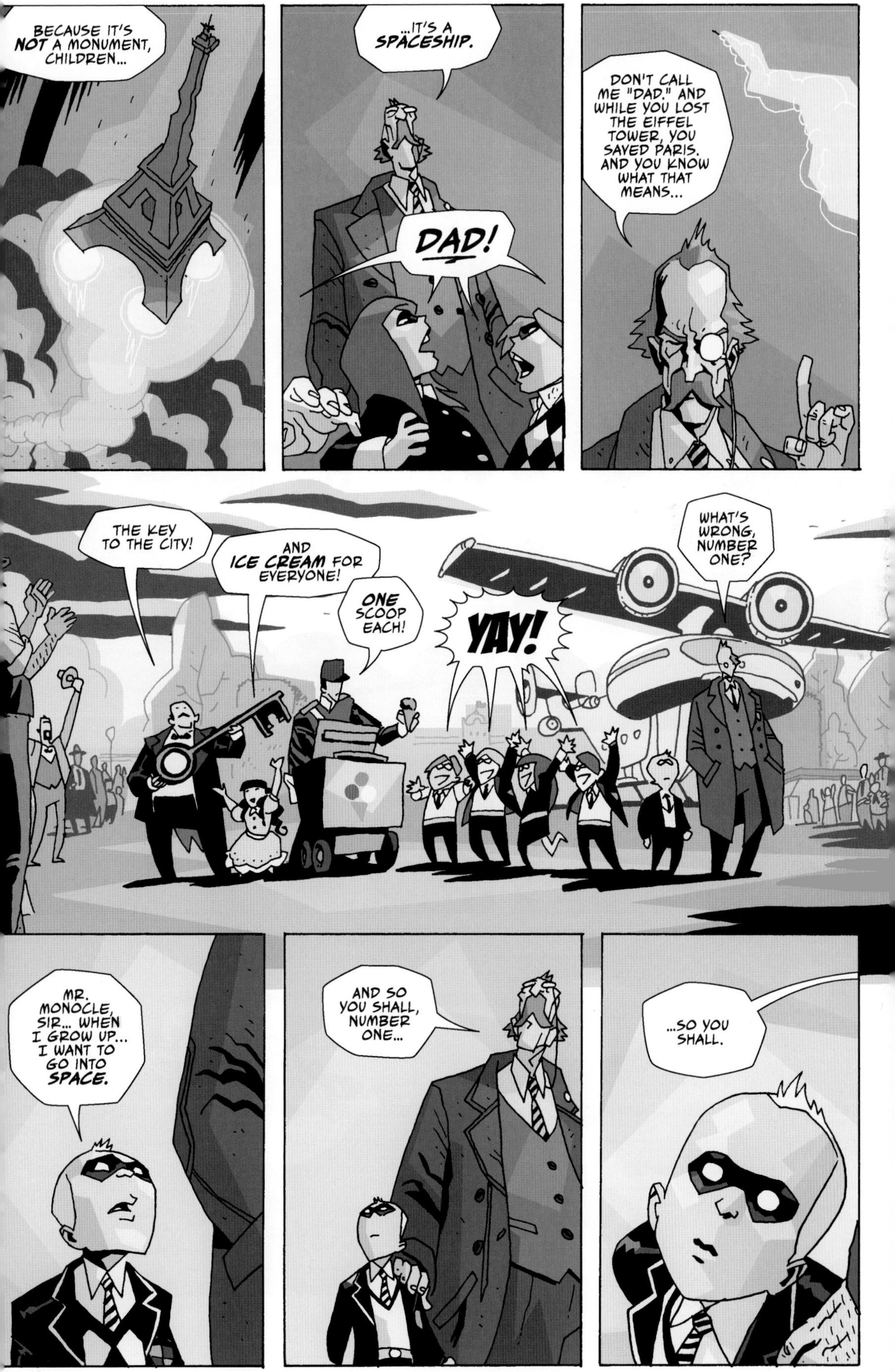
BECAUSE IT'S NOT A MONUMENT, CHILDREN...
...IT'S A SPACESHIP.
DAD!
DON'T CALL ME "DAD." AND WHILE YOU LOST THE EIFFEL TOWER, YOU SAVED PARIS. AND YOU KNOW WHAT THAT MEANS...
THE KEY TO THE CITY!
AND ICE CREAM FOR EVERYONE!
ONE SCOOP EACH!
YAY!
WHAT'S WRONG, NUMBER ONE?
MR. MONOCLE, SIR... WHEN I GROW UP... I WANT TO GO INTO SPACE.
AND SO YOU SHALL, NUMBER ONE...
...SO YOU SHALL.

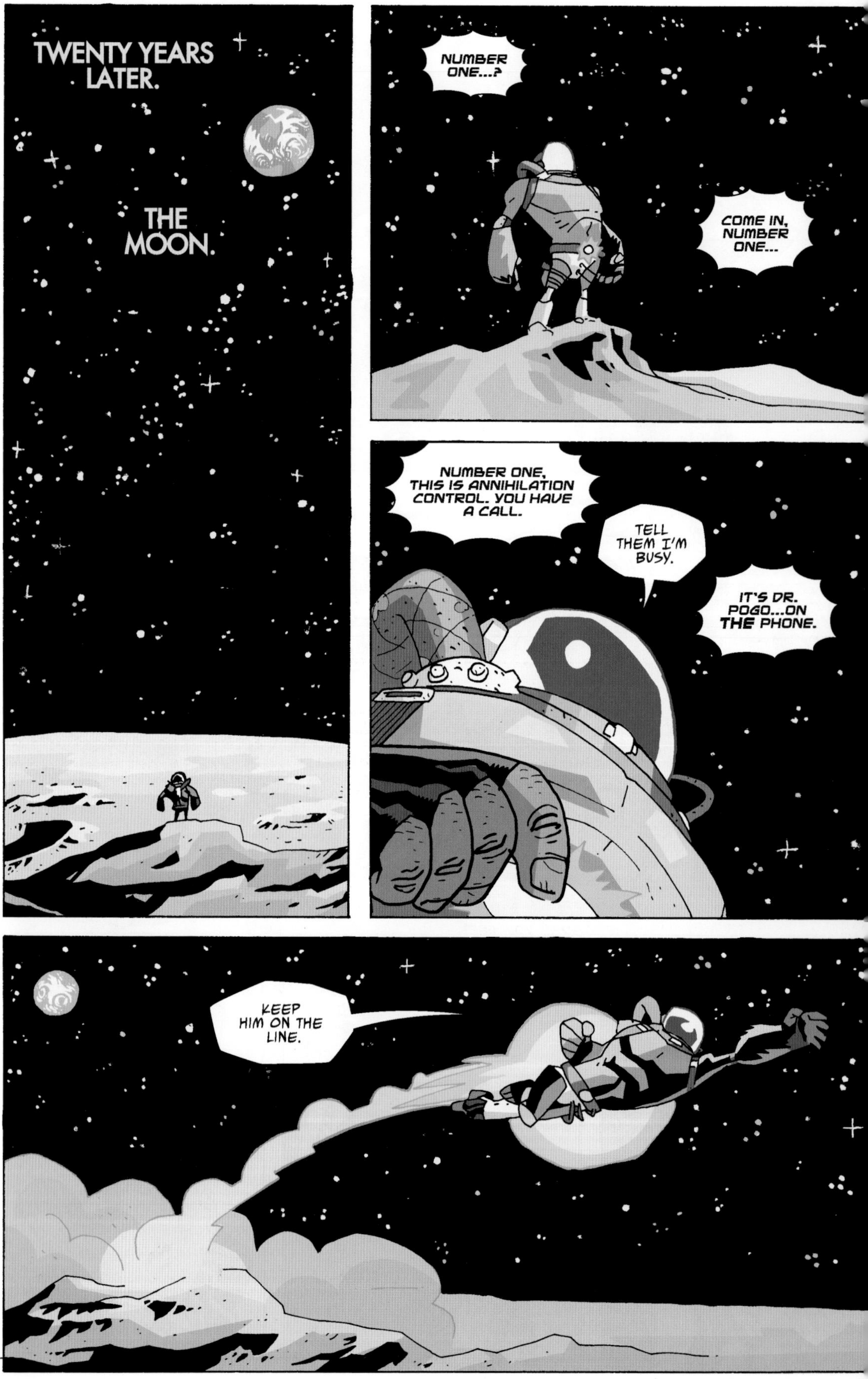
TWENTY YEARS LATER.
THE MOON.
NUMBER ONE...?
COME IN, NUMBER ONE...
NUMBER ONE, THIS IS ANNIHILATION CONTROL. YOU HAVE A CALL.
TELL THEM I'M BUSY.
IT'S DR. POGO...ON THE PHONE.
KEEP HIM ON THE LINE.

SPACEBOY
First boy in space.

POGO-- ANY NEWS FROM EARTH? IS THIS IT...?

...

Here to save the Earth.

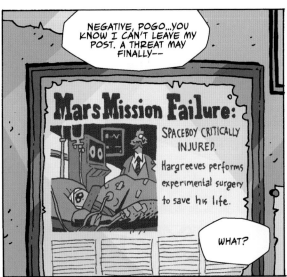

NEGATIVE, POGO...YOU KNOW I CAN'T LEAVE MY POST. A THREAT MAY FINALLY--

Mars Mission Failure:
SPACEBOY CRITICALLY INJURED. Hargreeves performs experimental surgery to save his life.

WHAT?

THE HORROR --DEAD!

SPACE LEAVE EARTH!

UMBRELLA ACADEMY DISBANDS!

THE JENNIFER INCIDENT!

Oh.

I SEE.

I'M ON MY WAY.

I'VE READIED YOUR SHIP, NUMBER ONE. WILL YOU BE REQUIRING YOUR LASER PISTOL?

YES, AND BEN? REMIND ME TO RE-PROGRAM YOU WHEN I GET BACK...

ONLY MY FATHER CALLS ME NUMBER ONE.

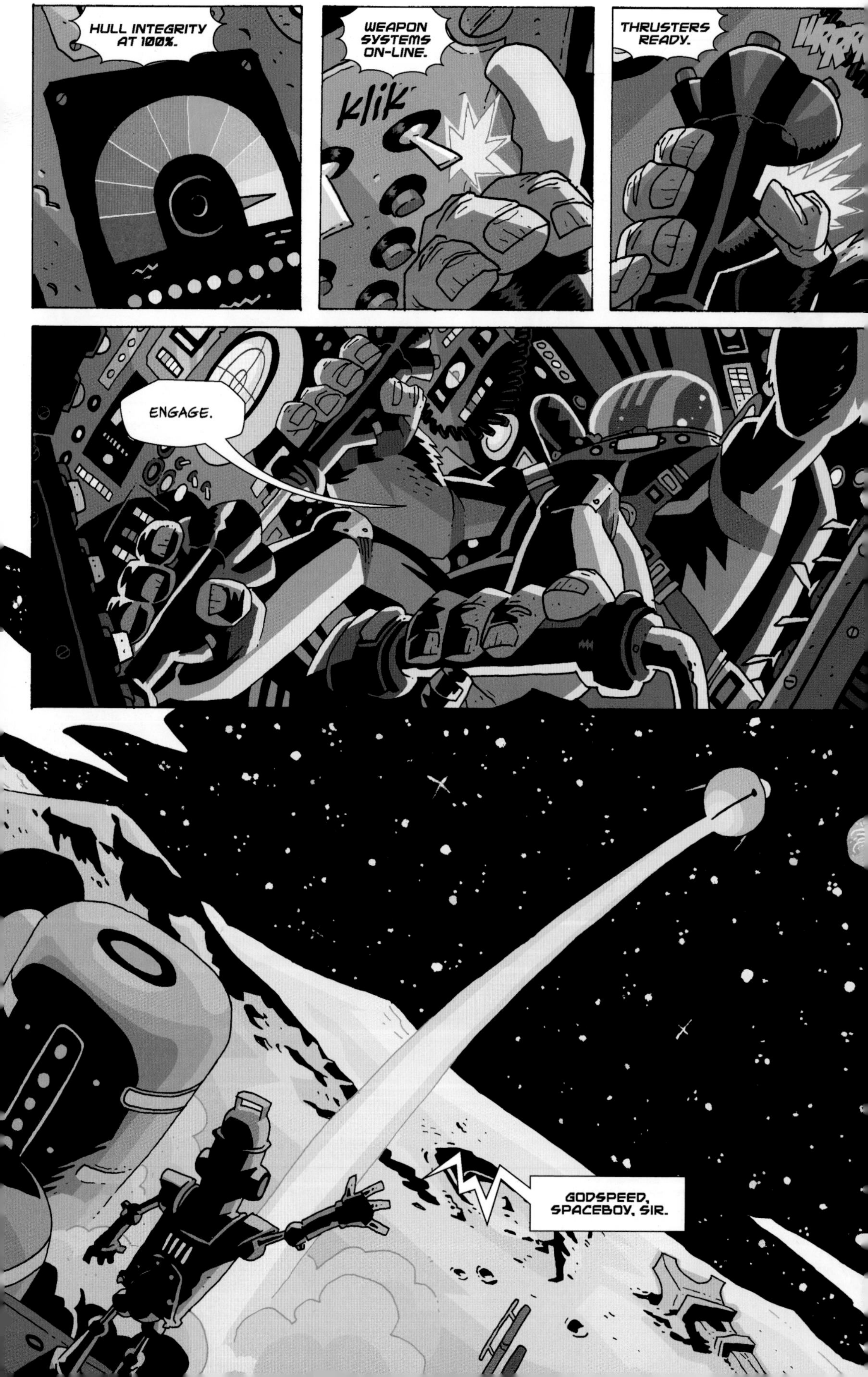
HULL INTEGRITY AT 100%.
WEAPON SYSTEMS ON-LINE.
KLIK
THRUSTERS READY.
ENGAGE.
GODSPEED, SPACEBOY, SIR.

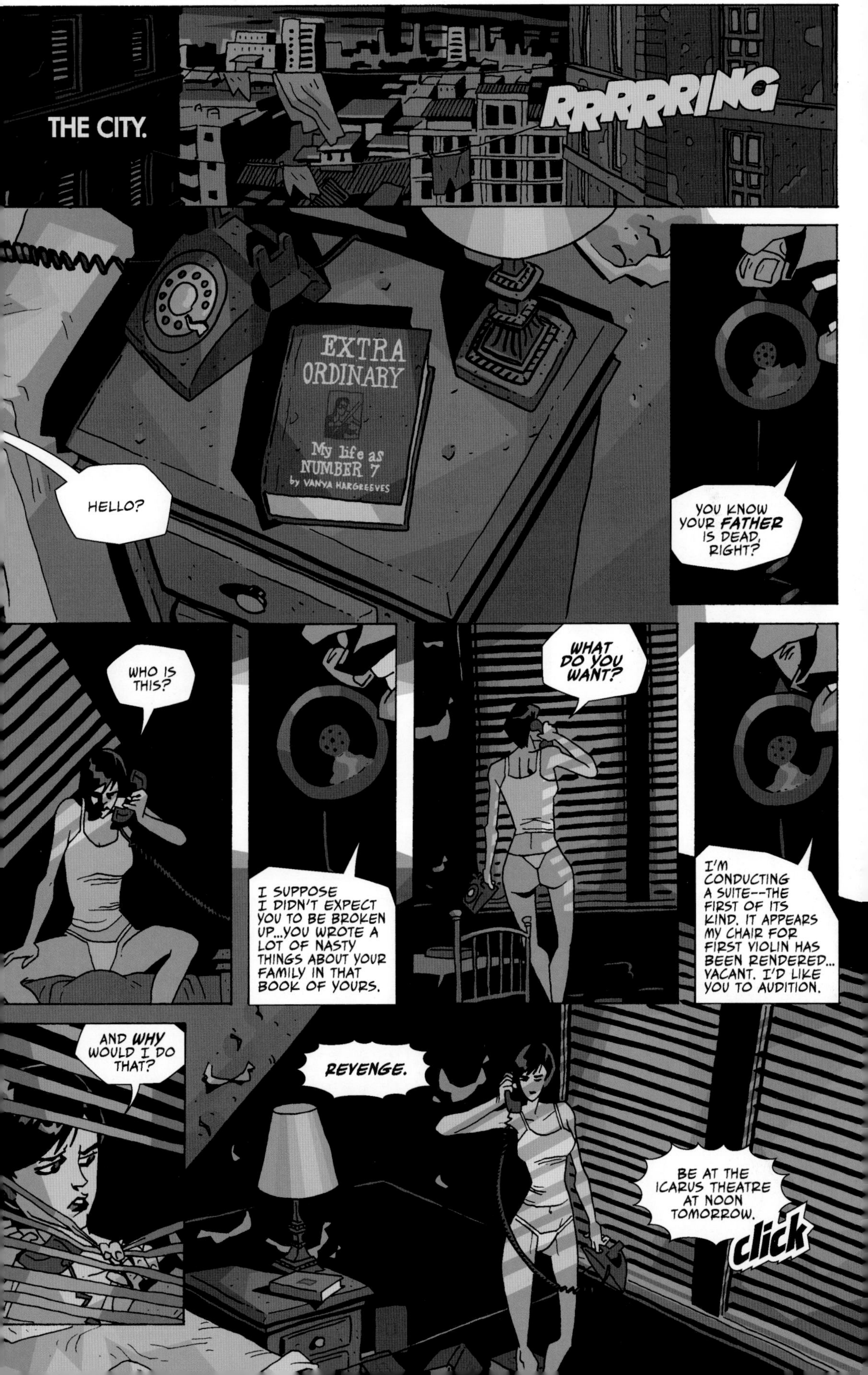
THE CITY.
RRRRRING
EXTRA ORDINARY
My life as NUMBER 7
by VANYA HARGREEVES
HELLO?
YOU KNOW YOUR FATHER IS DEAD, RIGHT?
WHO IS THIS?
I SUPPOSE I DIDN'T EXPECT YOU TO BE BROKEN UP...YOU WROTE A LOT OF NASTY THINGS ABOUT YOUR FAMILY IN THAT BOOK OF YOURS.
WHAT DO YOU WANT?
I'M CONDUCTING A SUITE--THE FIRST OF ITS KIND. IT APPEARS MY CHAIR FOR FIRST VIOLIN HAS BEEN RENDERED... VACANT. I'D LIKE YOU TO AUDITION.
AND WHY WOULD I DO THAT?
REVENGE.
BE AT THE ICARUS THEATRE AT NOON TOMORROW.
click

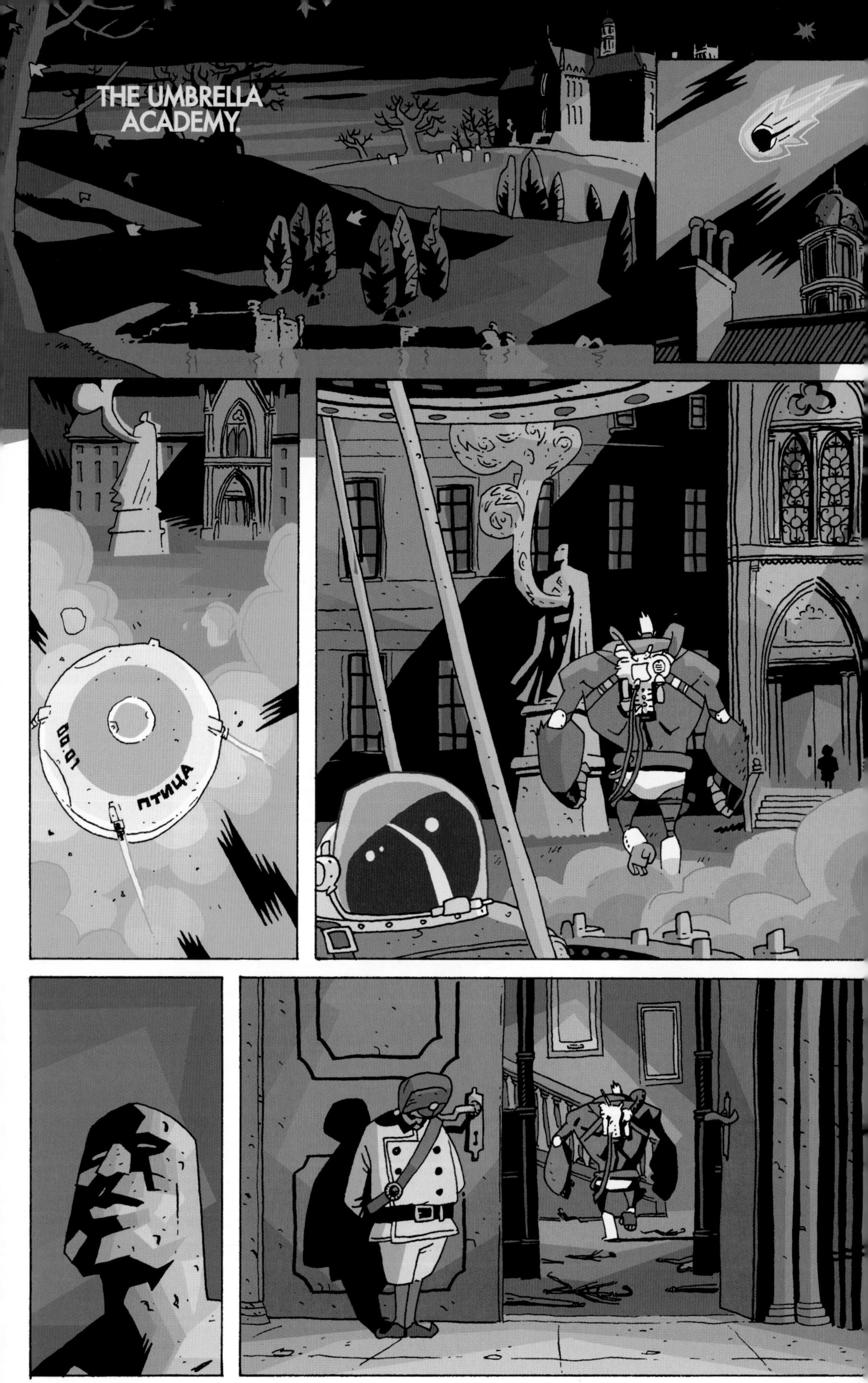

THE UMBRELLA ACADEMY.
00.01
ПТИЦА

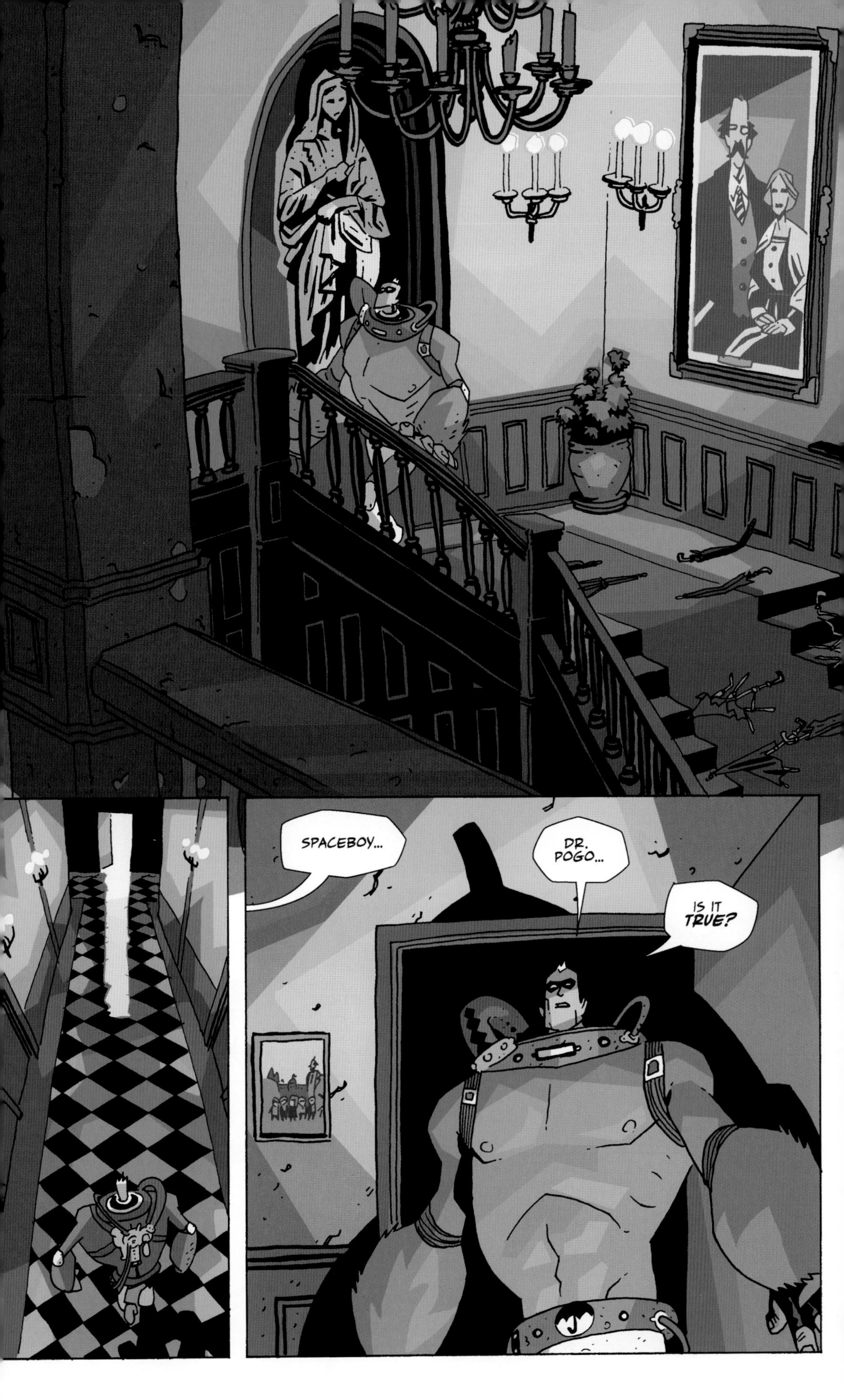
SPACEBOY...
DR. POGO...
IS IT TRUE?

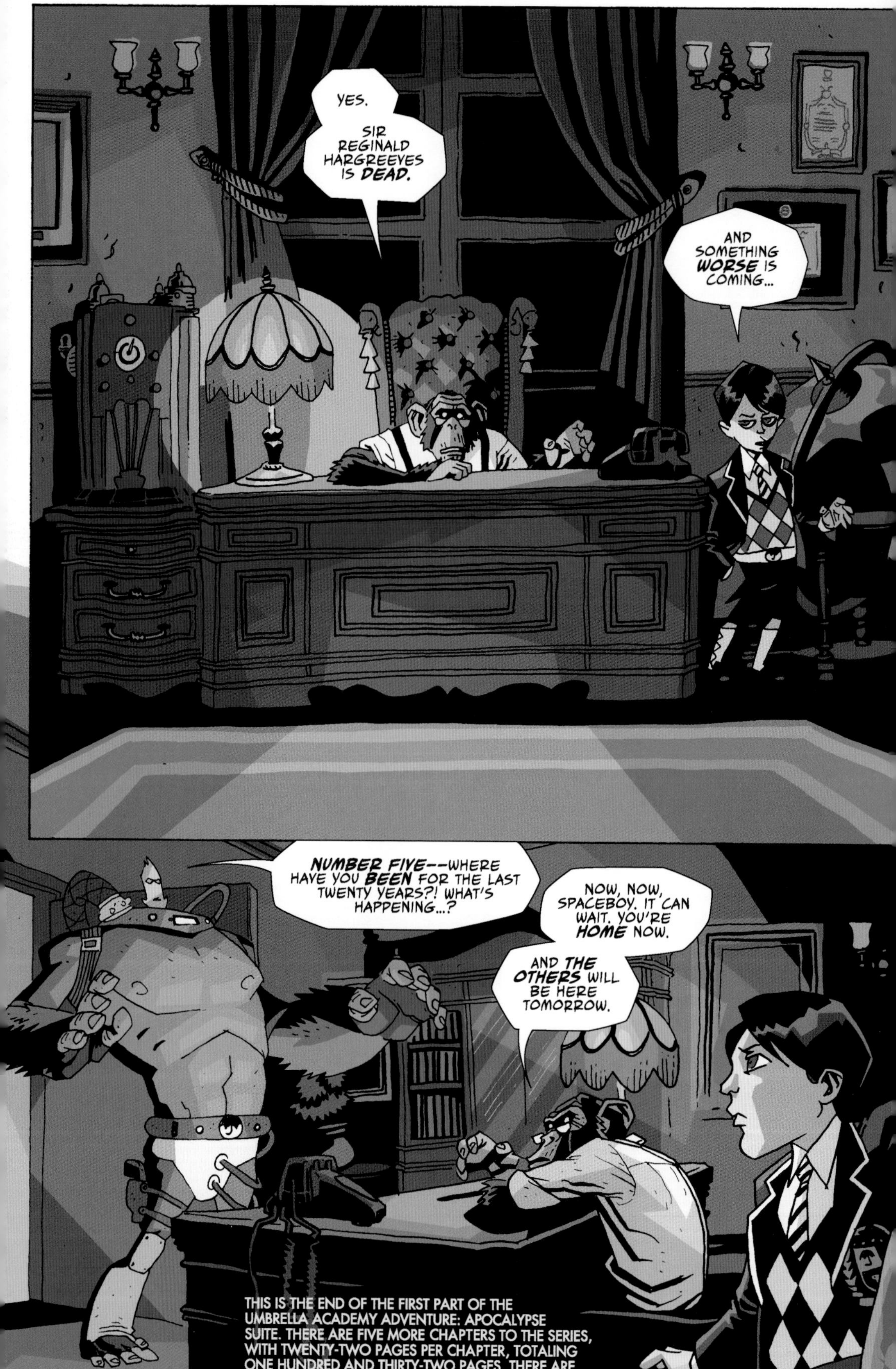
YES.
SIR REGINALD HARGREEVES IS DEAD.
AND SOMETHING WORSE IS COMING...
NUMBER FIVE--WHERE HAVE YOU BEEN FOR THE LAST TWENTY YEARS?! WHAT'S HAPPENING...?
NOW, NOW, SPACEBOY. IT CAN WAIT. YOU'RE HOME NOW.
AND THE OTHERS WILL BE HERE TOMORROW.
THIS IS THE END OF THE FIRST PART OF THE UMBRELLA ACADEMY ADVENTURE: APOCALYPSE SUITE. THERE ARE FIVE MORE CHAPTERS TO THE SERIES, WITH TWENTY-TWO PAGES PER CHAPTER, TOTALING ONE HUNDRED AND THIRTY-TWO PAGES. THERE ARE SEVEN MEMBERS OF THE UMBRELLA ACADEMY, AND SEVENTY-TWO NAMES ON THE EIFFEL TOWER. THERE IS NO CONNECTION BETWEEN THESE NUMBERS.

GABRIEL BÁ AND FÁBIO MOON!

"Twin Brazilian artists Fábio Moon and Gabriel Bá have made a huge mark on comics." —*Publisher's Weekly*

TWO BROTHERS
Fábio Moon & Gabriel Bá

THE UMBRELLA ACADEMY
APOCALYPSE SUITE

FÁBIO MOON
GABRIEL BÁ
De:
TALES

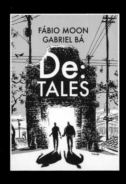

TWO BROTHERS
Story and art by Gabriel Bá
and Fábio Moon
ISBN 978-1-61655-856-7 | $24.99

DE:TALES
Story and art by Gabriel Bá and Fábio Moon
ISBN 978-1-59582-557-5 | $19.99

THE UMBRELLA ACADEMY: APOCALYPSE SUITE
Story by Gerard Way
Art by Gabriel Bá
TPB ISBN: 978-1-59307-978-9 | $17.99
Ltd. Ed. HC ISBN: 978-1-59582-163-8 | $79.95

THE UMBRELLA ACADEMY: DALLAS
Story by Gerard Way
Art by Gabriel Bá
TPB ISBN: 978-1-59582-345-8 | $17.99
Ltd. Ed. HC ISBN: 978-1-59582-344-1 | $79.95

PIXU: THE MARK OF EVIL
Story and art by Gabriel Bá, Becky Cloonan,
Vasilis Lolos, and Fábio Moon
ISBN 978-1-61655-813-0 | $14.99

B.P.R.D.: VAMPIRE
Story by Mike Mignola, Fábio Moon, and Gabriel Bá
Art by Fábio Moon and Gabriel Bá
ISBN 978-1-61655-196-4 | $19.99

B.P.R.D.: 1946–1948
Story by Mike Mignola, Joshua Dysart, and John Arcudi
Art by Fábio Moon, Gabriel Bá, Paul Azaceta, and Max Fiumara
ISBN 978-1-61655-646-4 | $34.99

AVAILABLE AT YOUR LOCAL COMICS SHOP OR BOOKSTORE!

To find a comics shop in your area, call 1-888-266-4226. For more information
or to order direct visit DarkHorse.com or call 1-800-862-0052 Mon.–Fri. 9 AM to 5 PM Pacific Time.

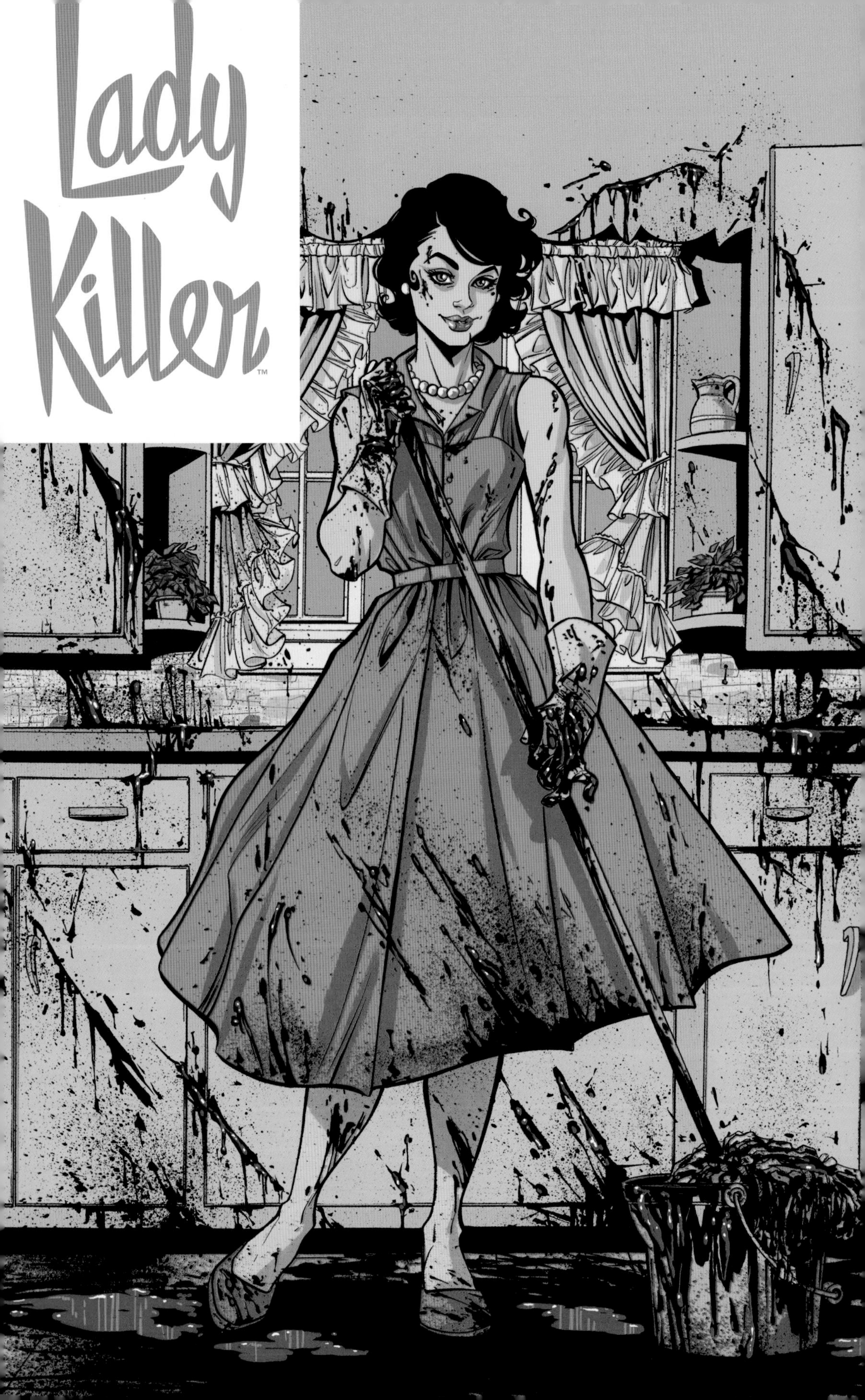
Lady Killer™

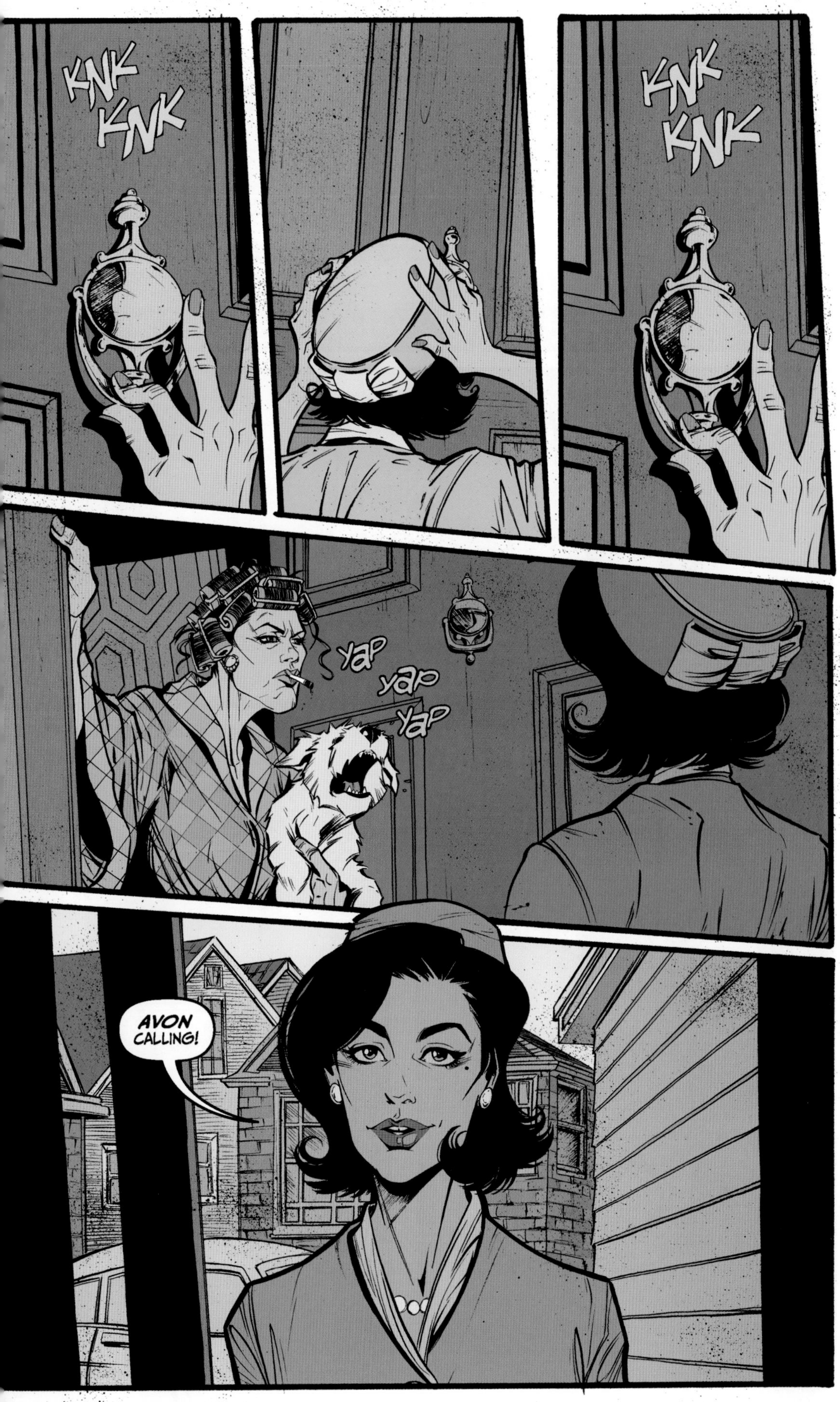
KNK KNK
KNK KNK
YAP YAP YAP
AVON CALLING!

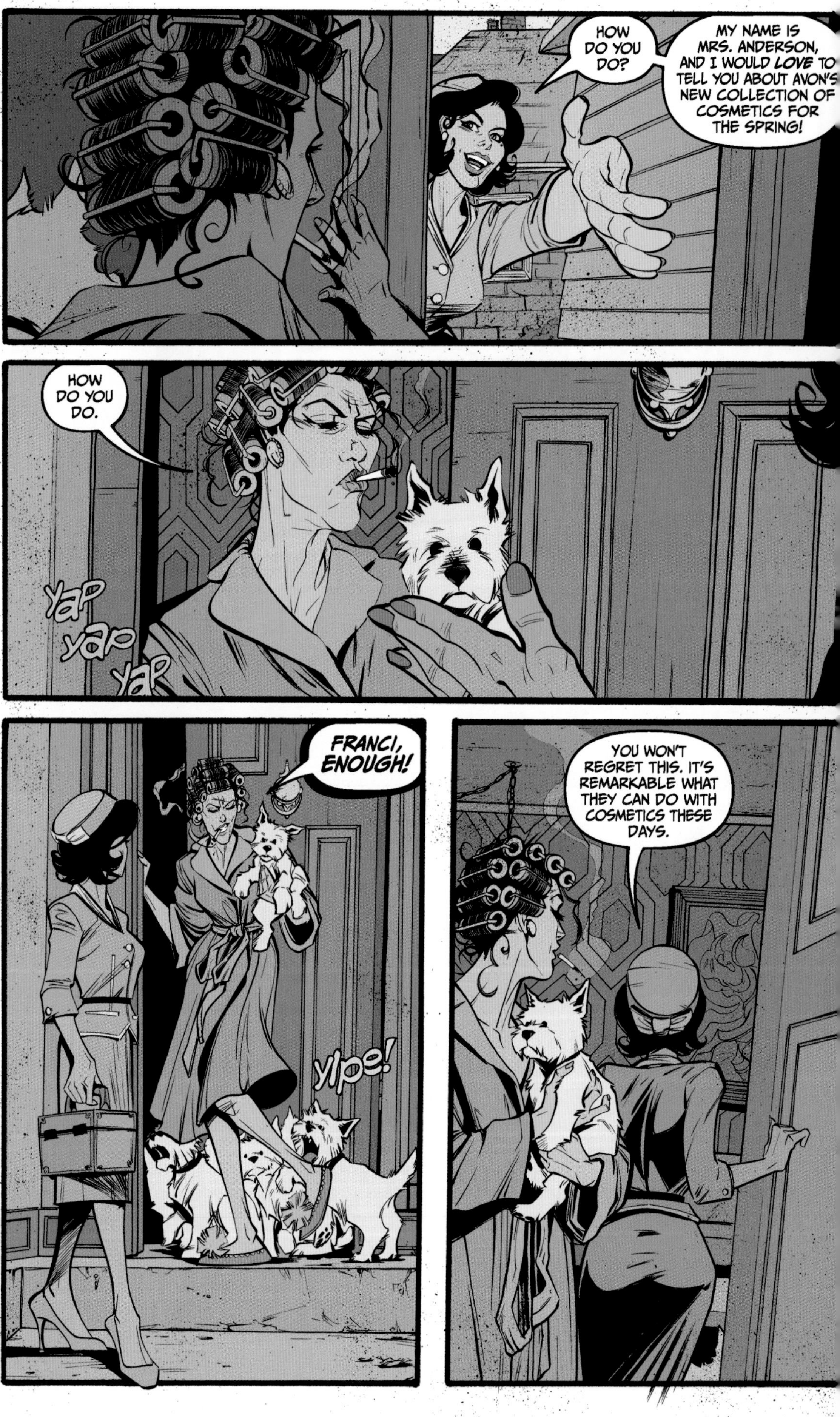
HOW DO YOU DO?
MY NAME IS MRS. ANDERSON, AND I WOULD *LOVE* TO TELL YOU ABOUT AVON'S NEW COLLECTION OF COSMETICS FOR THE SPRING!
HOW DO YOU DO.
YAP YAP YAP
FRANCI, ENOUGH!
YIPE!
YOU WON'T REGRET THIS. IT'S REMARKABLE WHAT THEY CAN DO WITH COSMETICS THESE DAYS.

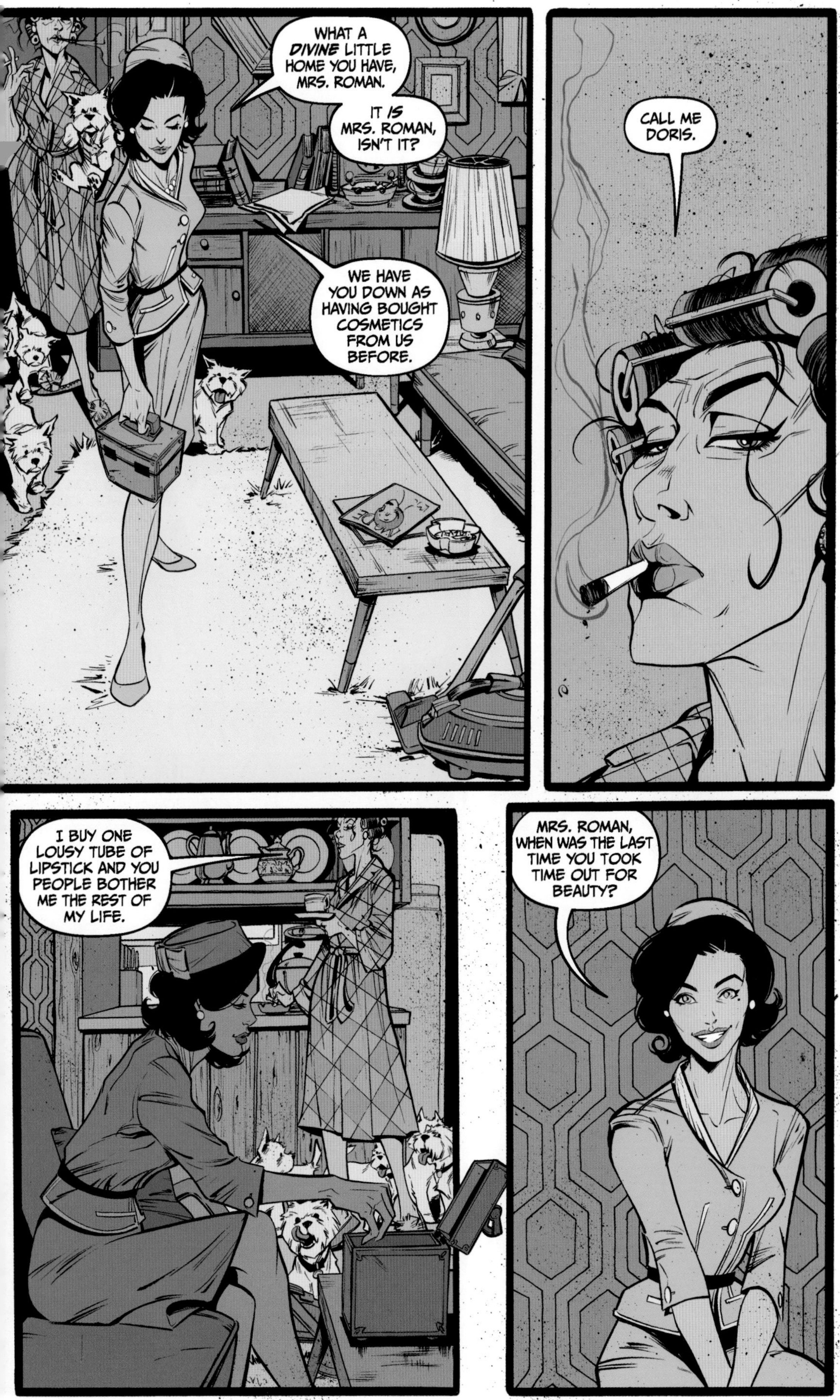
WHAT A *DIVINE* LITTLE HOME YOU HAVE, MRS. ROMAN.
IT *IS* MRS. ROMAN, ISN'T IT?
WE HAVE YOU DOWN AS HAVING BOUGHT COSMETICS FROM US BEFORE.
CALL ME DORIS.
I BUY ONE LOUSY TUBE OF LIPSTICK AND YOU PEOPLE BOTHER ME THE REST OF MY LIFE.
MRS. ROMAN, WHEN WAS THE LAST TIME YOU TOOK TIME OUT FOR BEAUTY?

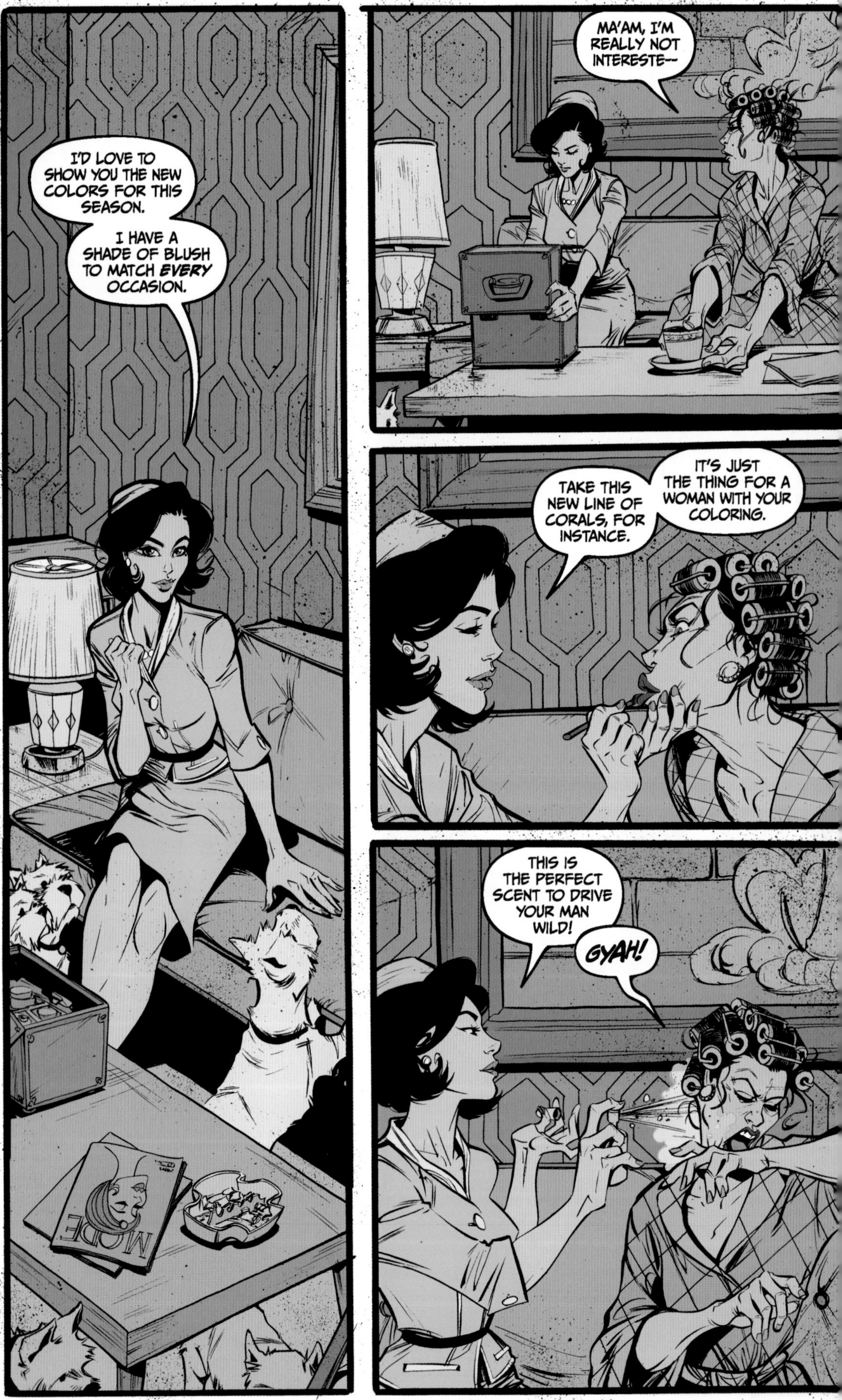
I'D LOVE TO SHOW YOU THE NEW COLORS FOR THIS SEASON.
I HAVE A SHADE OF BLUSH TO MATCH *EVERY* OCCASION.
MA'AM, I'M REALLY NOT INTERESTE--
TAKE THIS NEW LINE OF CORALS, FOR INSTANCE.
IT'S JUST THE THING FOR A WOMAN WITH YOUR COLORING.
MODE
THIS IS THE PERFECT SCENT TO DRIVE YOUR MAN WILD!
GYAH!

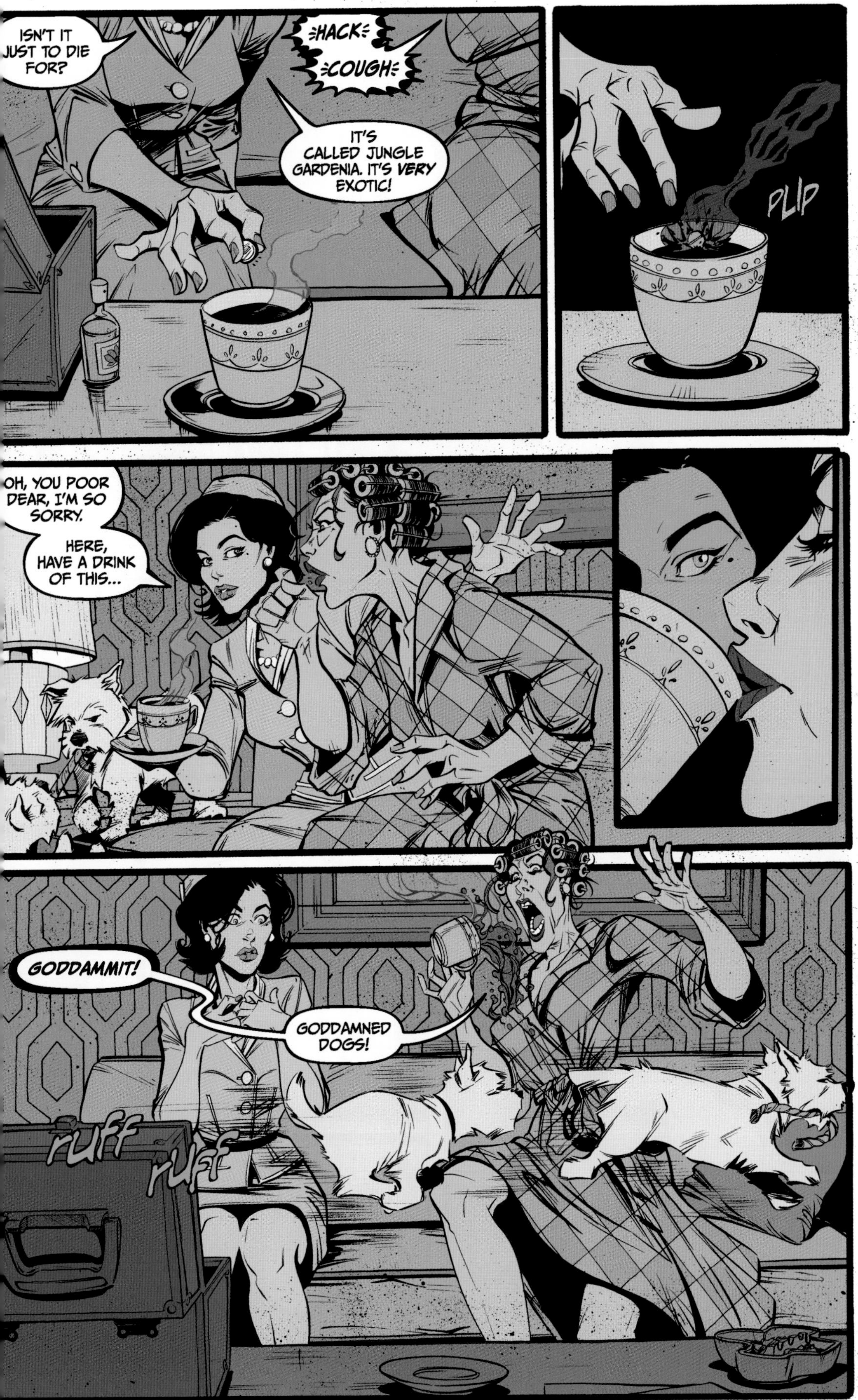
ISN'T IT JUST TO DIE FOR?
HACK
COUGH
IT'S CALLED JUNGLE GARDENIA. IT'S VERY EXOTIC!
PLIP
OH, YOU POOR DEAR, I'M SO SORRY.
HERE, HAVE A DRINK OF THIS...
GODDAMMIT!
GODDAMNED DOGS!
ruff
ruff

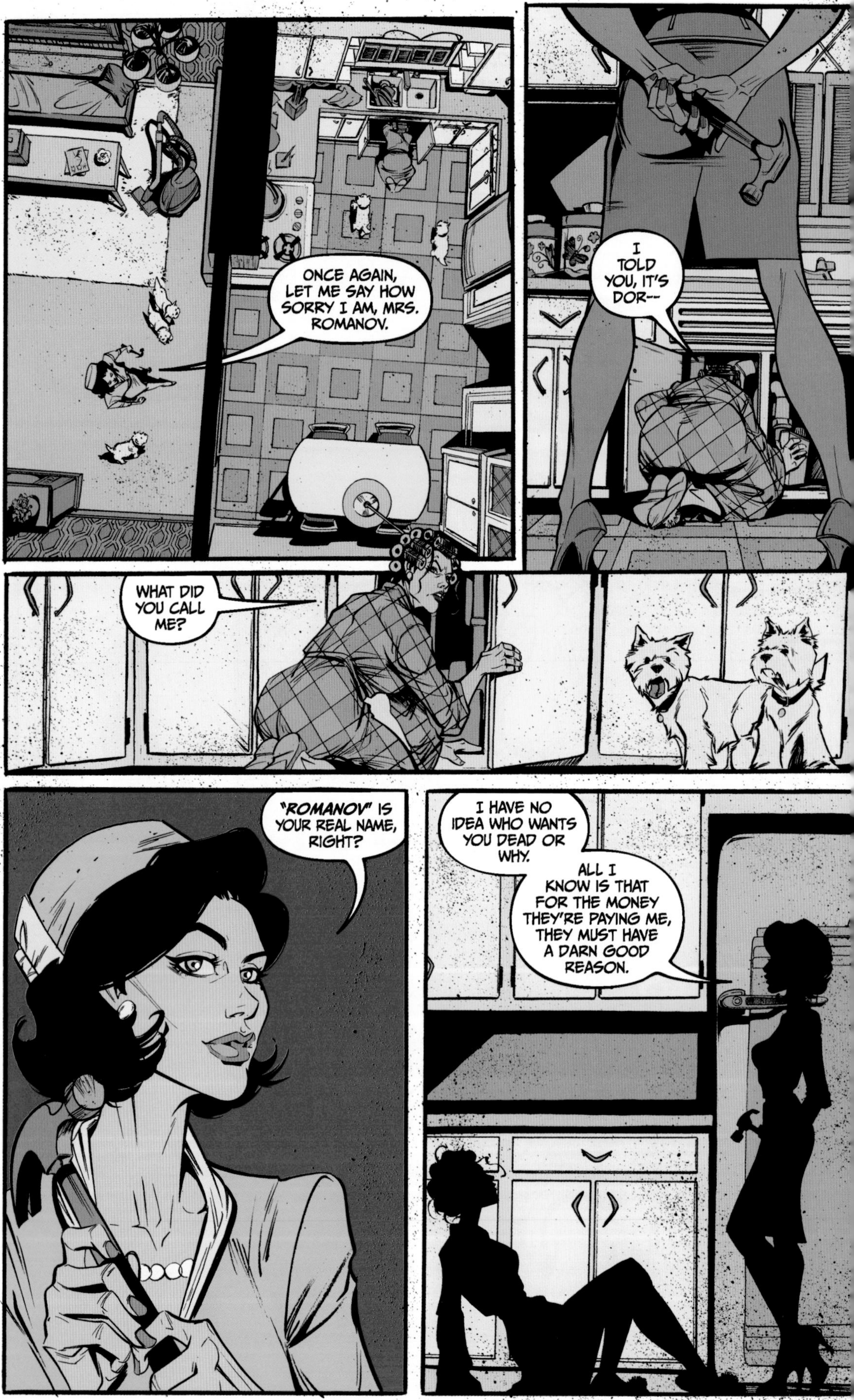
ONCE AGAIN, LET ME SAY HOW SORRY I AM, MRS. ROMANOV.
I TOLD YOU, IT'S DOR--
WHAT DID YOU CALL ME?
"ROMANOV" IS YOUR REAL NAME, RIGHT?
I HAVE NO IDEA WHO WANTS YOU DEAD OR WHY.
ALL I KNOW IS THAT FOR THE MONEY THEY'RE PAYING ME, THEY MUST HAVE A DARN GOOD REASON.

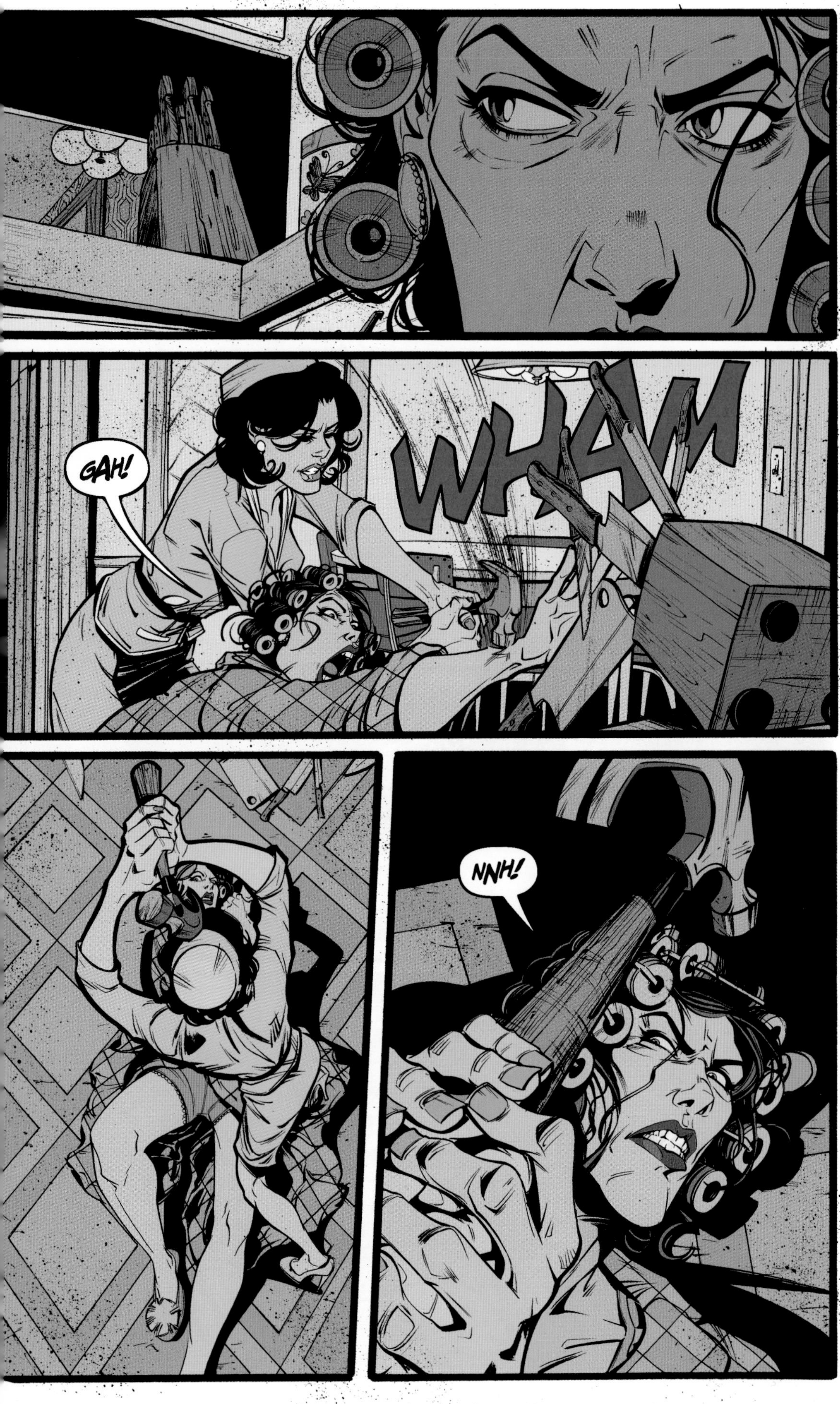
GAH!
WHAM
NNH!

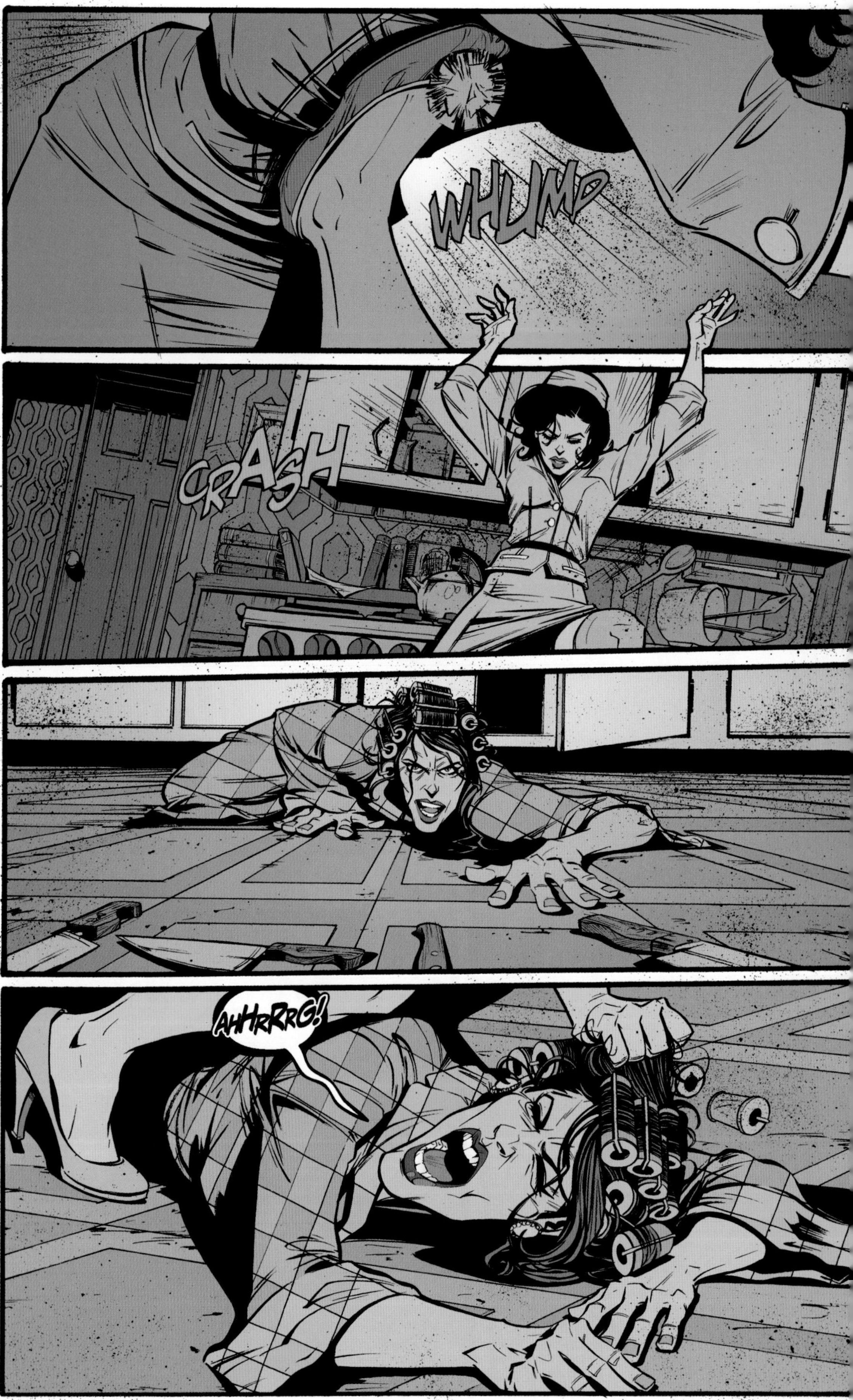
WHUMP
CRASH
AHHRRRG!

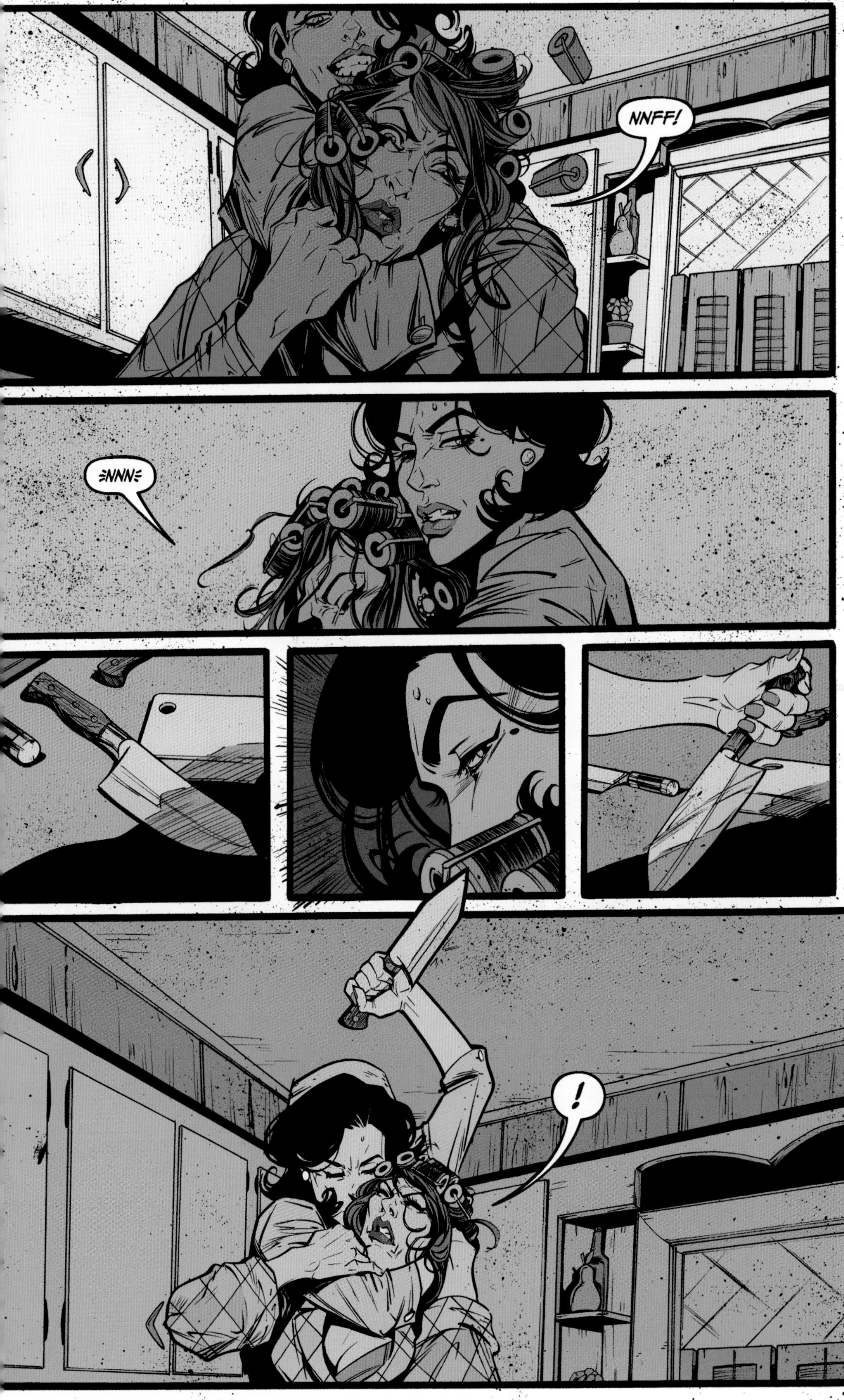
NNFF!
NNN
!

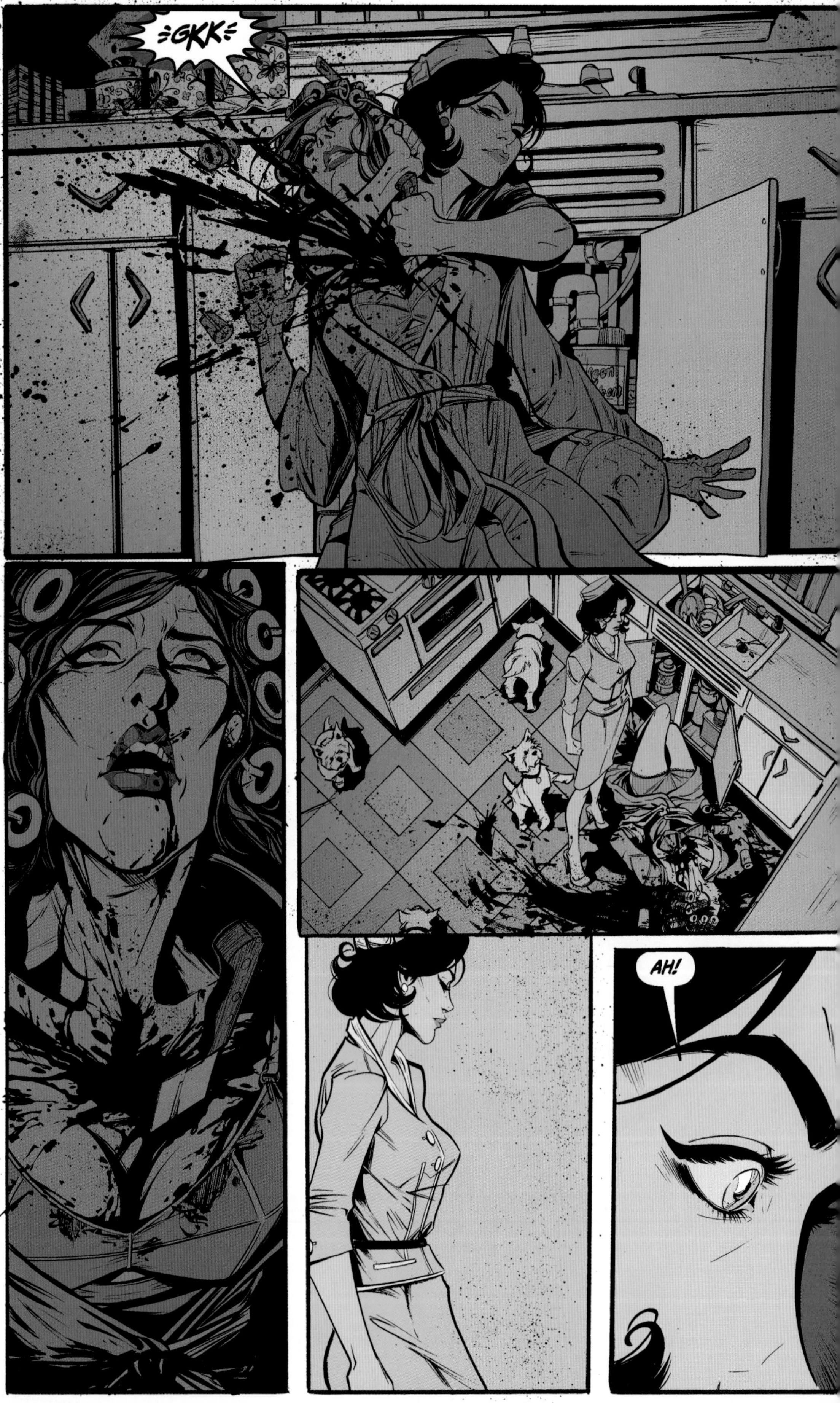
GKK
AH!

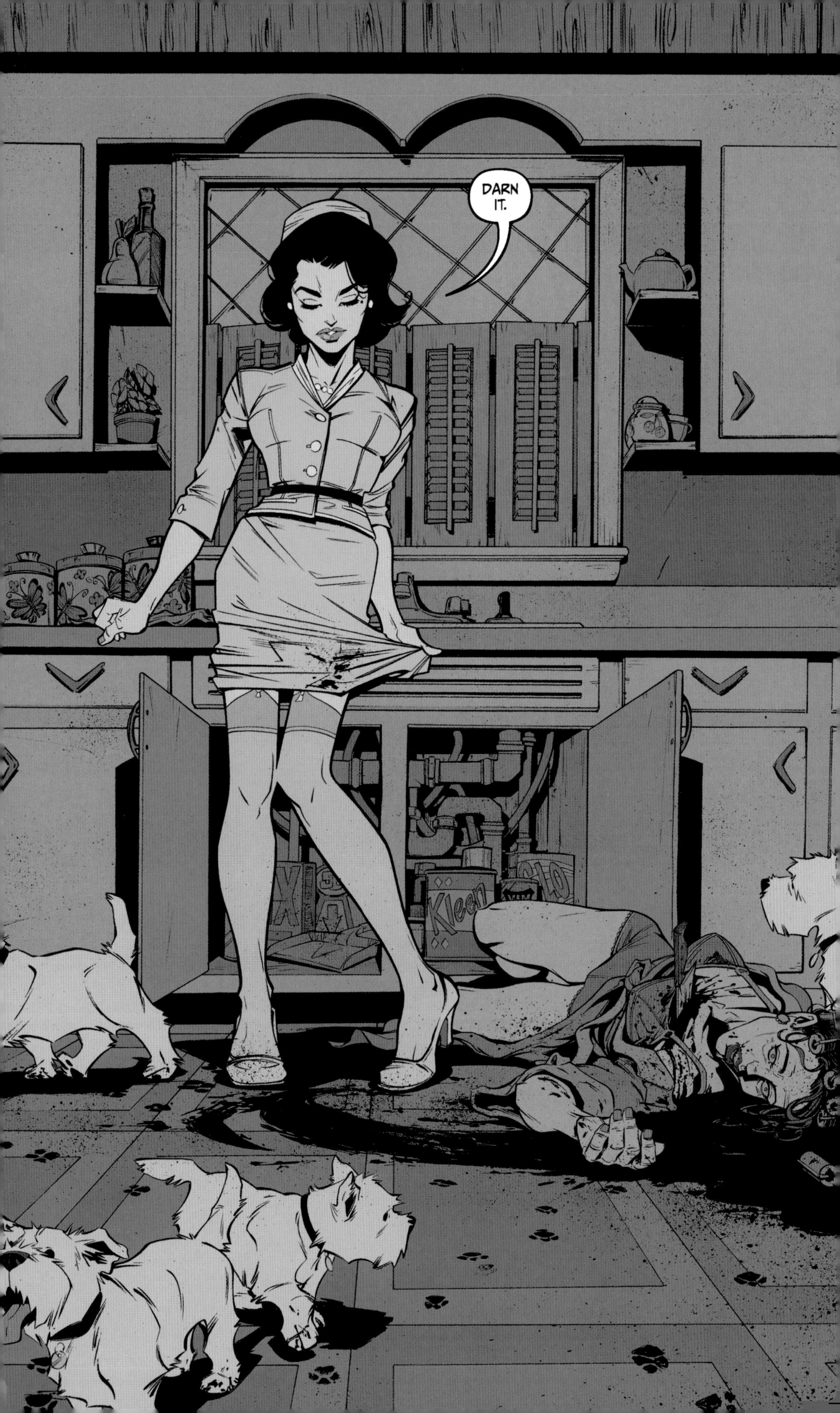
DARN IT.
Kleen

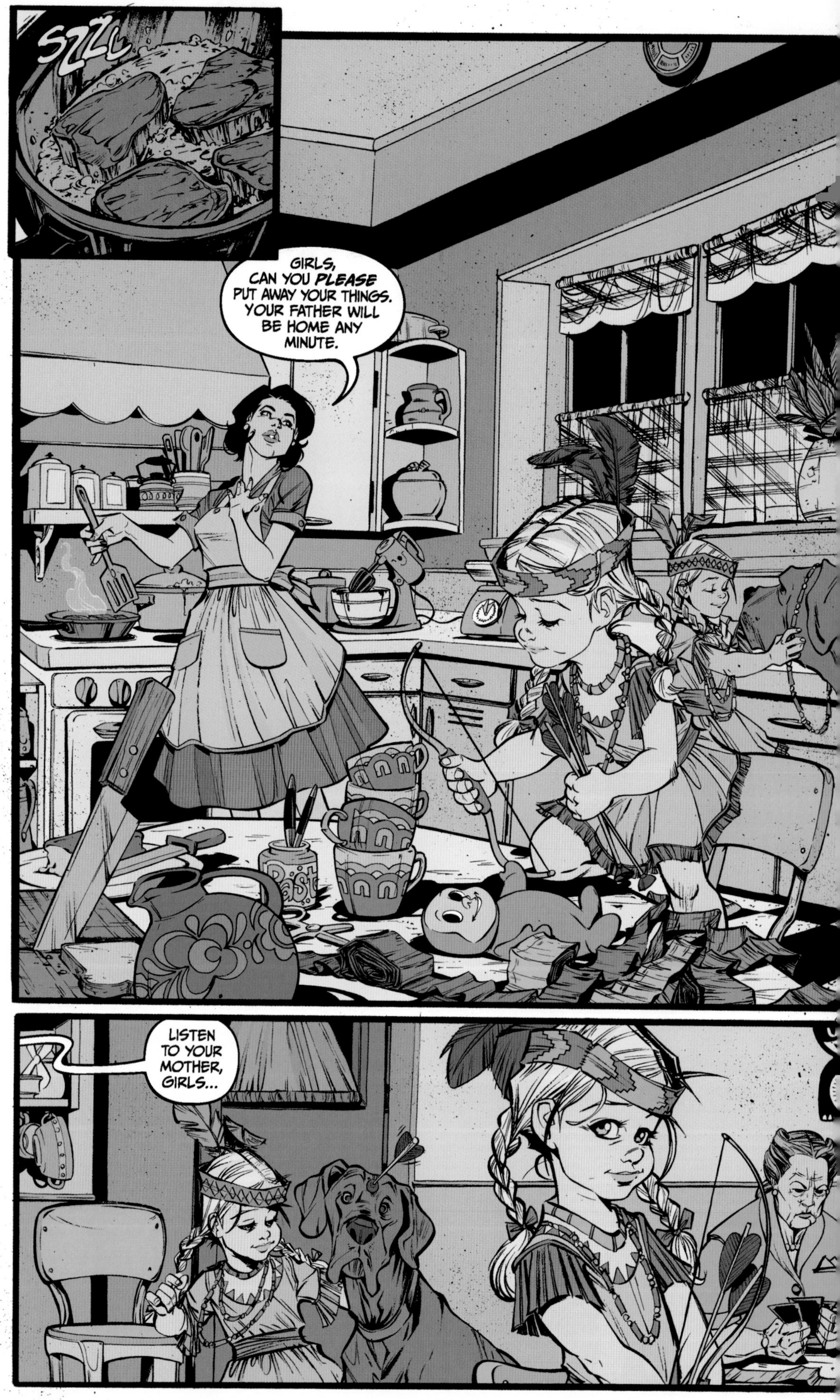
SZZL
GIRLS, CAN YOU PLEASE PUT AWAY YOUR THINGS. YOUR FATHER WILL BE HOME ANY MINUTE.
LISTEN TO YOUR MOTHER, GIRLS...

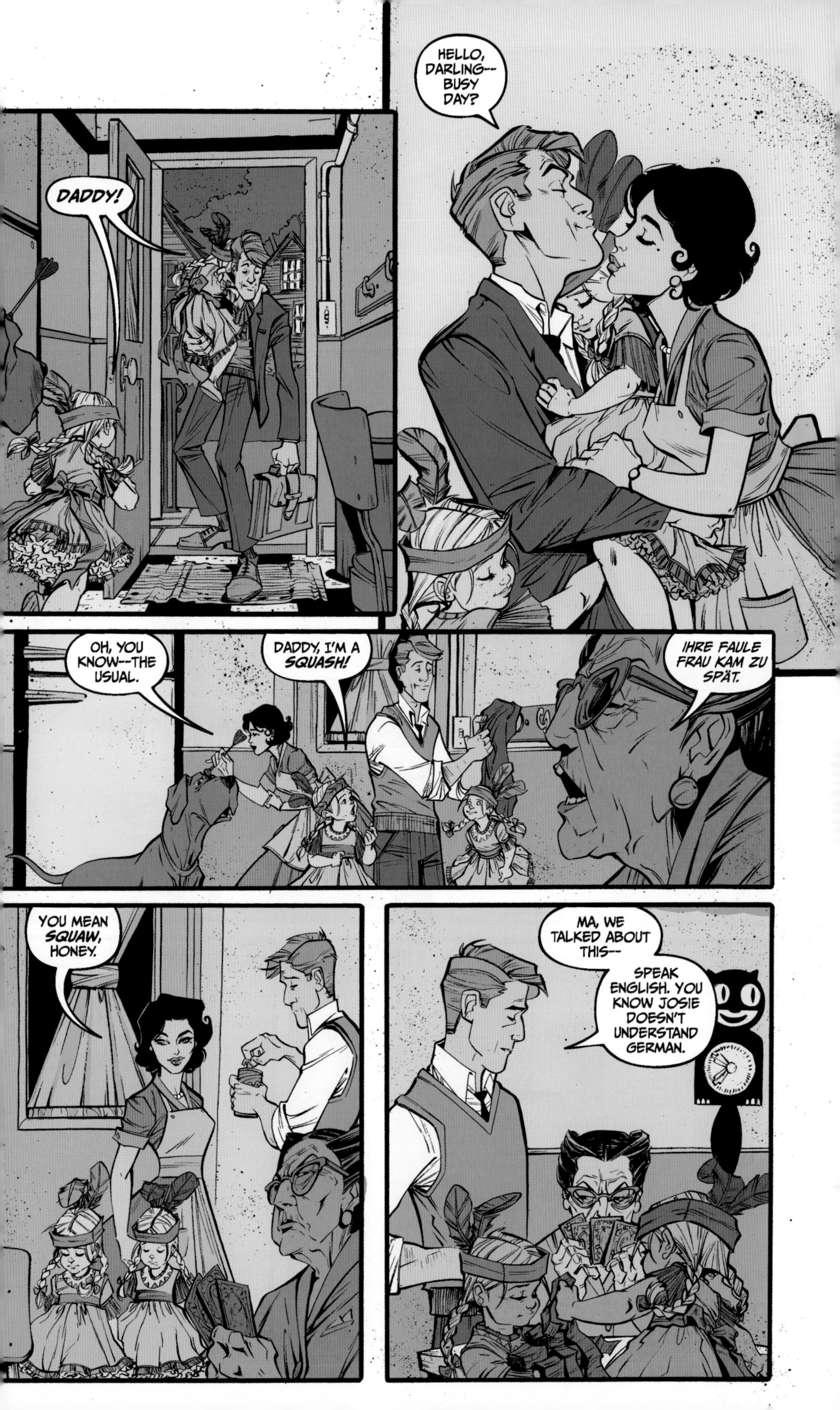
DADDY!
HELLO, DARLING-- BUSY DAY?
OH, YOU KNOW--THE USUAL.
DADDY, I'M A SQUASH!
IHRE FAULE FRAU KAM ZU SPÄT.
YOU MEAN SQUAW, HONEY.
MA, WE TALKED ABOUT THIS--
SPEAK ENGLISH. YOU KNOW JOSIE DOESN'T UNDERSTAND GERMAN.

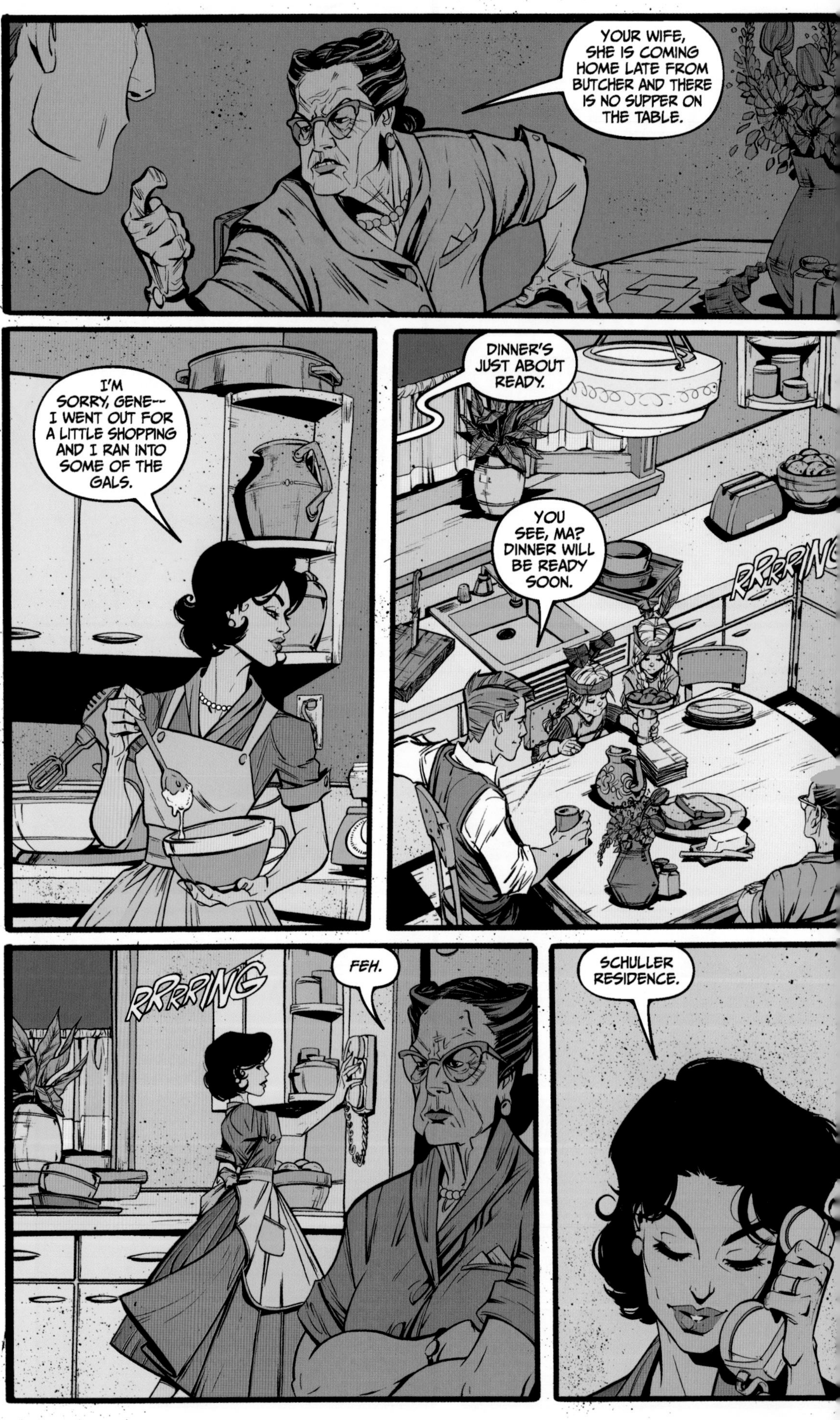
YOUR WIFE, SHE IS COMING HOME LATE FROM BUTCHER AND THERE IS NO SUPPER ON THE TABLE.
I'M SORRY, GENE-- I WENT OUT FOR A LITTLE SHOPPING AND I RAN INTO SOME OF THE GALS.
DINNER'S JUST ABOUT READY.
YOU SEE, MA? DINNER WILL BE READY SOON.
RRRRING
RRRRING
FEH.
SCHULLER RESIDENCE.

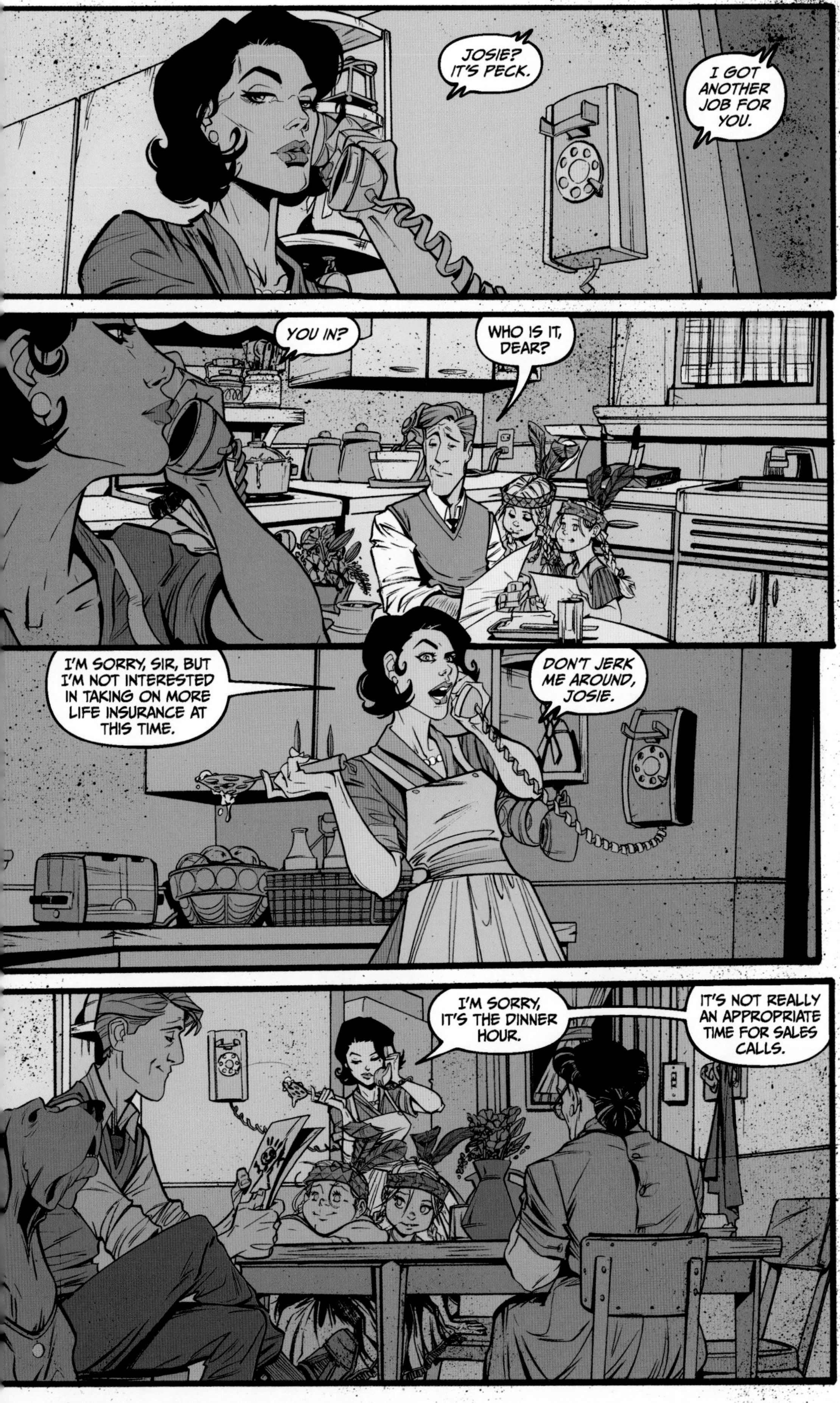
JOSIE? IT'S PECK.
I GOT ANOTHER JOB FOR YOU.
YOU IN?
WHO IS IT, DEAR?
I'M SORRY, SIR, BUT I'M NOT INTERESTED IN TAKING ON MORE LIFE INSURANCE AT THIS TIME.
DON'T JERK ME AROUND, JOSIE.
I'M SORRY, IT'S THE DINNER HOUR.
IT'S NOT REALLY AN APPROPRIATE TIME FOR SALES CALLS.

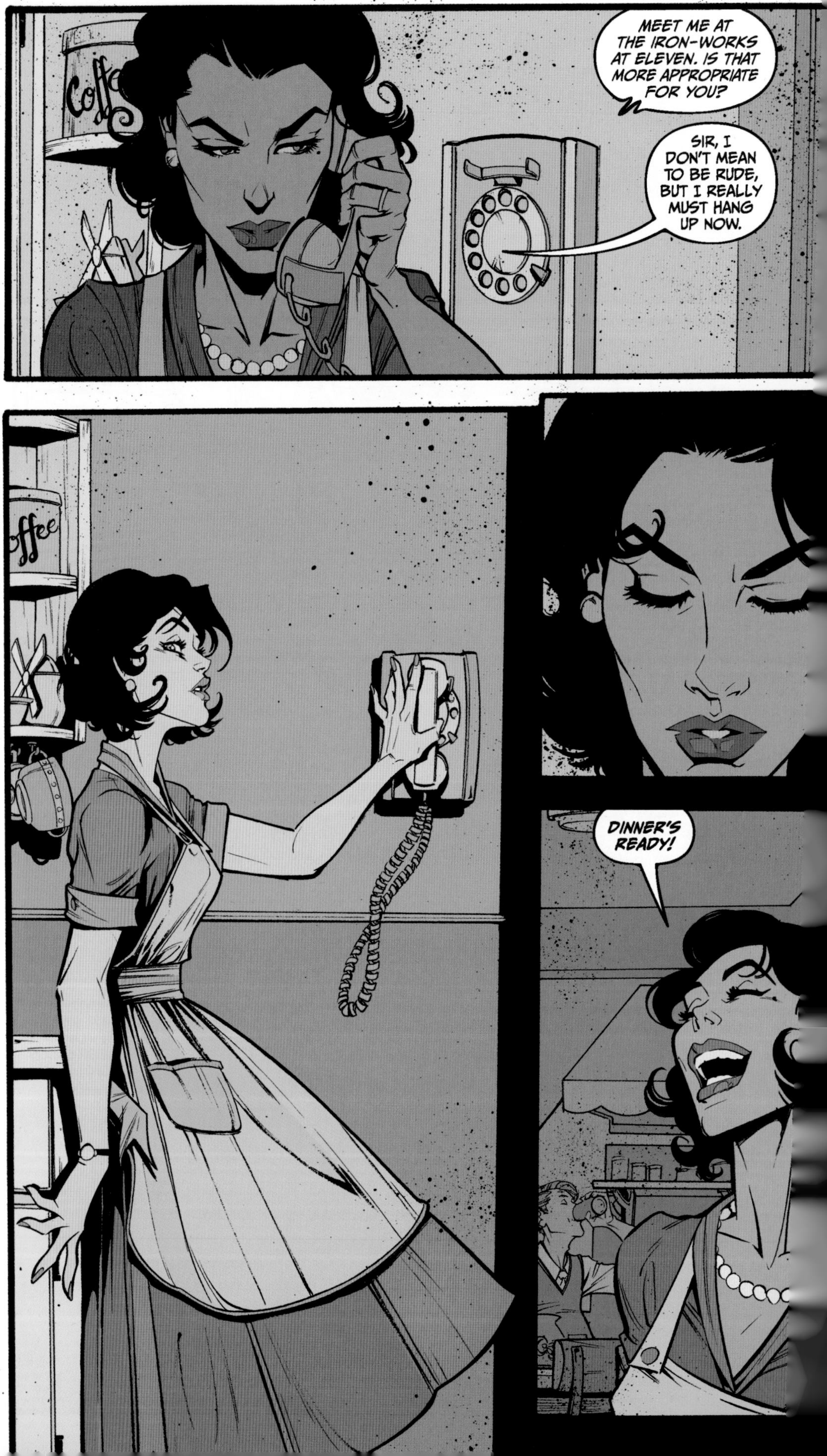
MEET ME AT THE IRON-WORKS AT ELEVEN. IS THAT MORE APPROPRIATE FOR YOU?
SIR, I DON'T MEAN TO BE RUDE, BUT I REALLY MUST HANG UP NOW.
Coffee
Coffee
DINNER'S READY!

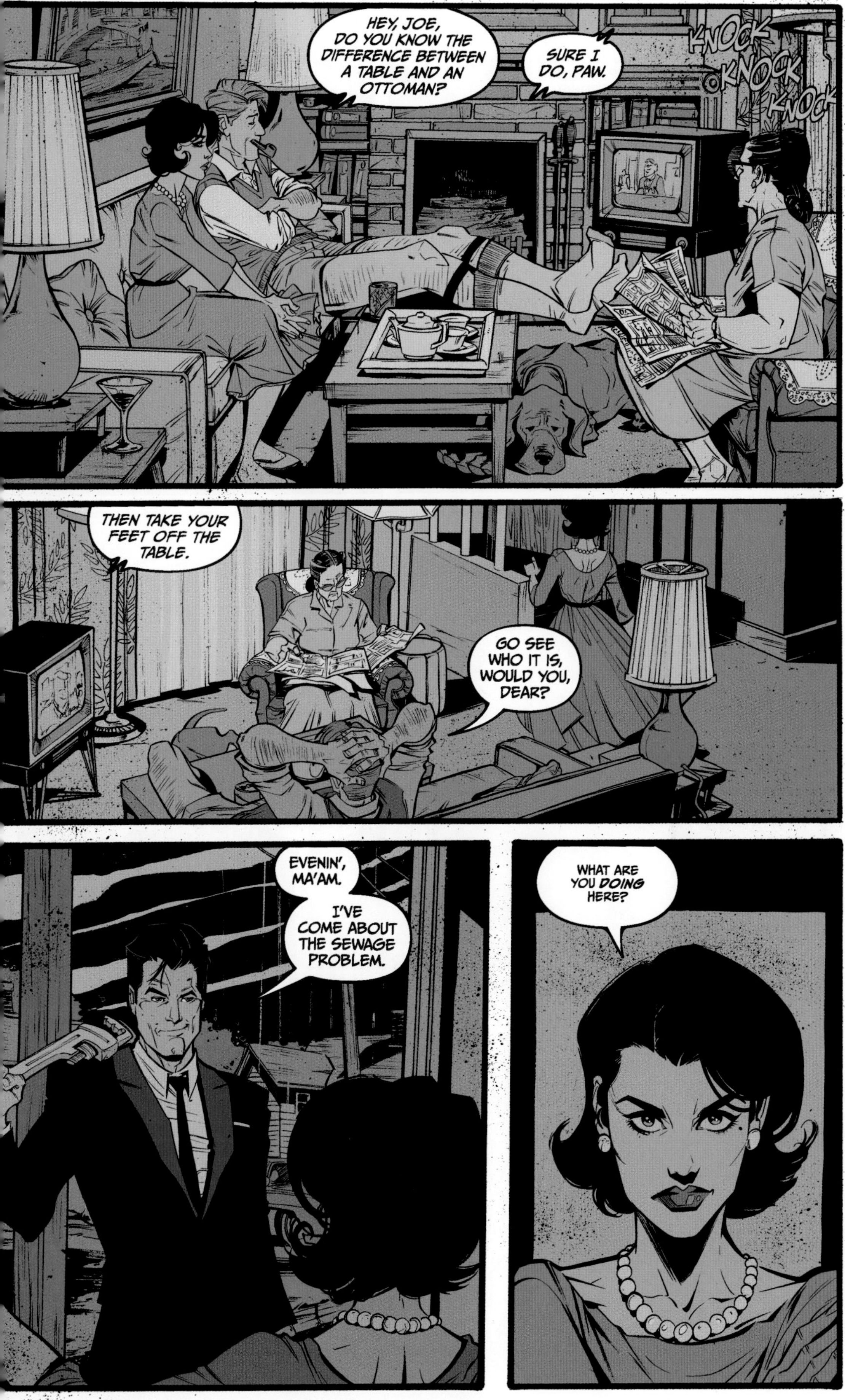
HEY, JOE, DO YOU KNOW THE DIFFERENCE BETWEEN A TABLE AND AN OTTOMAN?
SURE I DO, PAW.
KNOCK KNOCK KNOCK
THEN TAKE YOUR FEET OFF THE TABLE.
GO SEE WHO IT IS, WOULD YOU, DEAR?
EVENIN', MA'AM.
I'VE COME ABOUT THE SEWAGE PROBLEM.
WHAT ARE YOU DOING HERE?

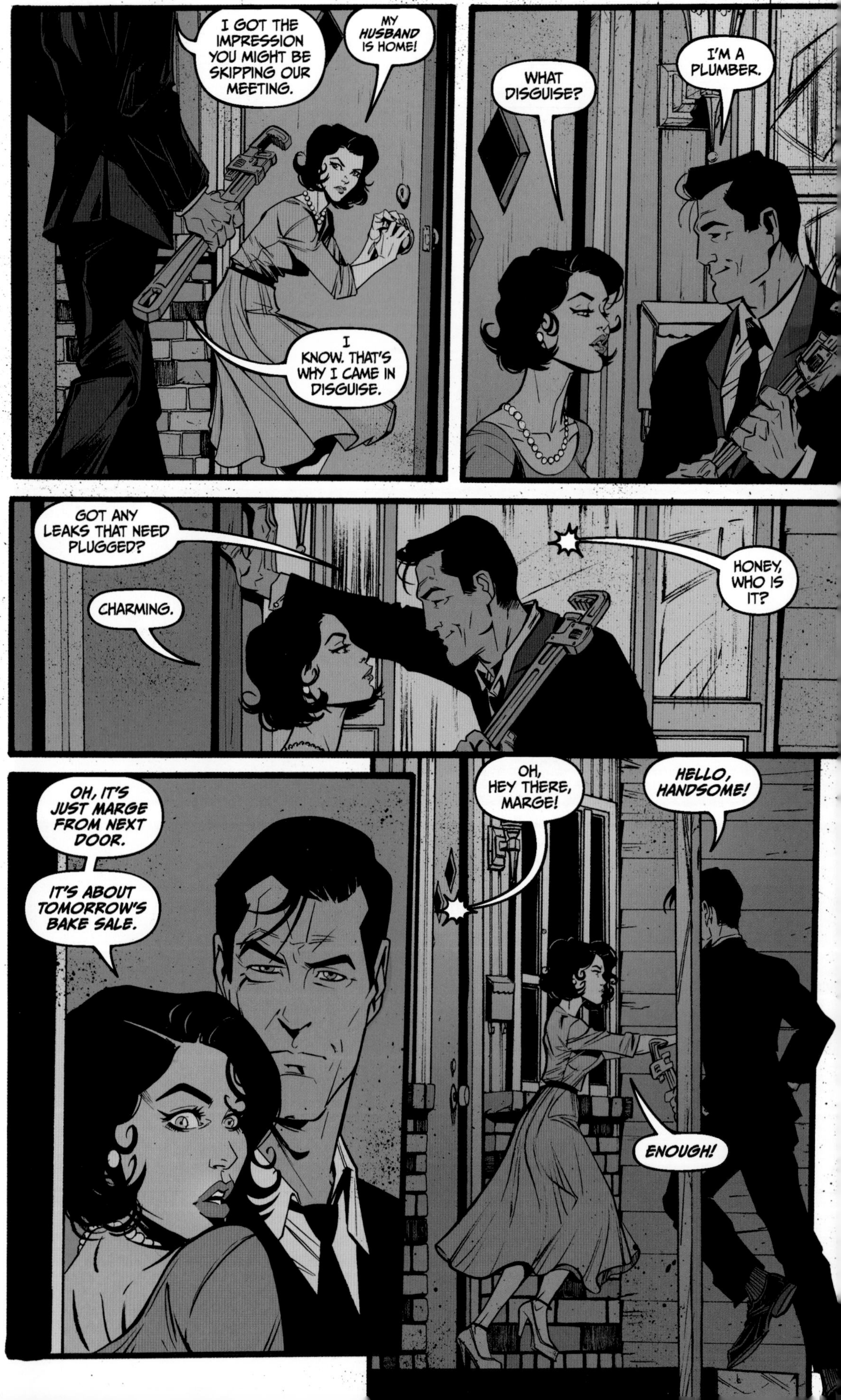

I GOT THE IMPRESSION YOU MIGHT BE SKIPPING OUR MEETING.
MY *HUSBAND* IS HOME!
I KNOW. THAT'S WHY I CAME IN DISGUISE.
WHAT DISGUISE?
I'M A PLUMBER.
GOT ANY LEAKS THAT NEED PLUGGED?
CHARMING.
HONEY, WHO IS IT?
OH, IT'S JUST MARGE FROM NEXT DOOR.
IT'S ABOUT TOMORROW'S BAKE SALE.
OH, HEY THERE, MARGE!
HELLO, HANDSOME!
ENOUGH!

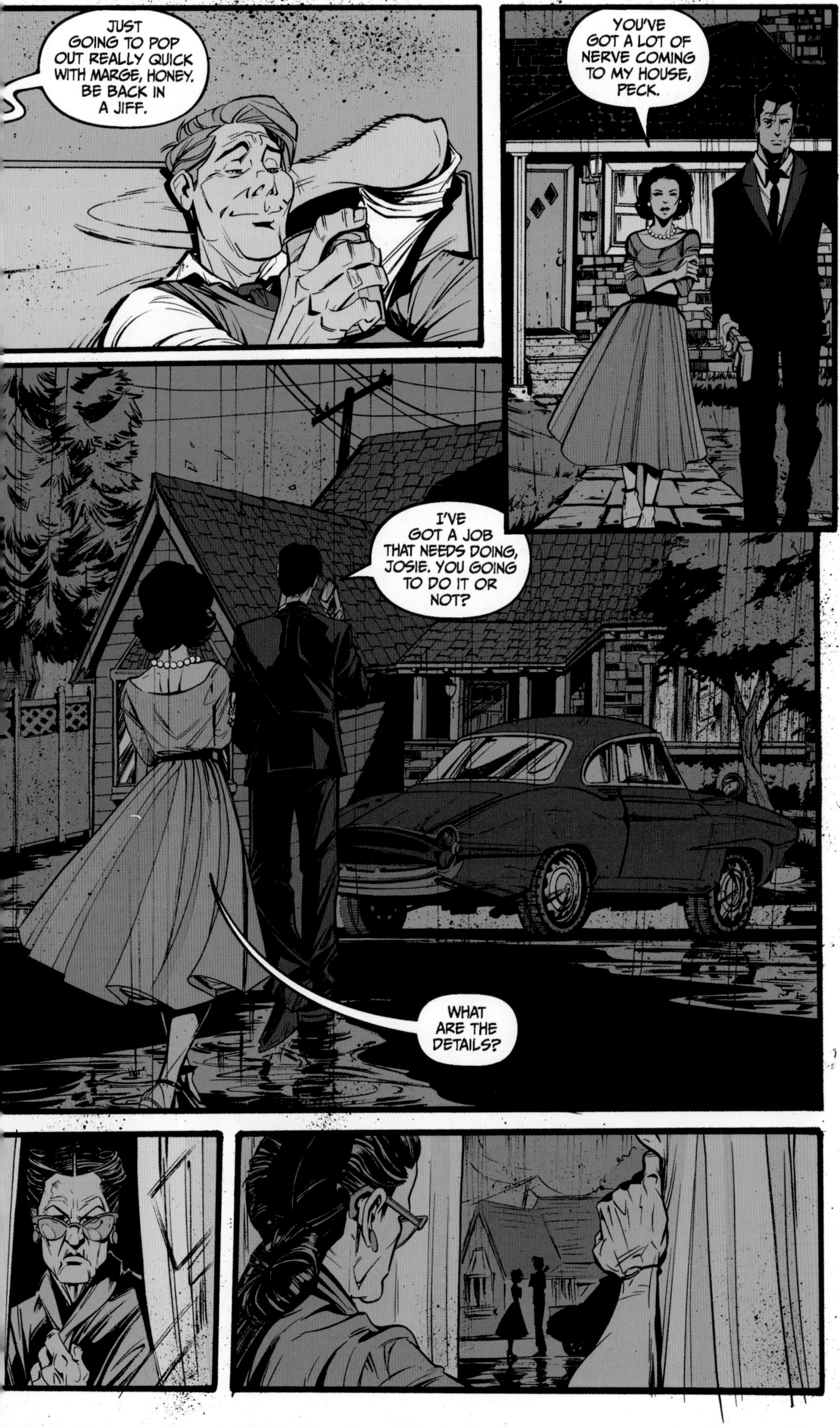
JUST GOING TO POP OUT REALLY QUICK WITH MARGE, HONEY. BE BACK IN A JIFF.
YOU'VE GOT A LOT OF NERVE COMING TO MY HOUSE, PECK.
I'VE GOT A JOB THAT NEEDS DOING, JOSIE. YOU GOING TO DO IT OR NOT?
WHAT ARE THE DETAILS?

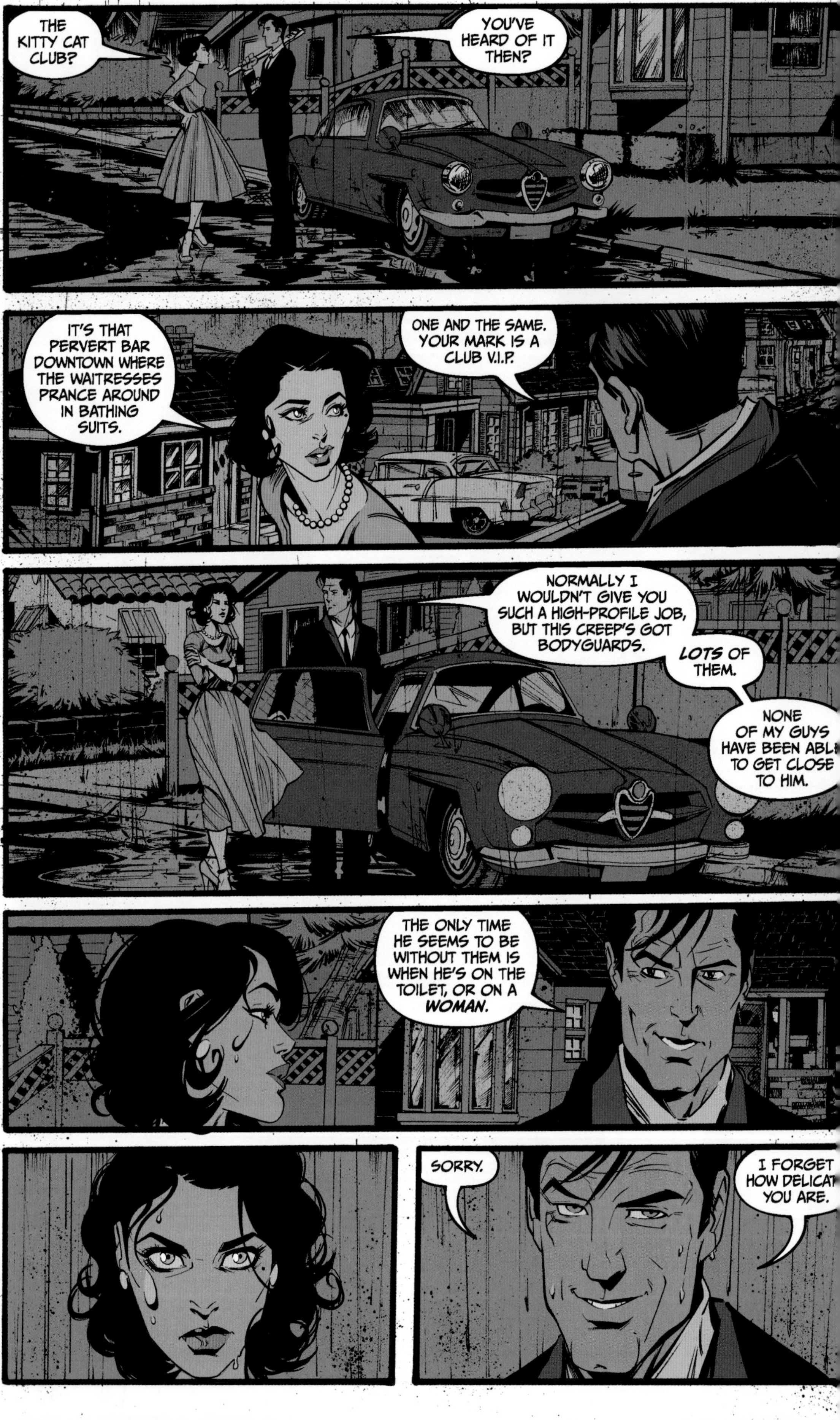
THE KITTY CAT CLUB?
YOU'VE HEARD OF IT THEN?
IT'S THAT PERVERT BAR DOWNTOWN WHERE THE WAITRESSES PRANCE AROUND IN BATHING SUITS.
ONE AND THE SAME. YOUR MARK IS A CLUB V.I.P.
NORMALLY I WOULDN'T GIVE YOU SUCH A HIGH-PROFILE JOB, BUT THIS CREEP'S GOT BODYGUARDS.
LOTS OF THEM.
NONE OF MY GUYS HAVE BEEN ABL TO GET CLOSE TO HIM.
THE ONLY TIME HE SEEMS TO BE WITHOUT THEM IS WHEN HE'S ON THE TOILET, OR ON A WOMAN.
SORRY.
I FORGET HOW DELICAT YOU ARE.

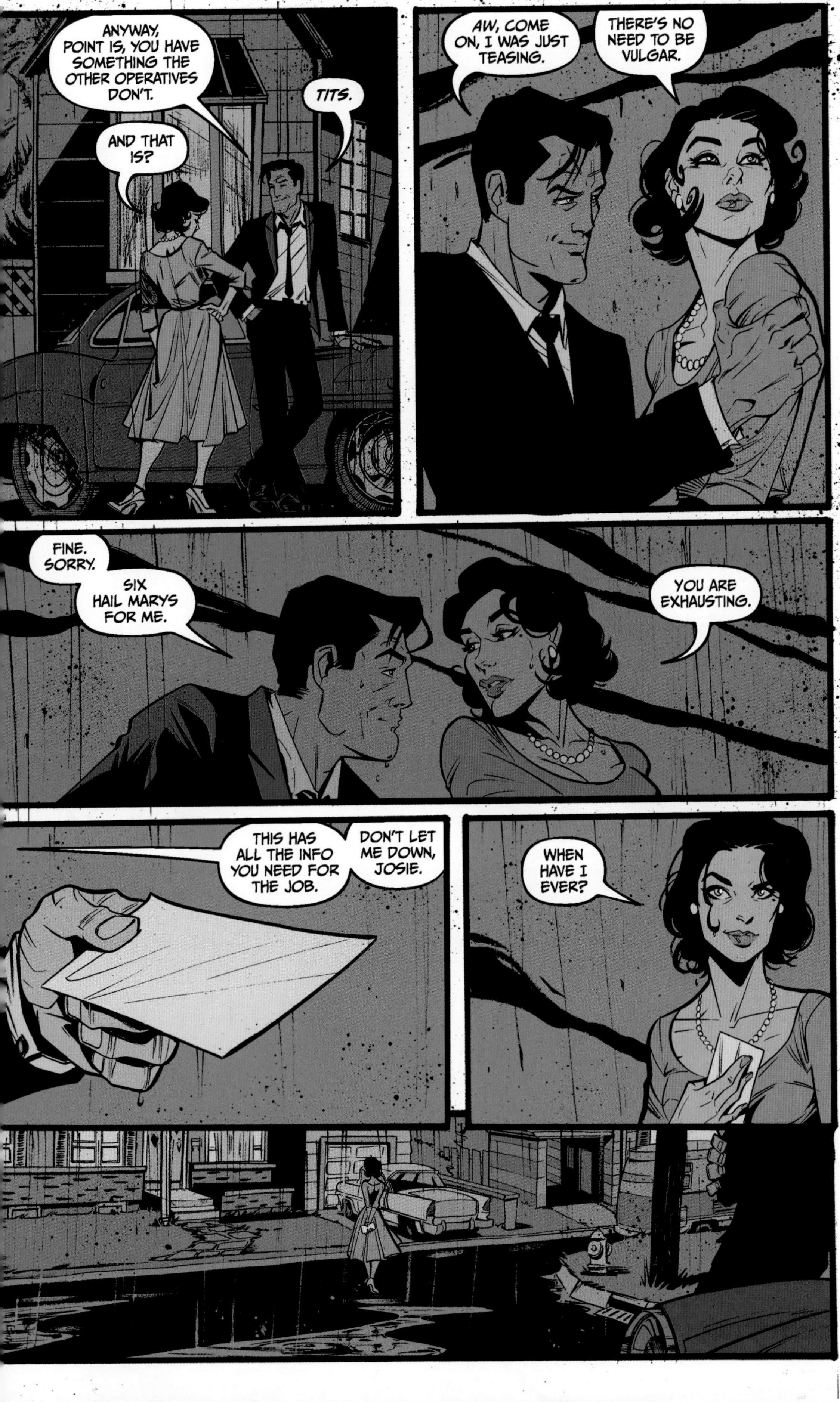
ANYWAY, POINT IS, YOU HAVE SOMETHING THE OTHER OPERATIVES DON'T.
AND THAT IS?
TITS.
AW, COME ON, I WAS JUST TEASING.
THERE'S NO NEED TO BE VULGAR.
FINE. SORRY.
SIX HAIL MARYS FOR ME.
YOU ARE EXHAUSTING.
THIS HAS ALL THE INFO YOU NEED FOR THE JOB.
DON'T LET ME DOWN, JOSIE.
WHEN HAVE I EVER?

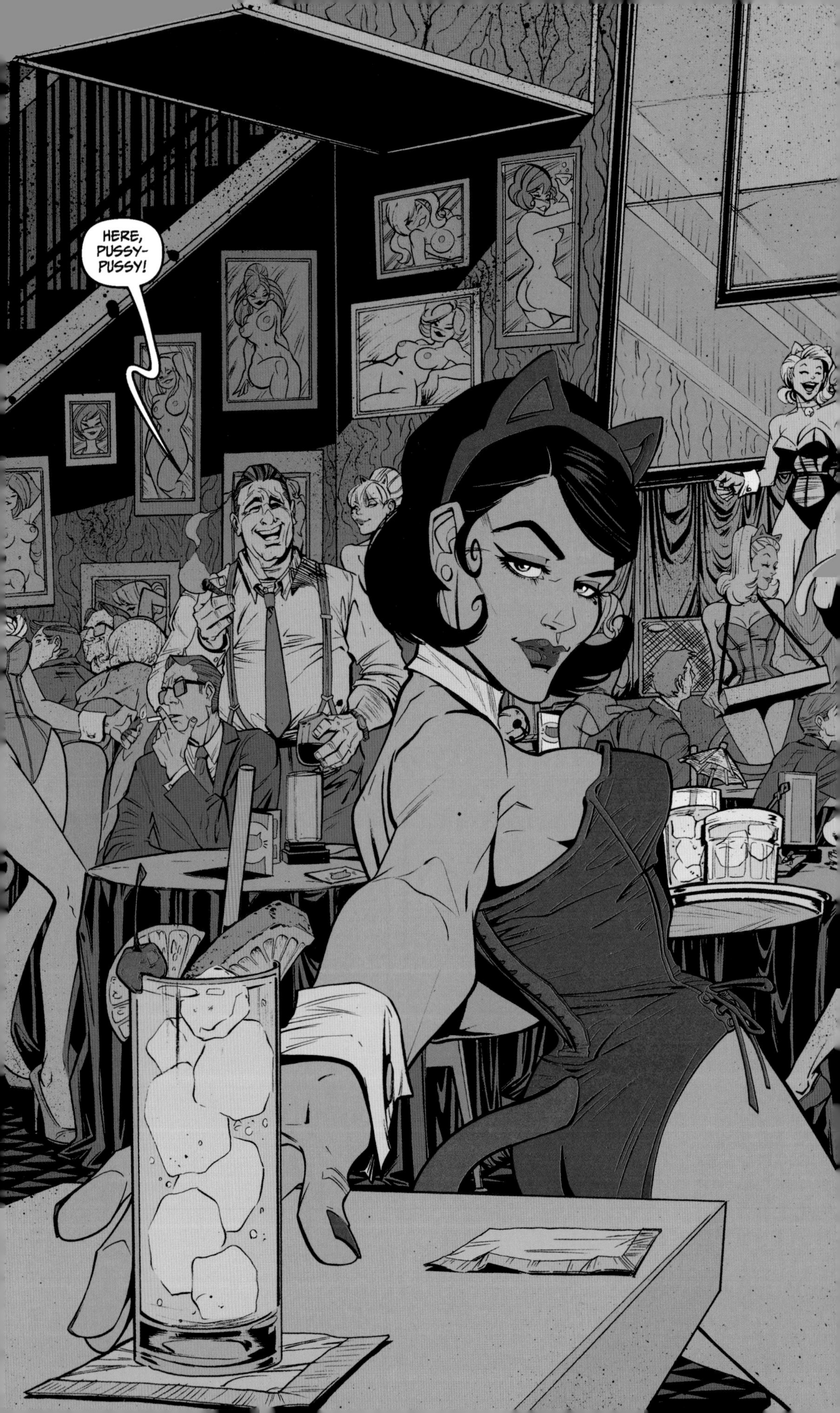
HERE, PUSSY-PUSSY!

darkhorse originals

"unique creators with unique visions"
—MIKE RICHARDSON, PUBLISHER

3 STORY: THE SECRET HISTORY OF THE GIANT MAN
978-1-59582-356-4 | $19.99

365 SAMURAI AND A FEW BOWLS OF RICE
978-1-59582-412-7 | $16.99

THE ADVENTURES OF BLANCHE
978-1-59582-258-1 | $15.99

APOCALYPTIGIRL: AN ARIA FOR THE END TIMES
978-1-61655-566-5 | $9.99

BEANWORLD
Volume 1: Wahoolazuma!
978-1-59582-240-6 | $19.99
Volume 2: A Gift Comes!
978-1-59582-299-4 | $19.99
Volume 3: Remember Here When You Are There!
978-1-59582-355-7 | $19.99
Volume 3.5: Tales of the Beanworld
978-1-59582-897-2 | $14.99

BLACKSAD
978-1-59582-393-9 | $29.99

BLACKSAD: A SILENT HELL
978-1-59582-931-3 | $19.99

BLOOD SONG: A SILENT BALLAD
978-1-59582-389-2 | $19.99

THE BOOK OF GRICKLE
978-1-59582-430-1 | $17.99

BRODY'S GHOST COLLECTED EDITION
978-1-61655-901-4 | $24.99

BUCKO
978-1-59582-973-3 | $19.99

CHANNEL ZERO
978-1-59582-936-8 | $19.99

CHERUBS
978-1-59582-984-9 | $19.99

CHIMICHANGA
978-1-59582-755-5 | $14.99

CITIZEN REX
978-1-59582-556-8 | $19.99

THE COMPLETE PISTOLWHIP
978-1-61655-720-1 | $27.99

CROSSING THE EMPTY QUARTER AND OTHER STORIES
978-1-59582-388-5 | $24.99

DE:TALES
HC: 978-1-59582-557-5 | $19.99
TPB: 978-1-59307-485-2 | $14.99

EVERYBODY GETS IT WRONG! AND OTHER STORIES: DAVID CHELSEA'S 24-HOUR COMICS
978-1-61655-155-1 | $19.99

EXURBIA
978-1-59582-339-7 | $9.99

FLUFFY
978-1-59307-972-7 | $19.99

GREEN RIVER KILLER
978-1-61655-812-3 | $19.99

HEART IN A BOX
978-1-61655-694-5 | $14.99

INSOMNIA CAFÉ
978-1-59582-357-1 | $14.99

THE MIGHTY SKULLBOY ARMY
Volume 2
978-1-59582-872-9 | $14.99

MILK AND CHEESE: DAIRY PRODUCTS GONE BAD
978-1-59582-805-7 | $19.99

MIND MGMT
Volume 1: The Manager
978-1-59582-797-5 | $19.99
Volume 2: The Futurist
978-1-61655-198-8 | $19.99
Volume 3: The Home Maker
978-1-61655-390-6 | $19.99
Volume 4: The Magician
978-1-61655-391-3 | $19.99
Volume 5: The Eraser
978-1-61655-696-9 | $19.99
Volume 6: The Immortals
978-1-61655-798-0 | $19.99

MOTEL ART IMPROVEMENT SERVICE
978-1-59582-550-6 | $19.99

THE NIGHT OF YOUR LIFE
978-1-59582-183-6 | $15.99

NINGEN'S NIGHTMARES
978-1-59582-859-0 | $12.99

NOIR
978-1-59582-358-8 | $12.99

PIXU: THE MARK OF EVIL
978-1-61655-813-0 | $14.99

RESET
978-1-61655-003-5 | $15.99

SACRIFICE
978-1-59582-985-6 | $19.99

SINFEST: VIVA LA RESISTANCE
978-1-59582-424-0 | $14.99

SPEAK OF THE DEVIL
978-1-59582-193-5 | $19.99

UNCLE SILAS
978-1-59582-566-7 | $9.99

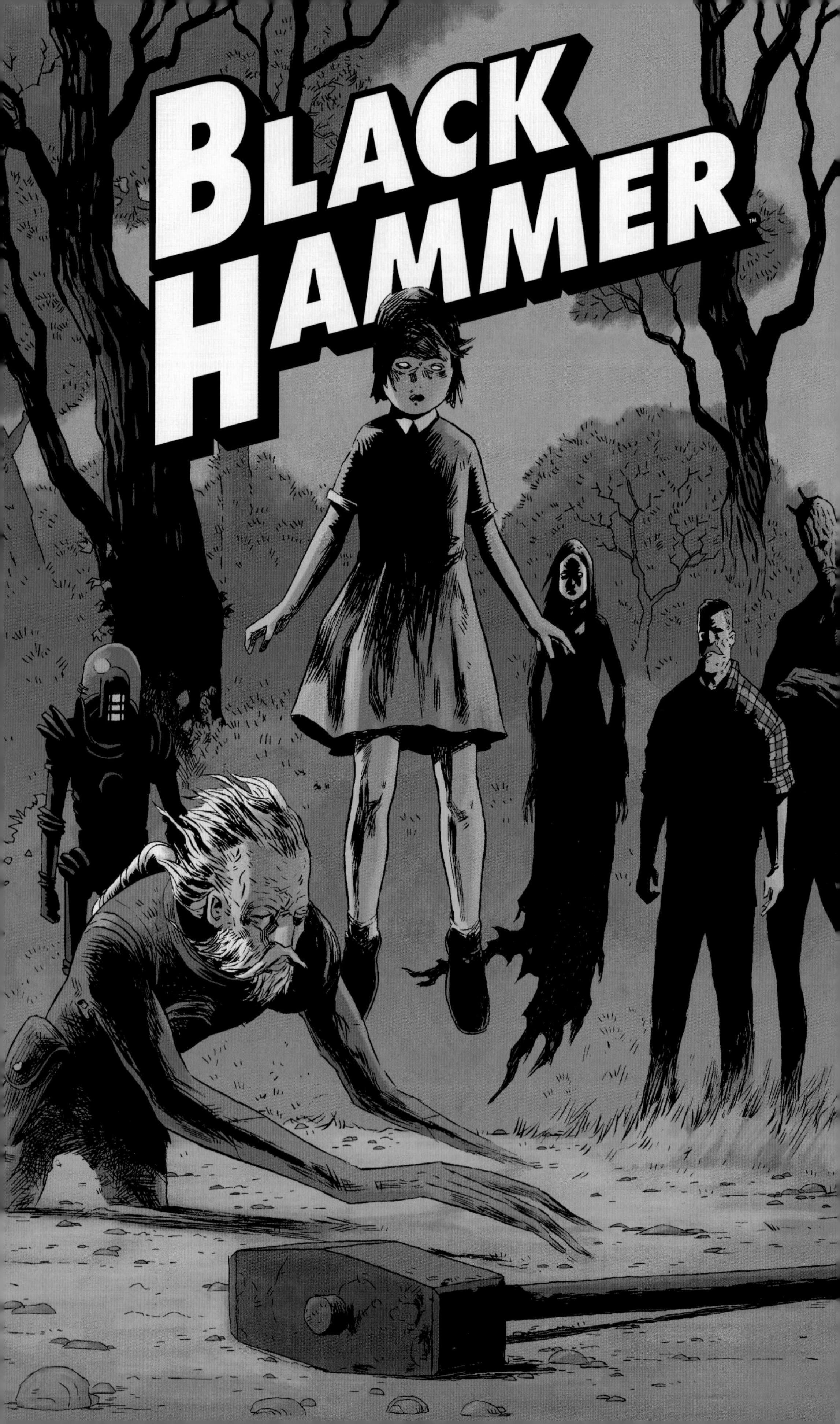
BLACK
HAMMER™

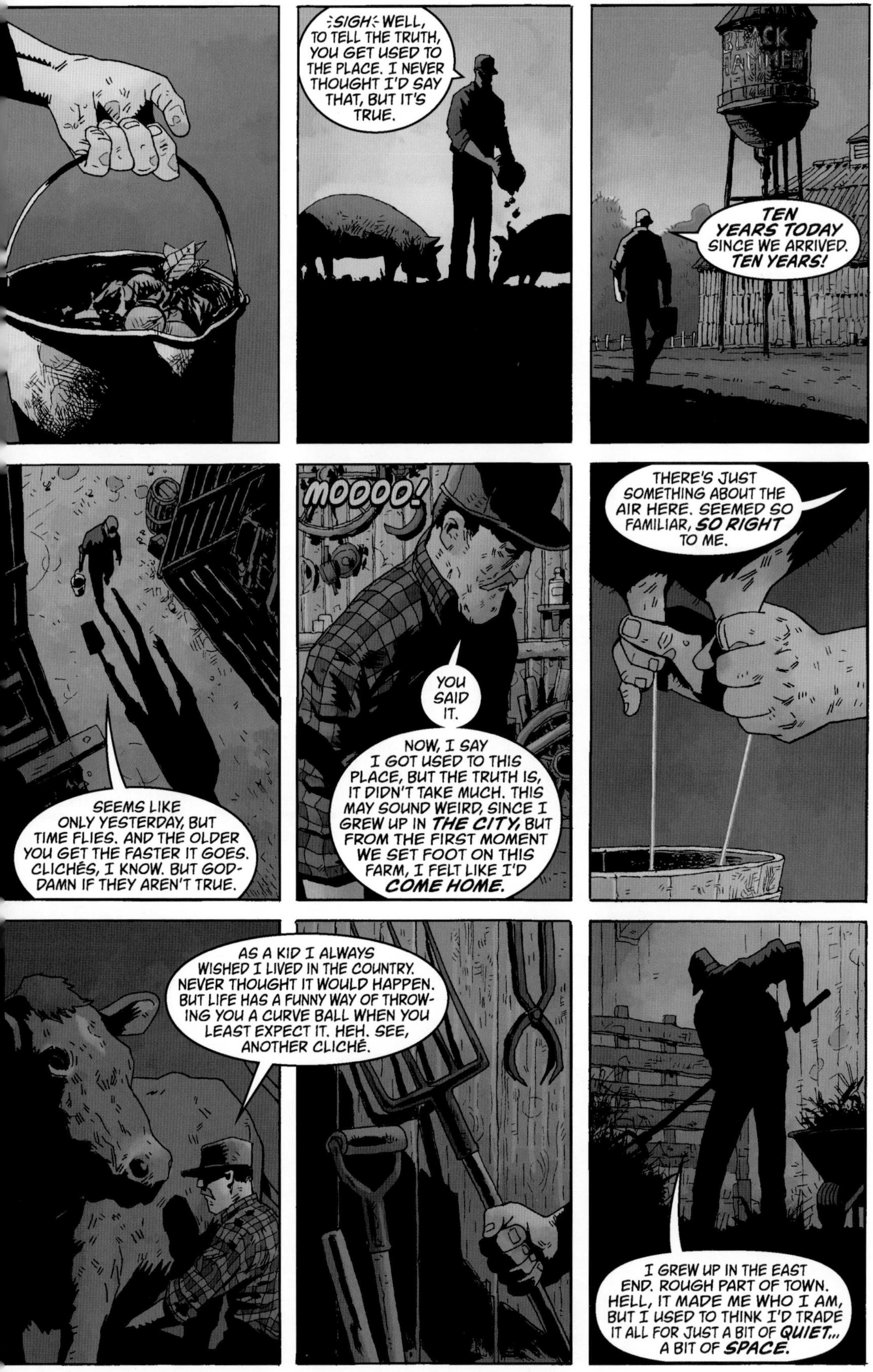
-SIGH- WELL, TO TELL THE TRUTH, YOU GET USED TO THE PLACE. I NEVER THOUGHT I'D SAY THAT, BUT IT'S TRUE.
BLACK HAMMER
TEN YEARS TODAY SINCE WE ARRIVED. TEN YEARS!
SEEMS LIKE ONLY YESTERDAY, BUT TIME FLIES. AND THE OLDER YOU GET THE FASTER IT GOES. CLICHÉS, I KNOW. BUT GOD-DAMN IF THEY AREN'T TRUE.
MOOOO!
YOU SAID IT.
NOW, I SAY I GOT USED TO THIS PLACE, BUT THE TRUTH IS, IT DIDN'T TAKE MUCH. THIS MAY SOUND WEIRD, SINCE I GREW UP IN THE CITY, BUT FROM THE FIRST MOMENT WE SET FOOT ON THIS FARM, I FELT LIKE I'D COME HOME.
THERE'S JUST SOMETHING ABOUT THE AIR HERE. SEEMED SO FAMILIAR, SO RIGHT TO ME.
AS A KID I ALWAYS WISHED I LIVED IN THE COUNTRY. NEVER THOUGHT IT WOULD HAPPEN. BUT LIFE HAS A FUNNY WAY OF THROWING YOU A CURVE BALL WHEN YOU LEAST EXPECT IT. HEH. SEE, ANOTHER CLICHÉ.
I GREW UP IN THE EAST END. ROUGH PART OF TOWN. HELL, IT MADE ME WHO I AM, BUT I USED TO THINK I'D TRADE IT ALL FOR JUST A BIT OF QUIET... A BIT OF SPACE.

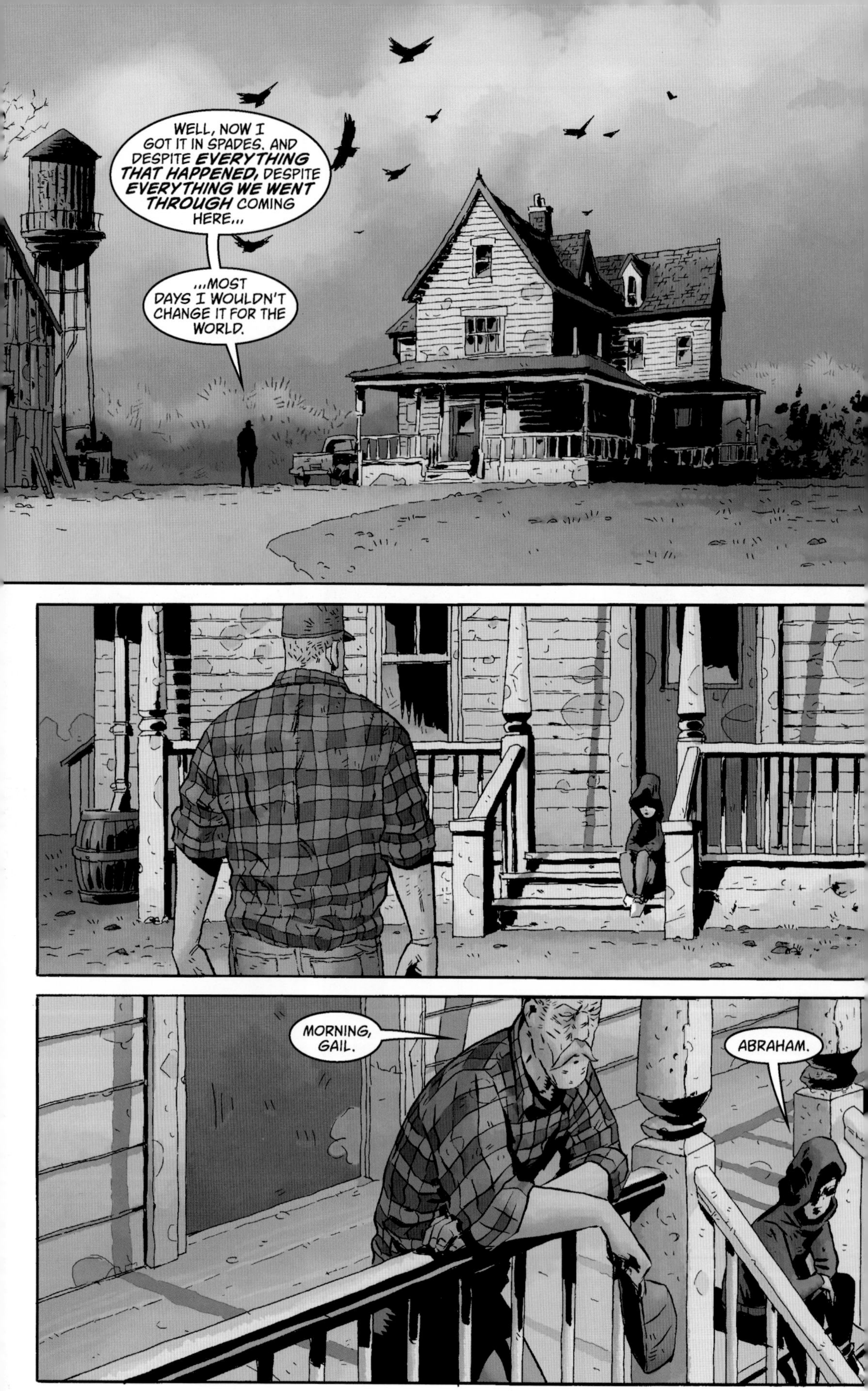
WELL, NOW I GOT IT IN SPADES. AND DESPITE **EVERYTHING THAT HAPPENED,** DESPITE **EVERYTHING WE WENT THROUGH** COMING HERE...
...MOST DAYS I WOULDN'T CHANGE IT FOR THE WORLD.
MORNING, GAIL.
ABRAHAM.

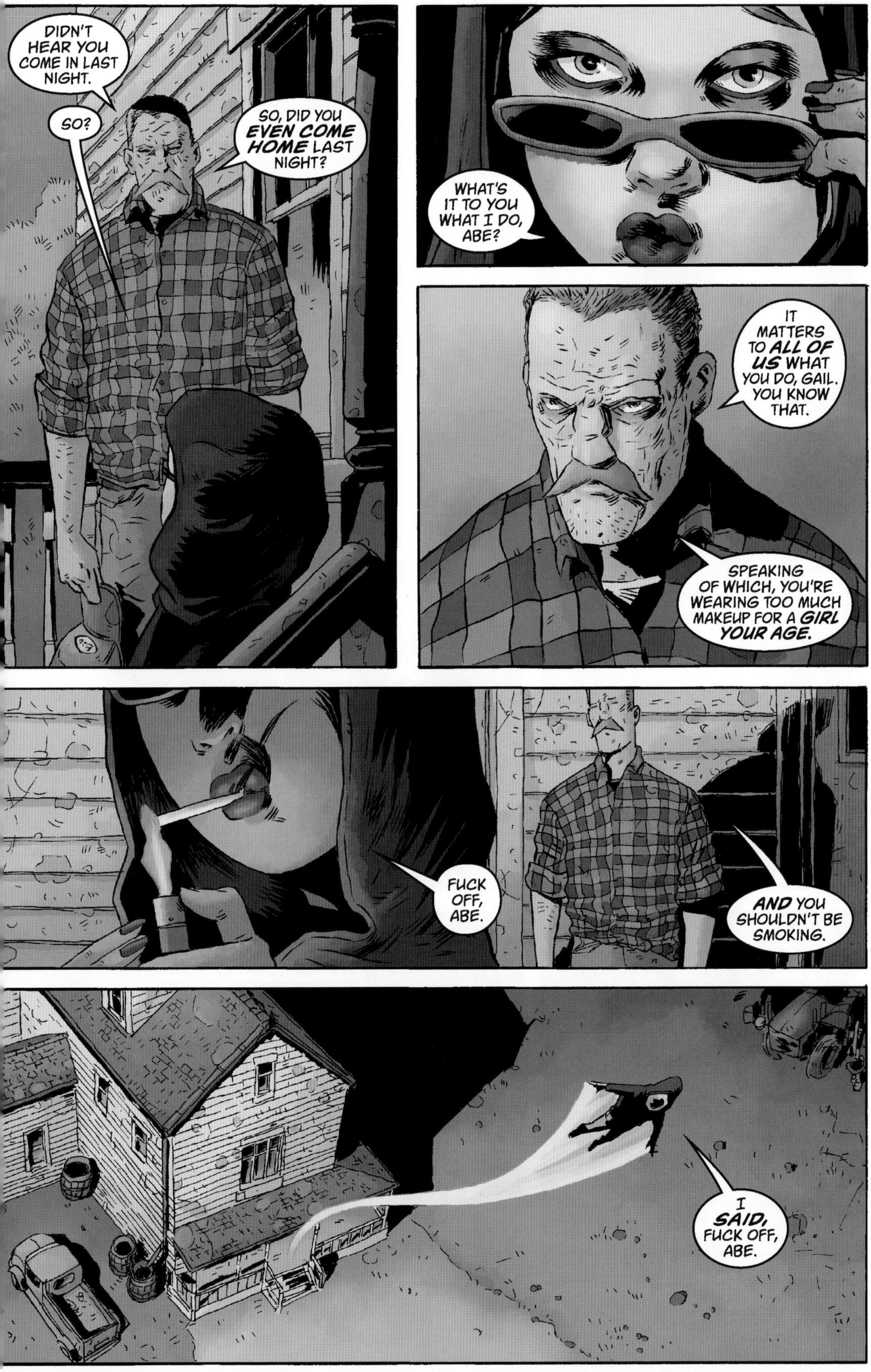
DIDN'T HEAR YOU COME IN LAST NIGHT.
SO?
SO, DID YOU EVEN COME HOME LAST NIGHT?
WHAT'S IT TO YOU WHAT I DO, ABE?
IT MATTERS TO ALL OF US WHAT YOU DO, GAIL. YOU KNOW THAT.
SPEAKING OF WHICH, YOU'RE WEARING TOO MUCH MAKEUP FOR A GIRL YOUR AGE.
FUCK OFF, ABE.
AND YOU SHOULDN'T BE SMOKING.
I SAID, FUCK OFF, ABE.

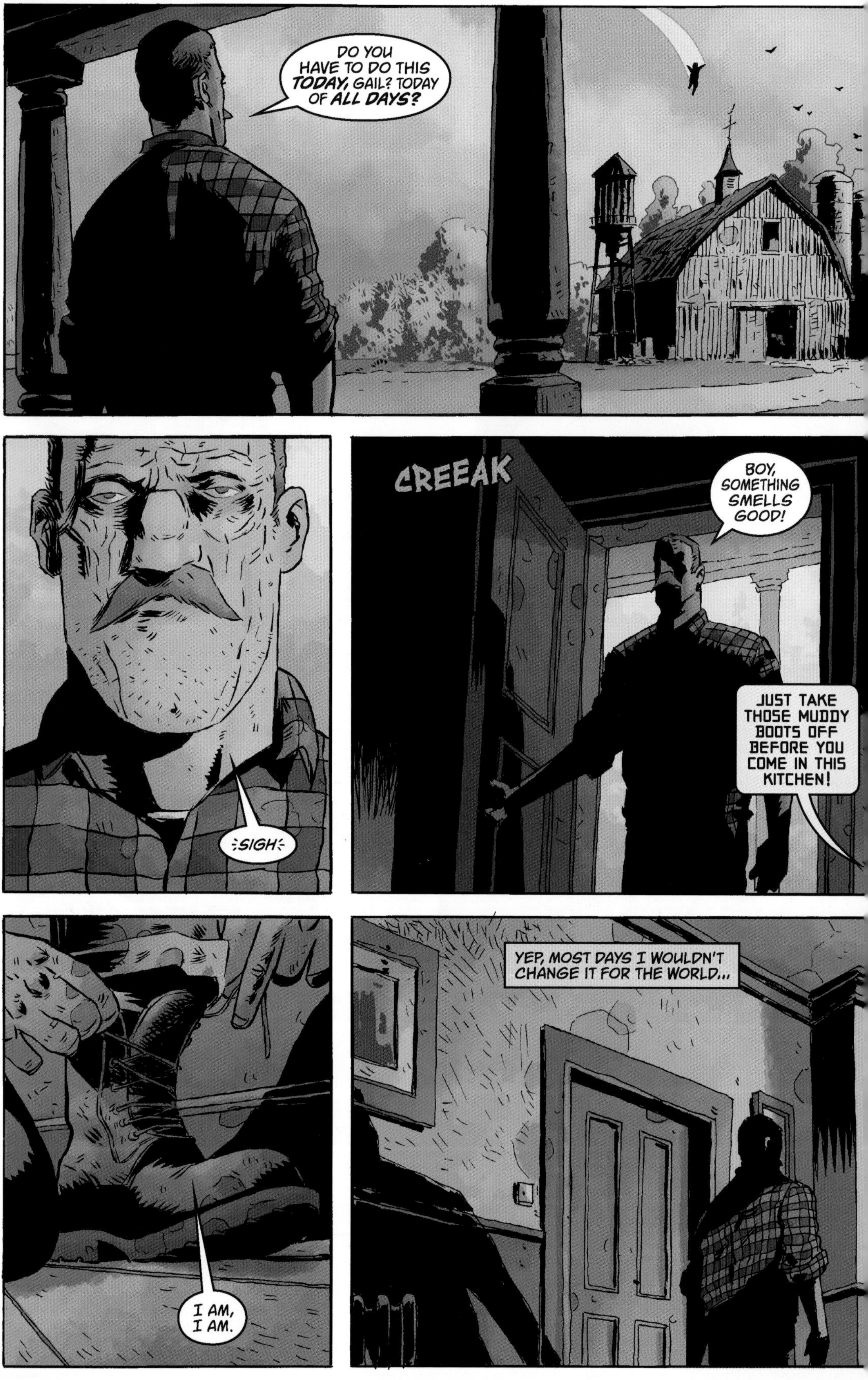

DO YOU HAVE TO DO THIS TODAY, GAIL? TODAY OF ALL DAYS?
SIGH
CREEAK
BOY, SOMETHING SMELLS GOOD!
JUST TAKE THOSE MUDDY BOOTS OFF BEFORE YOU COME IN THIS KITCHEN!
I AM, I AM.
YEP, MOST DAYS I WOULDN'T CHANGE IT FOR THE WORLD...

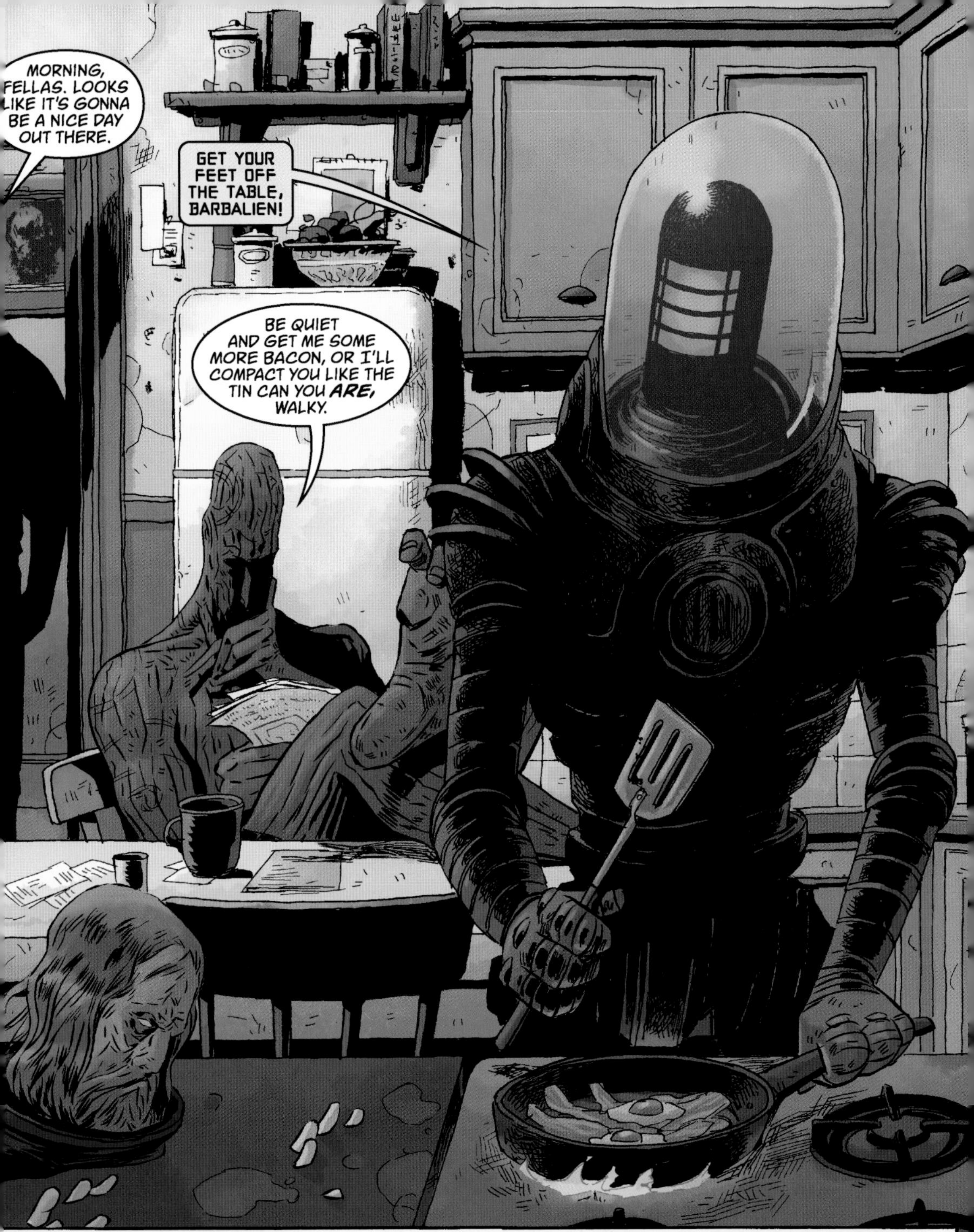
MORNING, FELLAS. LOOKS LIKE IT'S GONNA BE A NICE DAY OUT THERE.
GET YOUR FEET OFF THE TABLE, BARBALIEN!
BE QUIET AND GET ME SOME MORE BACON, OR I'LL COMPACT YOU LIKE THE TIN CAN YOU *ARE,* WALKY.

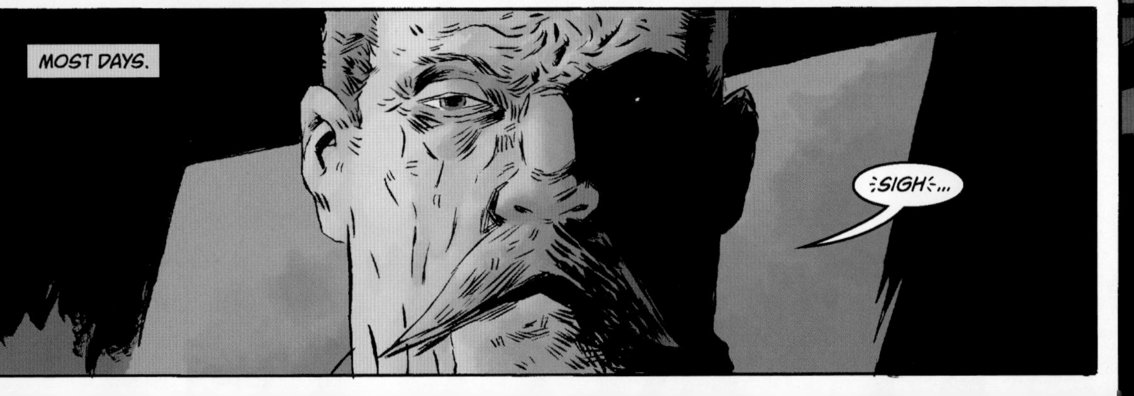
MOST DAYS.
SIGH...

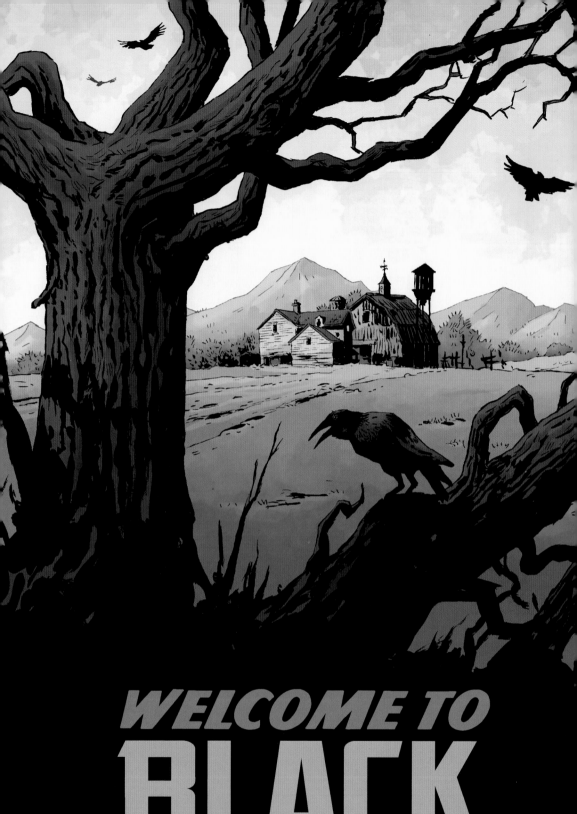

WELCOME TO BLACK HAMMER

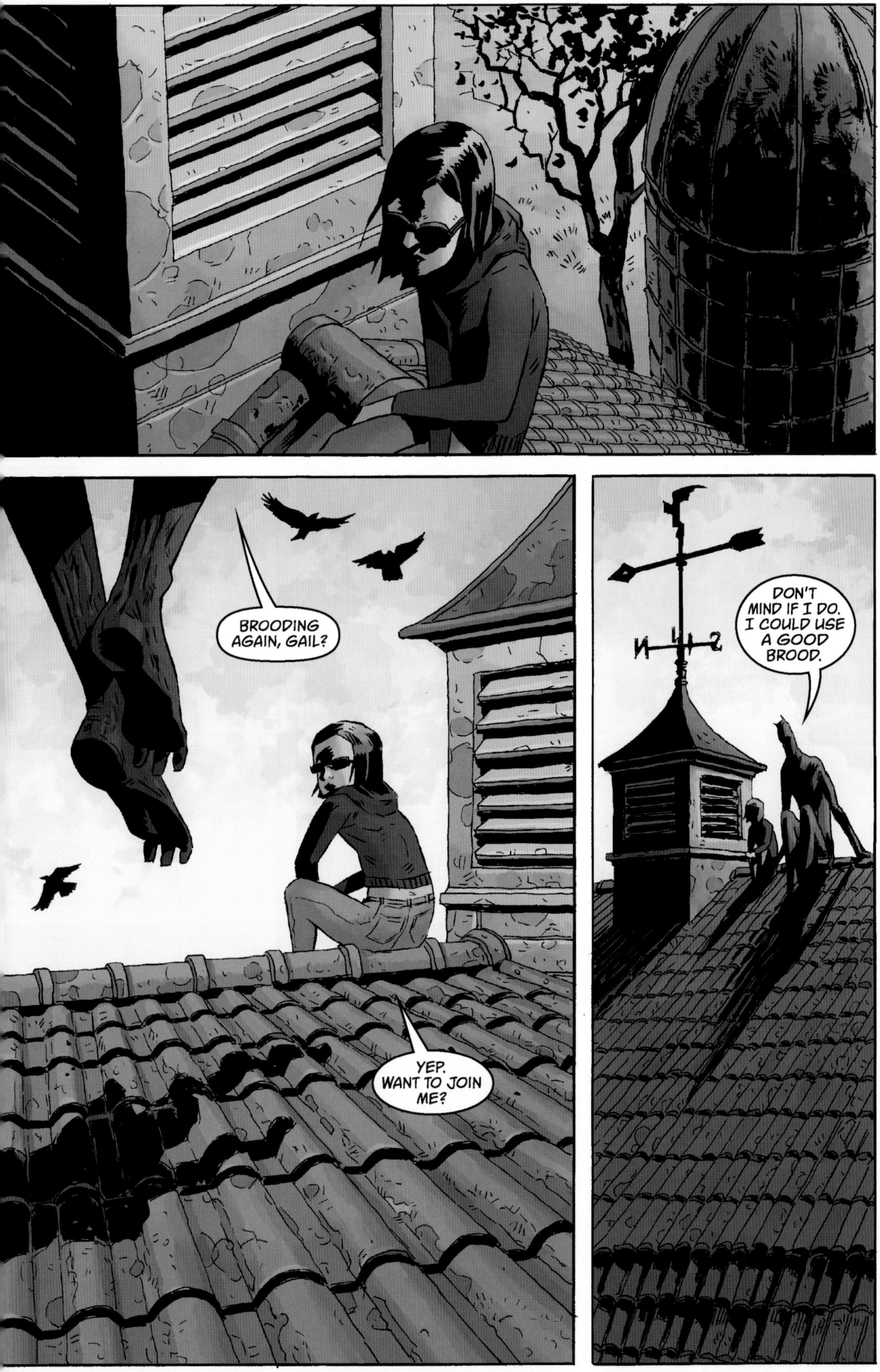
BROODING AGAIN, GAIL?
YEP. WANT TO JOIN ME?
DON'T MIND IF I DO. I COULD USE A GOOD BROOD.

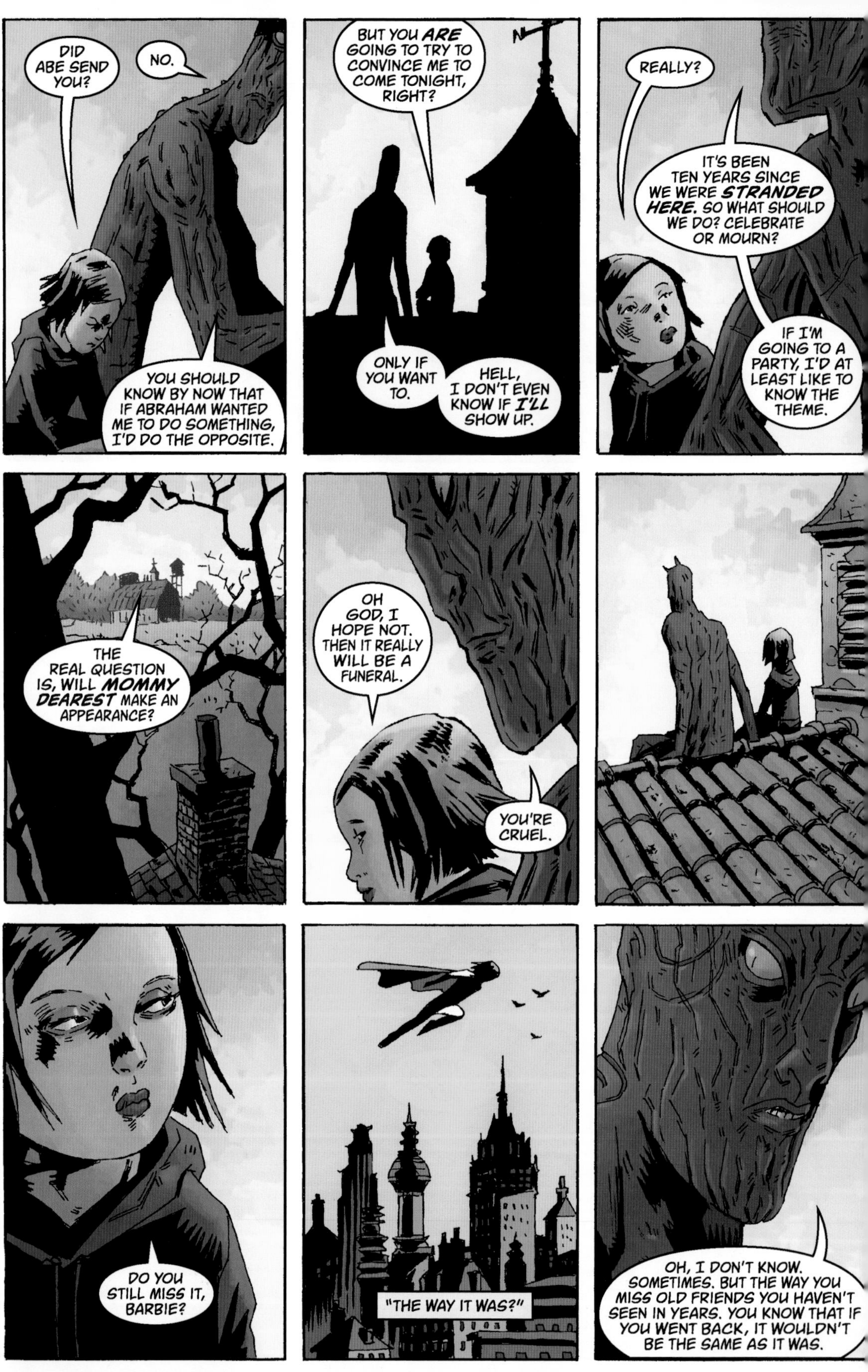
DID ABE SEND YOU?
NO.
YOU SHOULD KNOW BY NOW THAT IF ABRAHAM WANTED ME TO DO SOMETHING, I'D DO THE OPPOSITE.
BUT YOU ARE GOING TO TRY TO CONVINCE ME TO COME TONIGHT, RIGHT?
ONLY IF YOU WANT TO.
HELL, I DON'T EVEN KNOW IF I'LL SHOW UP.
REALLY?
IT'S BEEN TEN YEARS SINCE WE WERE STRANDED HERE. SO WHAT SHOULD WE DO? CELEBRATE OR MOURN?
IF I'M GOING TO A PARTY, I'D AT LEAST LIKE TO KNOW THE THEME.
THE REAL QUESTION IS, WILL MOMMY DEAREST MAKE AN APPEARANCE?
OH GOD, I HOPE NOT. THEN IT REALLY WILL BE A FUNERAL.
YOU'RE CRUEL.
DO YOU STILL MISS IT, BARBIE?
"THE WAY IT WAS?"
OH, I DON'T KNOW. SOMETIMES. BUT THE WAY YOU MISS OLD FRIENDS YOU HAVEN'T SEEN IN YEARS. YOU KNOW THAT IF YOU WENT BACK, IT WOULDN'T BE THE SAME AS IT WAS.

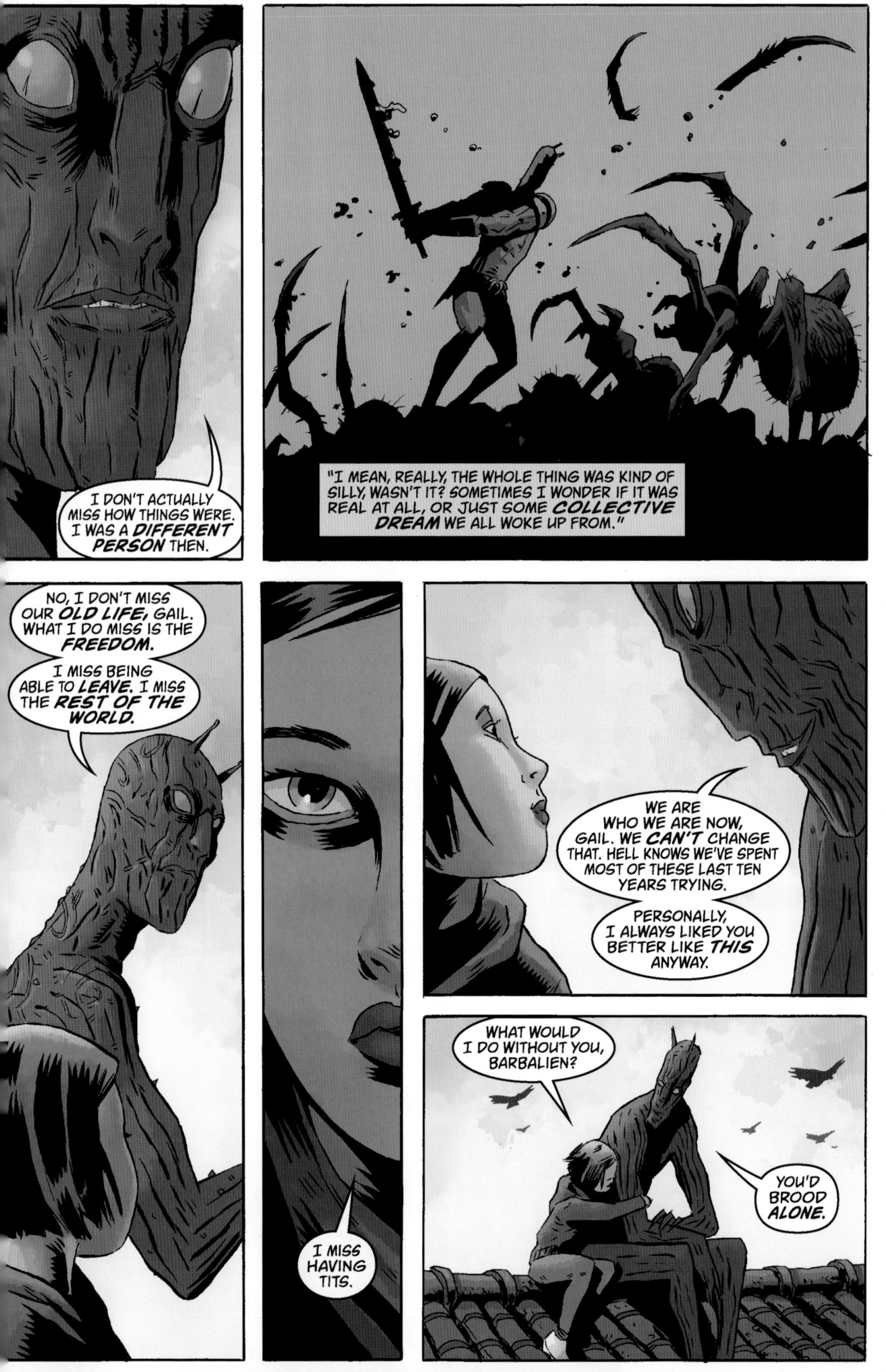
I DON'T ACTUALLY MISS HOW THINGS WERE. I WAS A DIFFERENT PERSON THEN.
"I MEAN, REALLY, THE WHOLE THING WAS KIND OF SILLY, WASN'T IT? SOMETIMES I WONDER IF IT WAS REAL AT ALL, OR JUST SOME COLLECTIVE DREAM WE ALL WOKE UP FROM."
NO, I DON'T MISS OUR OLD LIFE, GAIL. WHAT I DO MISS IS THE FREEDOM.
I MISS BEING ABLE TO LEAVE. I MISS THE REST OF THE WORLD.
I MISS HAVING TITS.
WE ARE WHO WE ARE NOW, GAIL. WE CAN'T CHANGE THAT. HELL KNOWS WE'VE SPENT MOST OF THESE LAST TEN YEARS TRYING.
PERSONALLY, I ALWAYS LIKED YOU BETTER LIKE THIS ANYWAY.
WHAT WOULD I DO WITHOUT YOU, BARBALIEN?
YOU'D BROOD ALONE.

AH, COLONEL WEIRD, I WASN'T SURE WE WOULD SEE YOU AGAIN TODAY.

KZT

Of course you'll see me, Talky Walky. I'm right here.

THAT'S NOT WHAT I--

IT'S JUST, YOU'VE BEEN SPENDING MORE AND MORE TIME *AWAY*, THESE PAST WEEKS.

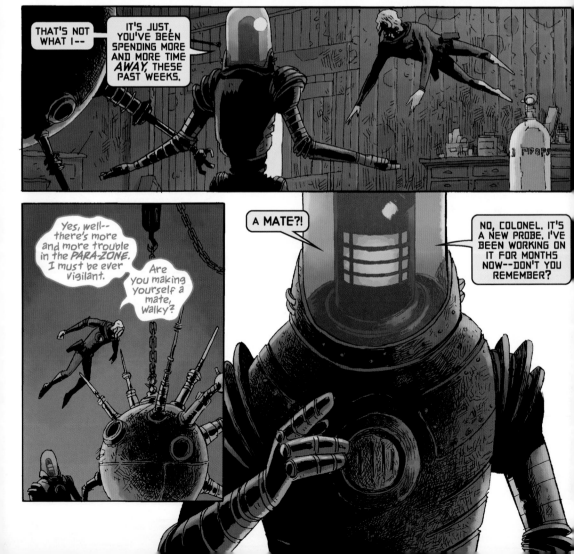

Yes, well-- there's more and more trouble in the *PARA-ZONE*. I must be ever vigilant.

Are you making yourself a mate, Walky?

A MATE?!

NO, COLONEL, IT'S A NEW PROBE. I'VE BEEN WORKING ON IT FOR MONTHS NOW--DON'T YOU REMEMBER?

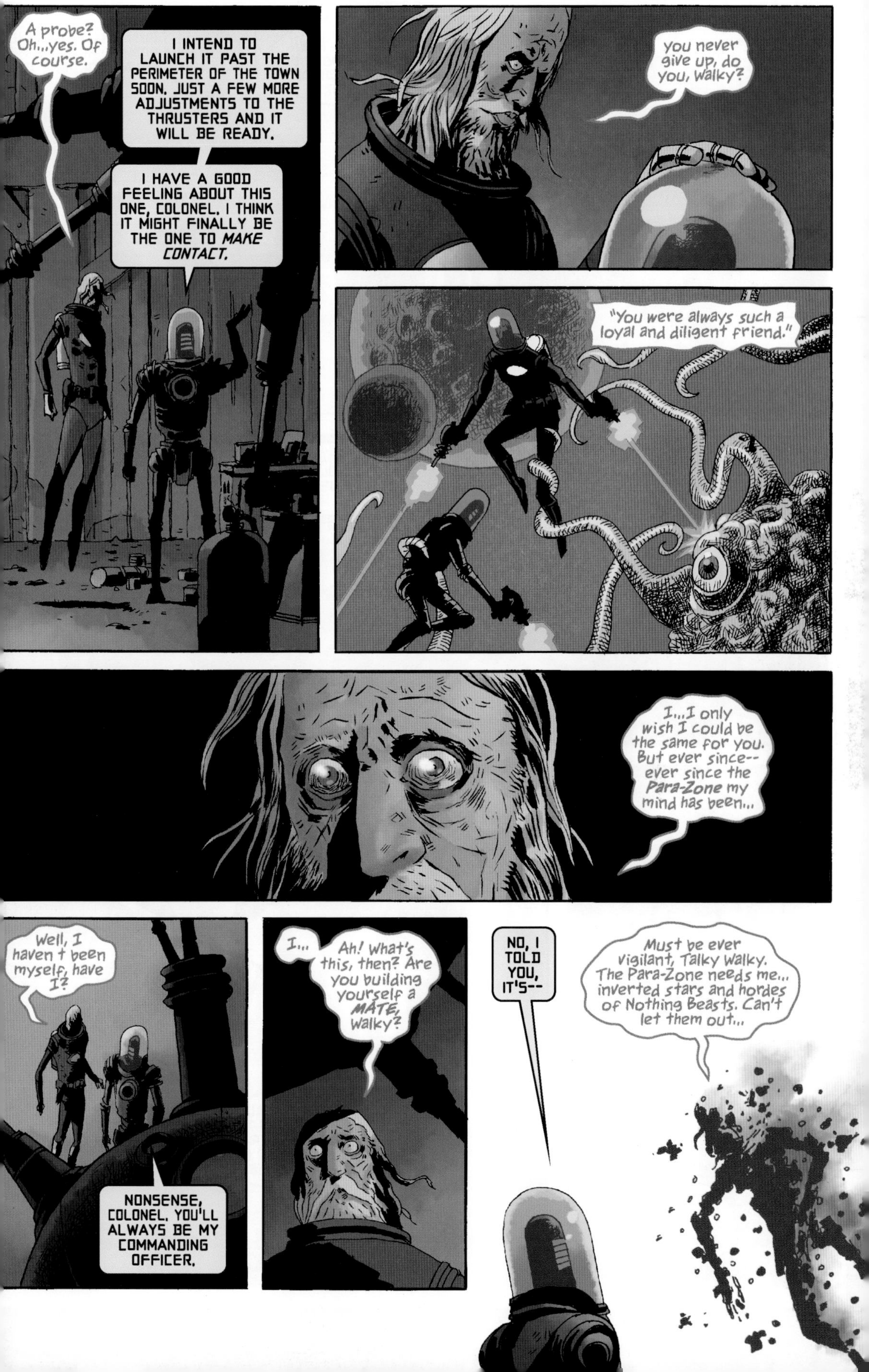
A probe? Oh...yes. Of course.
I INTEND TO LAUNCH IT PAST THE PERIMETER OF THE TOWN SOON. JUST A FEW MORE ADJUSTMENTS TO THE THRUSTERS AND IT WILL BE READY.
I HAVE A GOOD FEELING ABOUT THIS ONE, COLONEL. I THINK IT MIGHT FINALLY BE THE ONE TO MAKE CONTACT.
You never give up, do you, Walky?
"You were always such a loyal and diligent friend."
I...I only wish I could be the same for you. But ever since--ever since the Para-Zone my mind has been...
Well, I haven't been myself, have I?
NONSENSE, COLONEL. YOU'LL ALWAYS BE MY COMMANDING OFFICER.
I...
Ah! What's this, then? Are you building yourself a MATE, Walky?
NO, I TOLD YOU, IT'S--
Must be ever vigilant, Talky Walky. The Para-Zone needs me... inverted stars and hordes of Nothing Beasts. Can't let them out...

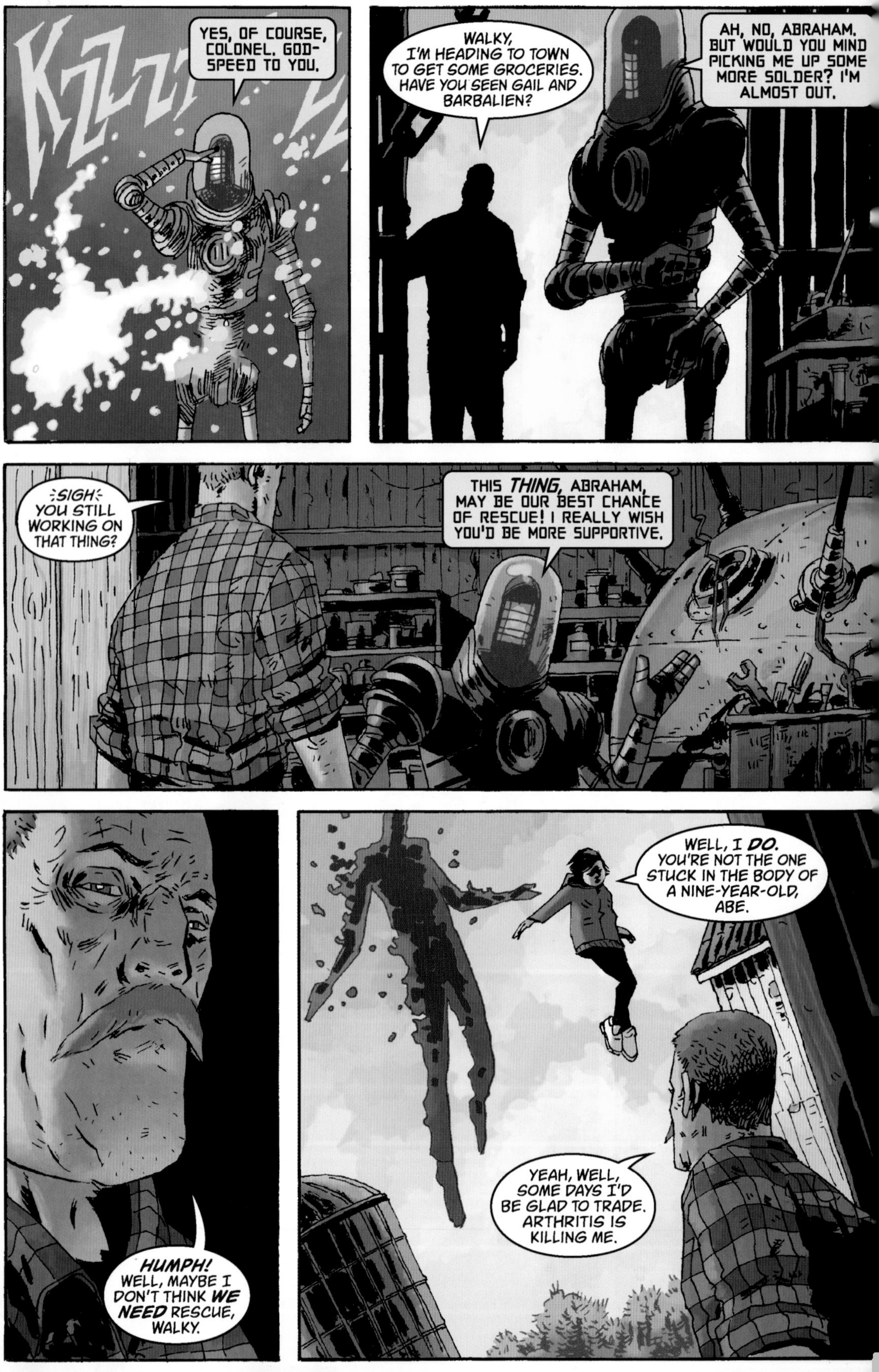
KZZZZZ
YES, OF COURSE, COLONEL. GOD-SPEED TO YOU.
WALKY, I'M HEADING TO TOWN TO GET SOME GROCERIES. HAVE YOU SEEN GAIL AND BARBALIEN?
AH, NO, ABRAHAM. BUT WOULD YOU MIND PICKING ME UP SOME MORE SOLDER? I'M ALMOST OUT.
SIGH YOU STILL WORKING ON THAT THING?
THIS THING, ABRAHAM, MAY BE OUR BEST CHANCE OF RESCUE! I REALLY WISH YOU'D BE MORE SUPPORTIVE.
HUMPH! WELL, MAYBE I DON'T THINK WE NEED RESCUE, WALKY.
WELL, I DO. YOU'RE NOT THE ONE STUCK IN THE BODY OF A NINE-YEAR-OLD, ABE.
YEAH, WELL, SOME DAYS I'D BE GLAD TO TRADE. ARTHRITIS IS KILLING ME.

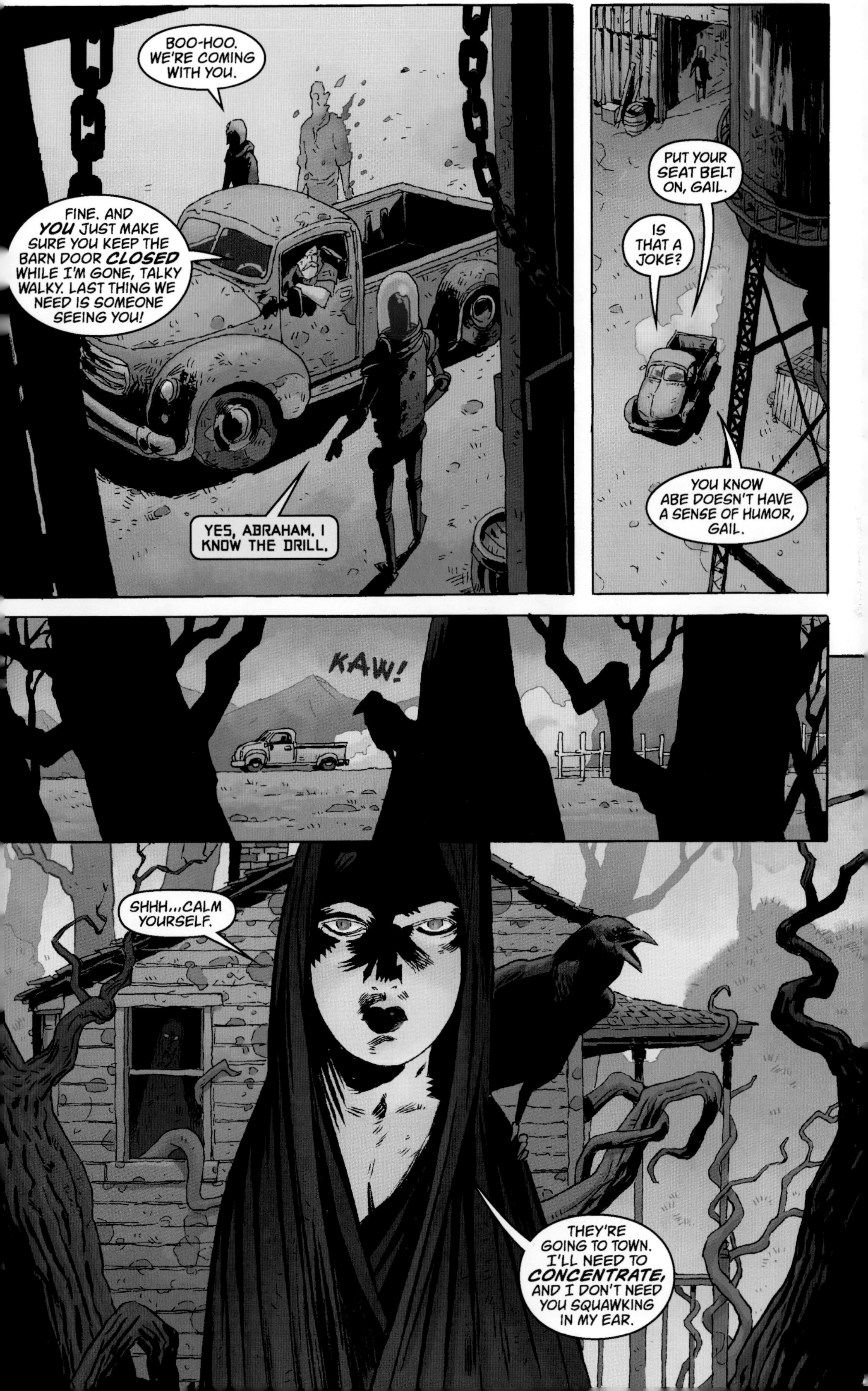
BOO-HOO. WE'RE COMING WITH YOU.
FINE. AND YOU JUST MAKE SURE YOU KEEP THE BARN DOOR CLOSED WHILE I'M GONE, TALKY WALKY. LAST THING WE NEED IS SOMEONE SEEING YOU!
YES, ABRAHAM. I KNOW THE DRILL.
PUT YOUR SEAT BELT ON, GAIL.
IS THAT A JOKE?
YOU KNOW ABE DOESN'T HAVE A SENSE OF HUMOR, GAIL.
KAW!
SHHH...CALM YOURSELF.
THEY'RE GOING TO TOWN. I'LL NEED TO CONCENTRATE, AND I DON'T NEED YOU SQUAWKING IN MY EAR.

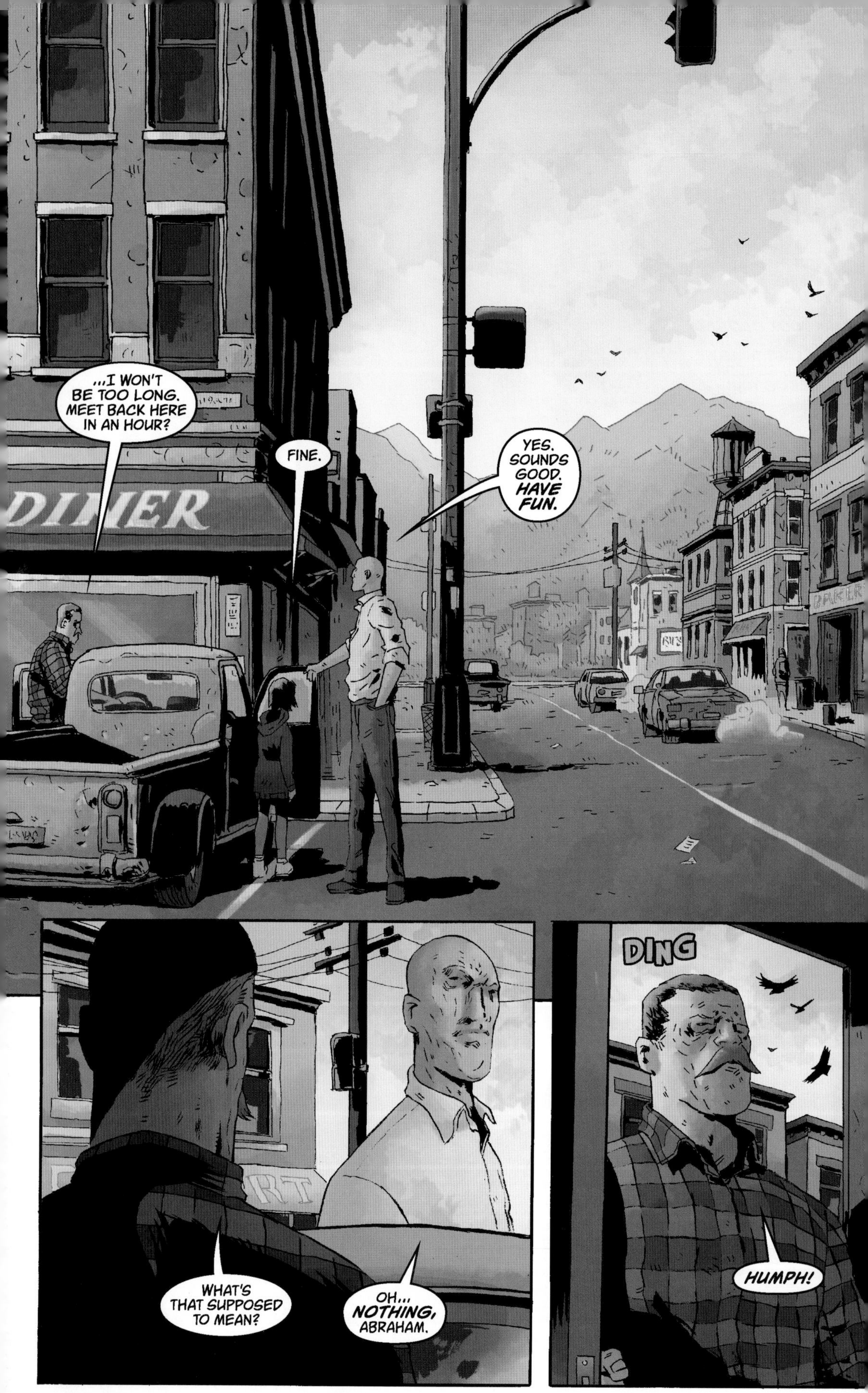
...I WON'T BE TOO LONG. MEET BACK HERE IN AN HOUR?
FINE.
YES. SOUNDS GOOD. HAVE FUN.
DINER
WHAT'S THAT SUPPOSED TO MEAN?
OH... NOTHING, ABRAHAM.
DING
HUMPH!

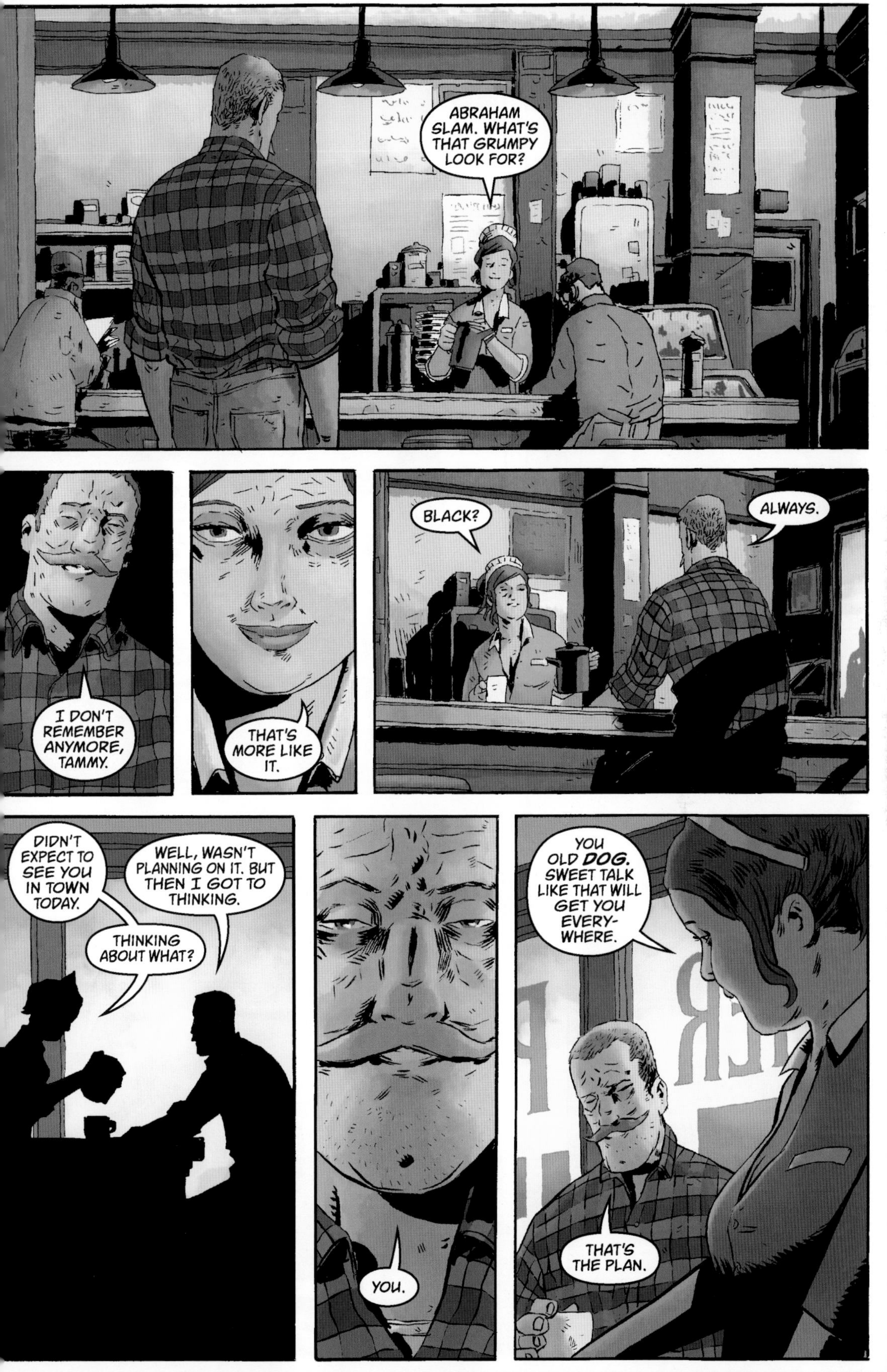
ABRAHAM SLAM. WHAT'S THAT GRUMPY LOOK FOR?
I DON'T REMEMBER ANYMORE, TAMMY.
THAT'S MORE LIKE IT.
BLACK?
ALWAYS.
DIDN'T EXPECT TO SEE YOU IN TOWN TODAY.
WELL, WASN'T PLANNING ON IT. BUT THEN I GOT TO THINKING.
THINKING ABOUT WHAT?
YOU.
YOU OLD DOG. SWEET TALK LIKE THAT WILL GET YOU EVERY-WHERE.
THAT'S THE PLAN.

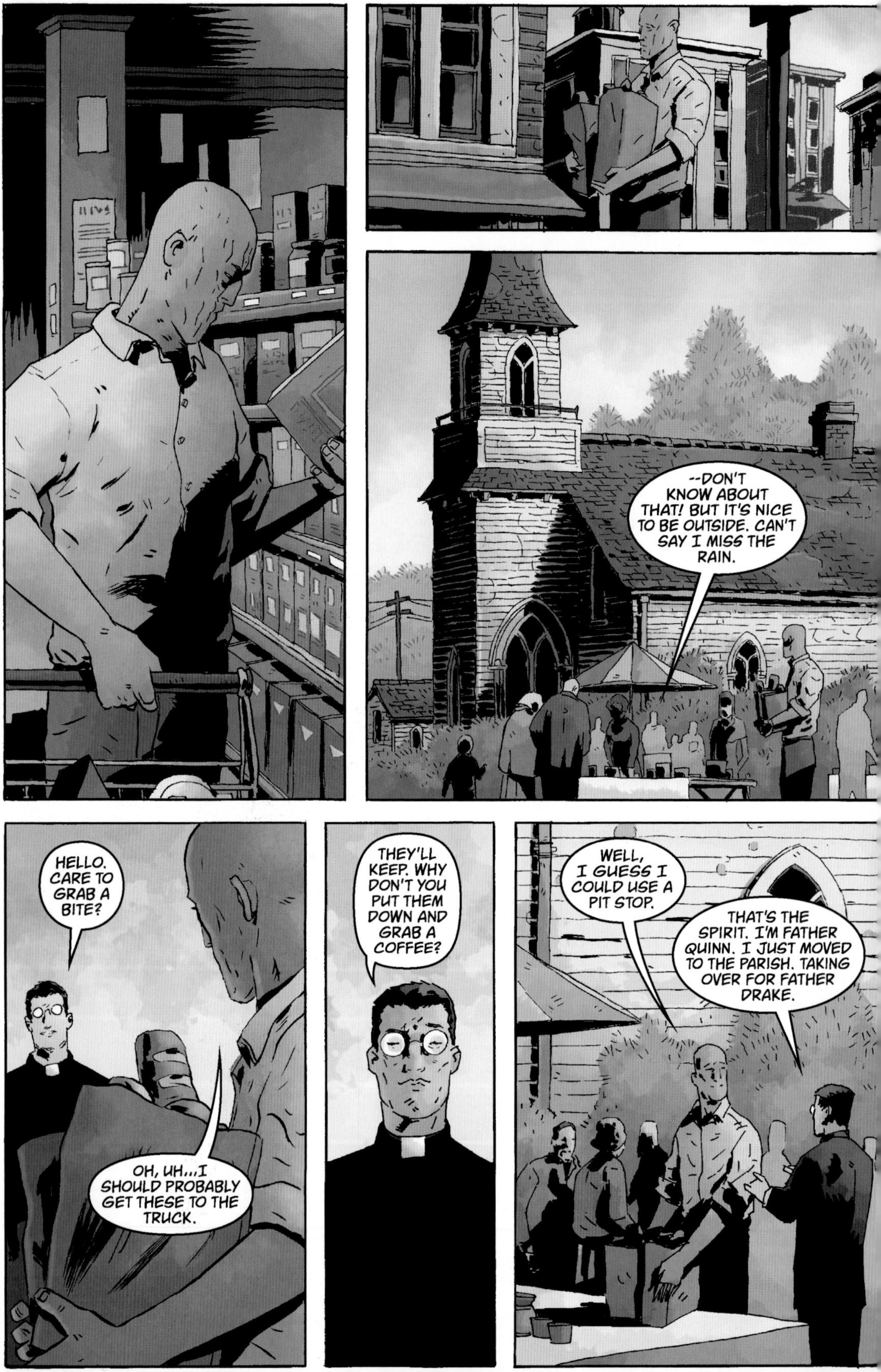
--DON'T KNOW ABOUT THAT! BUT IT'S NICE TO BE OUTSIDE. CAN'T SAY I MISS THE RAIN.
HELLO. CARE TO GRAB A BITE?
OH, UH...I SHOULD PROBABLY GET THESE TO THE TRUCK.
THEY'LL KEEP. WHY DON'T YOU PUT THEM DOWN AND GRAB A COFFEE?
WELL, I GUESS I COULD USE A PIT STOP.
THAT'S THE SPIRIT. I'M FATHER QUINN. I JUST MOVED TO THE PARISH. TAKING OVER FOR FATHER DRAKE.

OH, UH... MARK MARKZ. I, UH--I DIDN'T KNOW FATHER DRAKE VERY WELL, I'M AFRAID.

AH, NOT A CHURCHGOING MAN, THEN?

UH...NOT AS MUCH THESE DAYS. I'VE LAPSED.

WELL, YOU'LL HAVE TO PUT THE COFFEE BACK THEN, I'M AFRAID.

...

I'M JOKING.

AH, OKAY. GOOD.

SO...I GUESS I SHOULD MAKE MY SALES PITCH.

THE BOSS IS ALWAYS WATCHING, RIGHT?

HA, YES. BUT IT WOULD BE GREAT TO SEE YOU OUT AT *MASS*. NO PRESSURE, BUT MAYBE IT'S TIME YOU GAVE IT ANOTHER SHOT?

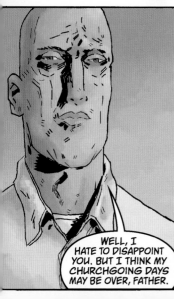

WELL, I HATE TO DISAPPOINT YOU. BUT I THINK MY CHURCHGOING DAYS MAY BE OVER, FATHER.

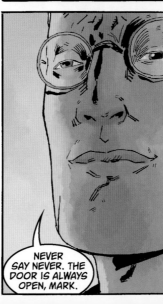

NEVER SAY NEVER. THE DOOR IS ALWAYS OPEN, MARK.

MARK MARKZ. WHAT IS THAT? EASTERN EUROPEAN?

UH...IT'S SWEDISH.

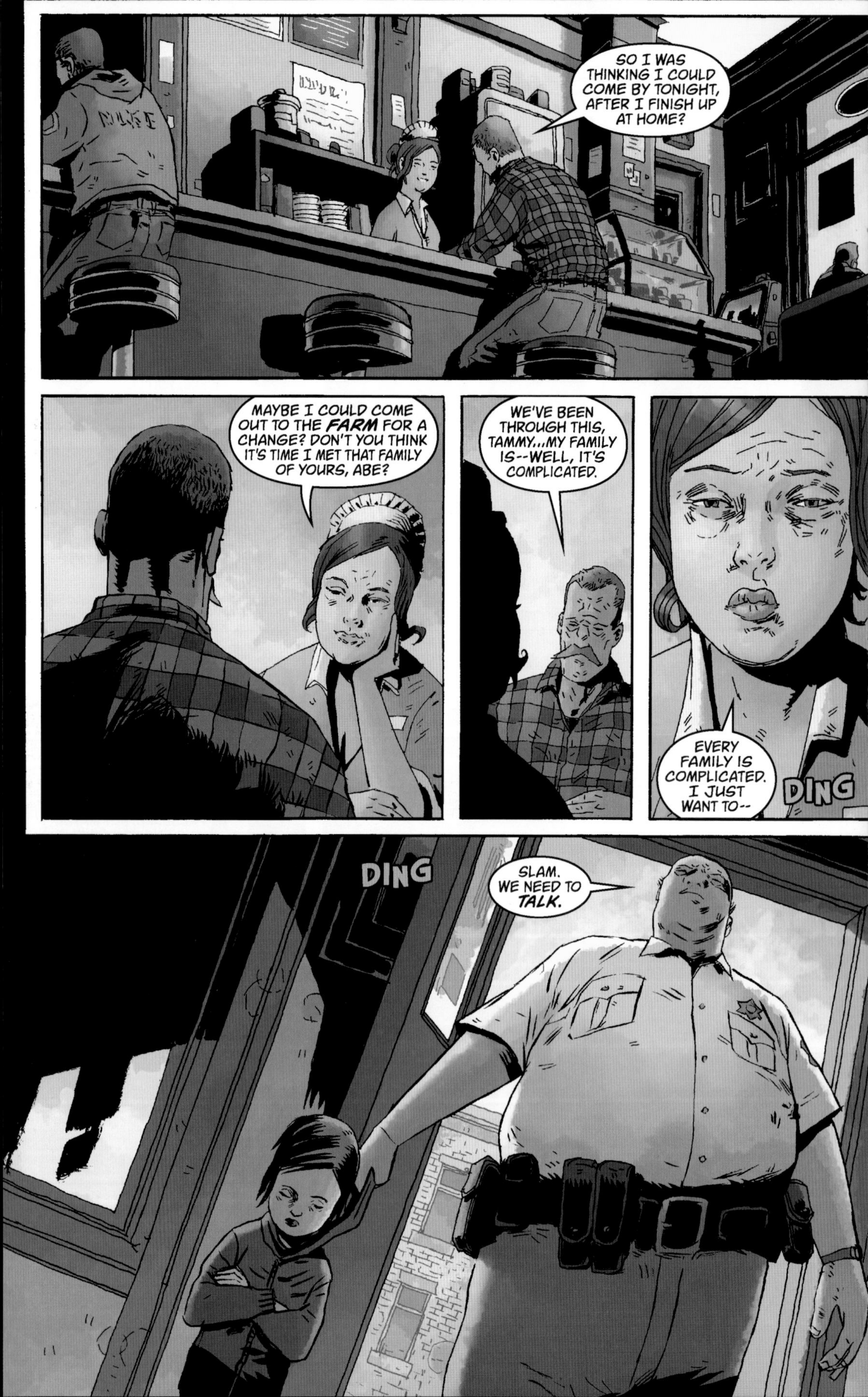
SO I WAS THINKING I COULD COME BY TONIGHT, AFTER I FINISH UP AT HOME?
MAYBE I COULD COME OUT TO THE FARM FOR A CHANGE? DON'T YOU THINK IT'S TIME I MET THAT FAMILY OF YOURS, ABE?
WE'VE BEEN THROUGH THIS, TAMMY...MY FAMILY IS--WELL, IT'S COMPLICATED.
EVERY FAMILY IS COMPLICATED. I JUST WANT TO--
DING
DING
SLAM. WE NEED TO TALK.

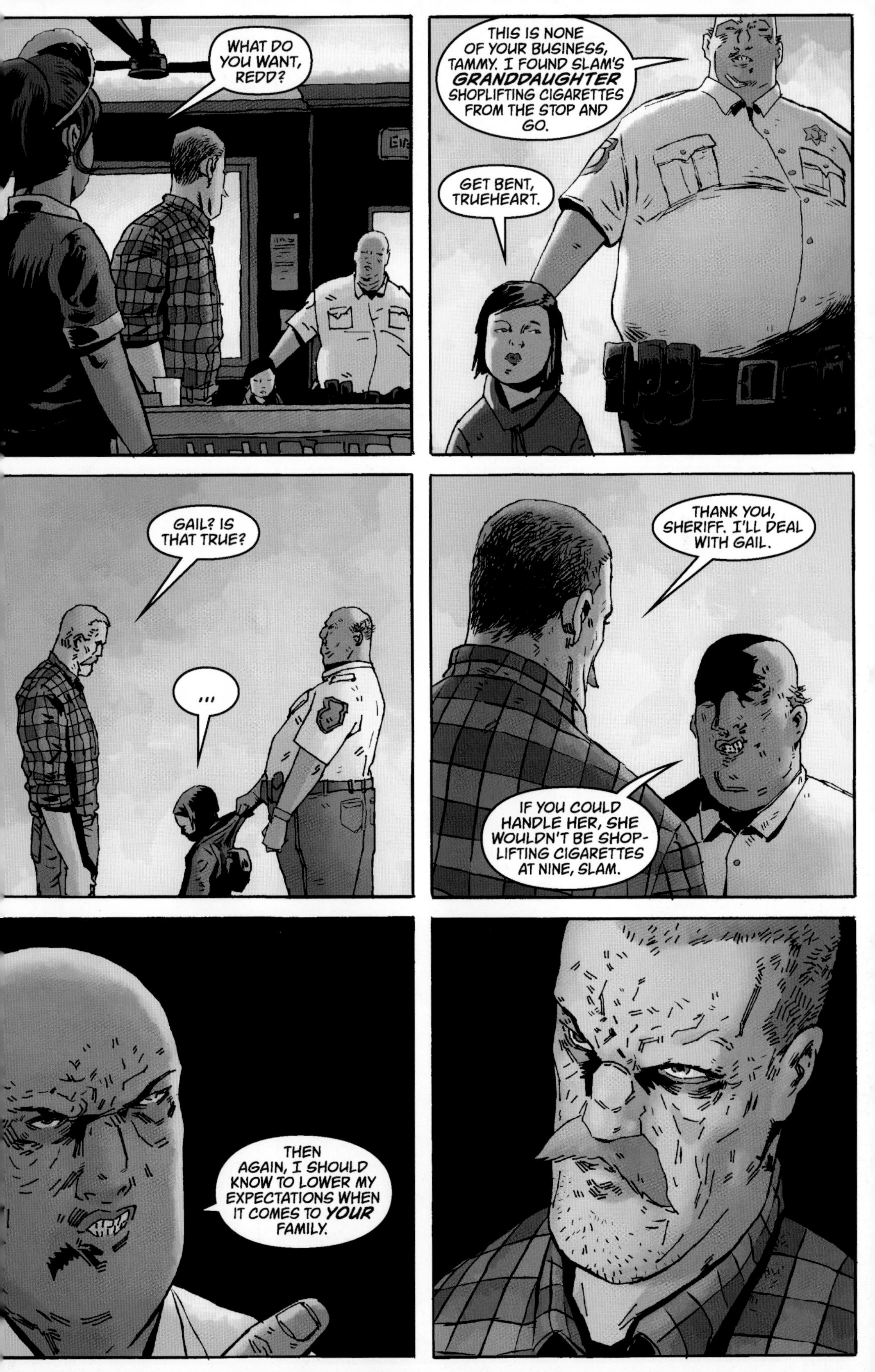
WHAT DO YOU WANT, REDD?
THIS IS NONE OF YOUR BUSINESS, TAMMY. I FOUND SLAM'S GRANDDAUGHTER SHOPLIFTING CIGARETTES FROM THE STOP AND GO.
GET BENT, TRUEHEART.
GAIL? IS THAT TRUE?
...
THANK YOU, SHERIFF. I'LL DEAL WITH GAIL.
IF YOU COULD HANDLE HER, SHE WOULDN'T BE SHOP-LIFTING CIGARETTES AT NINE, SLAM.
THEN AGAIN, I SHOULD KNOW TO LOWER MY EXPECTATIONS WHEN IT COMES TO YOUR FAMILY.

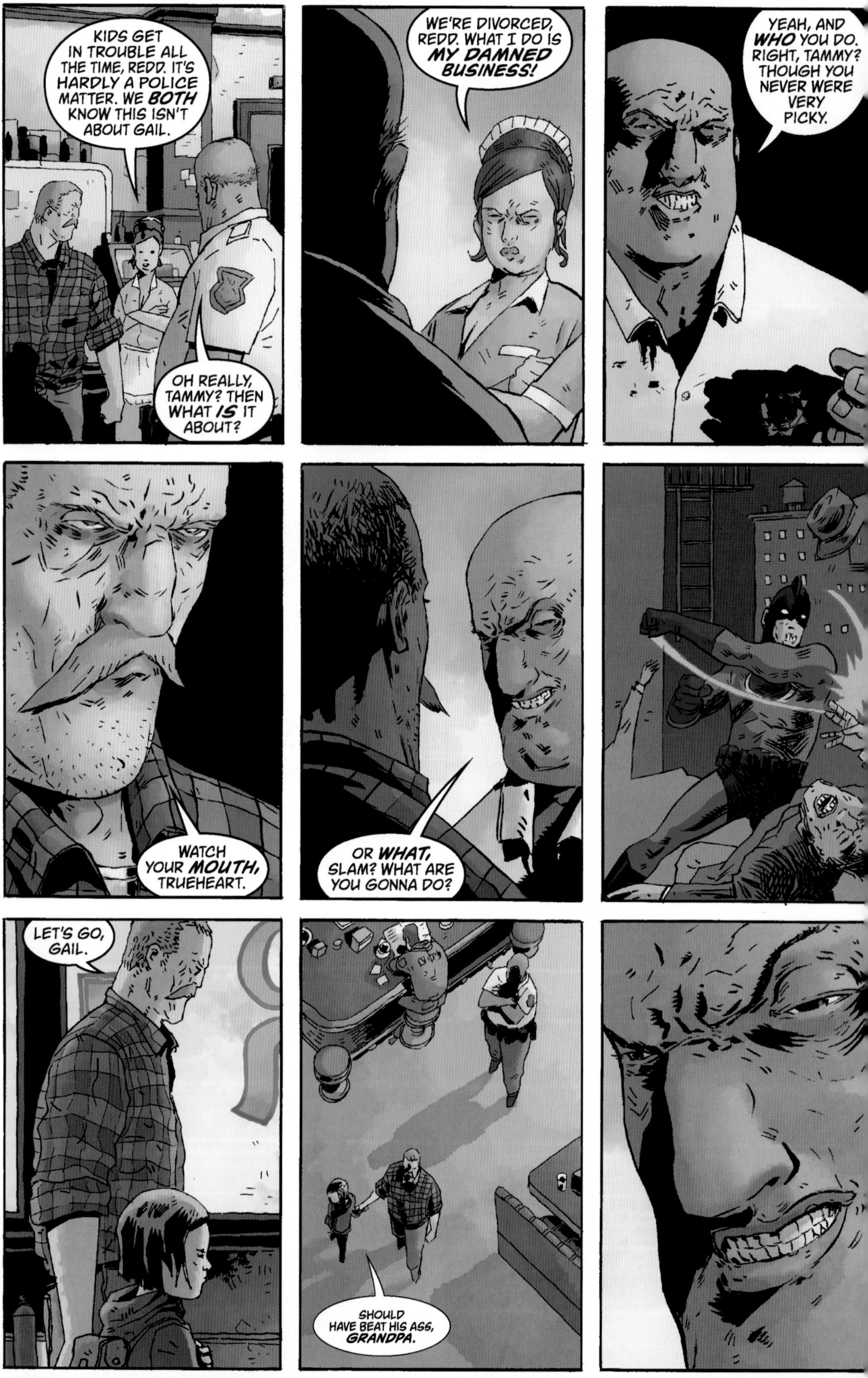
KIDS GET IN TROUBLE ALL THE TIME, REDD. IT'S HARDLY A POLICE MATTER. WE BOTH KNOW THIS ISN'T ABOUT GAIL.
OH REALLY, TAMMY? THEN WHAT IS IT ABOUT?
WE'RE DIVORCED, REDD. WHAT I DO IS MY DAMNED BUSINESS!
YEAH, AND WHO YOU DO. RIGHT, TAMMY? THOUGH YOU NEVER WERE VERY PICKY.
WATCH YOUR MOUTH, TRUEHEART.
OR WHAT, SLAM? WHAT ARE YOU GONNA DO?
LET'S GO, GAIL.
SHOULD HAVE BEAT HIS ASS, GRANDPA.

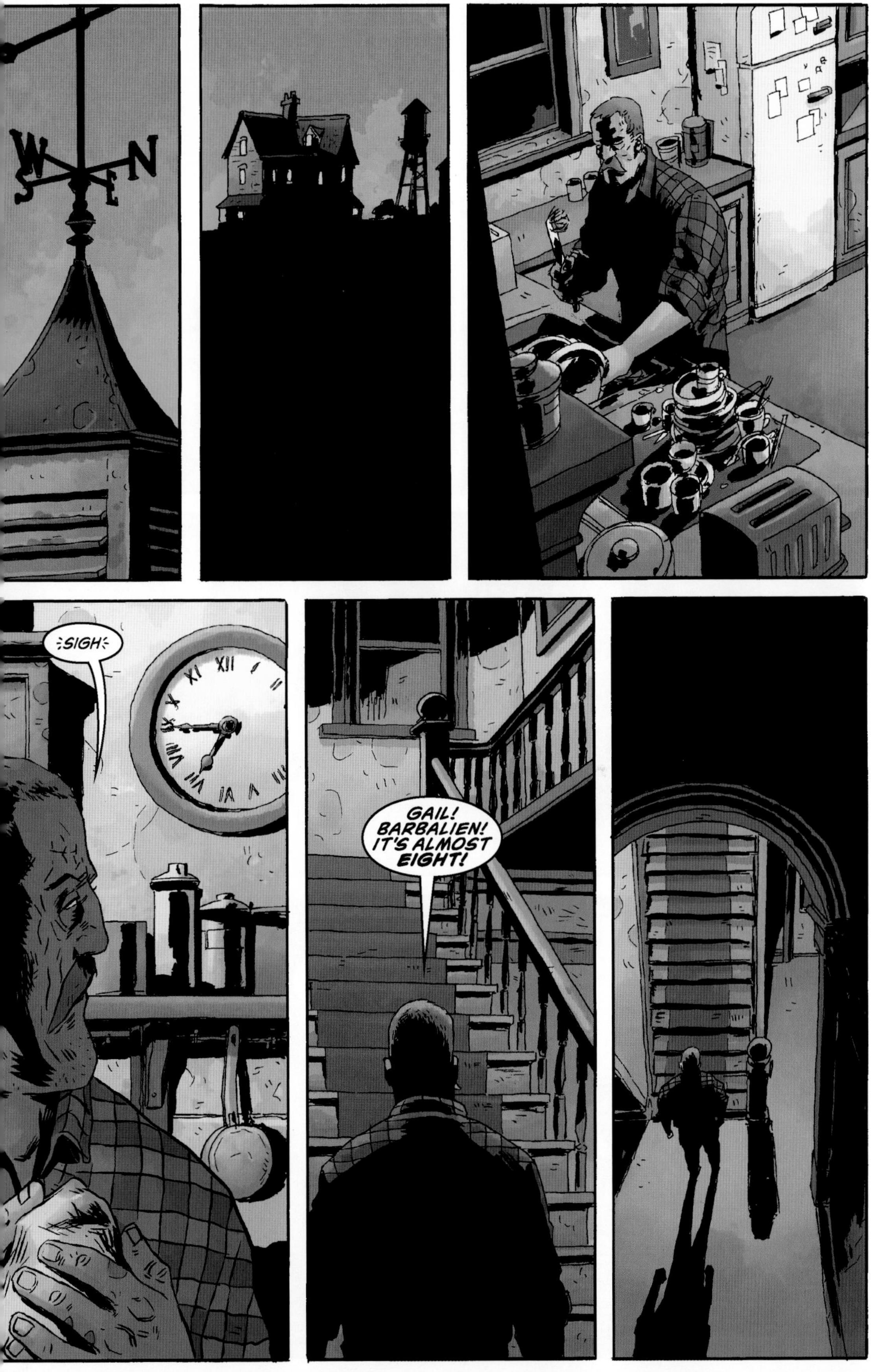
W
S
E
N
SIGH
GAIL! BARBALIEN! IT'S ALMOST EIGHT!

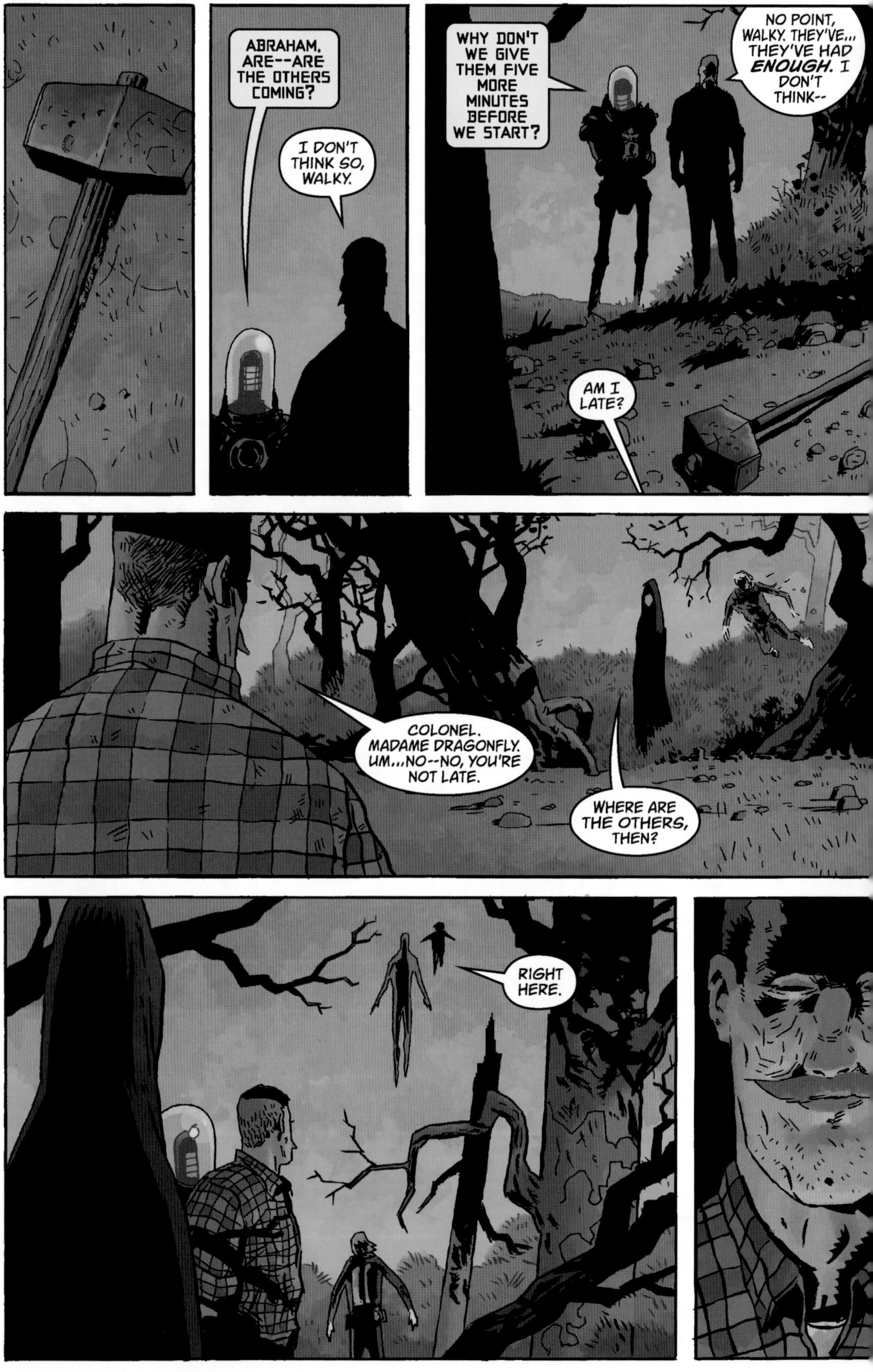
ABRAHAM, ARE--ARE THE OTHERS COMING?
I DON'T THINK SO, WALKY.
WHY DON'T WE GIVE THEM FIVE MORE MINUTES BEFORE WE START?
NO POINT, WALKY. THEY'VE... THEY'VE HAD *ENOUGH*. I DON'T THINK--
AM I LATE?
COLONEL. MADAME DRAGONFLY. UM...NO--NO, YOU'RE NOT LATE.
WHERE ARE THE OTHERS, THEN?
RIGHT HERE.

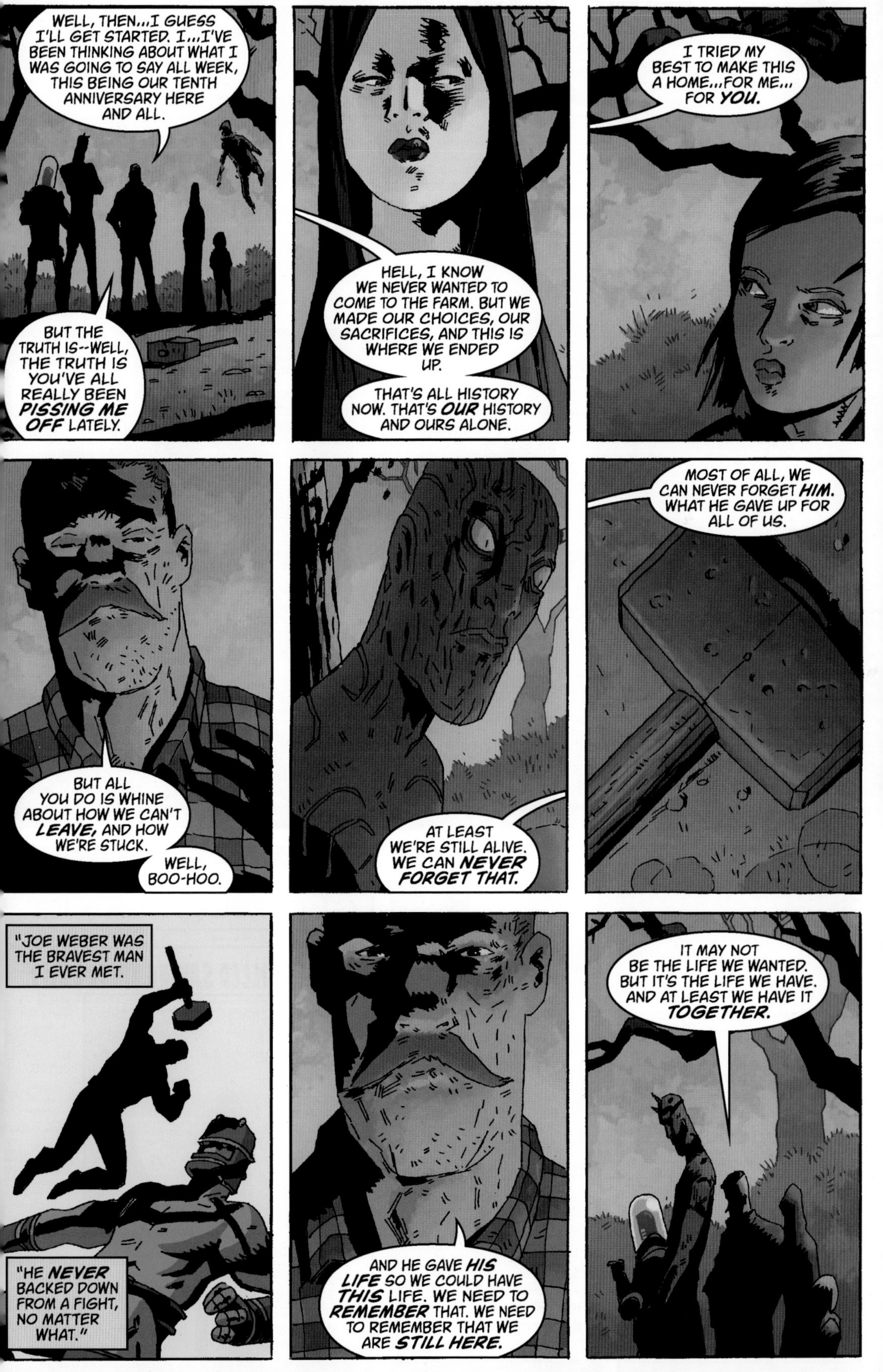
WELL, THEN...I GUESS I'LL GET STARTED. I...I'VE BEEN THINKING ABOUT WHAT I WAS GOING TO SAY ALL WEEK, THIS BEING OUR TENTH ANNIVERSARY HERE AND ALL.
BUT THE TRUTH IS--WELL, THE TRUTH IS YOU'VE ALL REALLY BEEN PISSING ME OFF LATELY.
HELL, I KNOW WE NEVER WANTED TO COME TO THE FARM. BUT WE MADE OUR CHOICES, OUR SACRIFICES, AND THIS IS WHERE WE ENDED UP.
THAT'S ALL HISTORY NOW. THAT'S OUR HISTORY AND OURS ALONE.
I TRIED MY BEST TO MAKE THIS A HOME...FOR ME... FOR YOU.
BUT ALL YOU DO IS WHINE ABOUT HOW WE CAN'T LEAVE, AND HOW WE'RE STUCK.
WELL, BOO-HOO.
AT LEAST WE'RE STILL ALIVE. WE CAN NEVER FORGET THAT.
MOST OF ALL, WE CAN NEVER FORGET HIM. WHAT HE GAVE UP FOR ALL OF US.
"JOE WEBER WAS THE BRAVEST MAN I EVER MET.
"HE NEVER BACKED DOWN FROM A FIGHT, NO MATTER WHAT."
AND HE GAVE HIS LIFE SO WE COULD HAVE THIS LIFE. WE NEED TO REMEMBER THAT. WE NEED TO REMEMBER THAT WE ARE STILL HERE.
IT MAY NOT BE THE LIFE WE WANTED. BUT IT'S THE LIFE WE HAVE. AND AT LEAST WE HAVE IT TOGETHER.

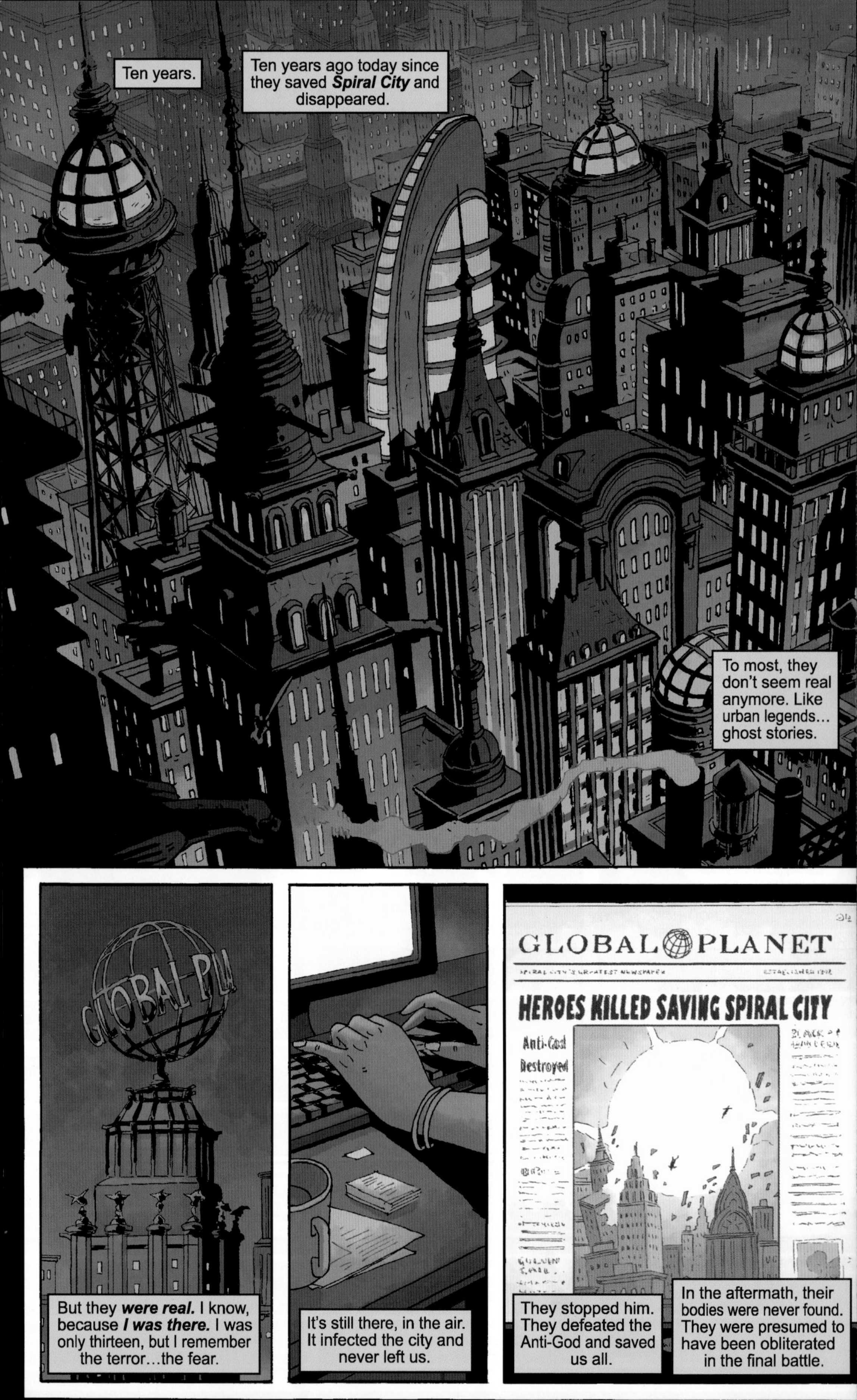
Ten years.
Ten years ago today since they saved ***Spiral City*** and disappeared.
To most, they don't seem real anymore. Like urban legends… ghost stories.
GLOBAL PLA
But they ***were real.*** I know, because ***I was there.*** I was only thirteen, but I remember the terror…the fear.
It's still there, in the air. It infected the city and never left us.
GLOBAL PLANET
HEROES KILLED SAVING SPIRAL CITY
Anti-God Destroyed
They stopped him. They defeated the Anti-God and saved us all.
In the aftermath, their bodies were never found. They were presumed to have been obliterated in the final battle.

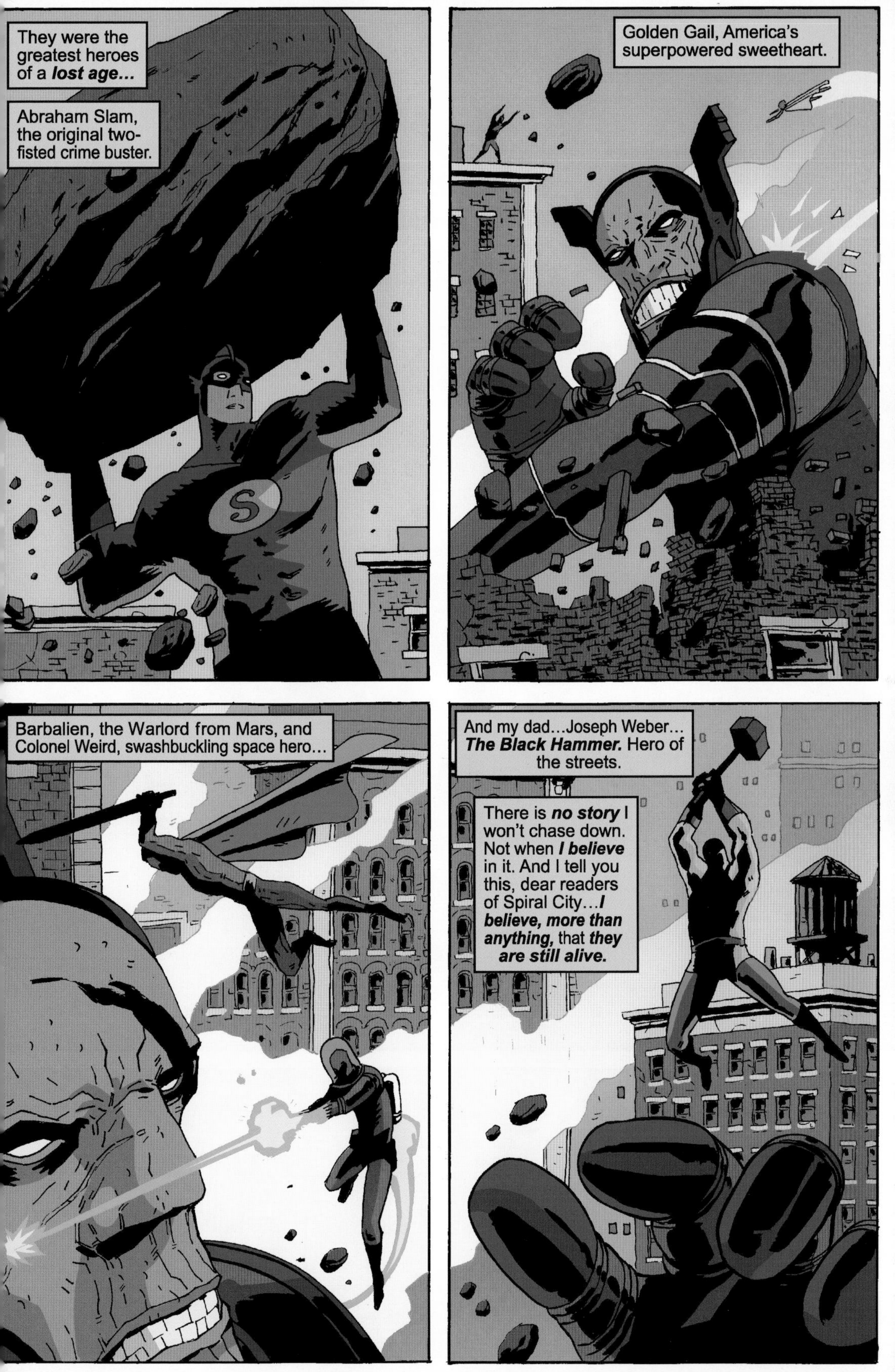
They were the greatest heroes of a ***lost age...***
Abraham Slam, the original two-fisted crime buster.
Golden Gail, America's superpowered sweetheart.
Barbalien, the Warlord from Mars, and Colonel Weird, swashbuckling space hero...
And my dad...Joseph Weber... ***The Black Hammer.*** Hero of the streets.
There is ***no story*** I won't chase down. Not when ***I believe*** in it. And I tell you this, dear readers of Spiral City...***I believe, more than anything,*** that ***they are still alive.***

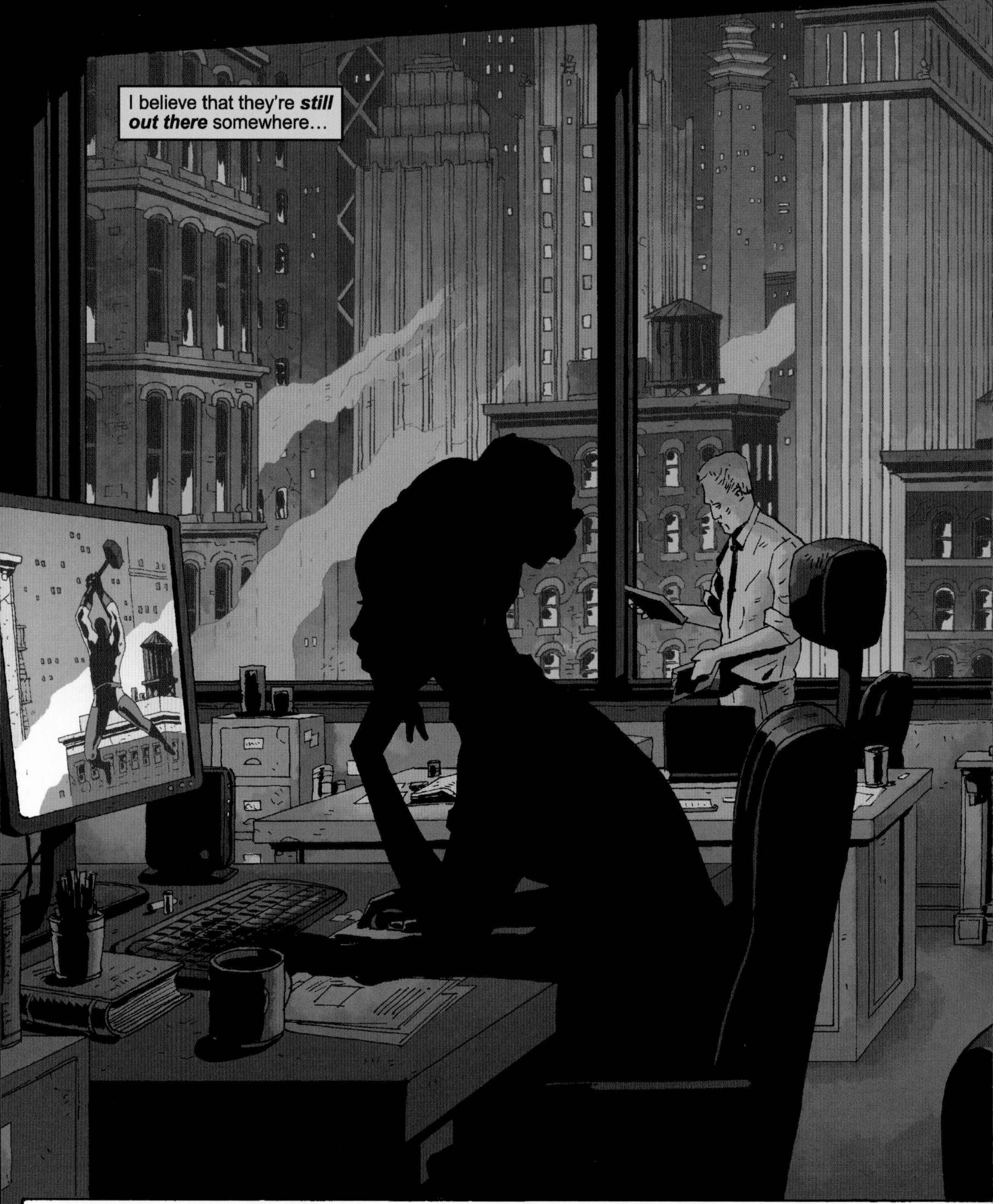
I believe that they're ***still out there*** somewhere…

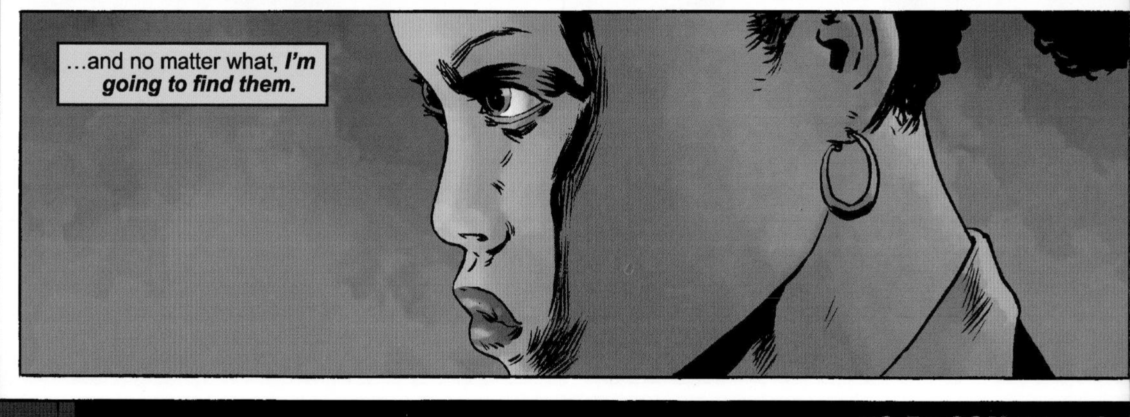
…and no matter what, ***I'm going to find them.***

TO BE CONTINUED…

SUPER:POWERED BY CREATORS!

"These superheroes ain't no boy scouts in spandex. They're a high-octane blend of the damaged, quixotic heroes of pulp and detective fiction and the do-gooders in capes from the Golden and Silver Ages." —Duane Swierczynski

ORIGINAL VISIONS— THRILLING TALES!

BLACK HAMMER
Jeff Lemire and Dean Ormston
VOLUME 1: SECRET ORIGINS
ISBN 978-1-61655-786-7 | $14.99

DREAM THIEF
Jai Nitz and Greg Smallwood
VOLUME 1
ISBN 978-1-61655-283-1 | $17.99

VOLUME 2: ESCAPE
ISBN 978-1-61655-513-9 | $17.99

BUZZKILL
Mark Reznicek, Donny Cates, and Geoff Shaw
ISBN 978-1-61655-305-0 | $14.99

THE BLACK BEETLE
Francesco Francavilla
VOLUME 1: NO WAY OUT
ISBN 978-1-61655-202-2 | $19.99

THE ANSWER!
Mike Norton and Dennis Hopeless
ISBN 978-1-61655-197-1 | $12.99

BLOODHOUND
Dan Jolley, Leonard Kirk, and Robin Riggs
VOLUME 1: BRASS KNUCKLE PSYCHOLOGY
ISBN 978-1-61655-125-4 | $19.99

VOLUME 2: CROWBAR MEDICINE
ISBN 978-1-61655-352-4 | $19.99

MICHAEL AVON OEMING'S THE VICTORIES
Michael Avon Oeming
VOLUME 1: TOUCHED
ISBN 978-1-61655-100-1 | $9.99

VOLUME 2: TRANSHUMAN
ISBN 978-1-61655-214-5 | $17.99

VOLUME 3: POSTHUMAN
ISBN 978-1-61655-445-3 | $17.99

VOLUME 4: METAHUMAN
ISBN 978-1-61655-517-7 | $17.99

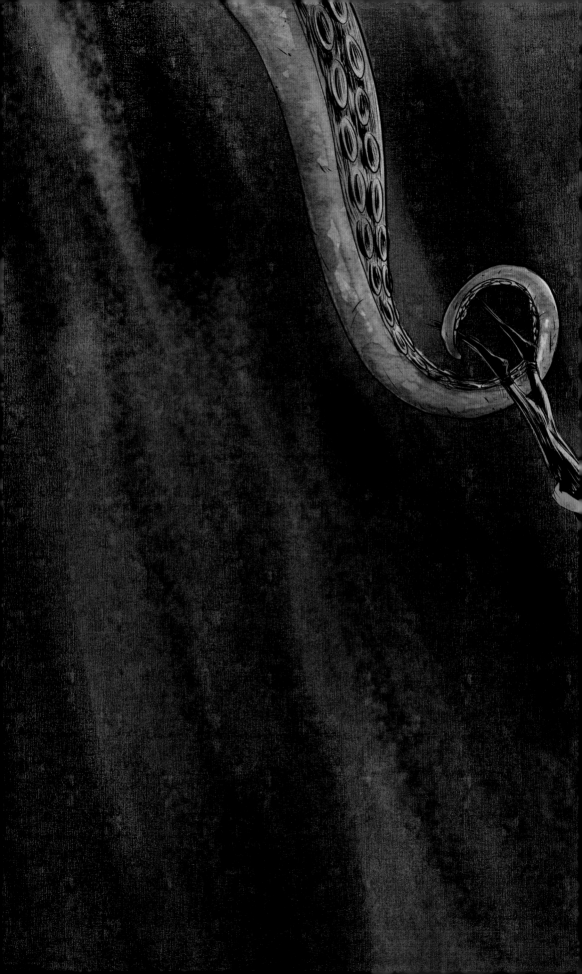

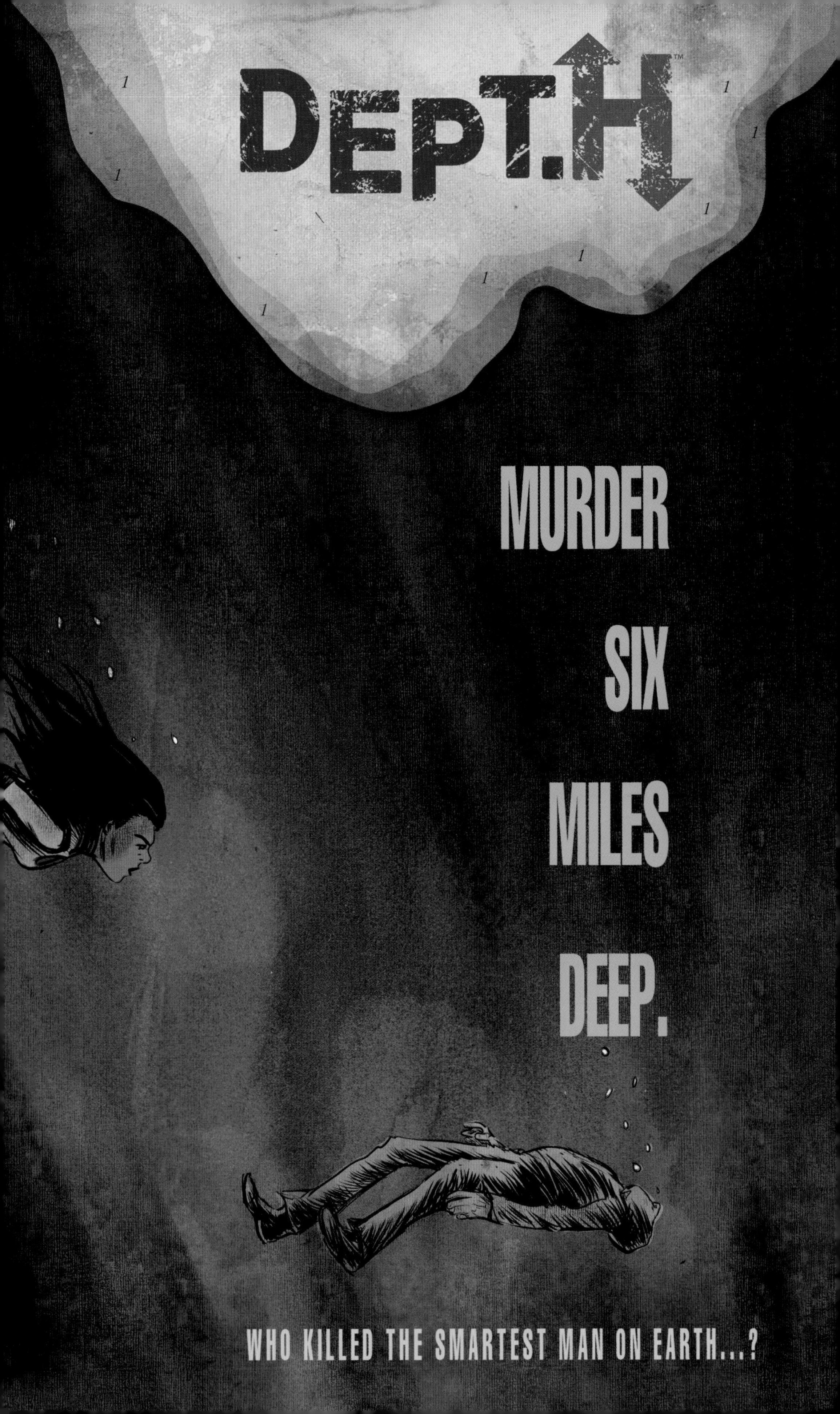
DEPT.H™
MURDER
SIX
MILES
DEEP.
WHO KILLED THE SMARTEST MAN ON EARTH...?

DARK HORSE NUMBER ONES

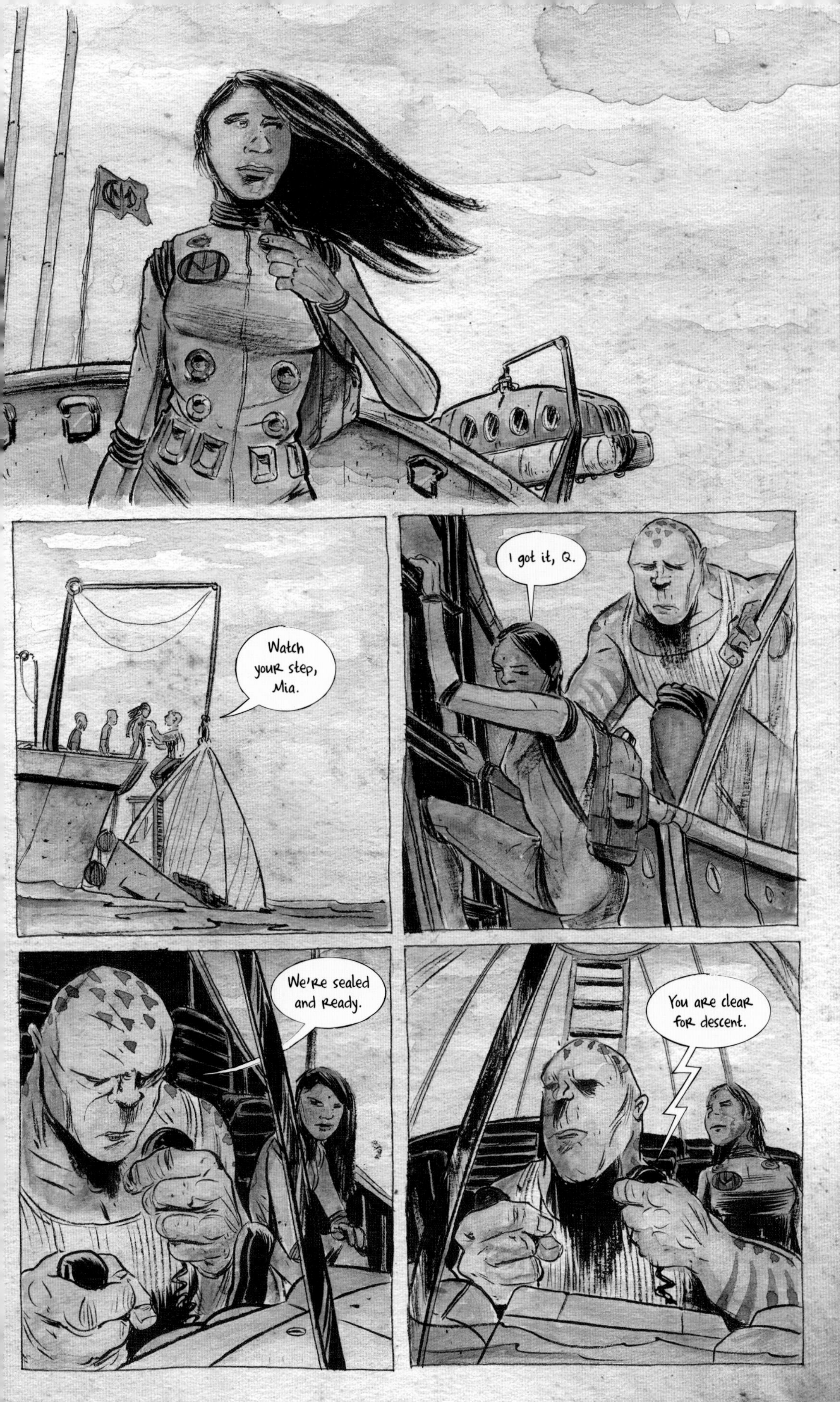
Watch your step, Mia.
I got it, Q.
We're sealed and ready.
You are clear for descent.

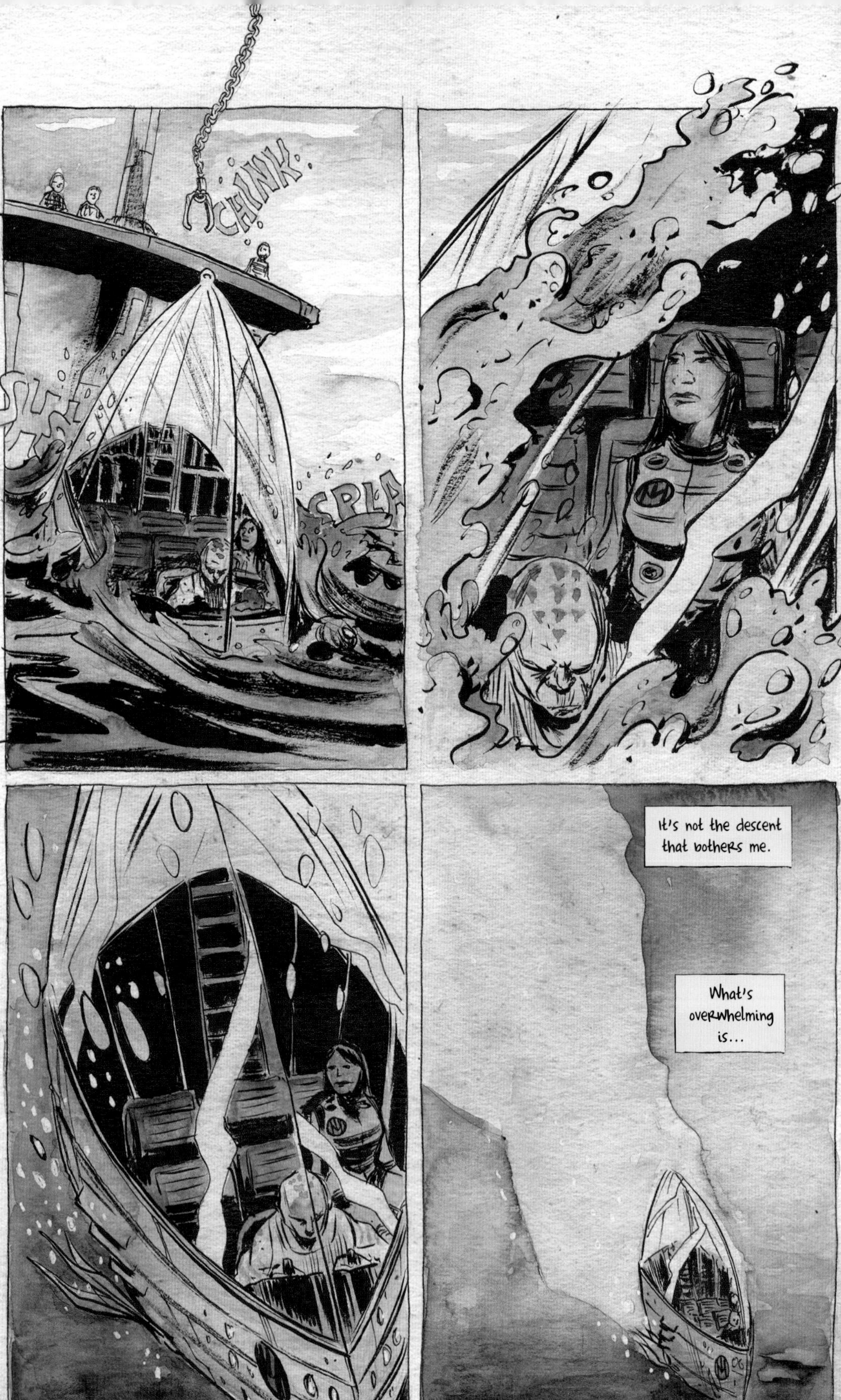
CHINK
SPLA
It's not the descent that bothers me.
What's overwhelming is...

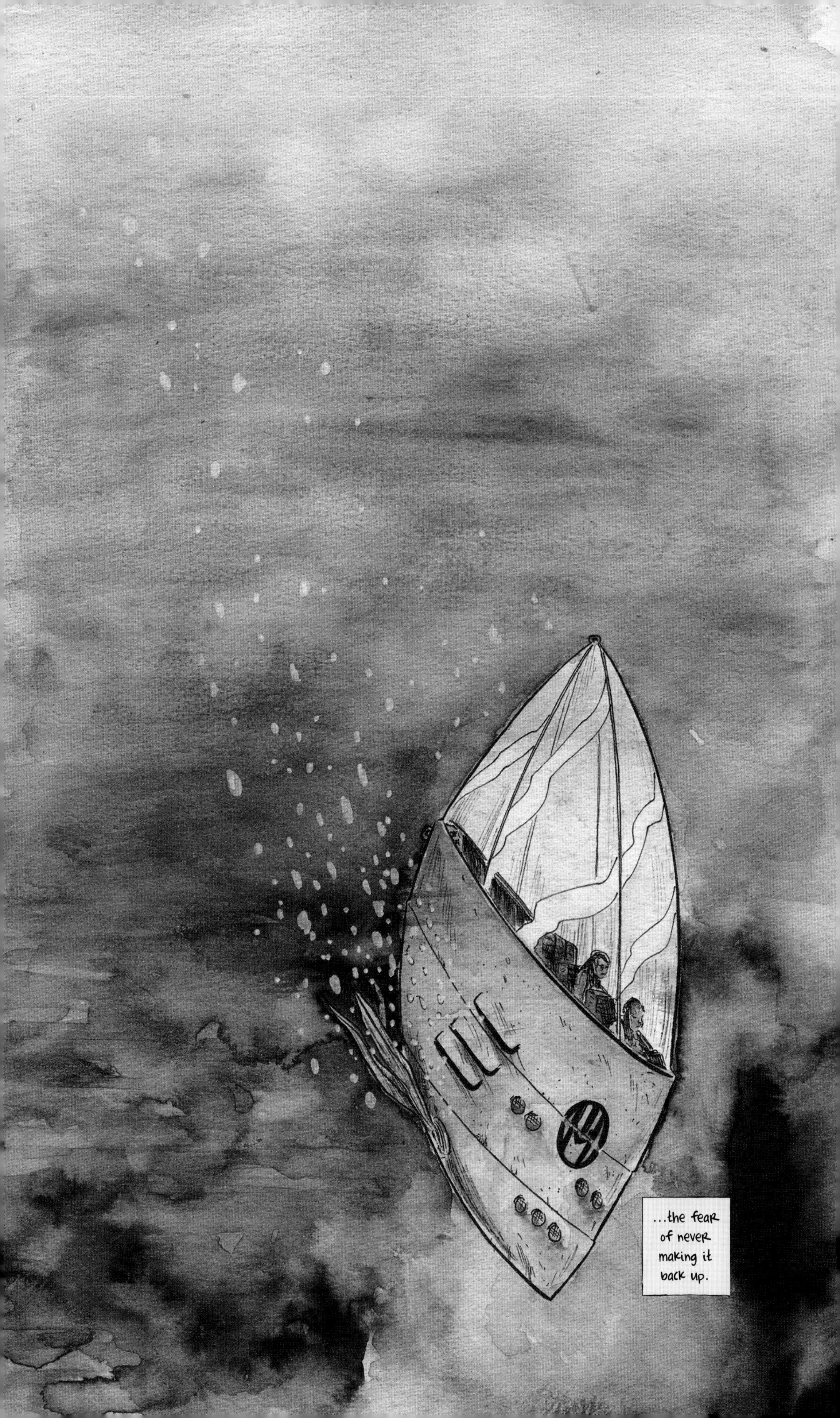
...the fear of never making it back up.

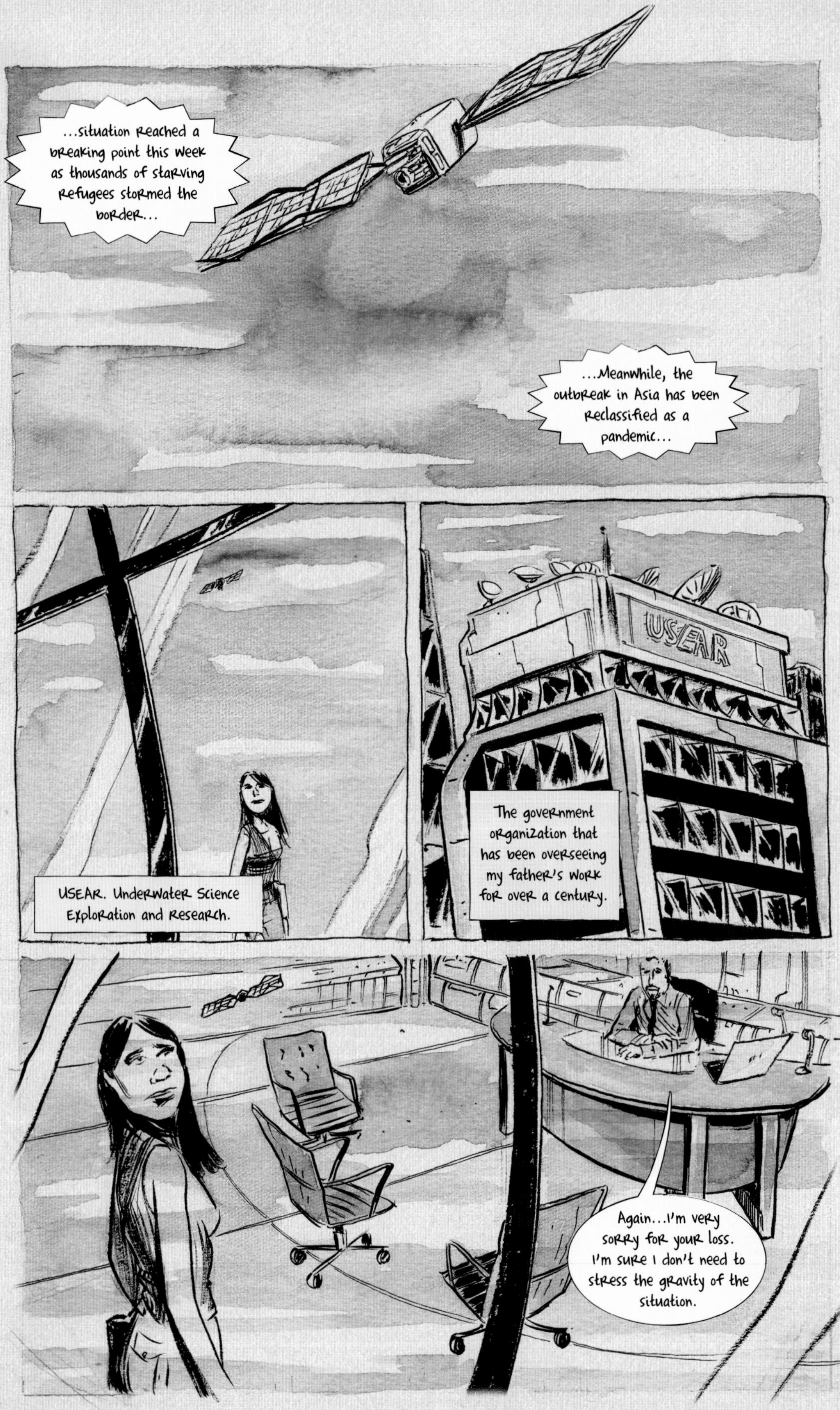
...situation reached a breaking point this week as thousands of starving refugees stormed the border...
...Meanwhile, the outbreak in Asia has been reclassified as a pandemic...
USEAR
USEAR. Underwater Science Exploration and Research.
The government organization that has been overseeing my father's work for over a century.
Again...I'm very sorry for your loss. I'm sure I don't need to stress the gravity of the situation.

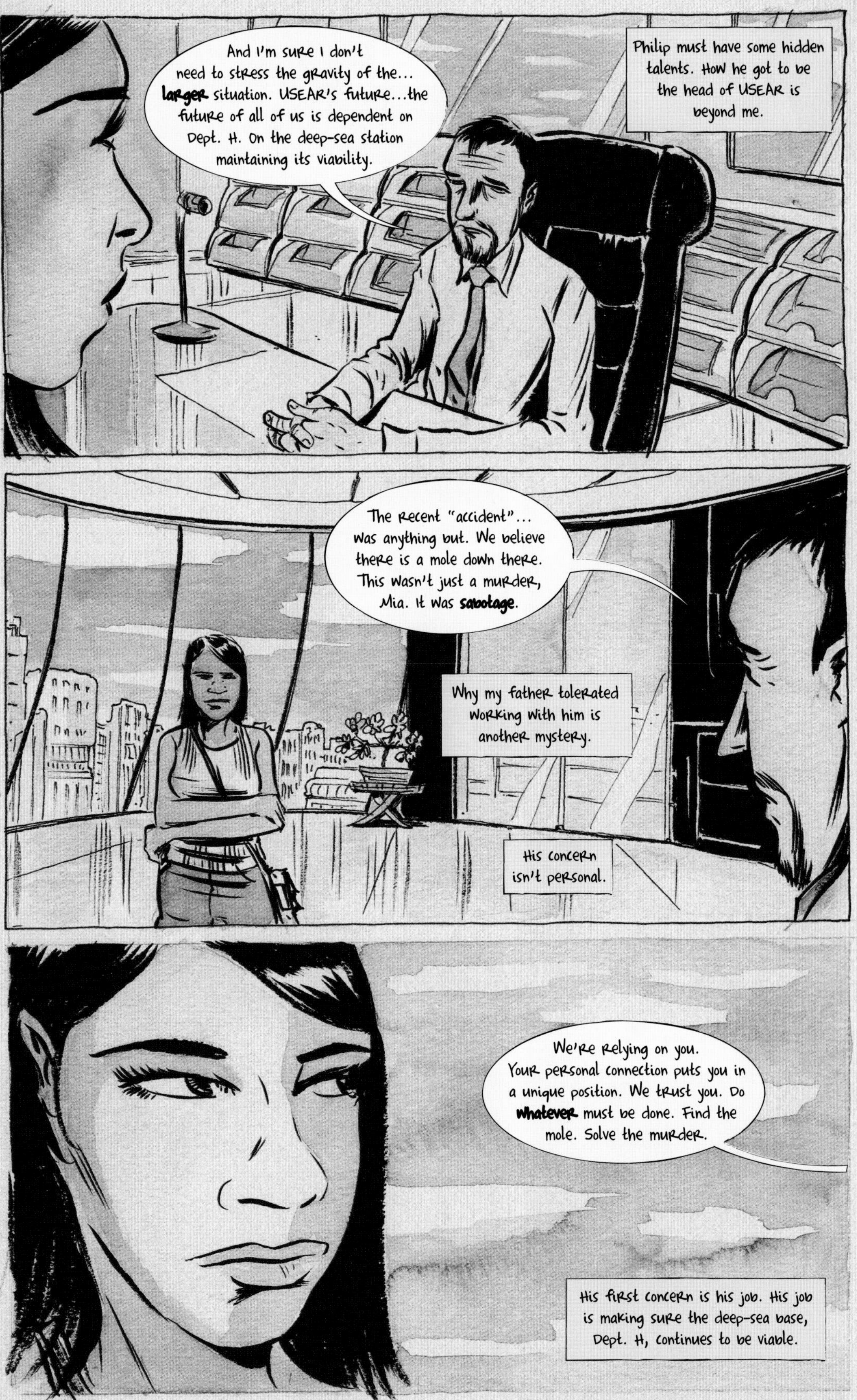
And I'm sure I don't need to stress the gravity of the... larger situation. USEAR's future...the future of all of us is dependent on Dept. H. On the deep-sea station maintaining its viability.
Philip must have some hidden talents. How he got to be the head of USEAR is beyond me.
The recent "accident"... was anything but. We believe there is a mole down there. This wasn't just a murder, Mia. It was sabotage.
Why my father tolerated working with him is another mystery.
His concern isn't personal.
We're relying on you. Your personal connection puts you in a unique position. We trust you. Do whatever must be done. Find the mole. Solve the murder.
His first concern is his job. His job is making sure the deep-sea base, Dept. H, continues to be viable.

"Treat everyone as a suspect."

It teeks a while ta get down there. We've got to rechahge the tanks and eleectreek.

"Eets naht like your space rockets, little miss."

Outer space is a breeze compared tah what yer ganna geet down heyah.

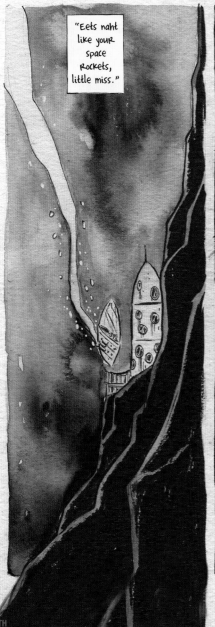

Ah seen it break strongha men than me.

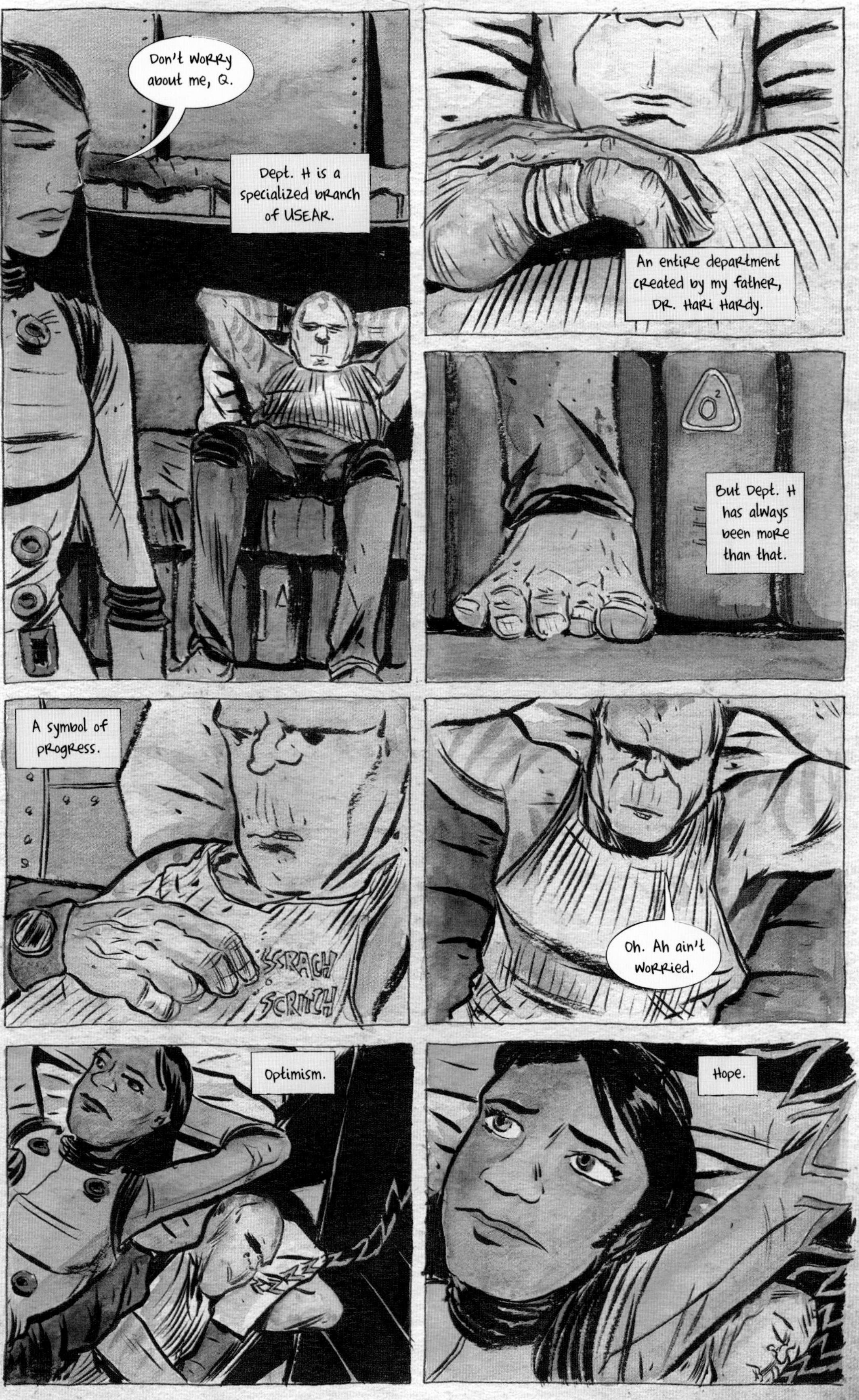
Don't worry about me, Q.
Dept. H is a specialized branch of USEAR.
An entire department created by my father, Dr. Hari Hardy.
But Dept. H has always been more than that.
A symbol of progress.
SCRACH
SCRITCH
Oh. Ah ain't worried.
Optimism.
Hope.

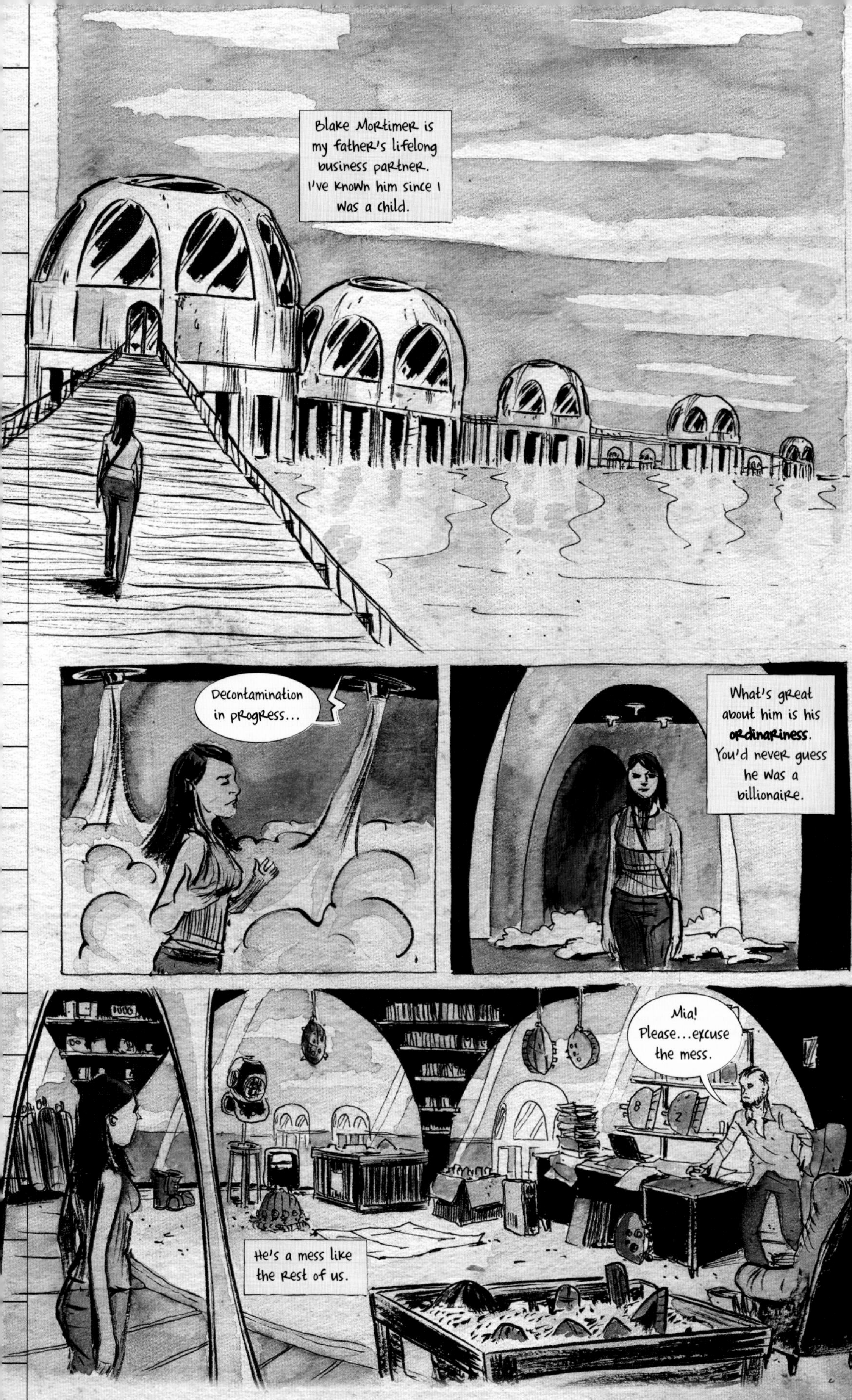
Blake Mortimer is my father's lifelong business partner. I've known him since I was a child.
Decontamination in progress...
What's great about him is his **ordinariness**. You'd never guess he was a billionaire.
Mia! Please...excuse the mess.
He's a mess like the rest of us.

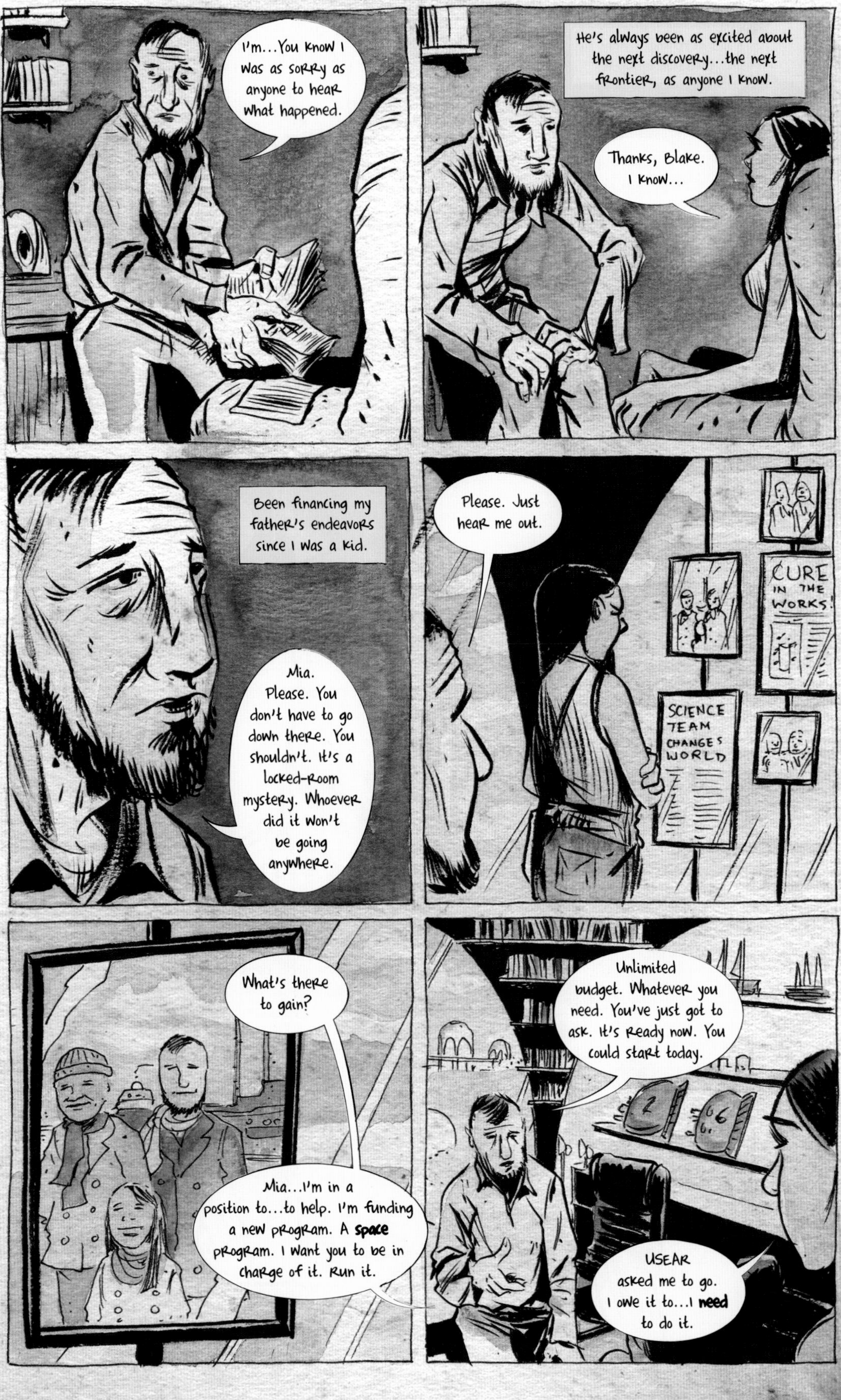
I'm...You know I was as sorry as anyone to hear what happened.
He's always been as excited about the next discovery...the next frontier, as anyone I know.
Thanks, Blake. I know...
Been financing my father's endeavors since I was a kid.
Mia. Please. You don't have to go down there. You shouldn't. It's a locked-room mystery. Whoever did it won't be going anywhere.
Please. Just hear me out.
CURE IN THE WORKS!
SCIENCE TEAM CHANGES WORLD
What's there to gain?
Mia...I'm in a position to...to help. I'm funding a new program. A **space** program. I want you to be in charge of it. Run it.
Unlimited budget. Whatever you need. You've just got to ask. It's ready now. You could start today.
USEAR asked me to go. I owe it to...I **need** to do it.

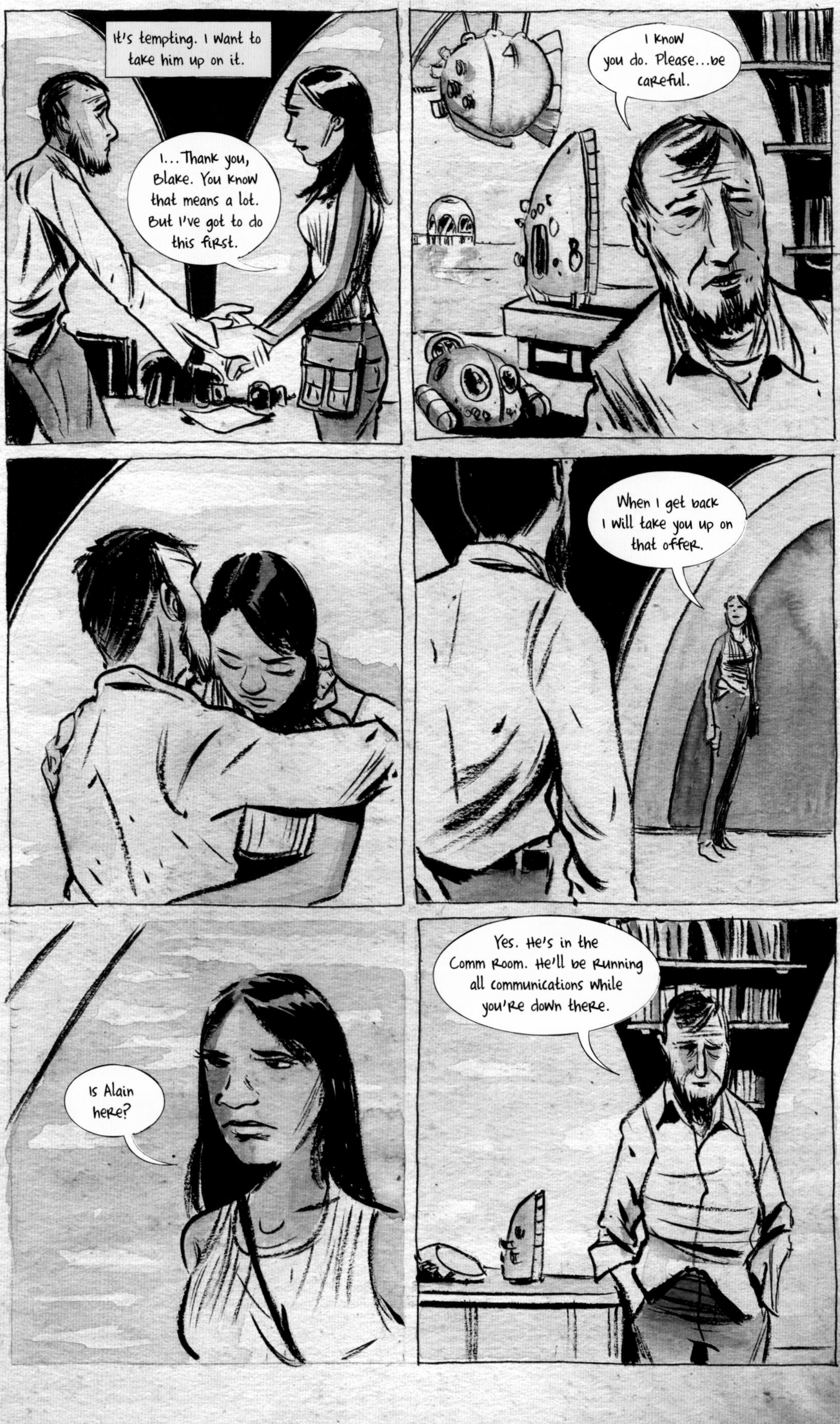
It's tempting. I want to take him up on it.
I... Thank you, Blake. You know that means a lot. But I've got to do this first.
I know you do. Please...be careful.
When I get back I will take you up on that offer.
Is Alain here?
Yes. He's in the Comm Room. He'll be running all communications while you're down there.

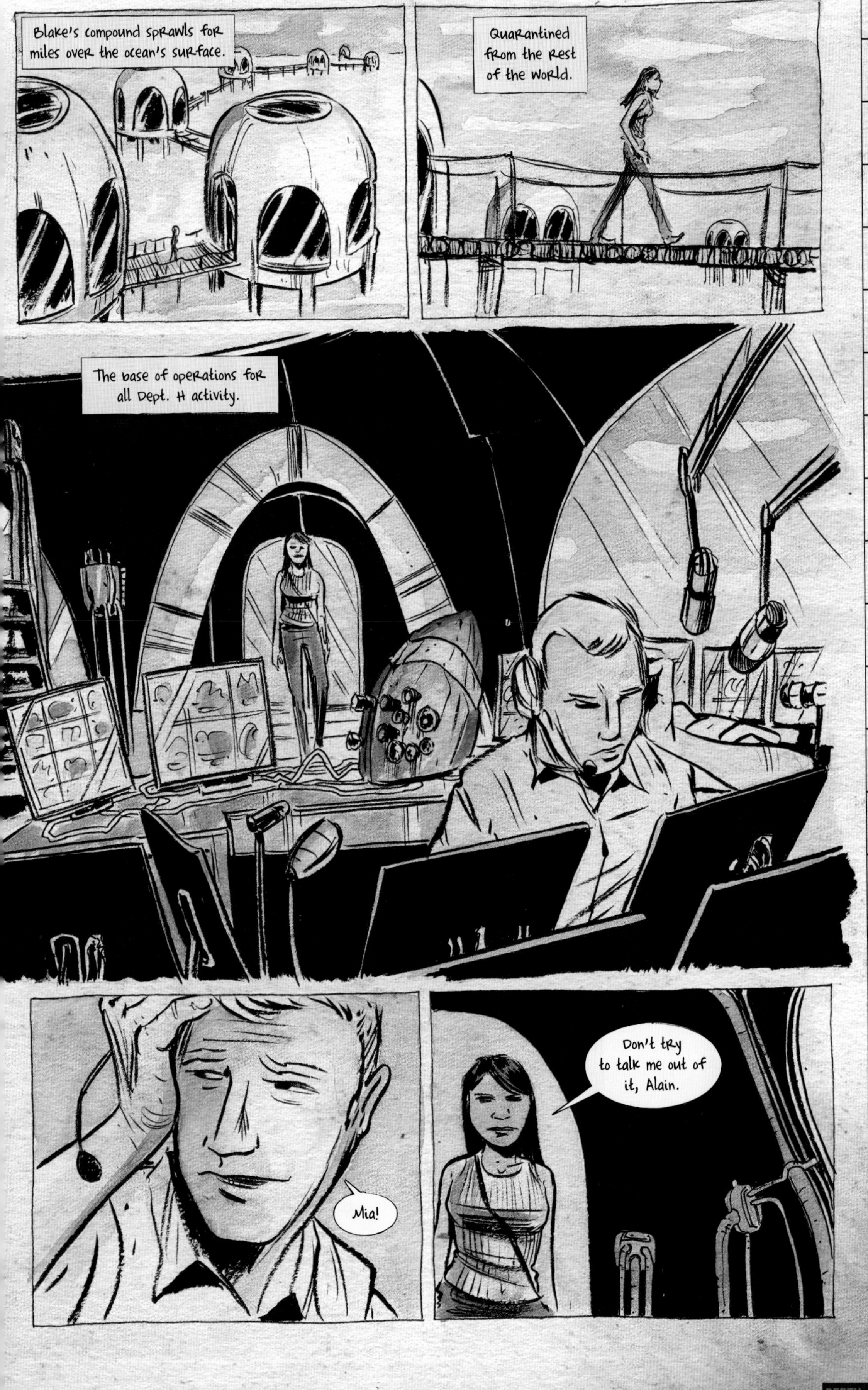
Blake's compound sprawls for miles over the ocean's surface.
Quarantined from the rest of the world.
The base of operations for all Dept. H activity.
Mia!
Don't try to talk me out of it, Alain.

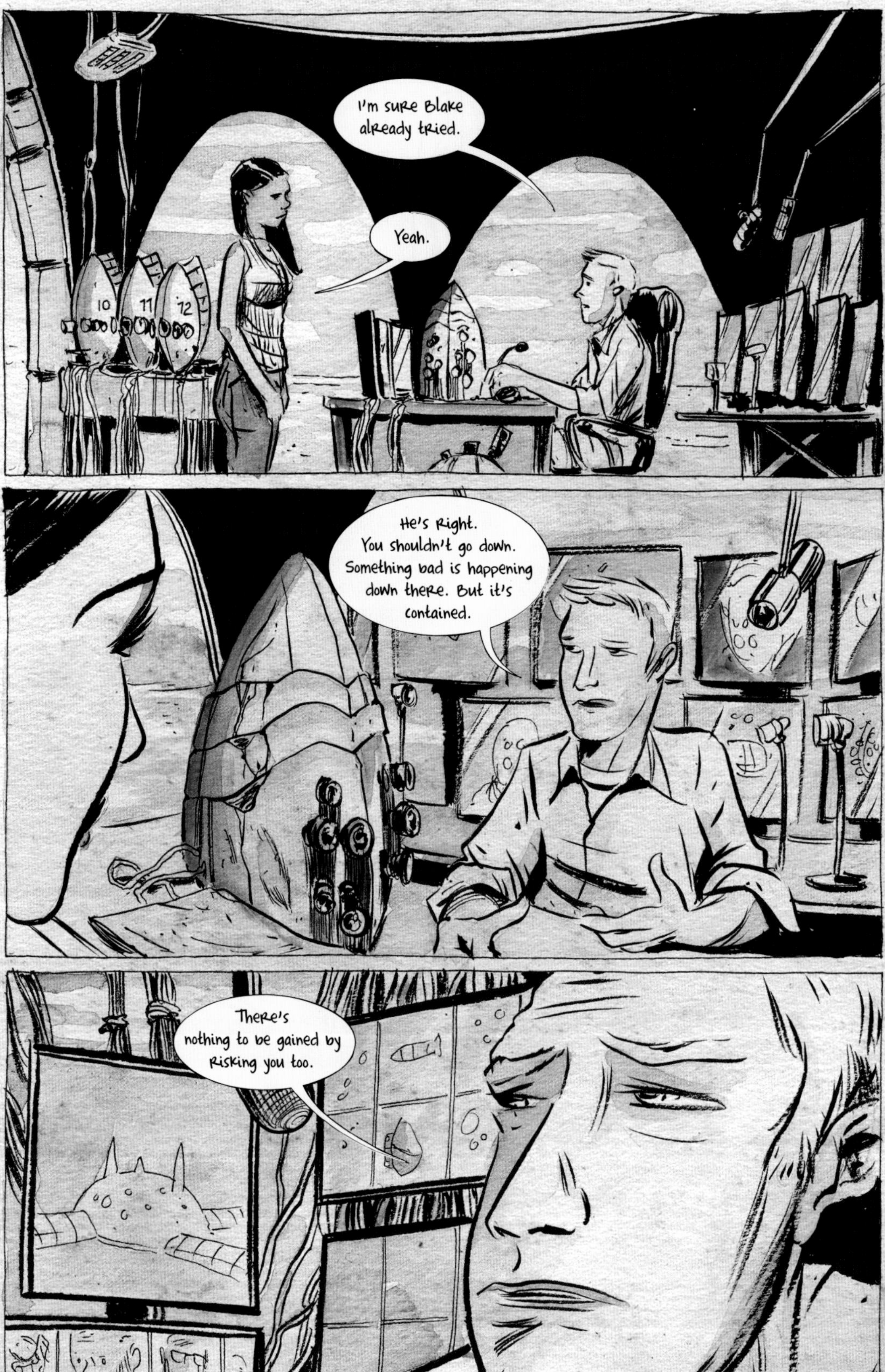
I'm sure Blake already tried.
Yeah.
He's right. You shouldn't go down. Something bad is happening down there. But it's contained.
There's nothing to be gained by risking you too.

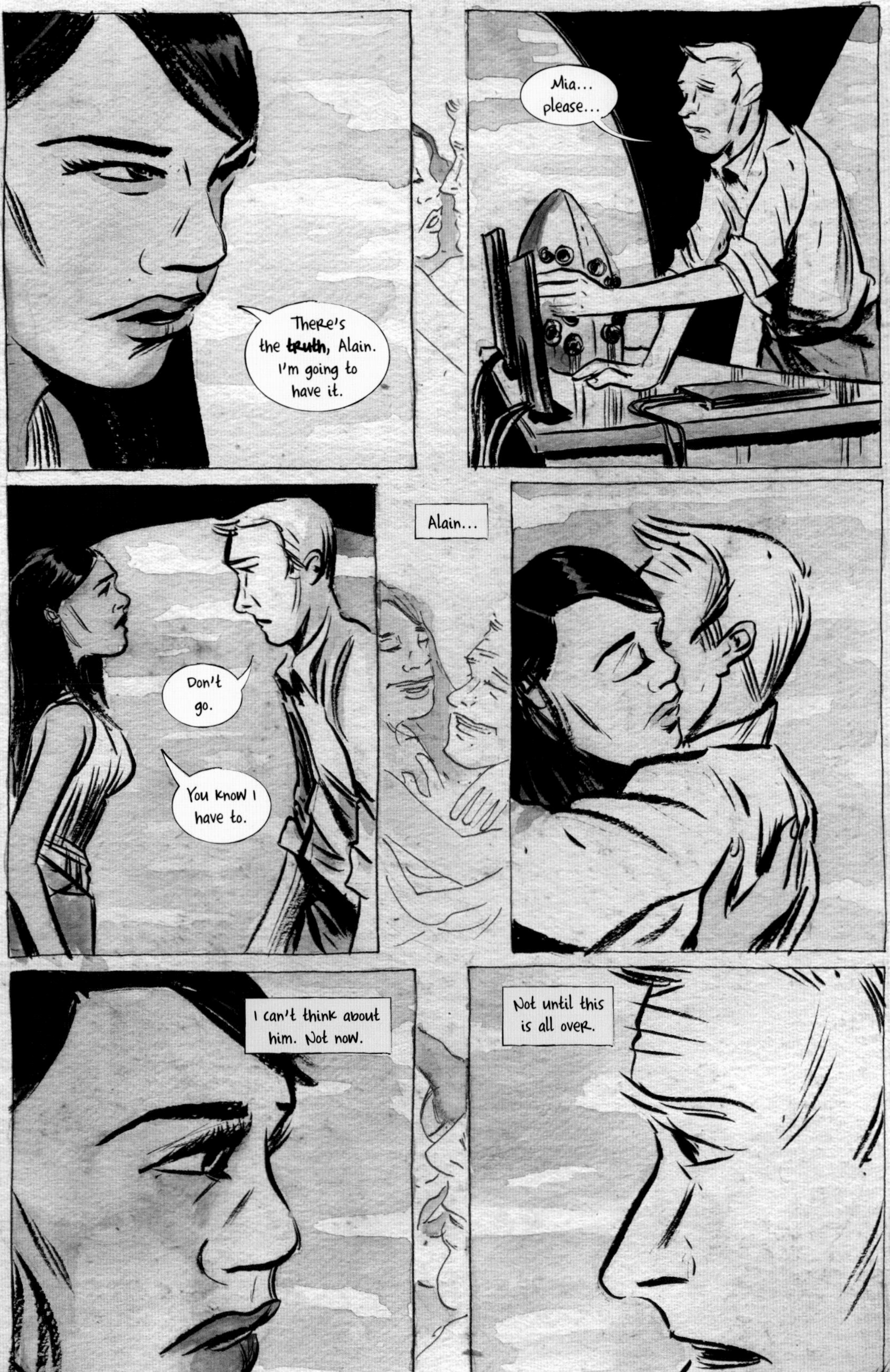
There's the truth, Alain. I'm going to have it.
Mia... please...
Don't go.
You know I have to.
Alain...
I can't think about him. Not now.
Not until this is all over.

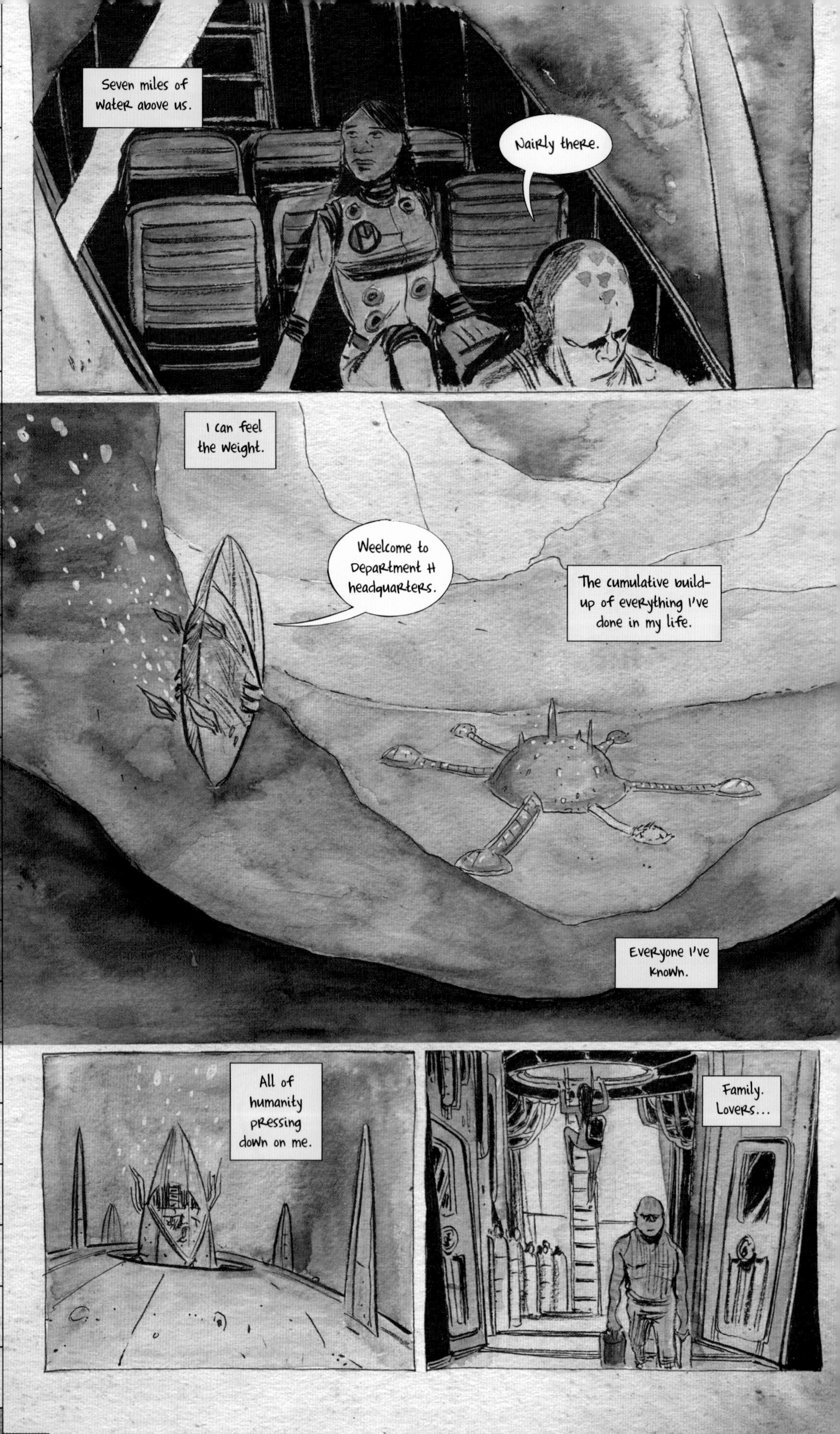

Seven miles of water above us.
Nairly there.
I can feel the weight.
Weelcome to Department H headquarters.
The cumulative build-up of everything I've done in my life.
Everyone I've known.
All of humanity pressing down on me.
Family. Lovers...

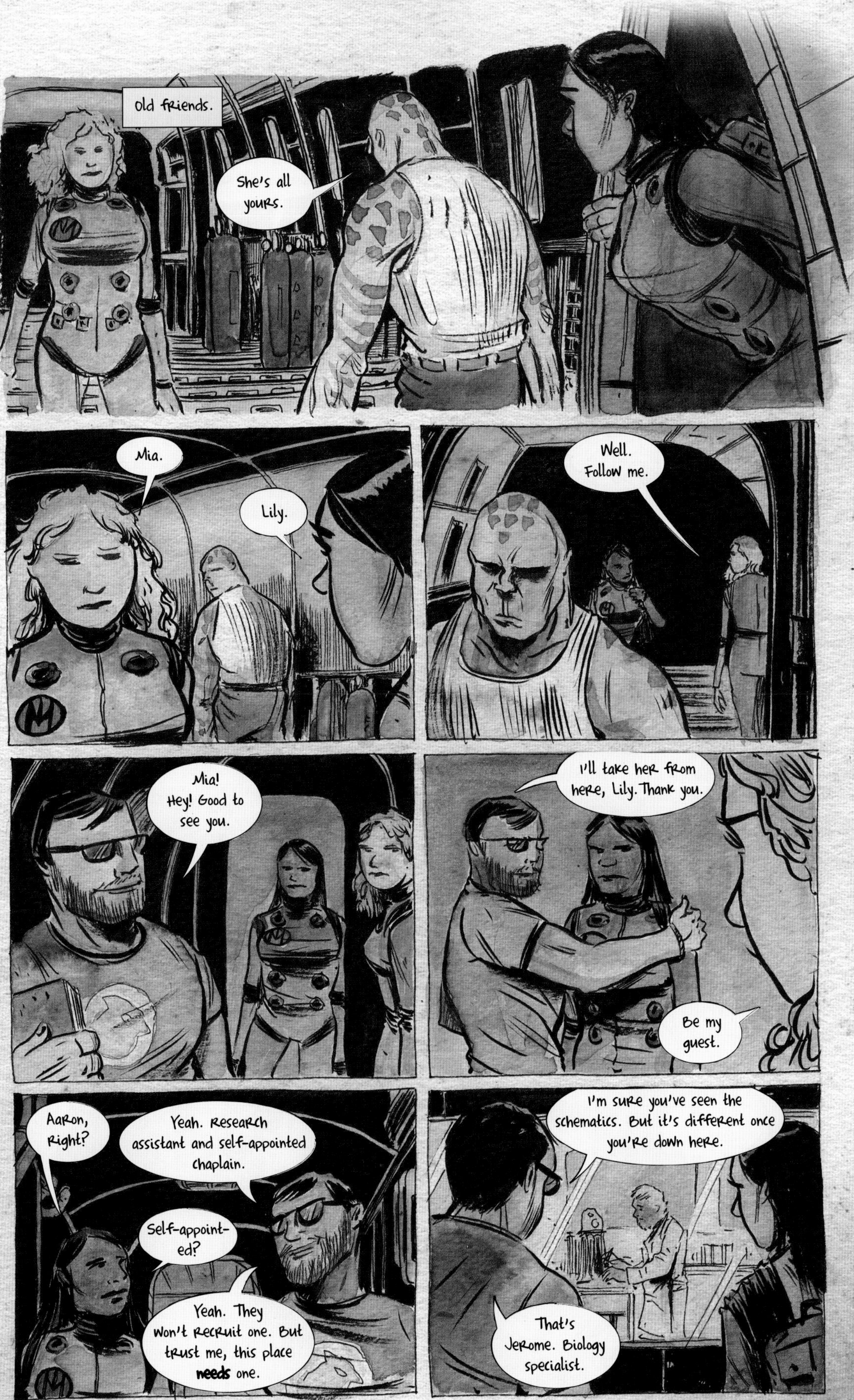
Old friends.
She's all yours.
Mia.
Lily.
Well. Follow me.
Mia! Hey! Good to see you.
I'll take her from here, Lily. Thank you.
Be my guest.
Aaron, right?
Yeah. Research assistant and self-appointed chaplain.
Self-appointed?
Yeah. They won't recruit one. But trust me, this place **needs** one.
I'm sure you've seen the schematics. But it's different once you're down here.
That's Jerome. Biology specialist.

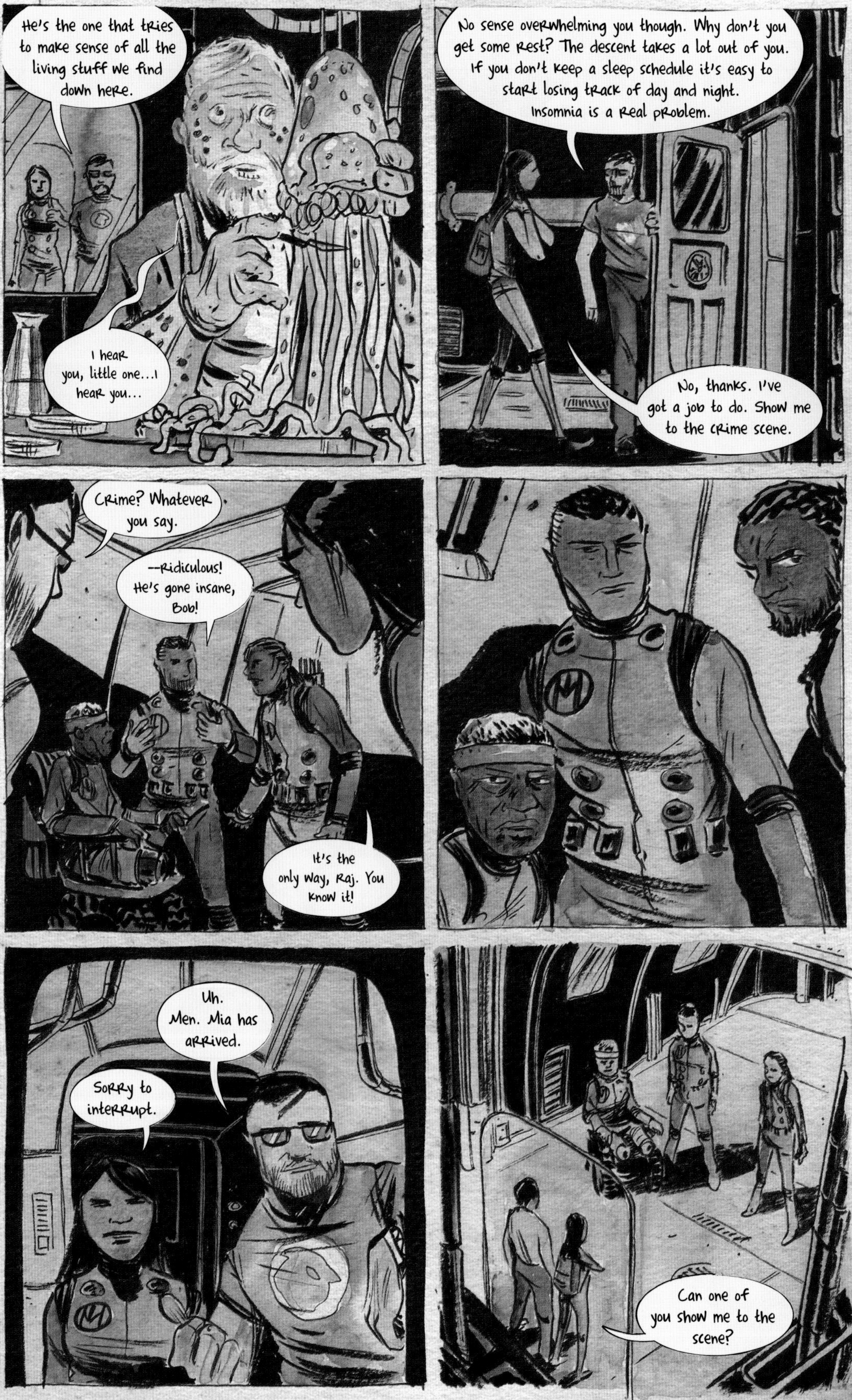
He's the one that tries to make sense of all the living stuff we find down here.
I hear you, little one... I hear you...
No sense overwhelming you though. Why don't you get some rest? The descent takes a lot out of you. If you don't keep a sleep schedule it's easy to start losing track of day and night. Insomnia is a real problem.
No, thanks. I've got a job to do. Show me to the crime scene.
Crime? Whatever you say.
--ridiculous! He's gone insane, Bob!
It's the only way, Raj. You know it!
Uh. Men. Mia has arrived.
Sorry to interrupt.
Can one of you show me to the scene?

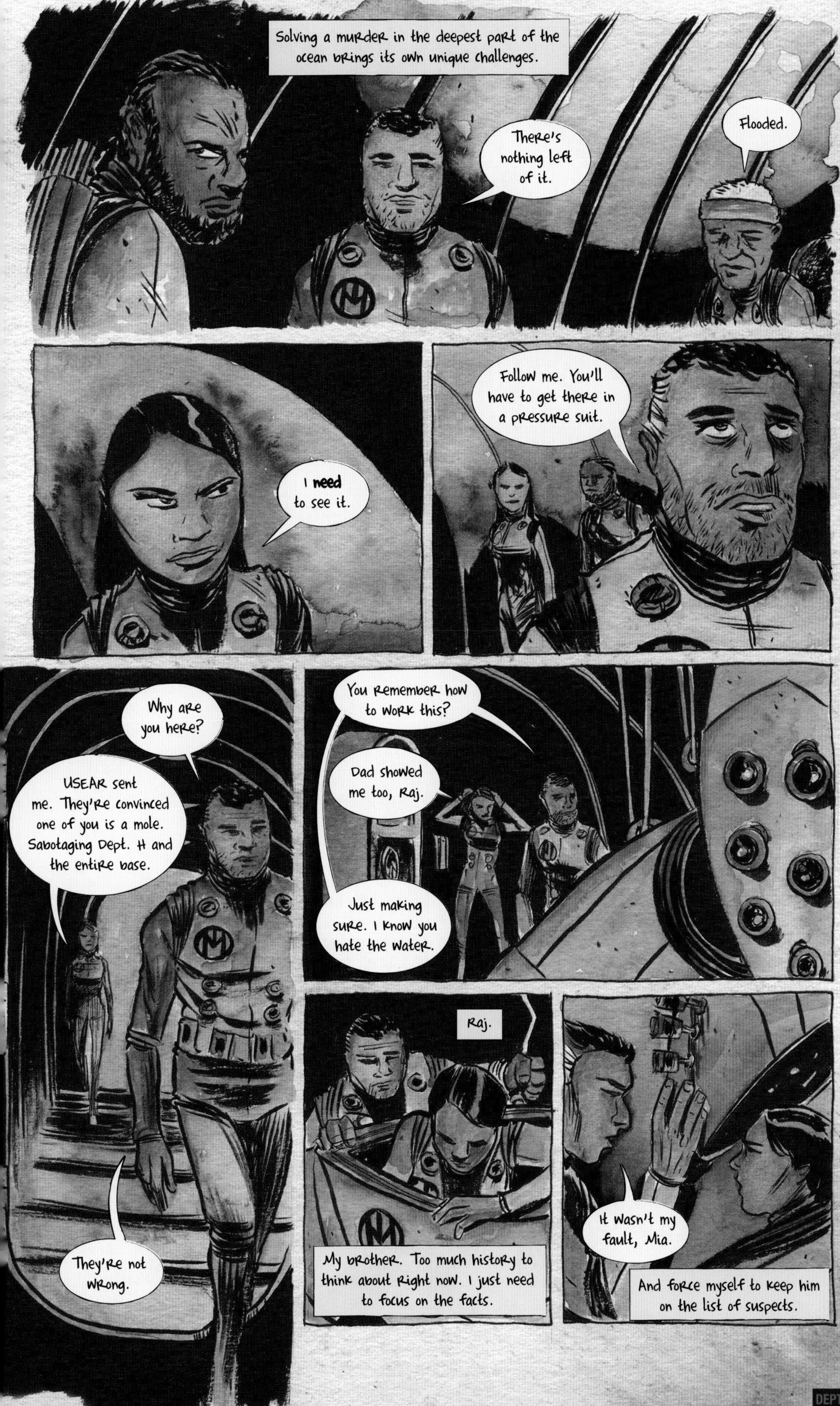
Solving a murder in the deepest part of the ocean brings its own unique challenges.
There's nothing left of it.
Flooded.
I **need** to see it.
Follow me. You'll have to get there in a pressure suit.
Why are you here?
USEAR sent me. They're convinced one of you is a mole. Sabotaging Dept. H and the entire base.
They're not wrong.
You remember how to work this?
Dad showed me too, Raj.
Just making sure. I know you hate the water.
Raj.
My brother. Too much history to think about right now. I just need to focus on the facts.
It wasn't my fault, Mia.
And force myself to keep him on the list of suspects.

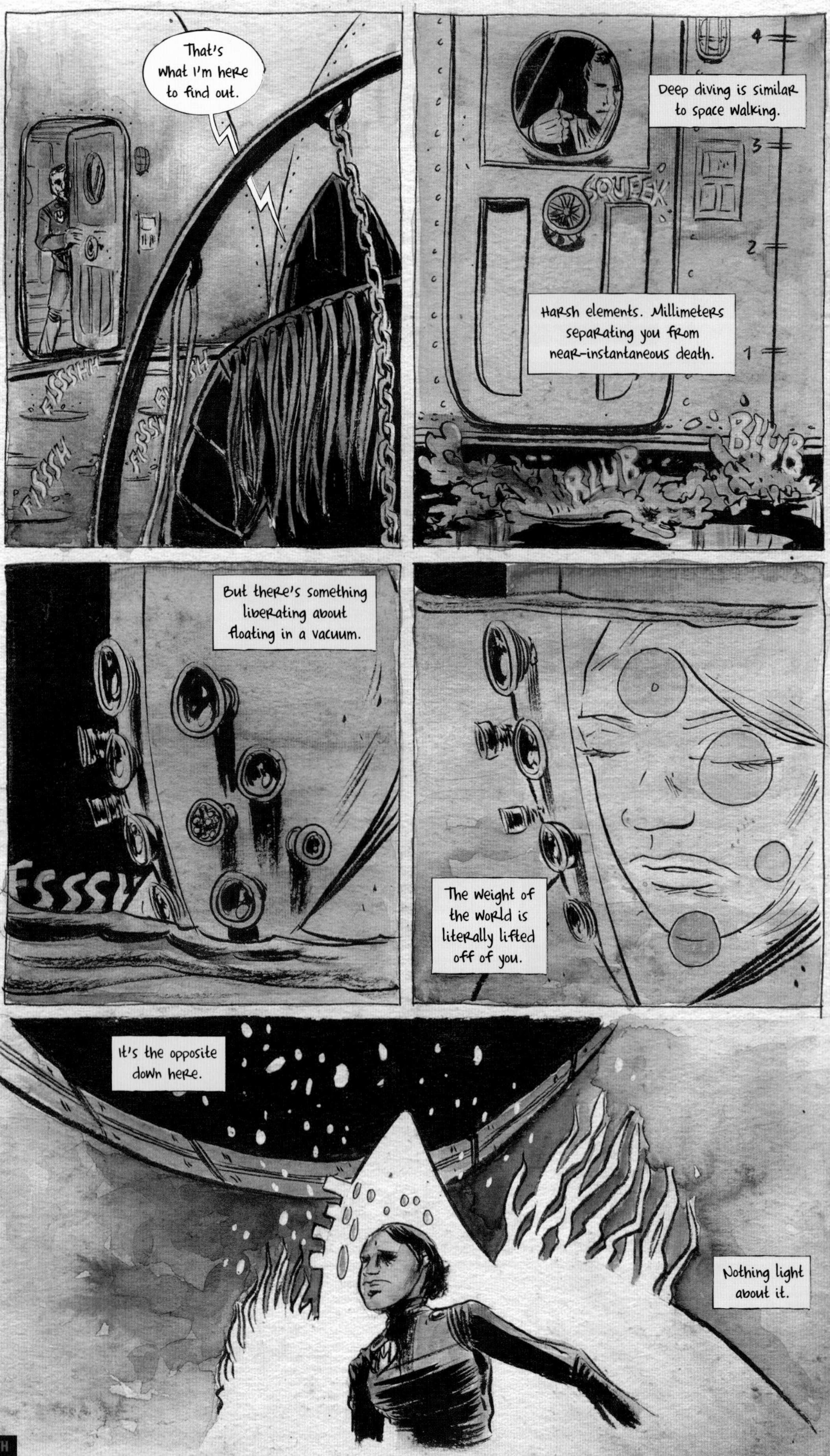
That's what I'm here to find out.
Deep diving is similar to space walking.
SQUEEK
Harsh elements. Millimeters separating you from near-instantaneous death.
BLUB
BLUB
But there's something liberating about floating in a vacuum.
The weight of the world is literally lifted off of you.
It's the opposite down here.
Nothing light about it.

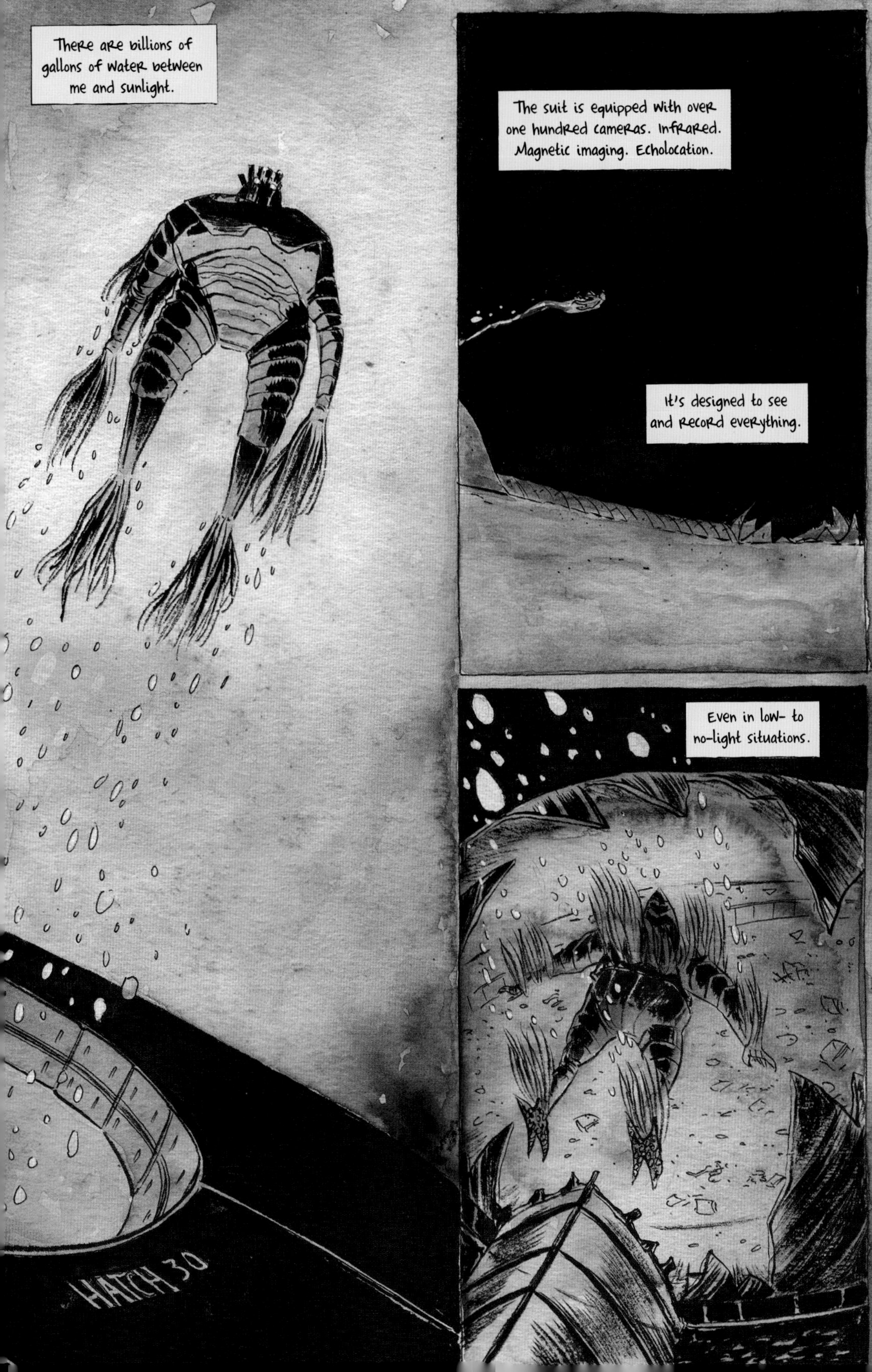
There are billions of gallons of water between me and sunlight.
HATCH 30
The suit is equipped with over one hundred cameras. Infrared. Magnetic imaging. Echolocation.
It's designed to see and record everything.
Even in low- to no-light situations.

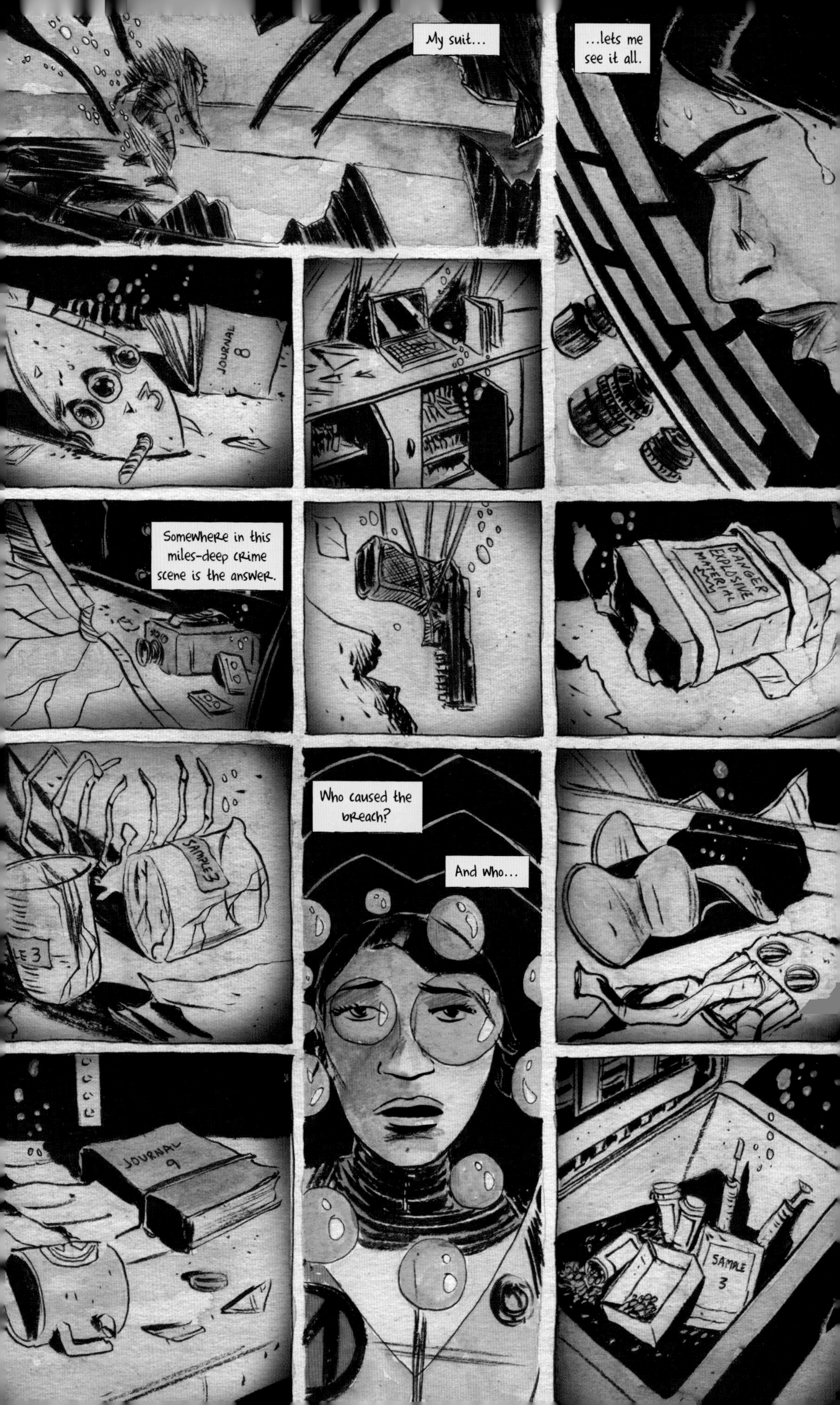
My suit...
...lets me see it all.
JOURNAL 8
Somewhere in this miles-deep crime scene is the answer.
DANGER EXPLOSIVE MATERIAL
SAMPLE 3
LE 3
Who caused the breach?
And who...
JOURNAL 9
SAMPLE 3

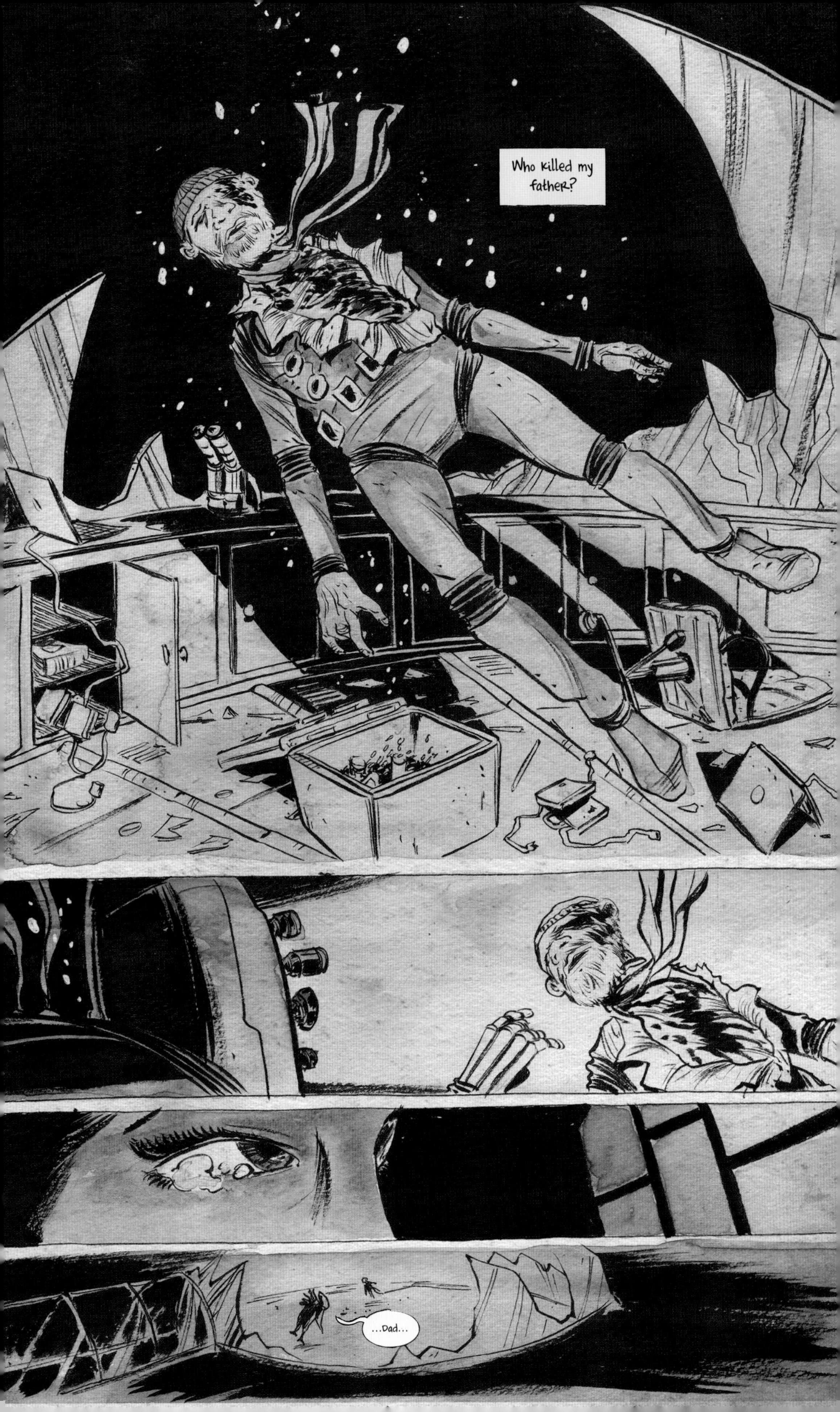
Who killed my father?
...Dad...

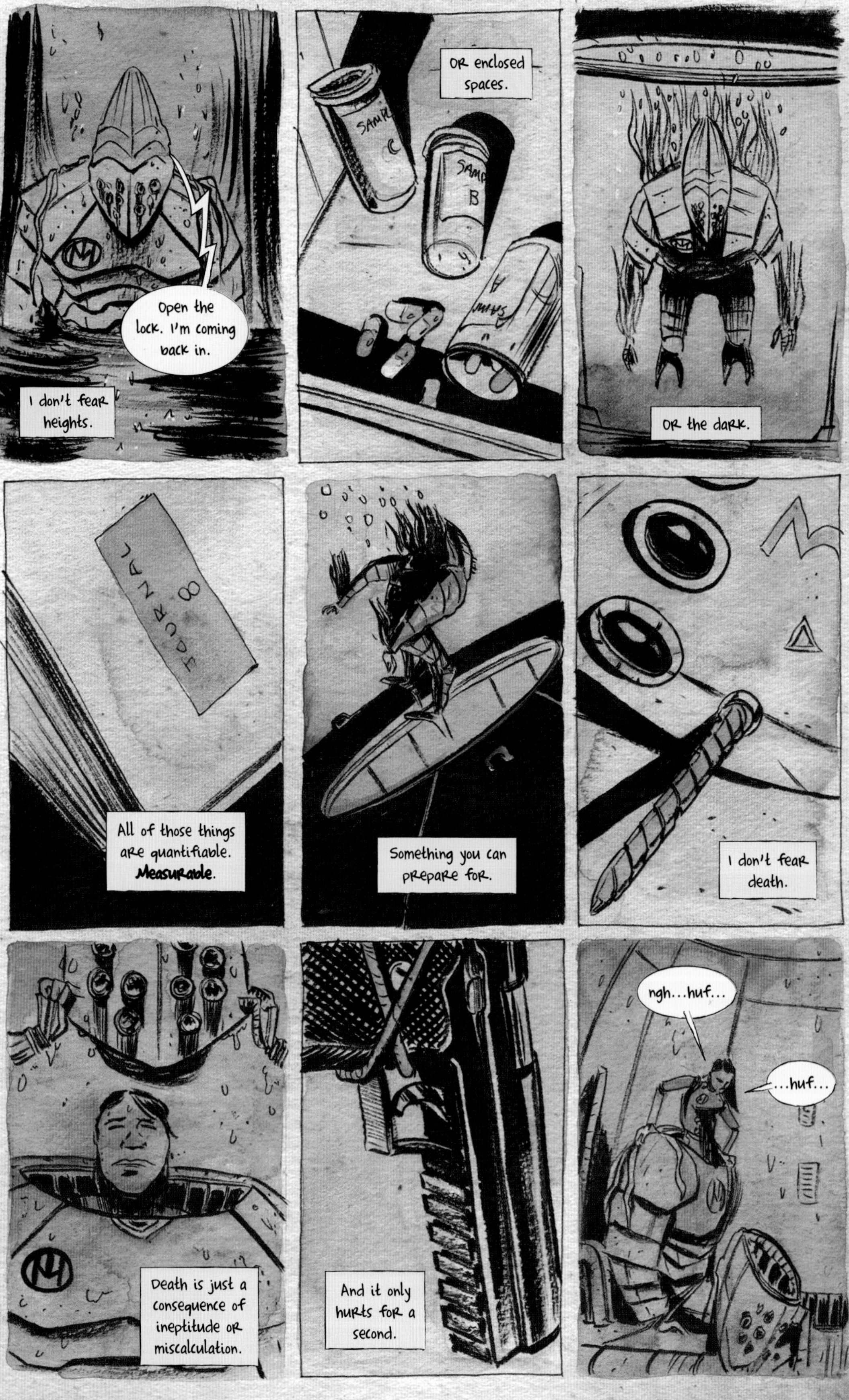
Open the lock. I'm coming back in.
I don't fear heights.
OR enclosed spaces.
SAMP
SAMP
B
SAMP
A
OR the dark.
JOURNAL
8
All of those things are quantifiable. Measurable.
Something you can prepare for.
I don't fear death.
Death is just a consequence of ineptitude or miscalculation.
And it only hurts for a second.
ngh...huf...
...huf...

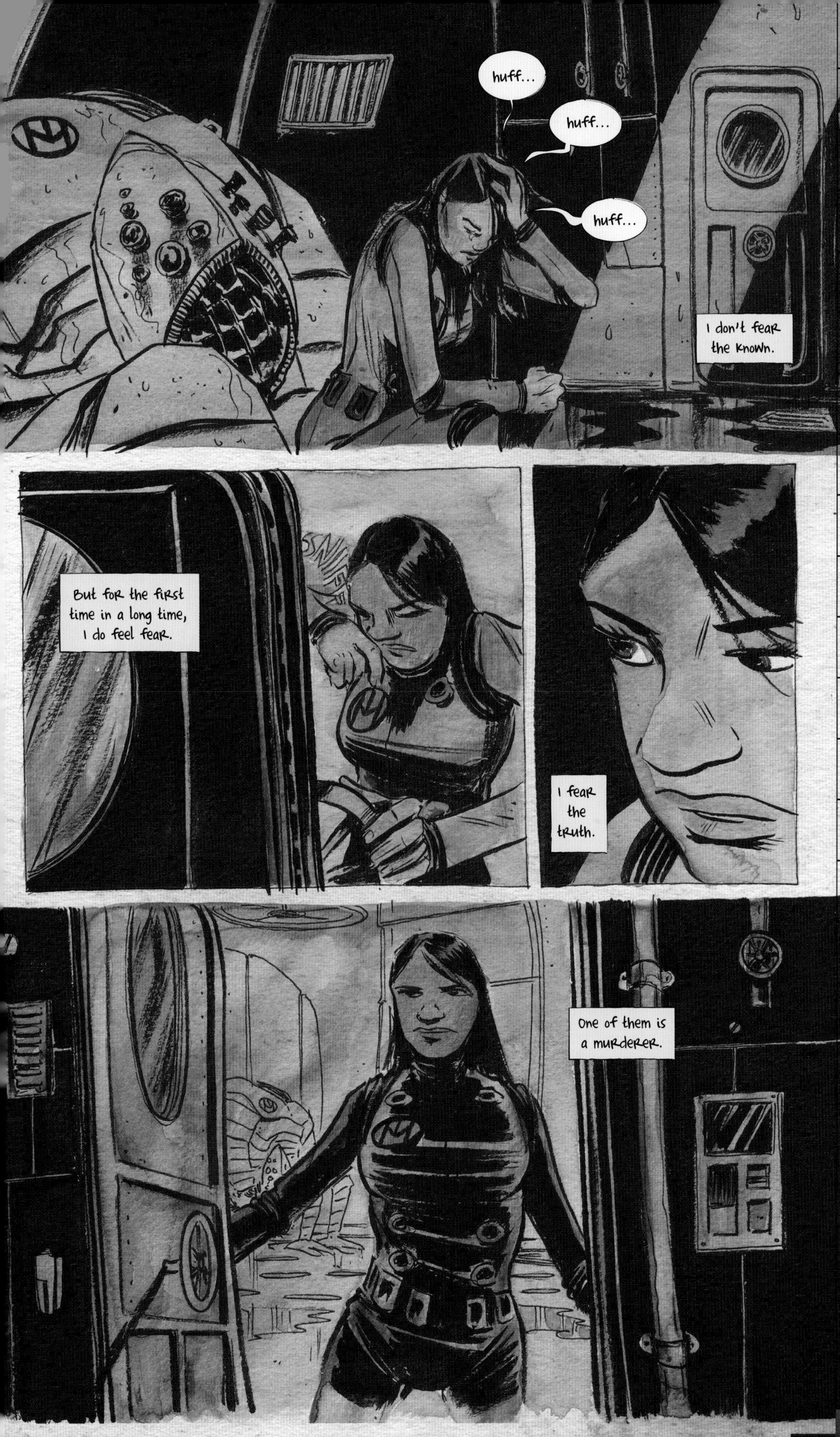
huff...
huff...
huff...
I don't fear the known.
But for the first time in a long time, I do feel fear.
I fear the truth.
One of them is a murderer.

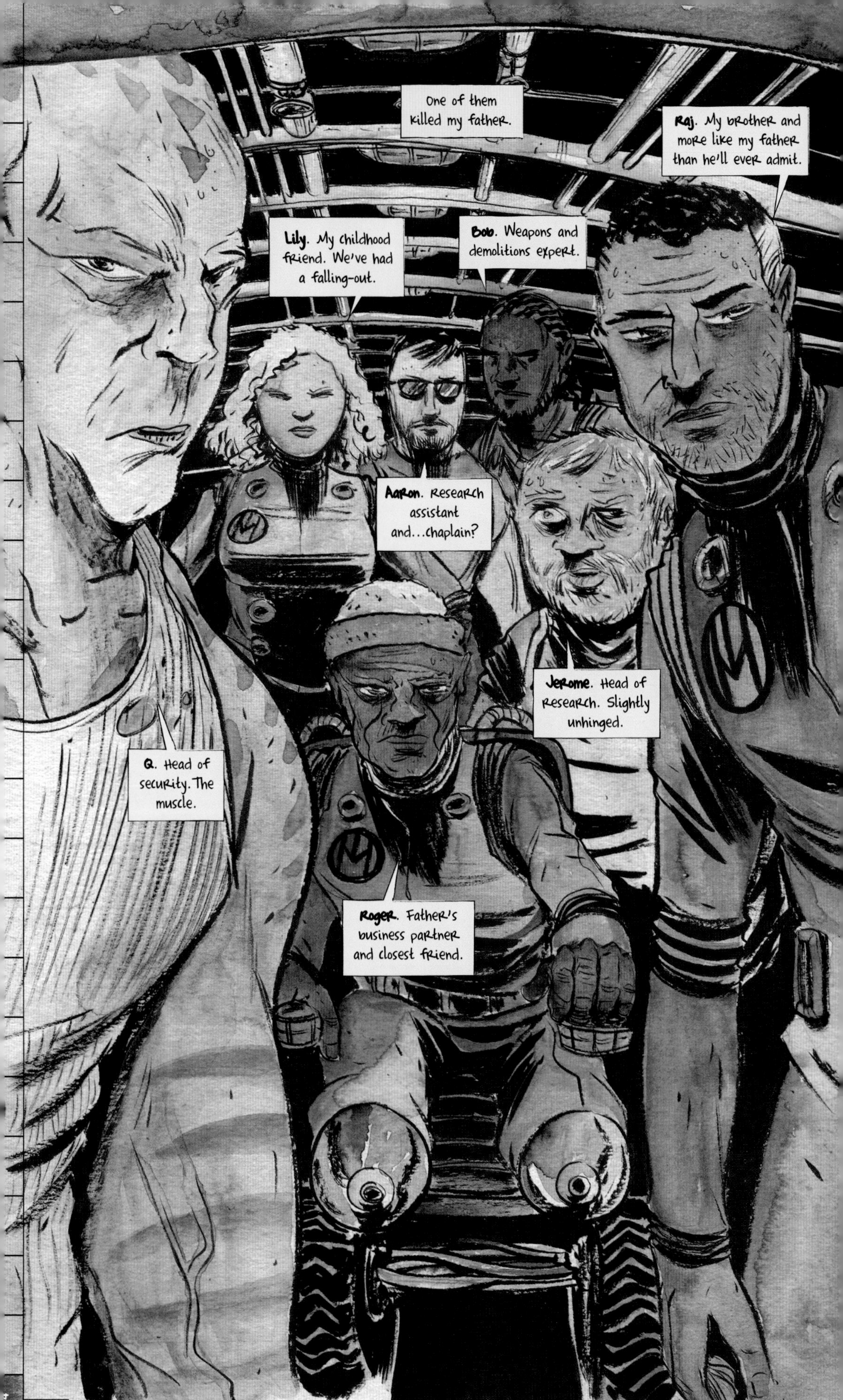
One of them killed my father.
Raj. My brother and more like my father than he'll ever admit.
Lily. My childhood friend. We've had a falling-out.
Bob. Weapons and demolitions expert.
Aaron. Research assistant and...chaplain?
Jerome. Head of Research. Slightly unhinged.
Q. Head of security. The muscle.
Roger. Father's business partner and closest friend.

matt kindt

"I'll read anything Kindt does." —Douglas Wolk, author of *Reading Comics*

MIND MGMT
VOLUME 1: THE MANAGER
ISBN 978-1-59582-797-5
$19.99
VOLUME 2: THE FUTURIST
ISBN 978-1-61655-198-8
$19.99
VOLUME 3: THE HOME MAKER
ISBN 978-1-61655-390-6
$19.99
VOLUME 4: THE MAGICIAN
ISBN 978-1-61655-391-3
$19.99
VOLUME 5: THE ERASER
ISBN 978-1-61655-696-9
$19.99
VOLUME 6: THE IMMORTALS
ISBN 978-1-61655-798-0
$19.99

**POPPY! AND THE
LOST LAGOON**
With Brian Hurtt
ISBN 978-1-61655-943-4
$14.99

PAST AWAYS
With Scott Kolins
ISBN 978-1-61655-792-8
$12.99

**THE COMPLETE
PISTOLWHIP**
With Jason Hall
ISBN 978-1-61655-720-1
$27.99

**3 STORY: THE
SECRET HISTORY
OF THE GIANT MAN**
ISBN 978-1-59582-356-4
$19.99

2 SISTERS
ISBN 978-1-61655-721-8
$27.99

**DEPT. H VOLUME 1:
PRESSURE**
ISBN 978-1-61655-989-2
$19.99

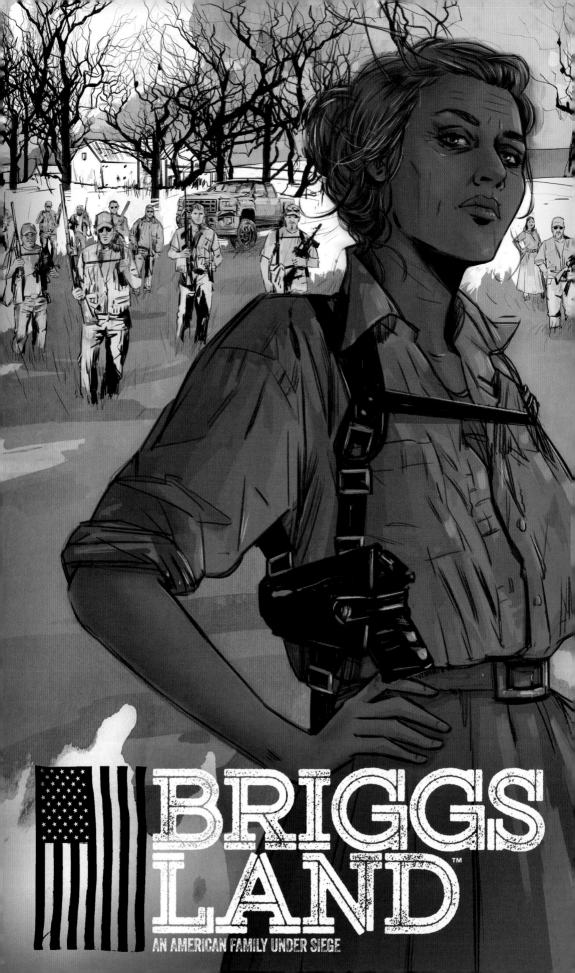

BRIGGS LAND

AN AMERICAN FAMILY UNDER SIEGE

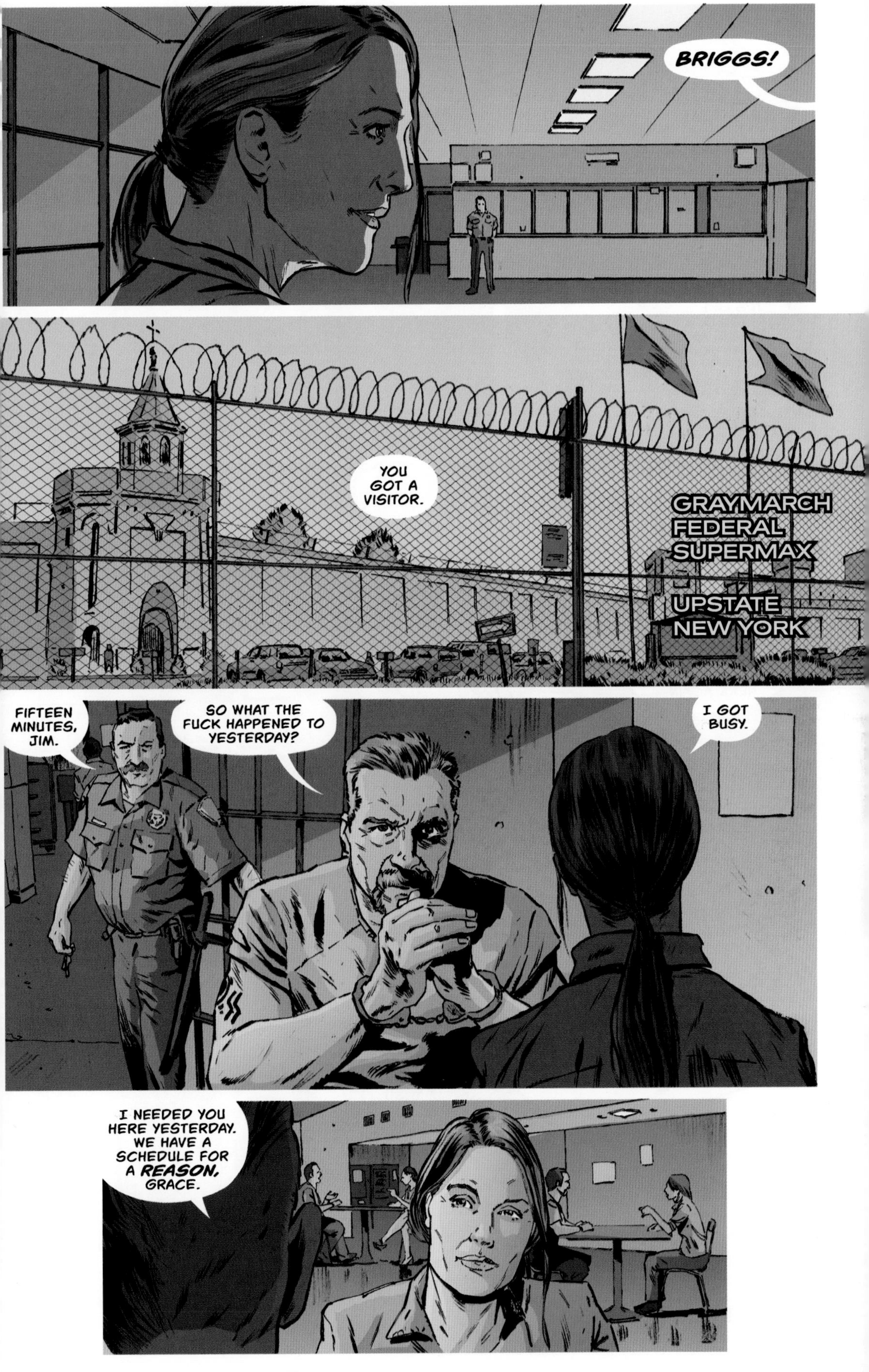
BRIGGS!
YOU GOT A VISITOR.
GRAYMARCH FEDERAL SUPERMAX
UPSTATE NEW YORK
FIFTEEN MINUTES, JIM.
SO WHAT THE FUCK HAPPENED TO YESTERDAY?
I GOT BUSY.
I NEEDED YOU HERE YESTERDAY. WE HAVE A SCHEDULE FOR A REASON, GRACE.

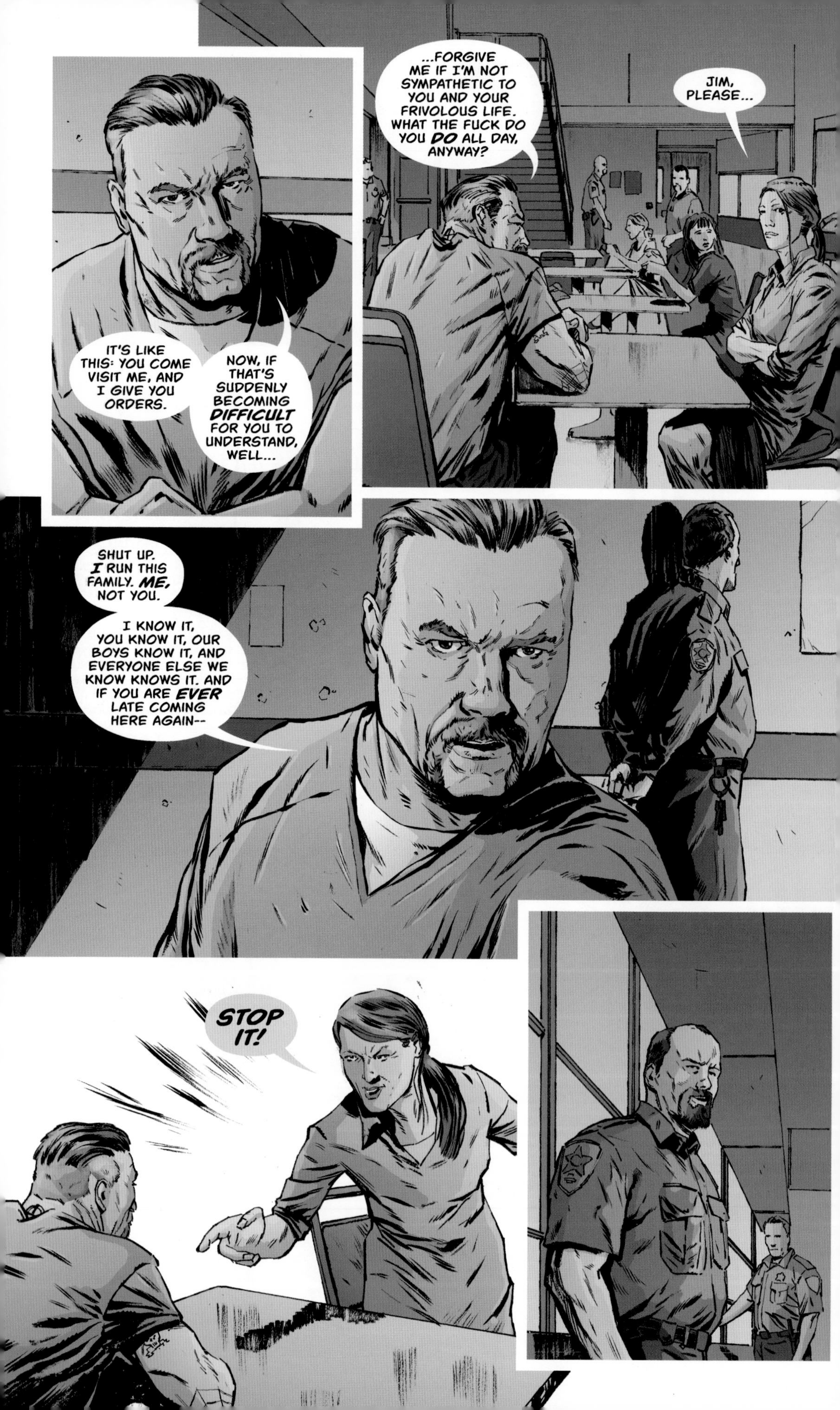
IT'S LIKE THIS: YOU COME VISIT ME, AND I GIVE YOU ORDERS.
NOW, IF THAT'S SUDDENLY BECOMING DIFFICULT FOR YOU TO UNDERSTAND, WELL...
...FORGIVE ME IF I'M NOT SYMPATHETIC TO YOU AND YOUR FRIVOLOUS LIFE. WHAT THE FUCK DO YOU DO ALL DAY, ANYWAY?
JIM, PLEASE...
SHUT UP. I RUN THIS FAMILY. ME, NOT YOU.
I KNOW IT, YOU KNOW IT, OUR BOYS KNOW IT, AND EVERYONE ELSE WE KNOW KNOWS IT. AND IF YOU ARE EVER LATE COMING HERE AGAIN--
STOP IT!

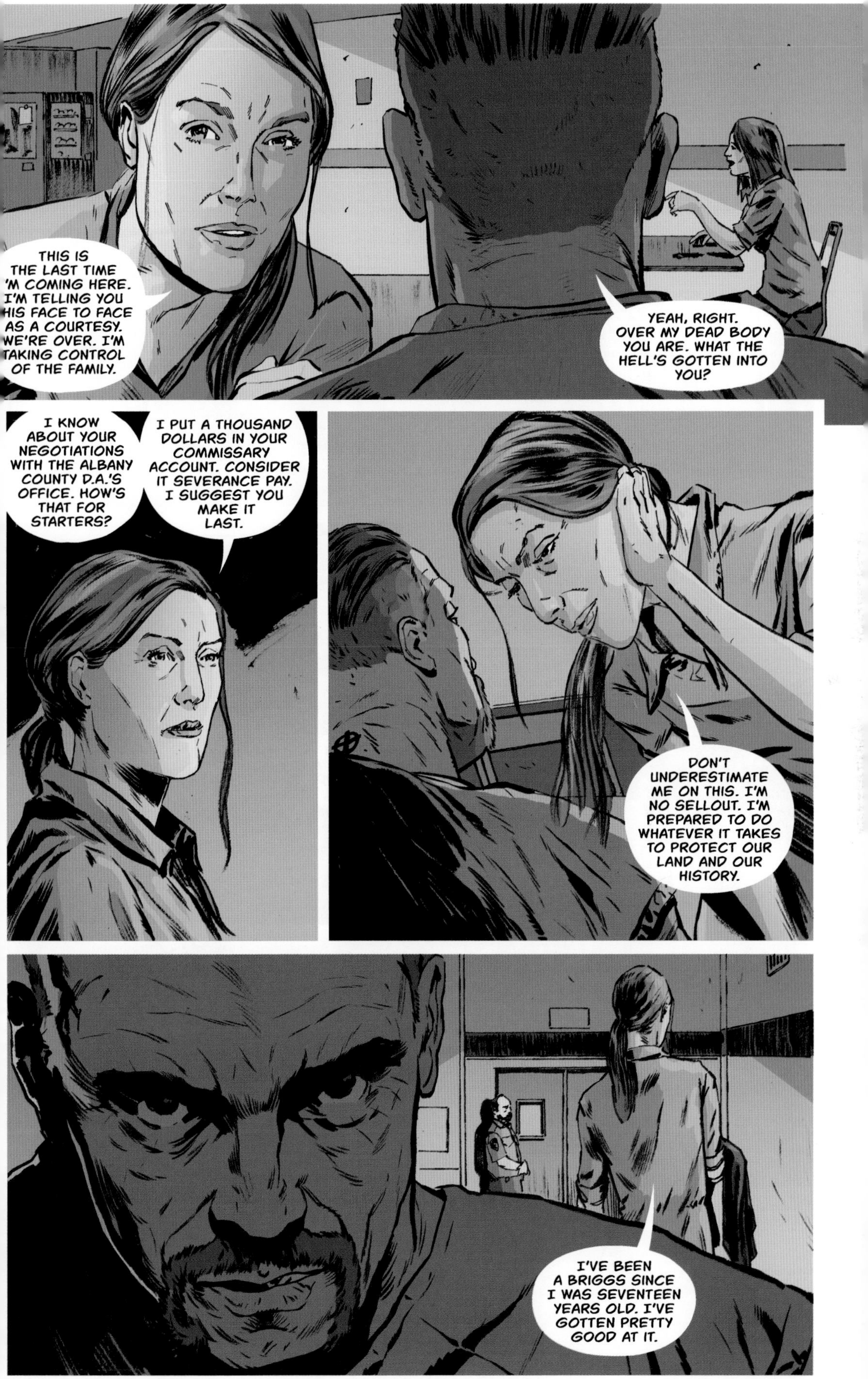
THIS IS THE LAST TIME 'M COMING HERE. I'M TELLING YOU HIS FACE TO FACE AS A COURTESY. WE'RE OVER. I'M TAKING CONTROL OF THE FAMILY.
YEAH, RIGHT. OVER MY DEAD BODY YOU ARE. WHAT THE HELL'S GOTTEN INTO YOU?
I KNOW ABOUT YOUR NEGOTIATIONS WITH THE ALBANY COUNTY D.A.'S OFFICE. HOW'S THAT FOR STARTERS?
I PUT A THOUSAND DOLLARS IN YOUR COMMISSARY ACCOUNT. CONSIDER IT SEVERANCE PAY. I SUGGEST YOU MAKE IT LAST.
DON'T UNDERESTIMATE ME ON THIS. I'M NO SELLOUT. I'M PREPARED TO DO WHATEVER IT TAKES TO PROTECT OUR LAND AND OUR HISTORY.
I'VE BEEN A BRIGGS SINCE I WAS SEVENTEEN YEARS OLD. I'VE GOTTEN PRETTY GOOD AT IT.

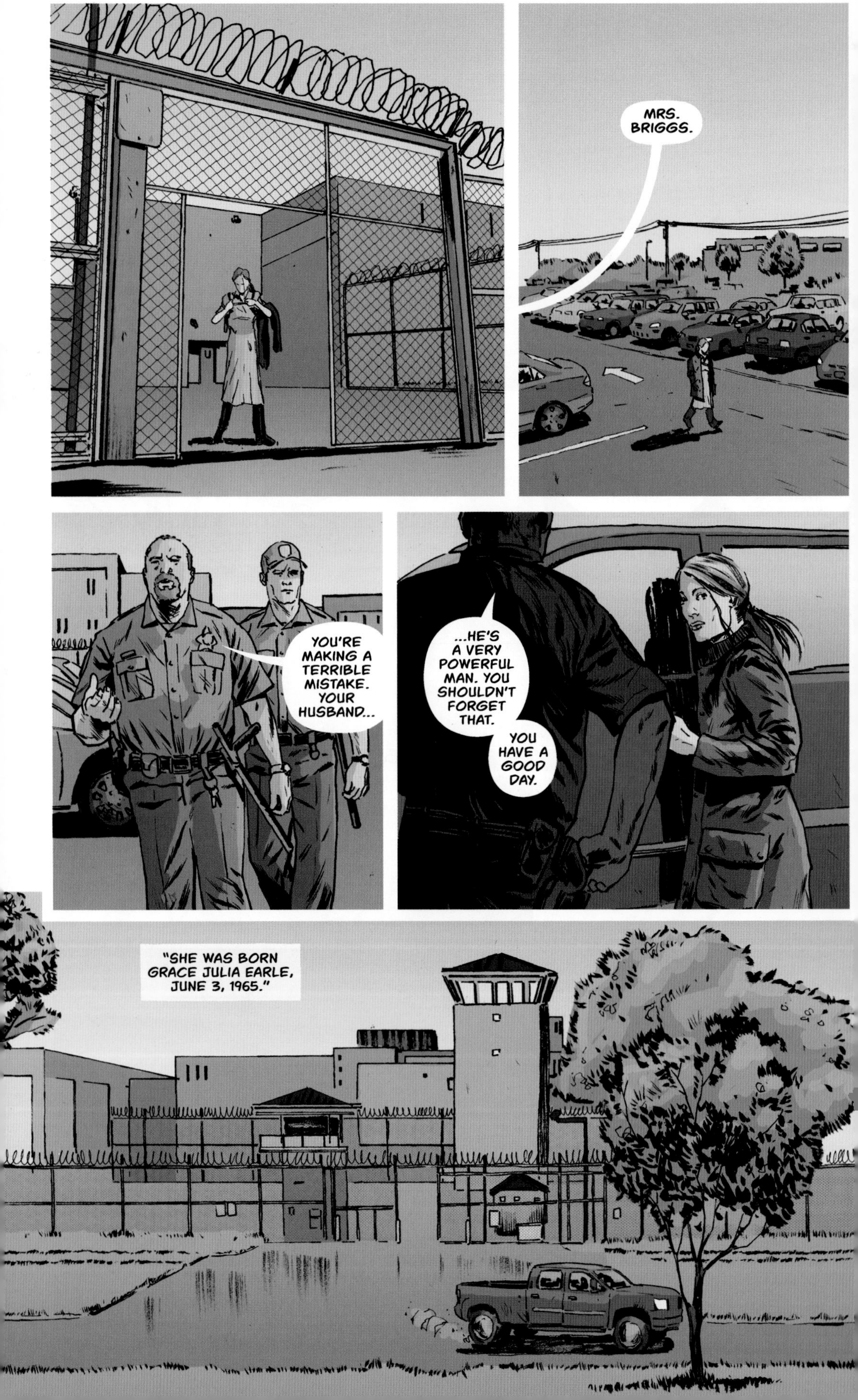
MRS. BRIGGS.
YOU'RE MAKING A TERRIBLE MISTAKE. YOUR HUSBAND...
...HE'S A VERY POWERFUL MAN. YOU SHOULDN'T FORGET THAT.
YOU HAVE A GOOD DAY.
"SHE WAS BORN GRACE JULIA EARLE, JUNE 3, 1965."

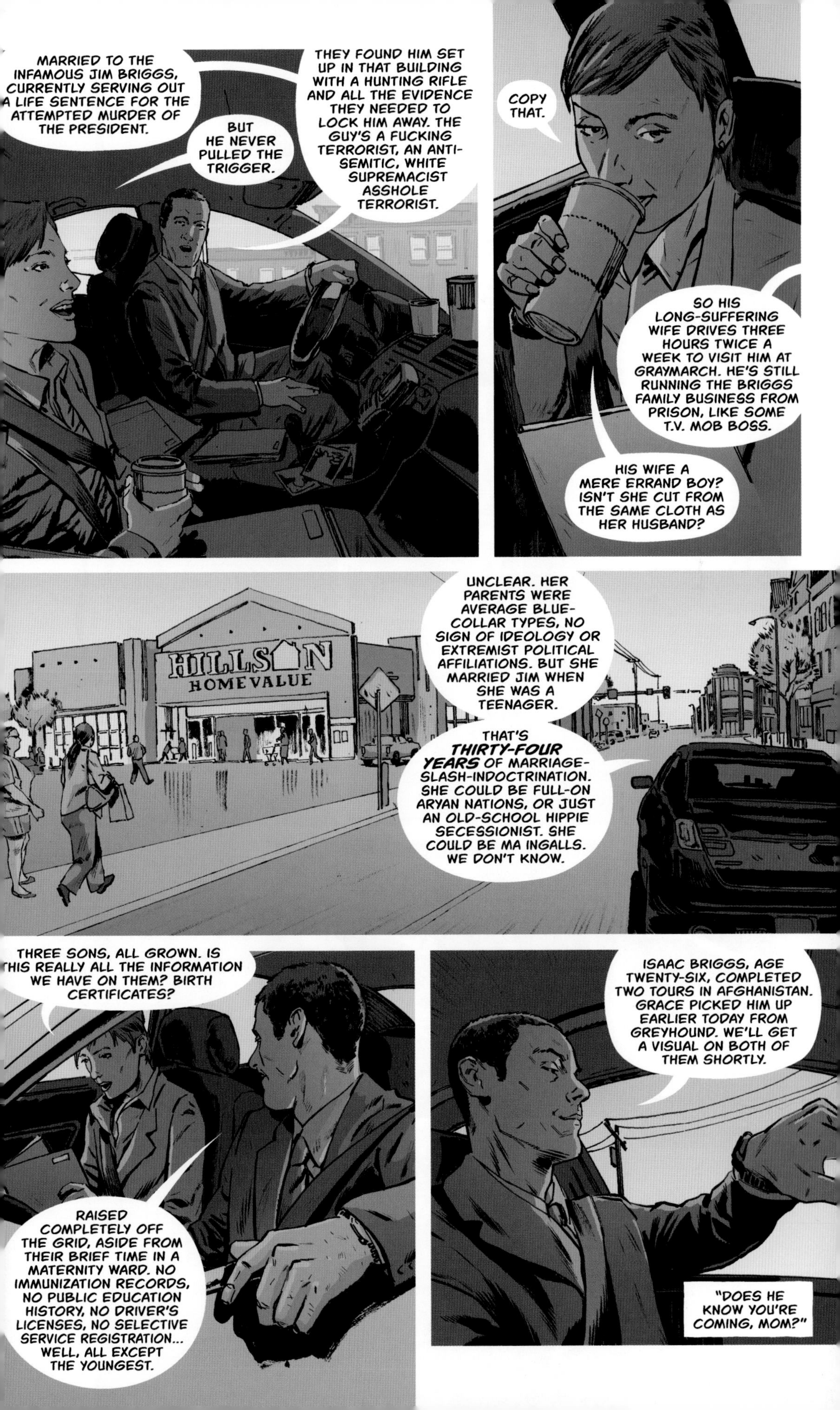
MARRIED TO THE INFAMOUS JIM BRIGGS, CURRENTLY SERVING OUT A LIFE SENTENCE FOR THE ATTEMPTED MURDER OF THE PRESIDENT.
BUT HE NEVER PULLED THE TRIGGER.
THEY FOUND HIM SET UP IN THAT BUILDING WITH A HUNTING RIFLE AND ALL THE EVIDENCE THEY NEEDED TO LOCK HIM AWAY. THE GUY'S A FUCKING TERRORIST, AN ANTI-SEMITIC, WHITE SUPREMACIST ASSHOLE TERRORIST.
COPY THAT.
SO HIS LONG-SUFFERING WIFE DRIVES THREE HOURS TWICE A WEEK TO VISIT HIM AT GRAYMARCH. HE'S STILL RUNNING THE BRIGGS FAMILY BUSINESS FROM PRISON, LIKE SOME T.V. MOB BOSS.
HIS WIFE A MERE ERRAND BOY? ISN'T SHE CUT FROM THE SAME CLOTH AS HER HUSBAND?
HILLSON HOMEVALUE
UNCLEAR. HER PARENTS WERE AVERAGE BLUE-COLLAR TYPES, NO SIGN OF IDEOLOGY OR EXTREMIST POLITICAL AFFILIATIONS. BUT SHE MARRIED JIM WHEN SHE WAS A TEENAGER.
THAT'S THIRTY-FOUR YEARS OF MARRIAGE-SLASH-INDOCTRINATION. SHE COULD BE FULL-ON ARYAN NATIONS, OR JUST AN OLD-SCHOOL HIPPIE SECESSIONIST. SHE COULD BE MA INGALLS. WE DON'T KNOW.
THREE SONS, ALL GROWN. IS THIS REALLY ALL THE INFORMATION WE HAVE ON THEM? BIRTH CERTIFICATES?
RAISED COMPLETELY OFF THE GRID, ASIDE FROM THEIR BRIEF TIME IN A MATERNITY WARD. NO IMMUNIZATION RECORDS, NO PUBLIC EDUCATION HISTORY, NO DRIVER'S LICENSES, NO SELECTIVE SERVICE REGISTRATION... WELL, ALL EXCEPT THE YOUNGEST.
ISAAC BRIGGS, AGE TWENTY-SIX, COMPLETED TWO TOURS IN AFGHANISTAN. GRACE PICKED HIM UP EARLIER TODAY FROM GREYHOUND. WE'LL GET A VISUAL ON BOTH OF THEM SHORTLY.
"DOES HE KNOW YOU'RE COMING, MOM?"

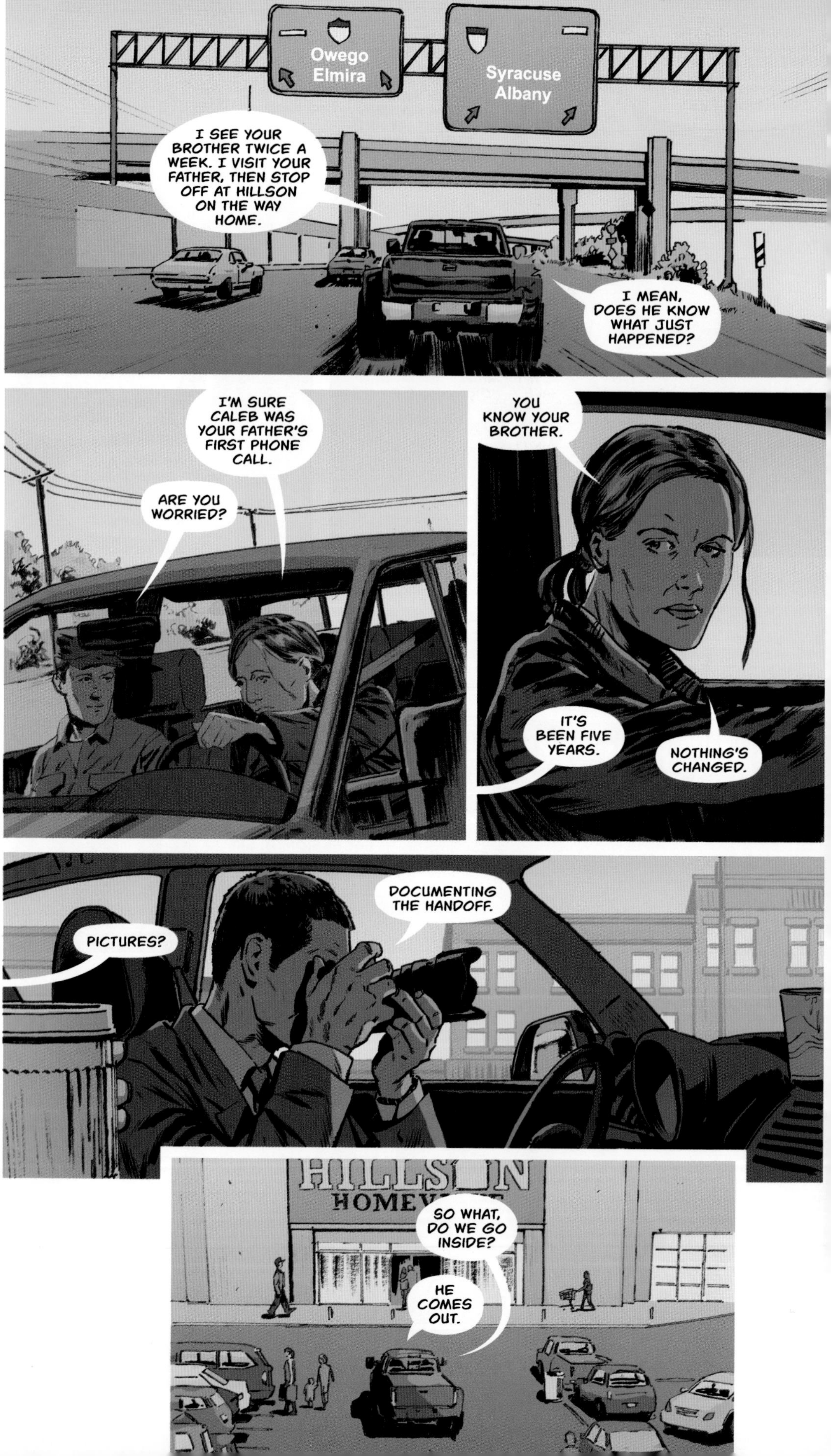
Owego
Elmira
Syracuse
Albany
I SEE YOUR BROTHER TWICE A WEEK. I VISIT YOUR FATHER, THEN STOP OFF AT HILLSON ON THE WAY HOME.
I MEAN, DOES HE KNOW WHAT JUST HAPPENED?
I'M SURE CALEB WAS YOUR FATHER'S FIRST PHONE CALL.
ARE YOU WORRIED?
YOU KNOW YOUR BROTHER.
IT'S BEEN FIVE YEARS.
NOTHING'S CHANGED.
PICTURES?
DOCUMENTING THE HANDOFF.
SO WHAT, DO WE GO INSIDE?
HE COMES OUT.

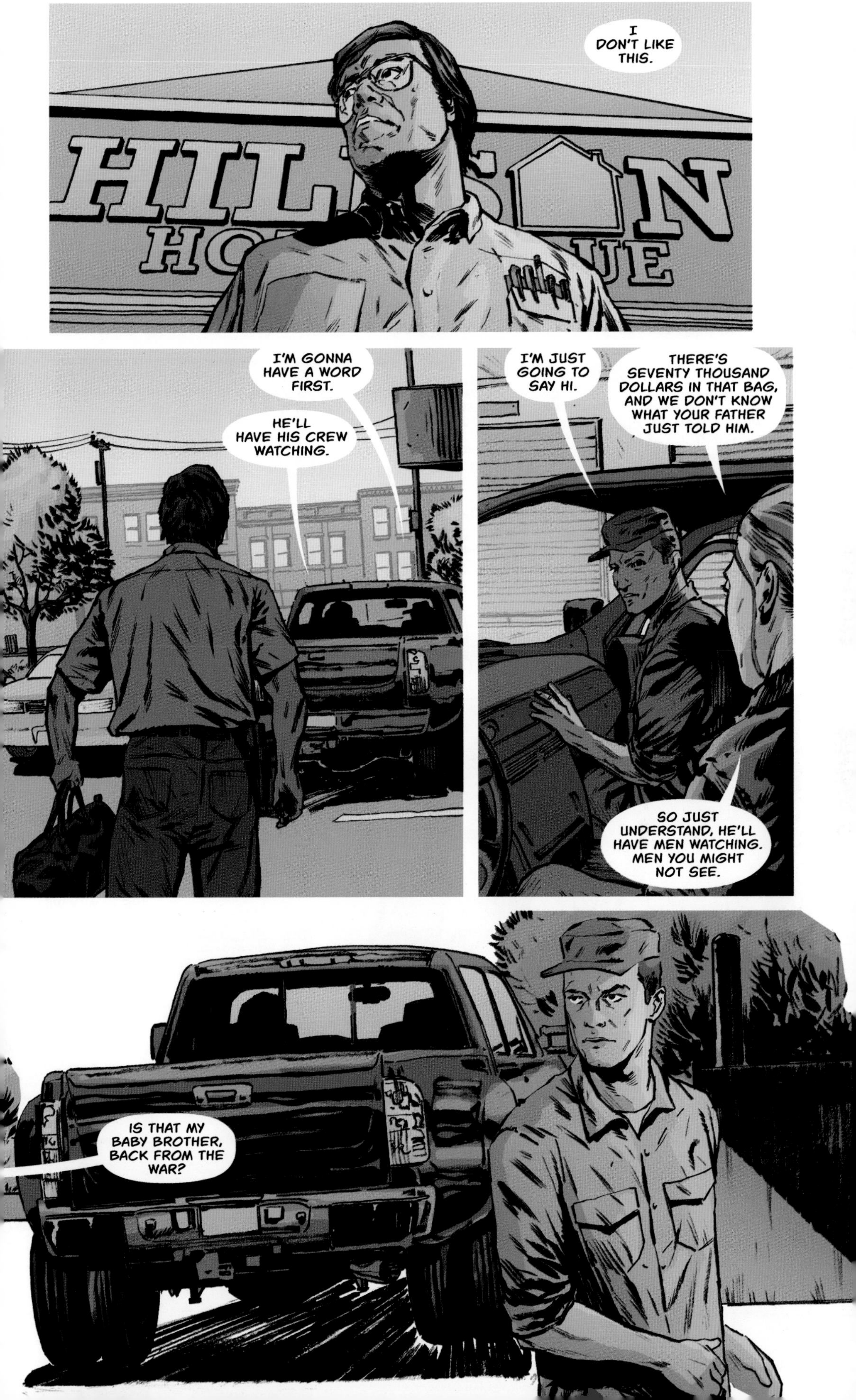
I DON'T LIKE THIS.
HILLSON
HO UE
I'M GONNA HAVE A WORD FIRST.
HE'LL HAVE HIS CREW WATCHING.
I'M JUST GOING TO SAY HI.
THERE'S SEVENTY THOUSAND DOLLARS IN THAT BAG, AND WE DON'T KNOW WHAT YOUR FATHER JUST TOLD HIM.
SO JUST UNDERSTAND, HE'LL HAVE MEN WATCHING. MEN YOU MIGHT NOT SEE.
IS THAT MY BABY BROTHER, BACK FROM THE WAR?

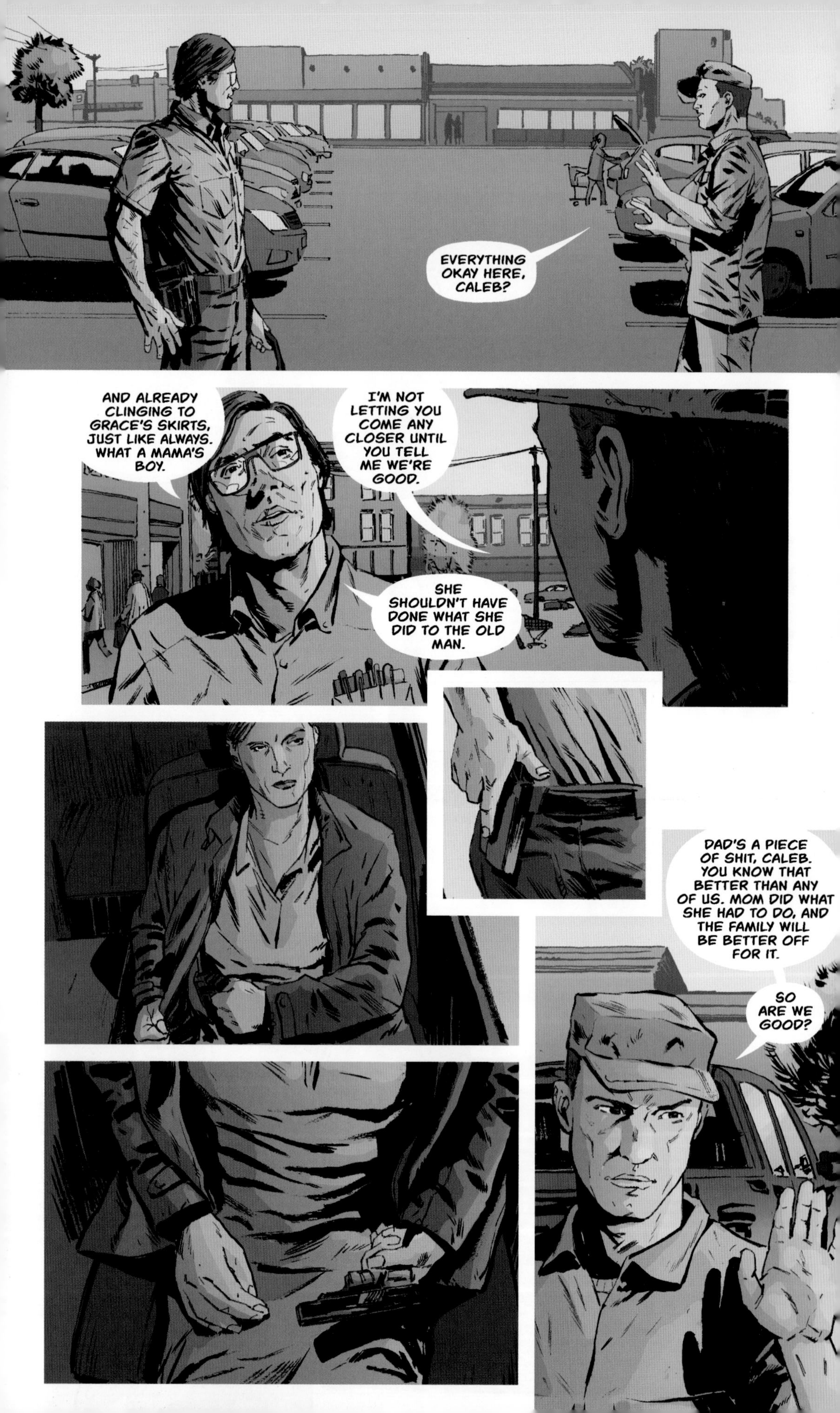
EVERYTHING OKAY HERE, CALEB?
AND ALREADY CLINGING TO GRACE'S SKIRTS, JUST LIKE ALWAYS. WHAT A MAMA'S BOY.
I'M NOT LETTING YOU COME ANY CLOSER UNTIL YOU TELL ME WE'RE GOOD.
SHE SHOULDN'T HAVE DONE WHAT SHE DID TO THE OLD MAN.
DAD'S A PIECE OF SHIT, CALEB. YOU KNOW THAT BETTER THAN ANY OF US. MOM DID WHAT SHE HAD TO DO, AND THE FAMILY WILL BE BETTER OFF FOR IT.
SO ARE WE GOOD?

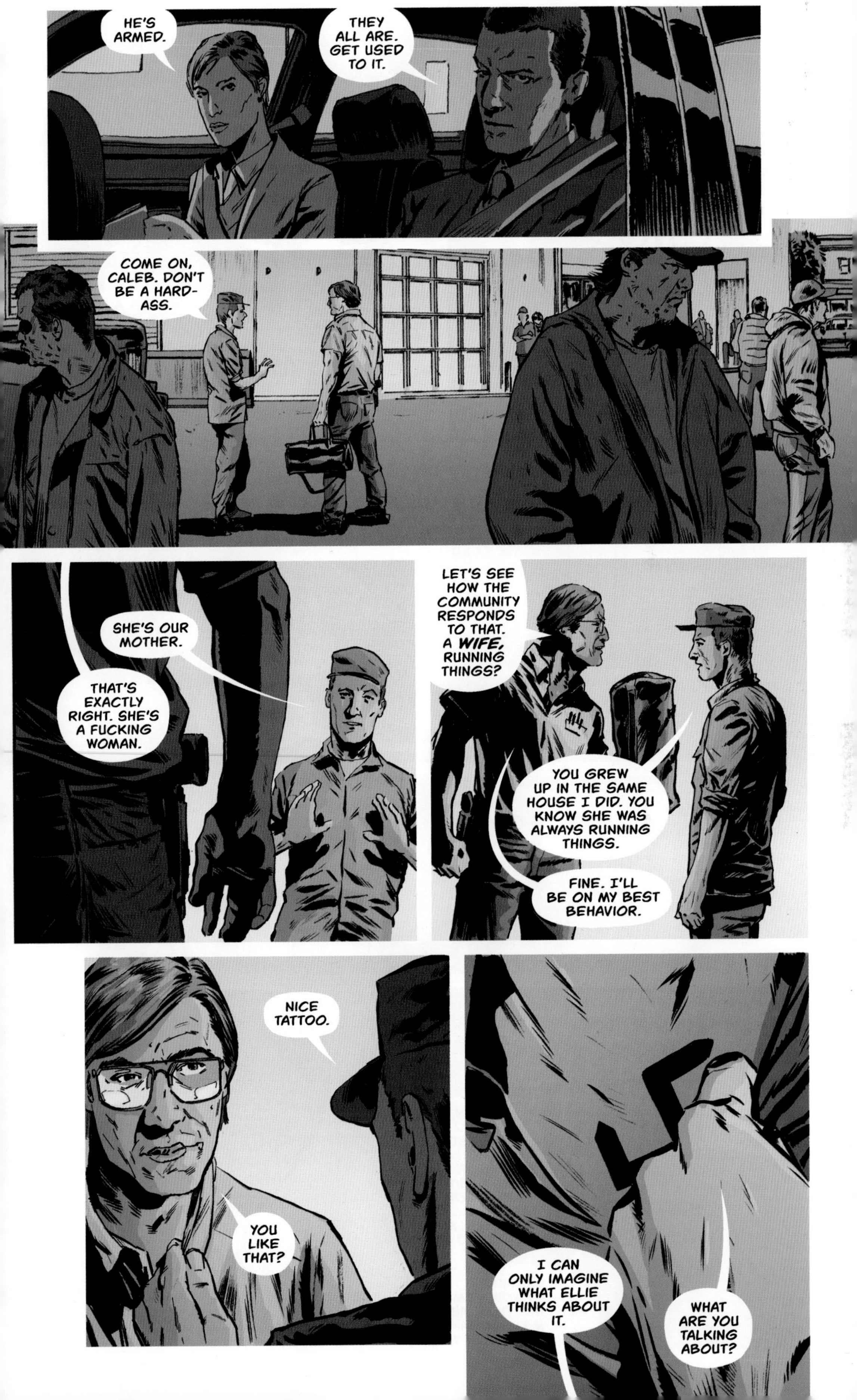
HE'S ARMED.
THEY ALL ARE. GET USED TO IT.
COME ON, CALEB. DON'T BE A HARD-ASS.
SHE'S OUR MOTHER.
THAT'S EXACTLY RIGHT. SHE'S A FUCKING WOMAN.
LET'S SEE HOW THE COMMUNITY RESPONDS TO THAT. A WIFE, RUNNING THINGS?
YOU GREW UP IN THE SAME HOUSE I DID. YOU KNOW SHE WAS ALWAYS RUNNING THINGS.
FINE. I'LL BE ON MY BEST BEHAVIOR.
NICE TATTOO.
YOU LIKE THAT?
I CAN ONLY IMAGINE WHAT ELLIE THINKS ABOUT IT.
WHAT ARE YOU TALKING ABOUT?

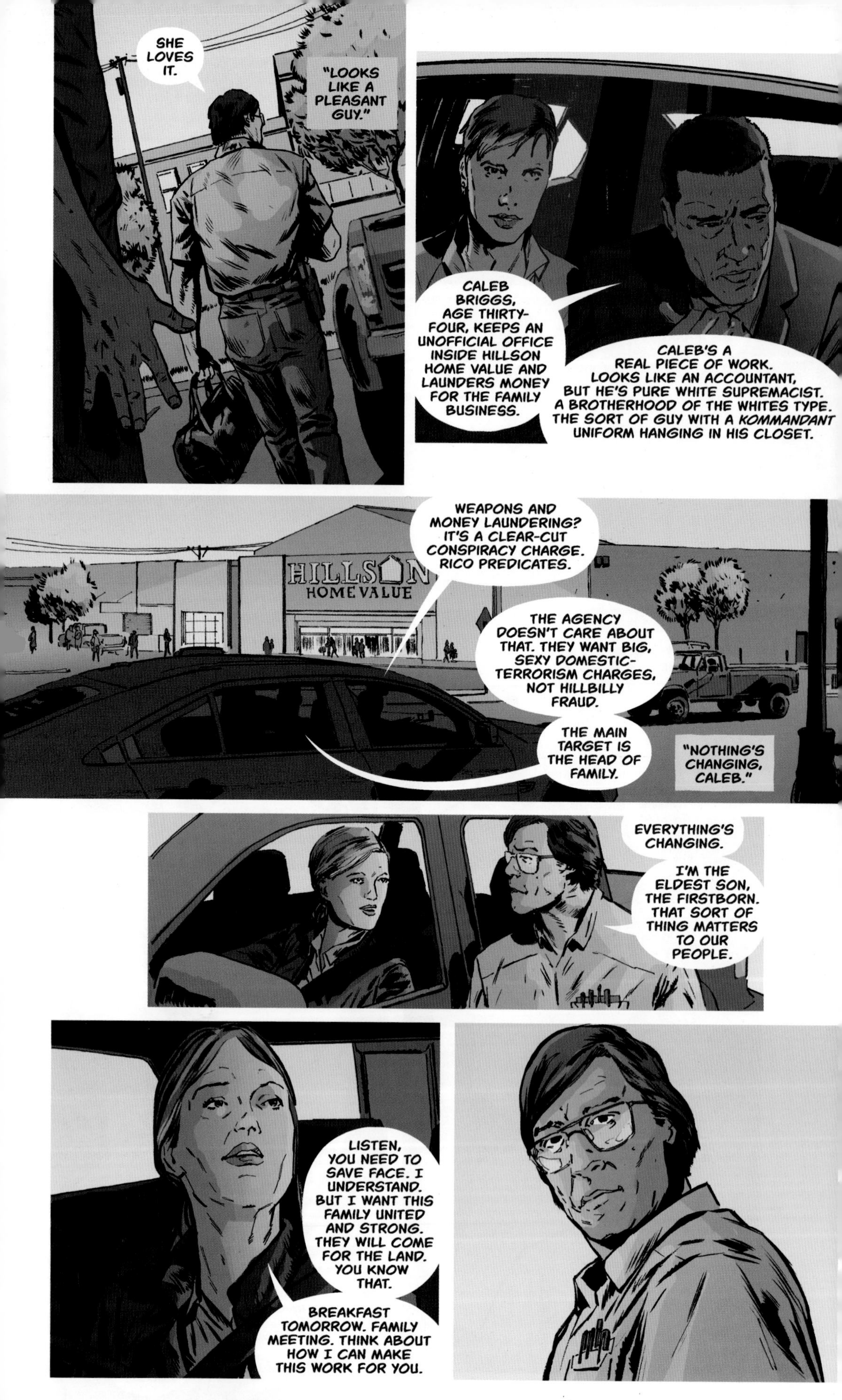
SHE LOVES IT.
"LOOKS LIKE A PLEASANT GUY."
CALEB BRIGGS, AGE THIRTY-FOUR, KEEPS AN UNOFFICIAL OFFICE INSIDE HILLSON HOME VALUE AND LAUNDERS MONEY FOR THE FAMILY BUSINESS.
CALEB'S A REAL PIECE OF WORK. LOOKS LIKE AN ACCOUNTANT, BUT HE'S PURE WHITE SUPREMACIST. A BROTHERHOOD OF THE WHITES TYPE. THE SORT OF GUY WITH A *KOMMANDANT* UNIFORM HANGING IN HIS CLOSET.
HILLSON HOME VALUE
WEAPONS AND MONEY LAUNDERING? IT'S A CLEAR-CUT CONSPIRACY CHARGE. RICO PREDICATES.
THE AGENCY DOESN'T CARE ABOUT THAT. THEY WANT BIG, SEXY DOMESTIC-TERRORISM CHARGES, NOT HILLBILLY FRAUD.
THE MAIN TARGET IS THE HEAD OF FAMILY.
"NOTHING'S CHANGING, CALEB."
EVERYTHING'S CHANGING.
I'M THE ELDEST SON, THE FIRSTBORN. THAT SORT OF THING MATTERS TO OUR PEOPLE.
LISTEN, YOU NEED TO SAVE FACE. I UNDERSTAND. BUT I WANT THIS FAMILY UNITED AND STRONG. THEY WILL COME FOR THE LAND. YOU KNOW THAT.
BREAKFAST TOMORROW. FAMILY MEETING. THINK ABOUT HOW I CAN MAKE THIS WORK FOR YOU.

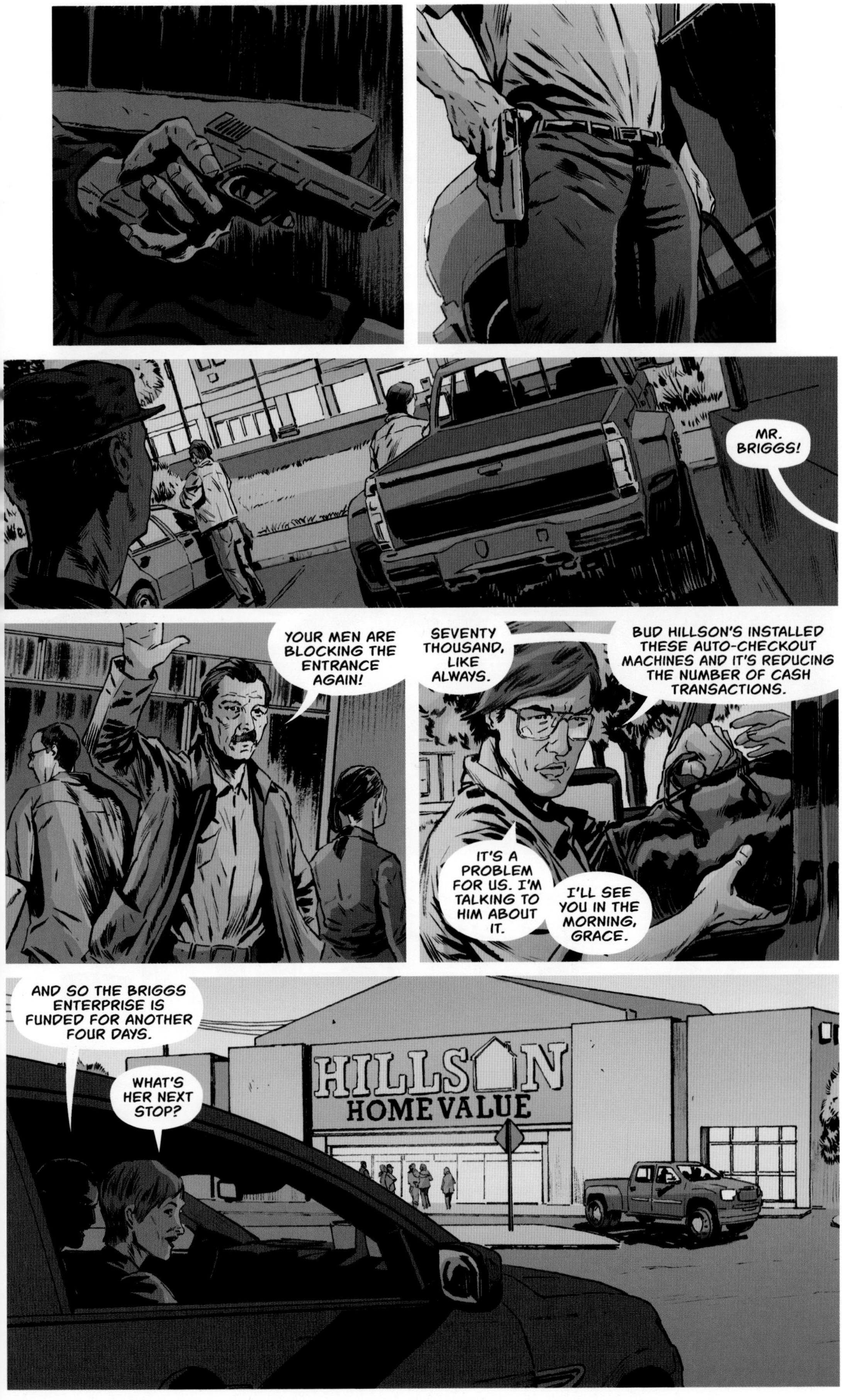
MR. BRIGGS!
YOUR MEN ARE BLOCKING THE ENTRANCE AGAIN!
SEVENTY THOUSAND, LIKE ALWAYS.
BUD HILLSON'S INSTALLED THESE AUTO-CHECKOUT MACHINES AND IT'S REDUCING THE NUMBER OF CASH TRANSACTIONS.
IT'S A PROBLEM FOR US. I'M TALKING TO HIM ABOUT IT.
I'LL SEE YOU IN THE MORNING, GRACE.
AND SO THE BRIGGS ENTERPRISE IS FUNDED FOR ANOTHER FOUR DAYS.
HILLSON HOME VALUE
WHAT'S HER NEXT STOP?

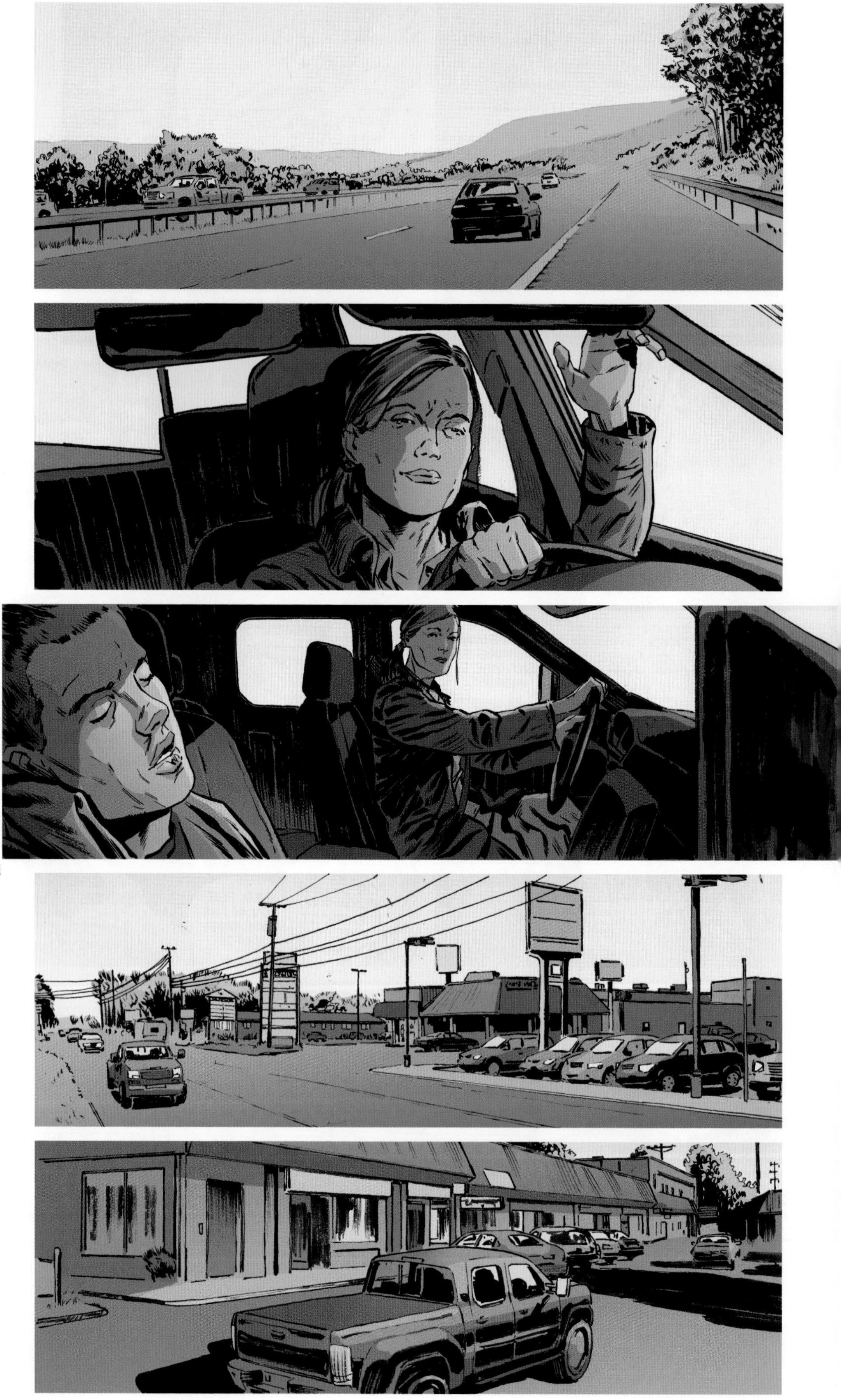

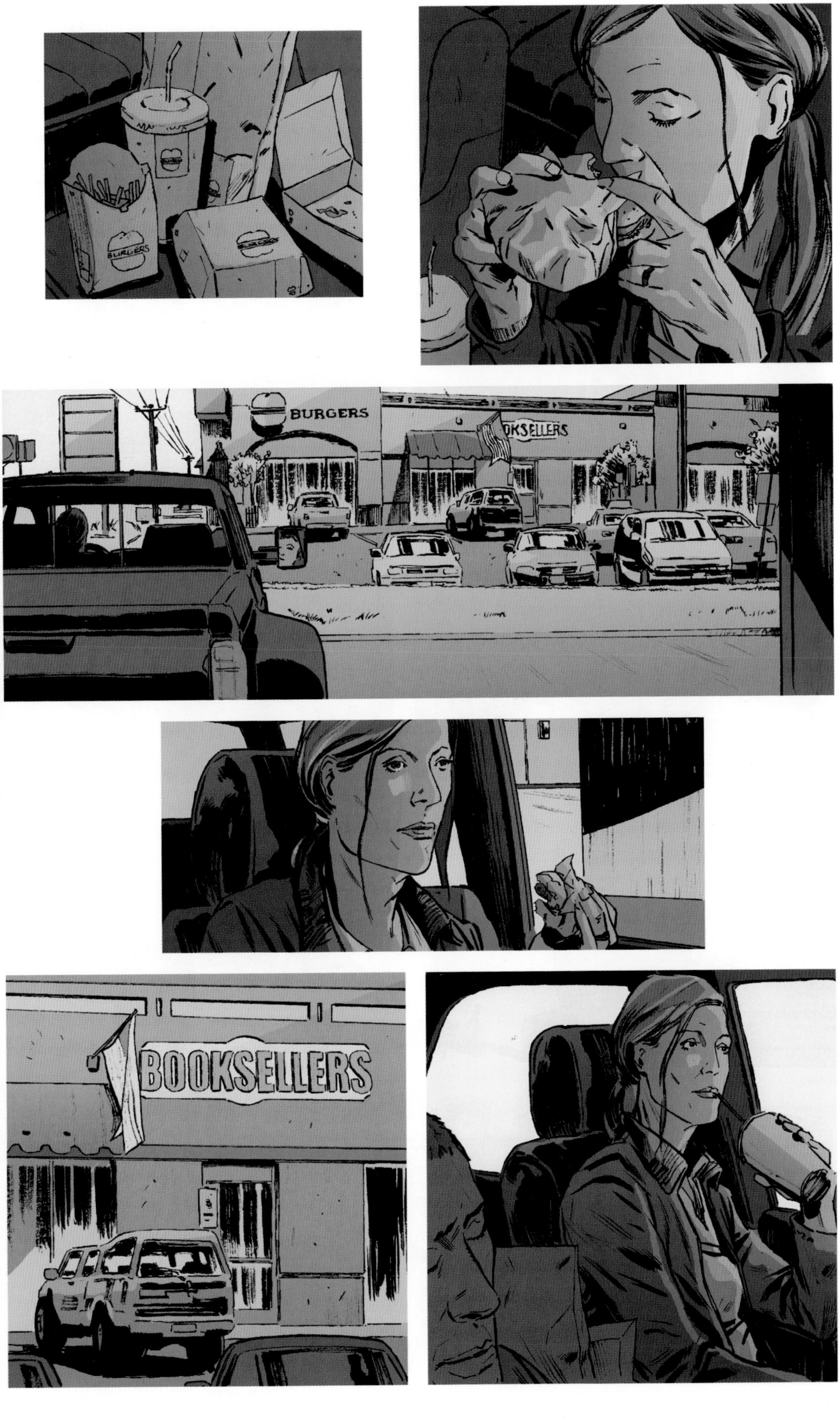
BURGERS
BURGERS
OKSELLERS
BOOKSELLERS

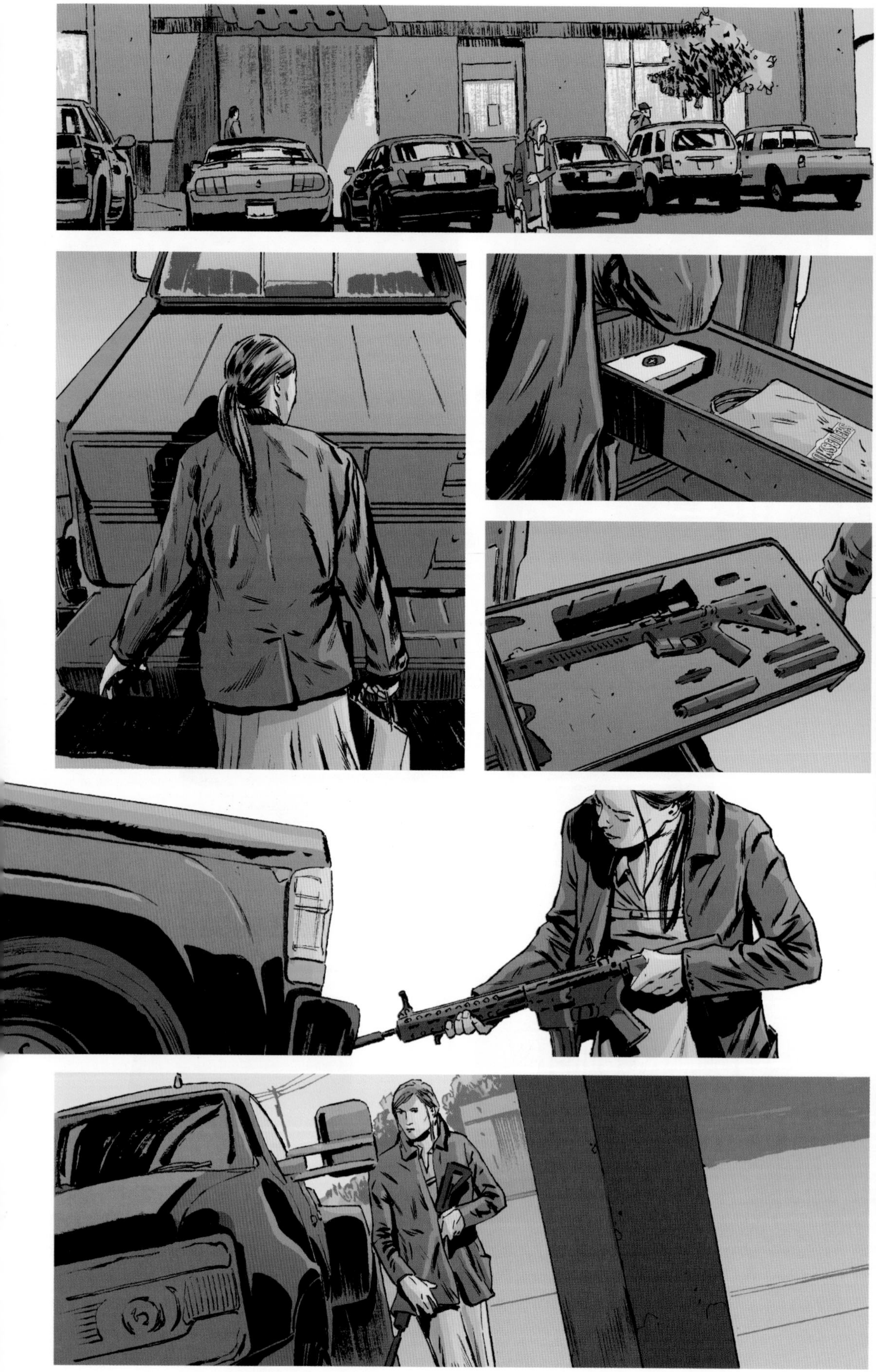

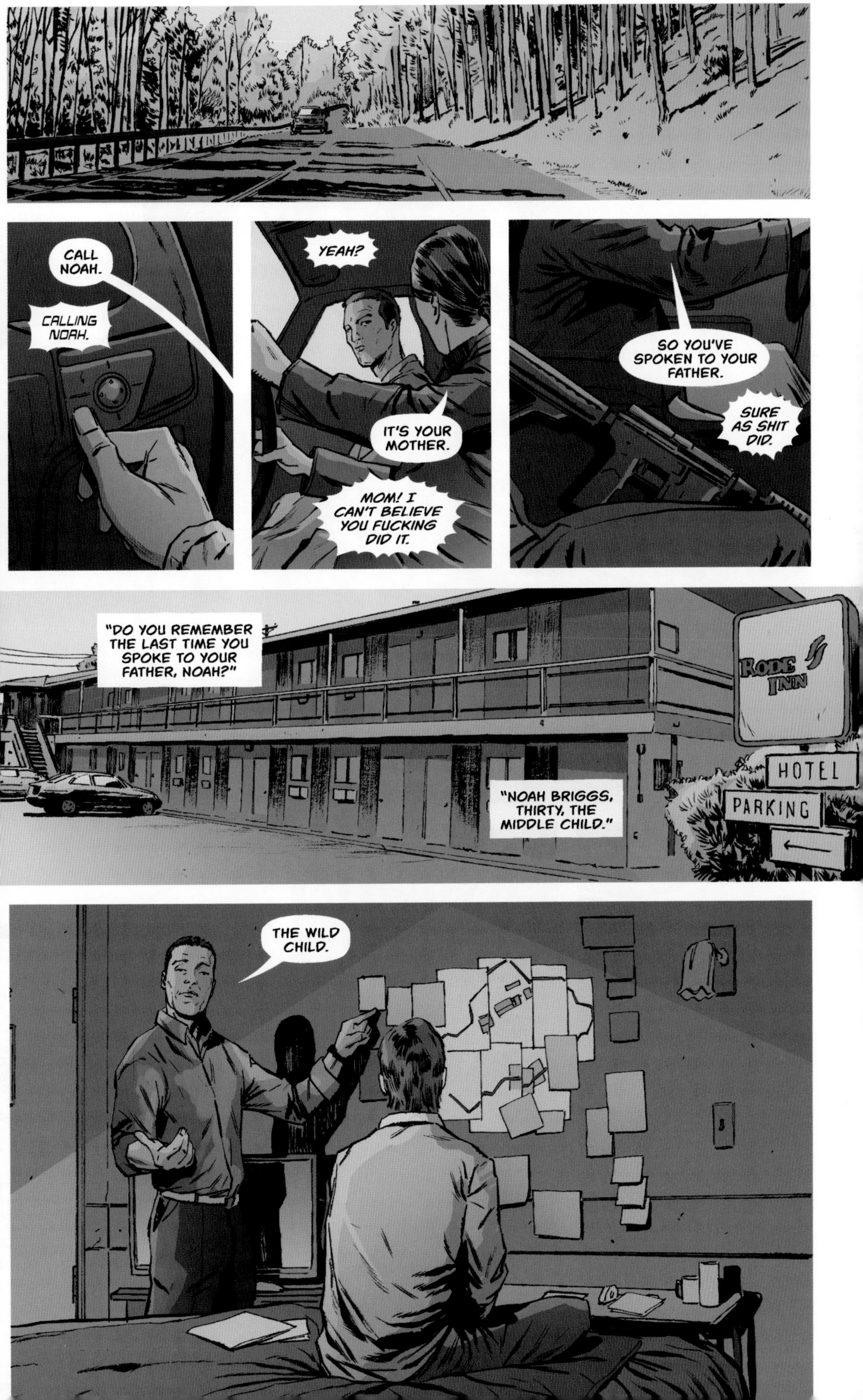

CALL NOAH.
CALLING NOAH.
YEAH?
IT'S YOUR MOTHER.
MOM! I CAN'T BELIEVE YOU FUCKING DID IT.
SO YOU'VE SPOKEN TO YOUR FATHER.
SURE AS SHIT DID.
"DO YOU REMEMBER THE LAST TIME YOU SPOKE TO YOUR FATHER, NOAH?"
RODE INN
HOTEL
PARKING
"NOAH BRIGGS, THIRTY, THE MIDDLE CHILD."
THE WILD CHILD.

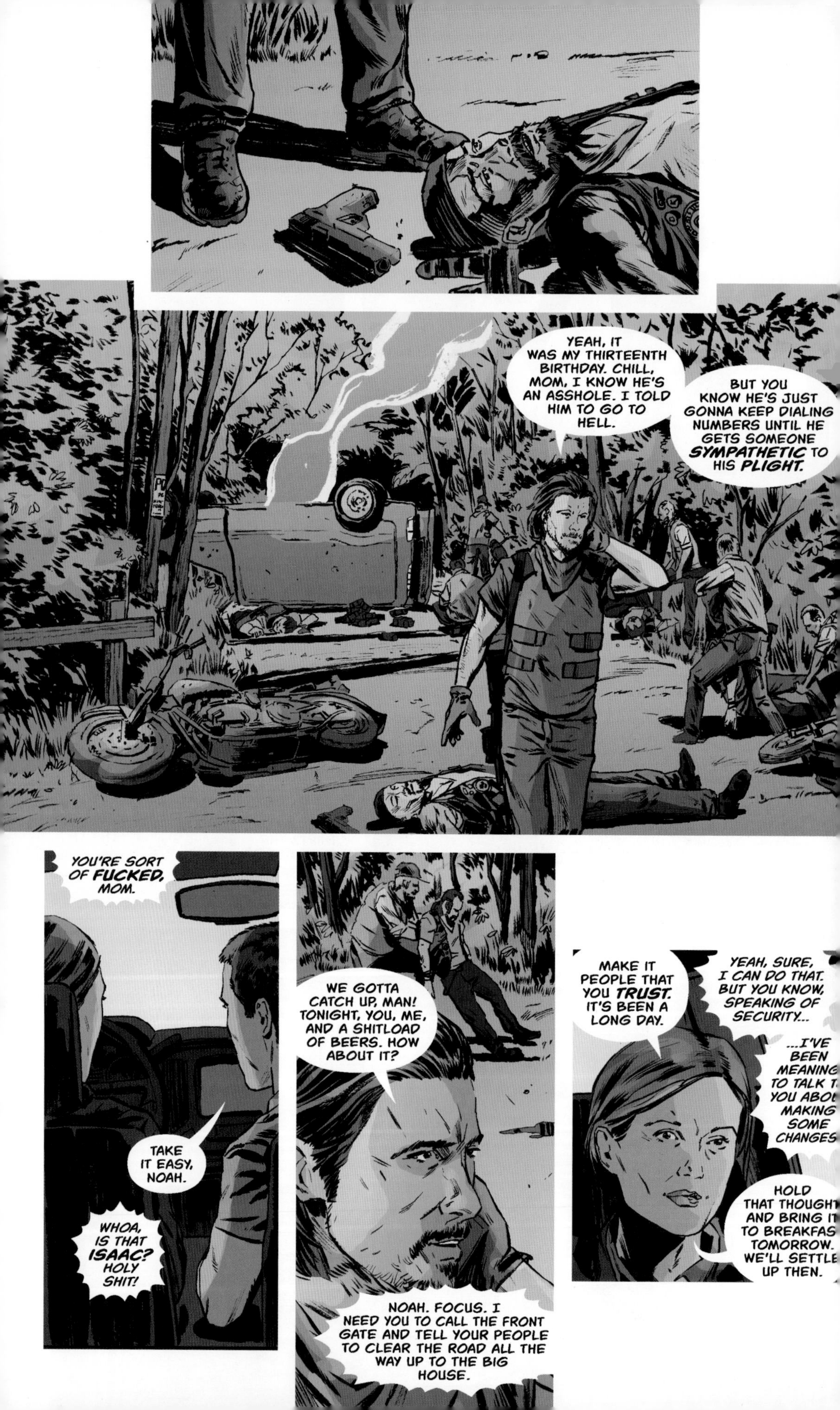
YEAH, IT WAS MY THIRTEENTH BIRTHDAY. CHILL, MOM, I KNOW HE'S AN ASSHOLE. I TOLD HIM TO GO TO HELL.
BUT YOU KNOW HE'S JUST GONNA KEEP DIALING NUMBERS UNTIL HE GETS SOMEONE SYMPATHETIC TO HIS PLIGHT.
YOU'RE SORT OF FUCKED, MOM.
TAKE IT EASY, NOAH.
WHOA, IS THAT ISAAC? HOLY SHIT!
WE GOTTA CATCH UP, MAN! TONIGHT, YOU, ME, AND A SHITLOAD OF BEERS. HOW ABOUT IT?
NOAH. FOCUS. I NEED YOU TO CALL THE FRONT GATE AND TELL YOUR PEOPLE TO CLEAR THE ROAD ALL THE WAY UP TO THE BIG HOUSE.
MAKE IT PEOPLE THAT YOU TRUST. IT'S BEEN A LONG DAY.
YEAH, SURE, I CAN DO THAT. BUT YOU KNOW, SPEAKING OF SECURITY...
...I'VE BEEN MEANING TO TALK T YOU ABOU MAKING SOME CHANGES
HOLD THAT THOUGH AND BRING I TO BREAKFAS TOMORROW. WE'LL SETTLE UP THEN.

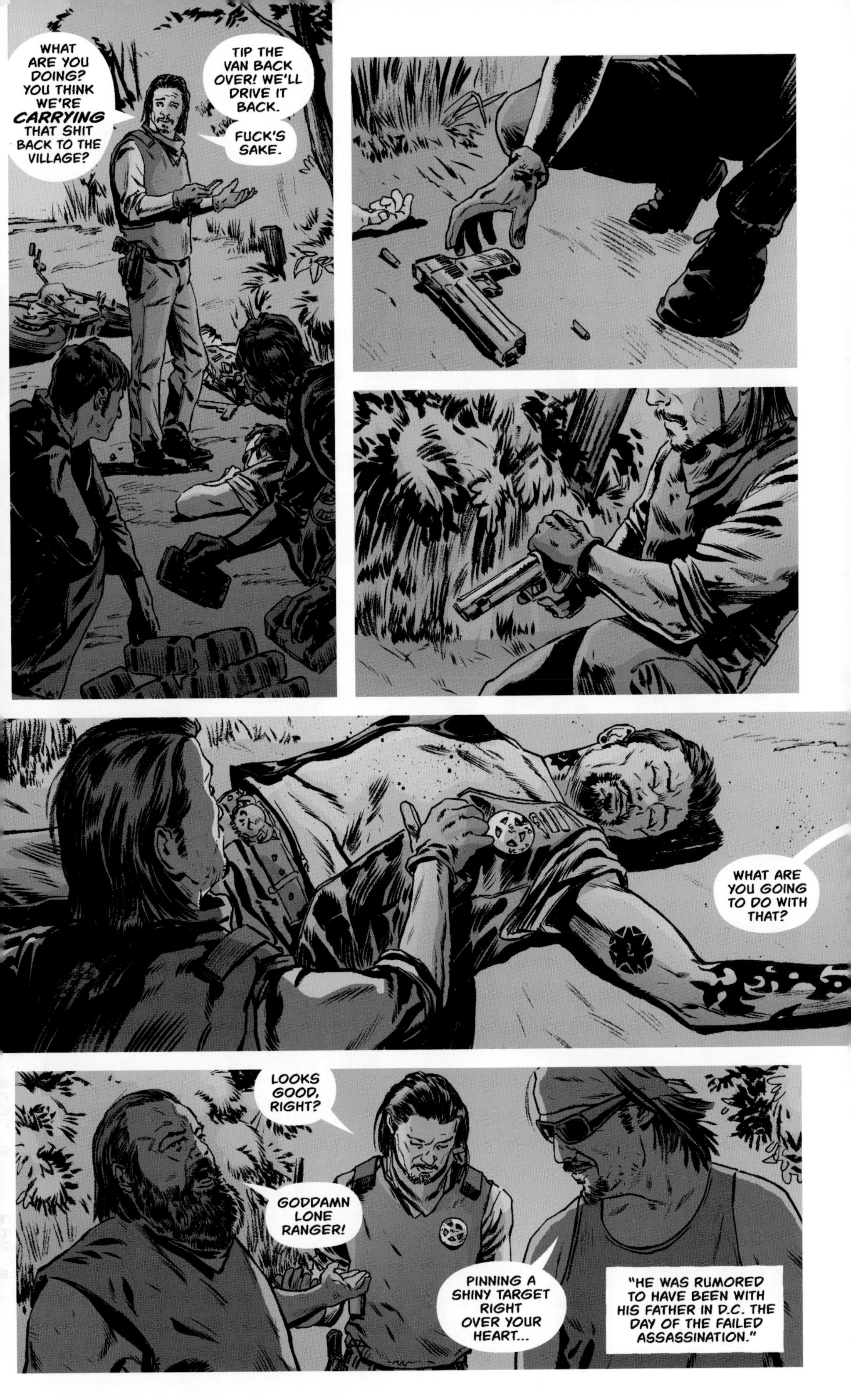
WHAT ARE YOU DOING? YOU THINK WE'RE CARRYING THAT SHIT BACK TO THE VILLAGE?
TIP THE VAN BACK OVER! WE'LL DRIVE IT BACK.
FUCK'S SAKE.
WHAT ARE YOU GOING TO DO WITH THAT?
LOOKS GOOD, RIGHT?
GODDAMN LONE RANGER!
PINNING A SHINY TARGET RIGHT OVER YOUR HEART...
"HE WAS RUMORED TO HAVE BEEN WITH HIS FATHER IN D.C. THE DAY OF THE FAILED ASSASSINATION."

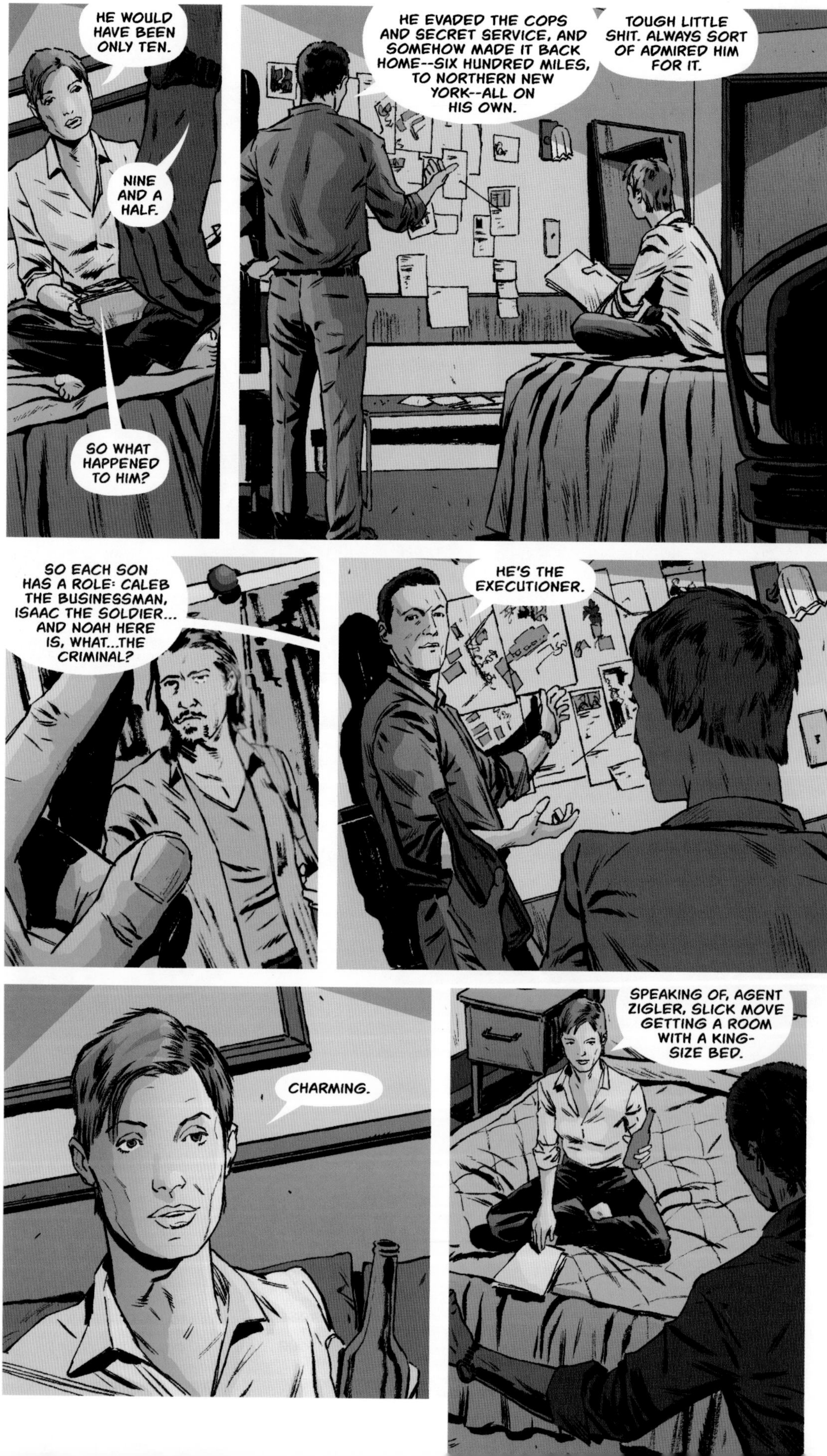
HE WOULD HAVE BEEN ONLY TEN.
NINE AND A HALF.
SO WHAT HAPPENED TO HIM?
HE EVADED THE COPS AND SECRET SERVICE, AND SOMEHOW MADE IT BACK HOME--SIX HUNDRED MILES, TO NORTHERN NEW YORK--ALL ON HIS OWN.
TOUGH LITTLE SHIT. ALWAYS SORT OF ADMIRED HIM FOR IT.
SO EACH SON HAS A ROLE: CALEB THE BUSINESSMAN, ISAAC THE SOLDIER... AND NOAH HERE IS, WHAT...THE CRIMINAL?
HE'S THE EXECUTIONER.
CHARMING.
SPEAKING OF, AGENT ZIGLER, SLICK MOVE GETTING A ROOM WITH A KING-SIZE BED.

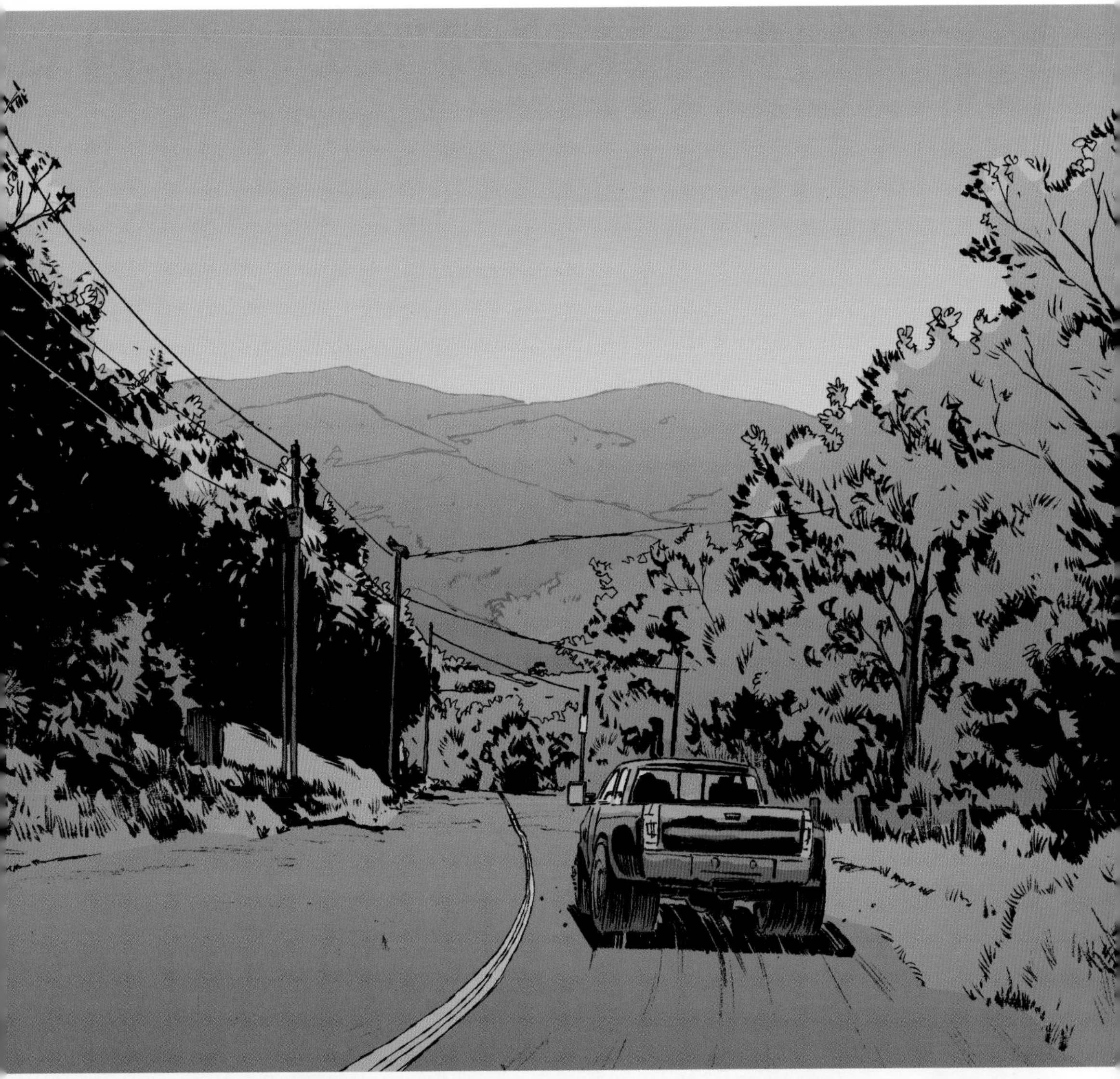

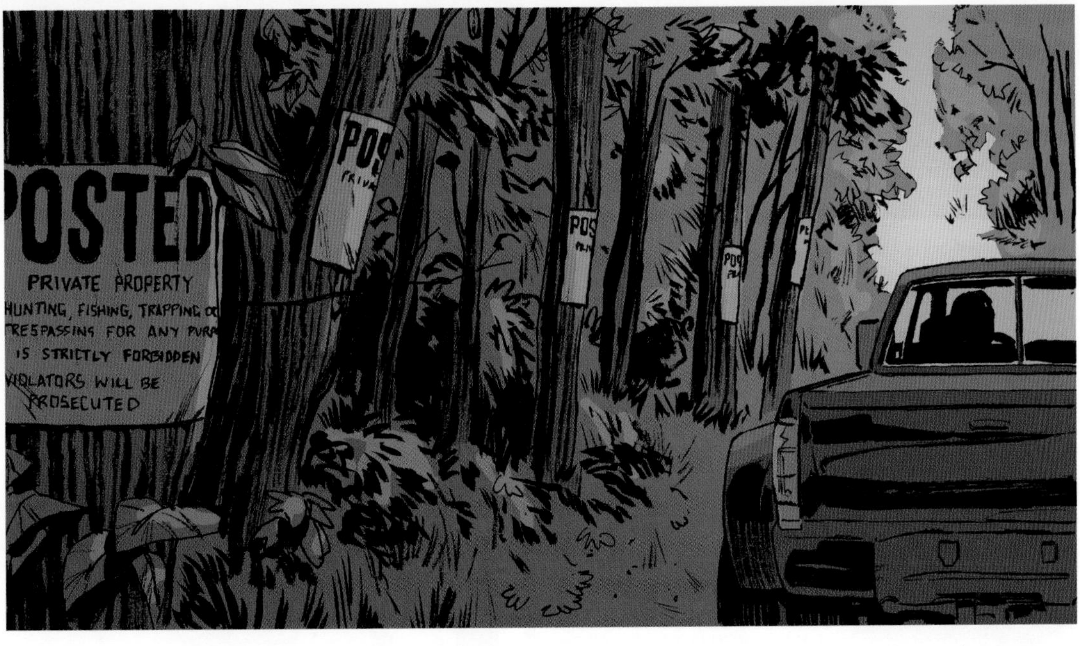

POSTED
PRIVATE PROPERTY
HUNTING, FISHING, TRAPPING
TRESPASSING FOR ANY
IS STRICTLY FORBIDDEN
VIOLATORS WILL BE
PROSECUTED

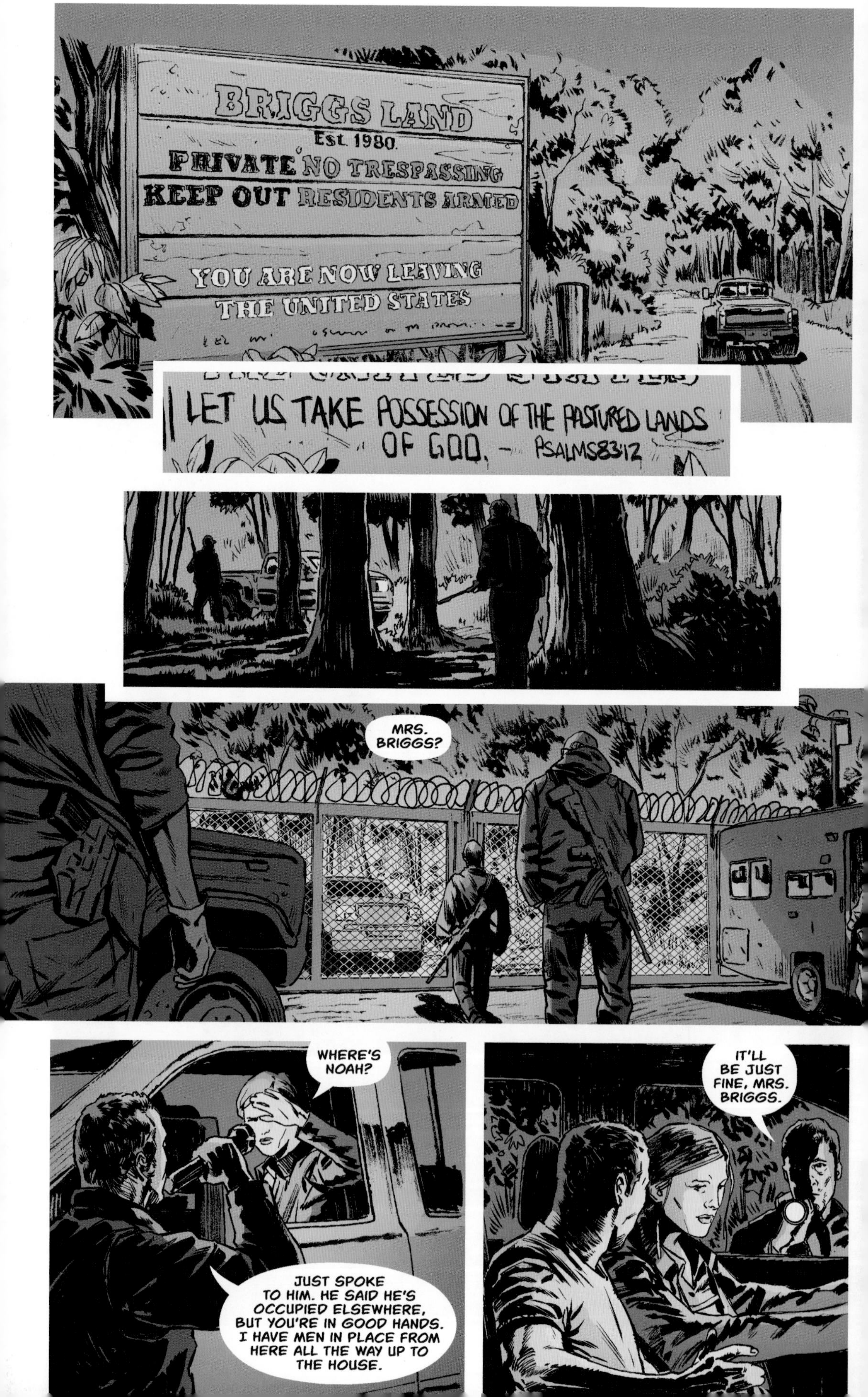

BRIGGS LAND
Est. 1980.
PRIVATE NO TRESPASSING
KEEP OUT RESIDENTS ARMED
YOU ARE NOW LEAVING
THE UNITED STATES
LET US TAKE POSSESSION OF THE PASTURED LANDS OF GOD. - PSALMS 83:12
MRS. BRIGGS?
WHERE'S NOAH?
JUST SPOKE TO HIM. HE SAID HE'S OCCUPIED ELSEWHERE, BUT YOU'RE IN GOOD HANDS. I HAVE MEN IN PLACE FROM HERE ALL THE WAY UP TO THE HOUSE.
IT'LL BE JUST FINE, MRS. BRIGGS.

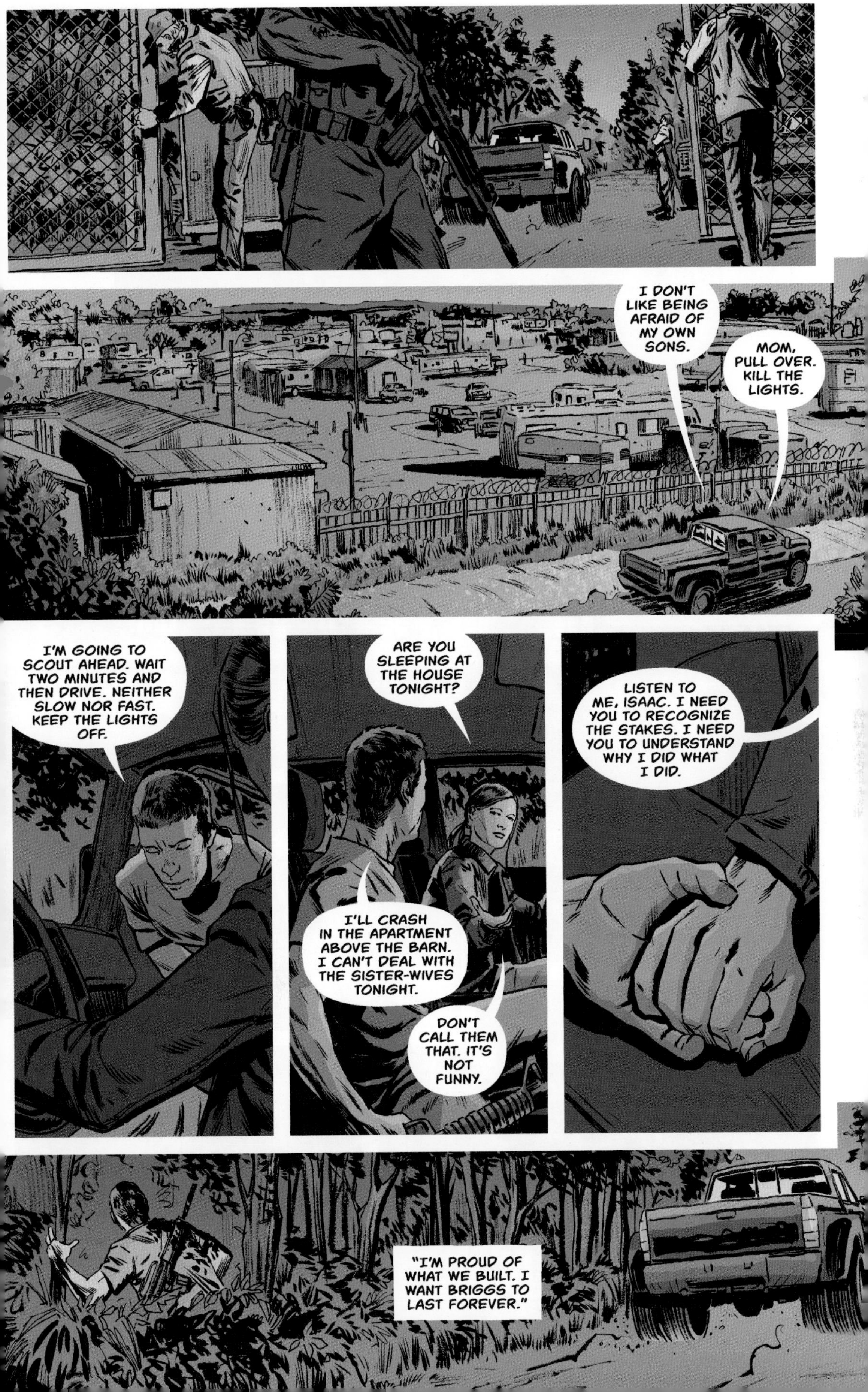
I DON'T LIKE BEING AFRAID OF MY OWN SONS.
MOM, PULL OVER. KILL THE LIGHTS.
I'M GOING TO SCOUT AHEAD. WAIT TWO MINUTES AND THEN DRIVE. NEITHER SLOW NOR FAST. KEEP THE LIGHTS OFF.
ARE YOU SLEEPING AT THE HOUSE TONIGHT?
I'LL CRASH IN THE APARTMENT ABOVE THE BARN. I CAN'T DEAL WITH THE SISTER-WIVES TONIGHT.
DON'T CALL THEM THAT. IT'S NOT FUNNY.
LISTEN TO ME, ISAAC. I NEED YOU TO RECOGNIZE THE STAKES. I NEED YOU TO UNDERSTAND WHY I DID WHAT I DID.
"I'M PROUD OF WHAT WE BUILT. I WANT BRIGGS TO LAST FOREVER."

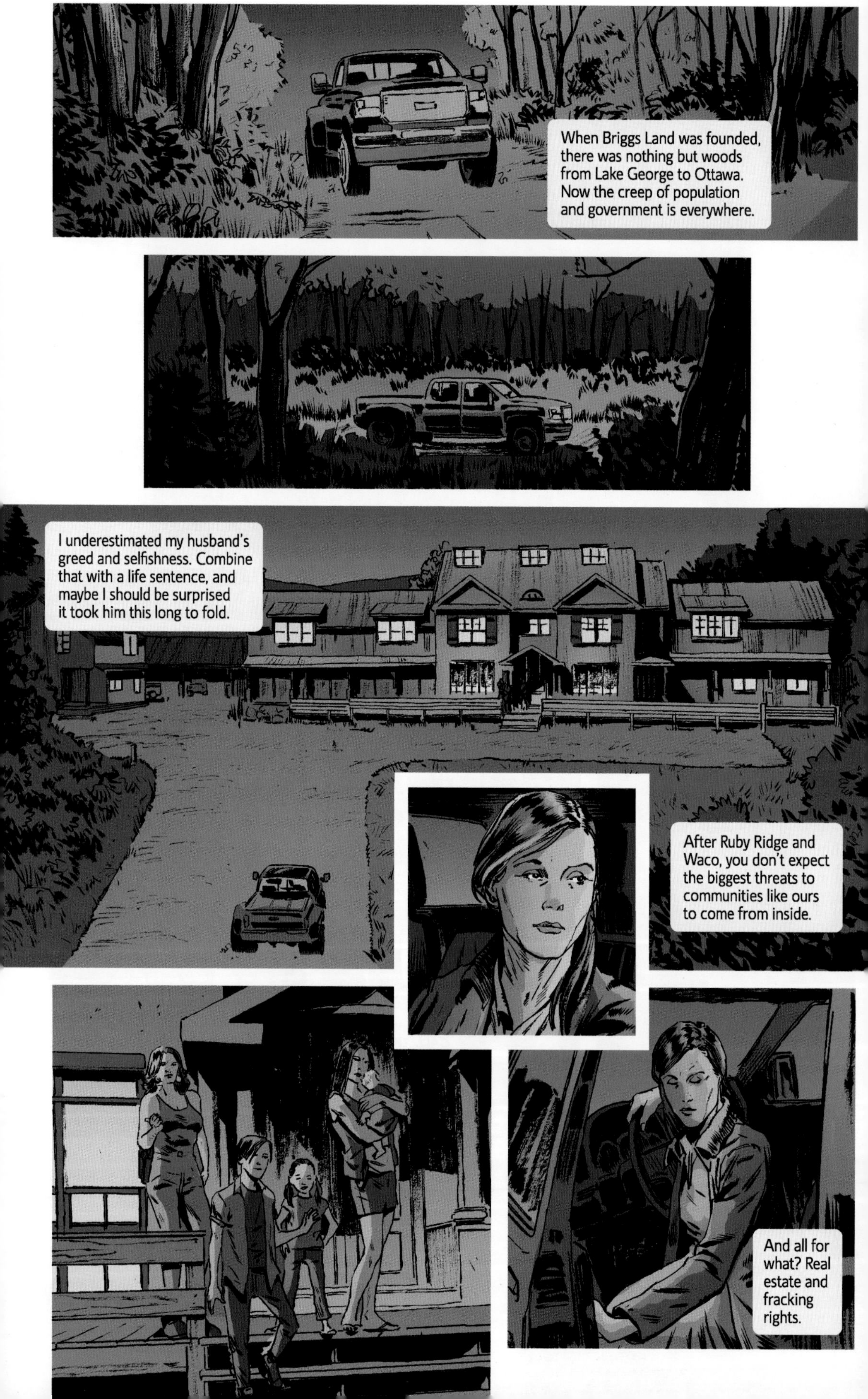
When Briggs Land was founded, there was nothing but woods from Lake George to Ottawa. Now the creep of population and government is everywhere.
I underestimated my husband's greed and selfishness. Combine that with a life sentence, and maybe I should be surprised it took him this long to fold.
After Ruby Ridge and Waco, you don't expect the biggest threats to communities like ours to come from inside.
And all for what? Real estate and fracking rights.

I was still a child when I married. I took to the home, raised three strong sons, and performed perfectly to expectations. I left the running of the business to Jim.

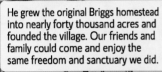

He grew the original Briggs homestead into nearly forty thousand acres and founded the village. Our friends and family could come and enjoy the same freedom and sanctuary we did.

That was supposed to be the endgame.

A closed loop, keeping within our means, carrying no debt, drawing nothing from the government-- a self-sufficient lifestyle.

I still believe in that. Not the violence, the racism, the hate... but the ideal.

Enough to do what I did. Enough to see it through.

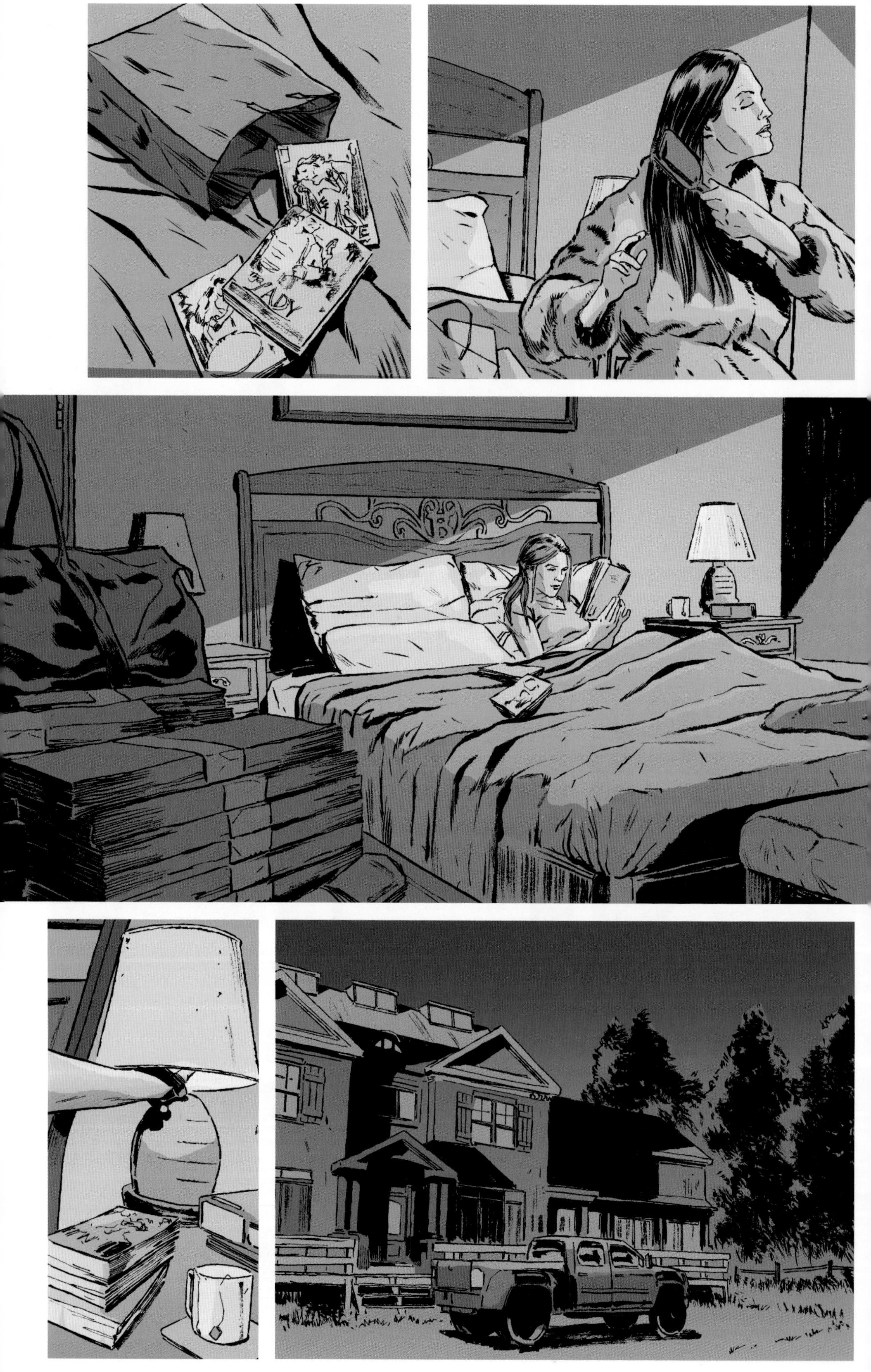
LADY

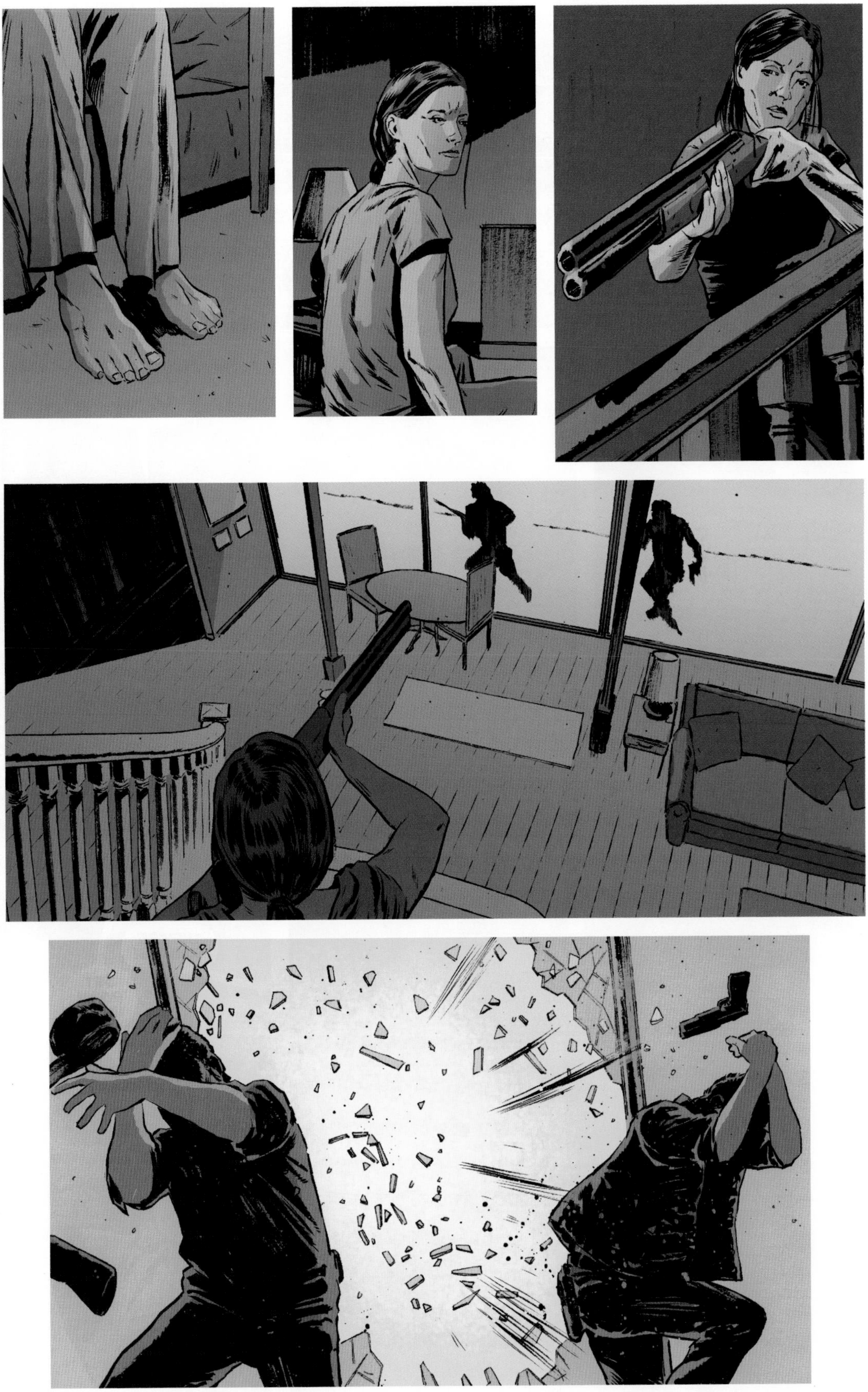

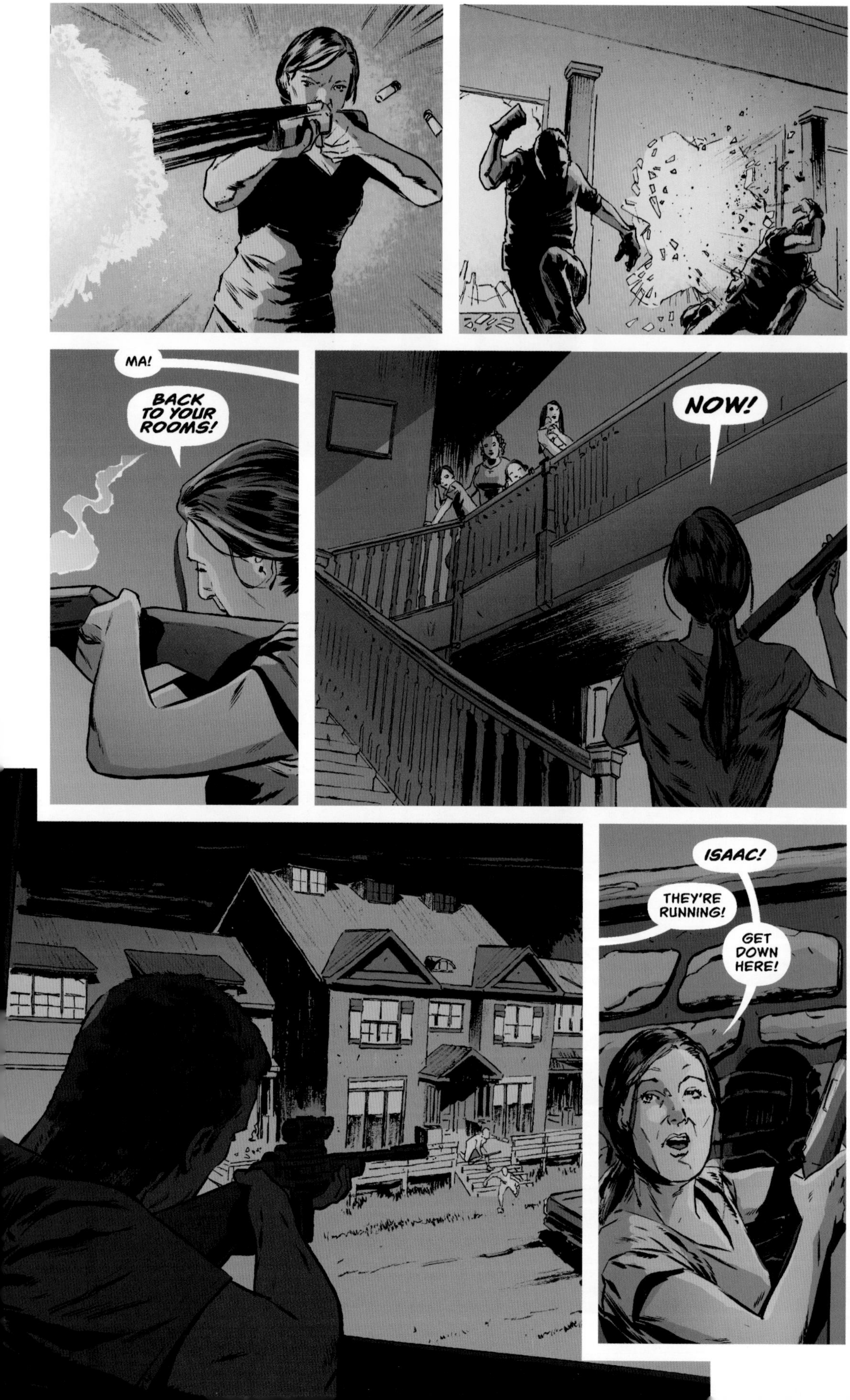
MA!
BACK TO YOUR ROOMS!
NOW!
ISAAC!
THEY'RE RUNNING!
GET DOWN HERE!

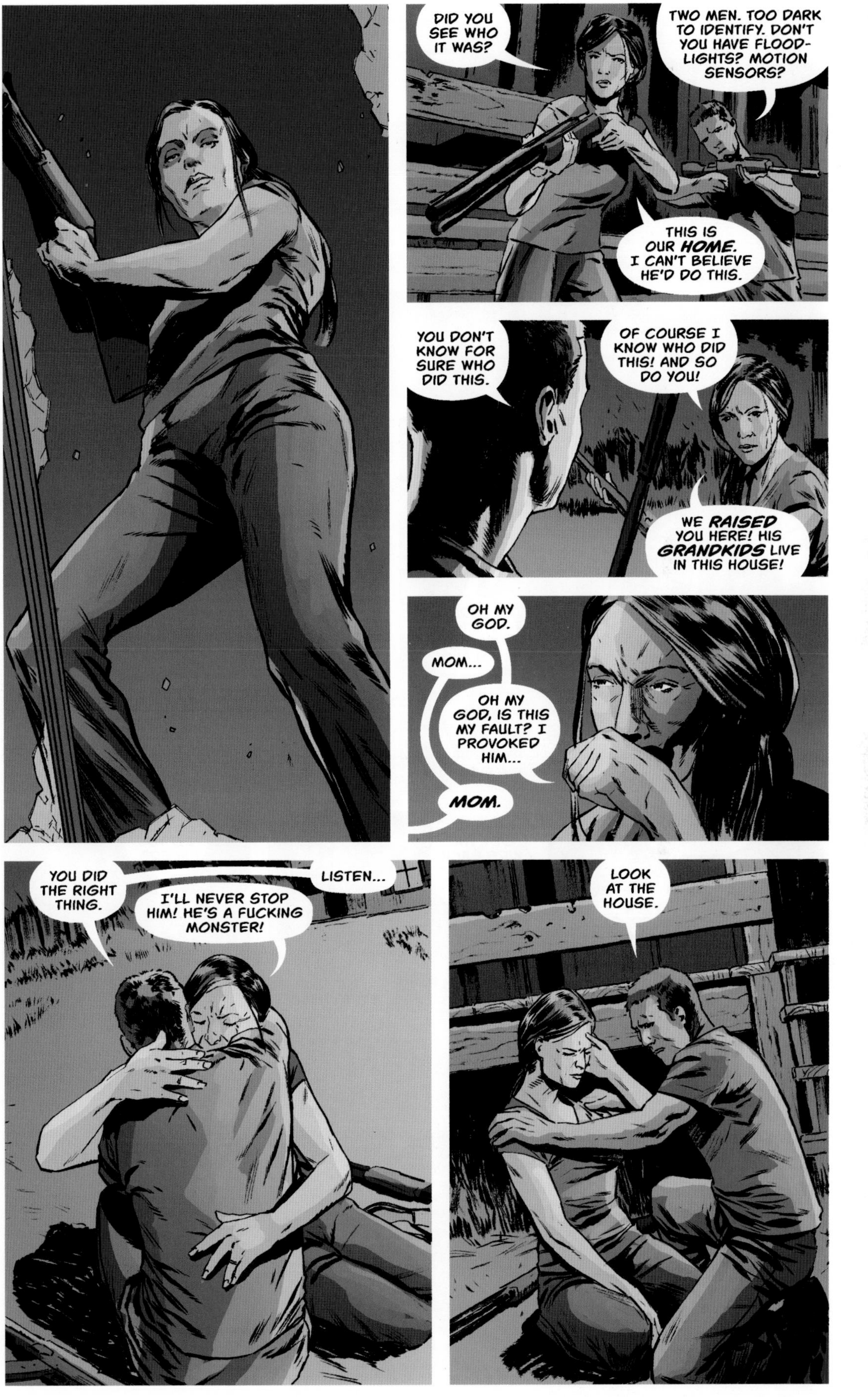
DID YOU SEE WHO IT WAS?
TWO MEN. TOO DARK TO IDENTIFY. DON'T YOU HAVE FLOOD-LIGHTS? MOTION SENSORS?
THIS IS OUR **HOME.** I CAN'T BELIEVE HE'D DO THIS.
YOU DON'T KNOW FOR SURE WHO DID THIS.
OF COURSE I KNOW WHO DID THIS! AND SO DO YOU!
WE **RAISED** YOU HERE! HIS **GRANDKIDS** LIVE IN THIS HOUSE!
OH MY GOD.
MOM...
OH MY GOD, IS THIS MY FAULT? I PROVOKED HIM...
MOM.
YOU DID THE RIGHT THING.
LISTEN...
I'LL NEVER STOP HIM! HE'S A FUCKING MONSTER!
LOOK AT THE HOUSE.

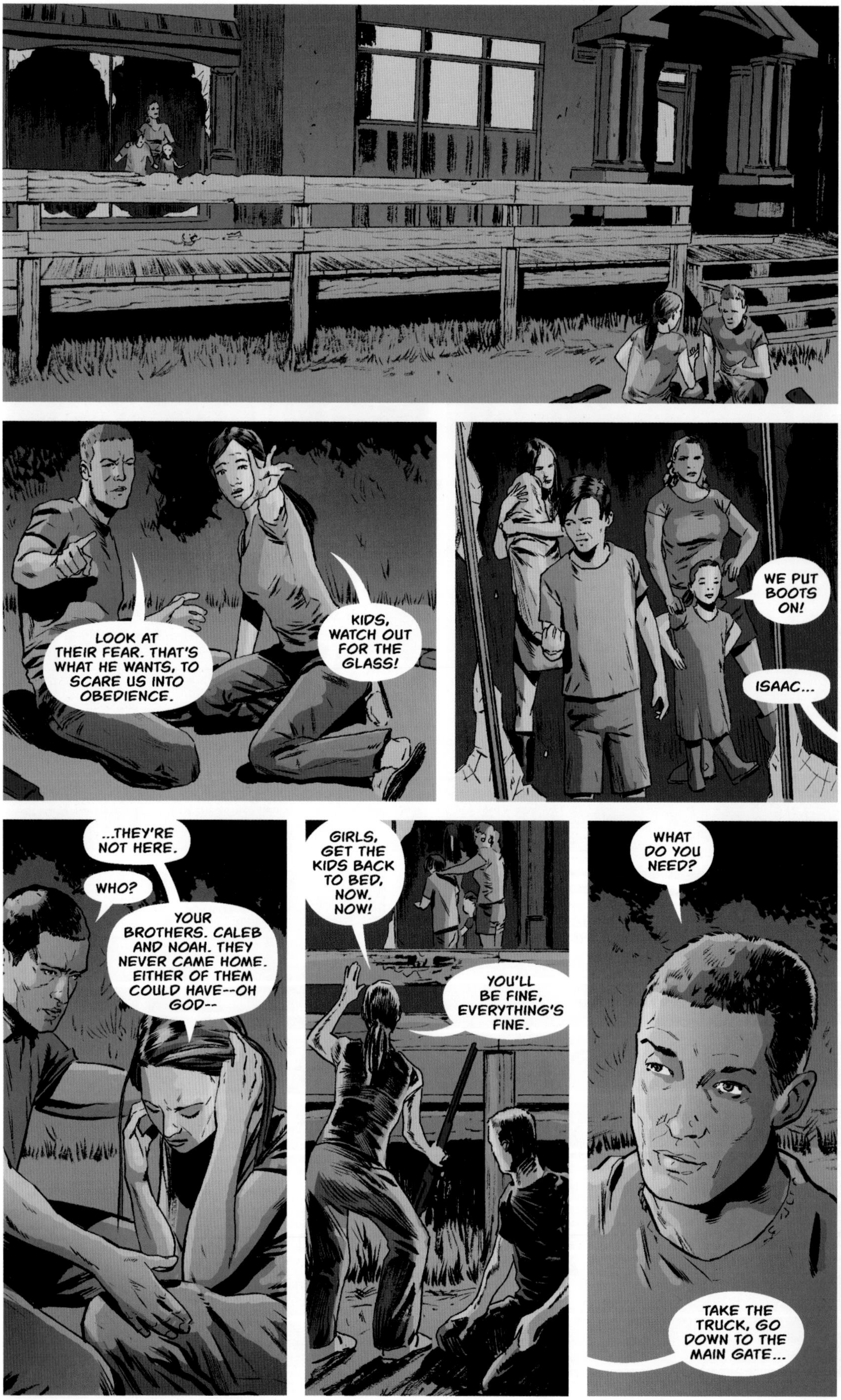

LOOK AT THEIR FEAR. THAT'S WHAT HE WANTS, TO SCARE US INTO OBEDIENCE.
KIDS, WATCH OUT FOR THE GLASS!
WE PUT BOOTS ON!
ISAAC...
...THEY'RE NOT HERE.
WHO?
YOUR BROTHERS. CALEB AND NOAH. THEY NEVER CAME HOME. EITHER OF THEM COULD HAVE--OH GOD--
GIRLS, GET THE KIDS BACK TO BED, NOW. NOW!
YOU'LL BE FINE, EVERYTHING'S FINE.
WHAT DO YOU NEED?
TAKE THE TRUCK, GO DOWN TO THE MAIN GATE...

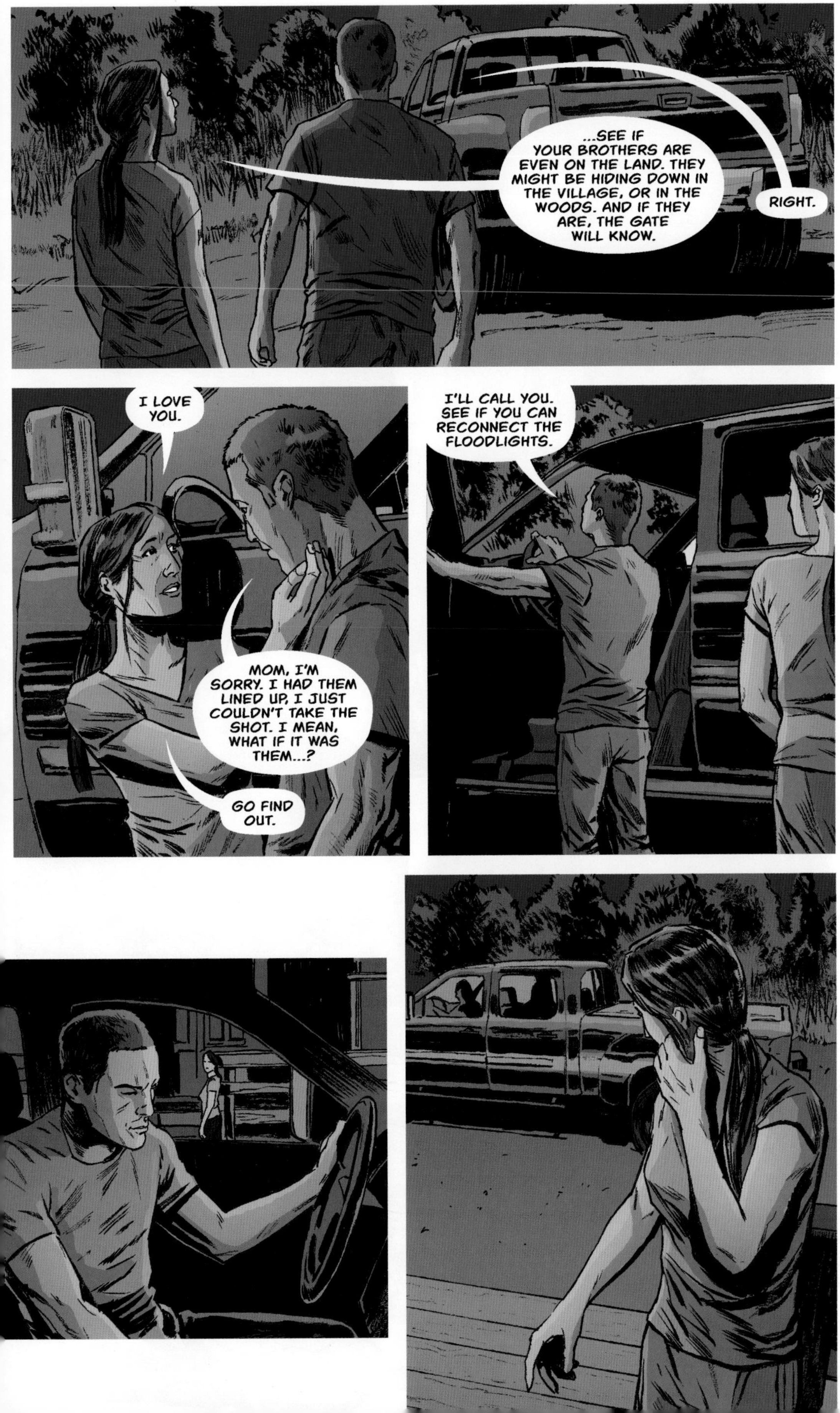
...SEE IF YOUR BROTHERS ARE EVEN ON THE LAND. THEY MIGHT BE HIDING DOWN IN THE VILLAGE, OR IN THE WOODS. AND IF THEY ARE, THE GATE WILL KNOW.
RIGHT.
I LOVE YOU.
MOM, I'M SORRY. I HAD THEM LINED UP, I JUST COULDN'T TAKE THE SHOT. I MEAN, WHAT IF IT WAS THEM...?
GO FIND OUT.
I'LL CALL YOU. SEE IF YOU CAN RECONNECT THE FLOODLIGHTS.

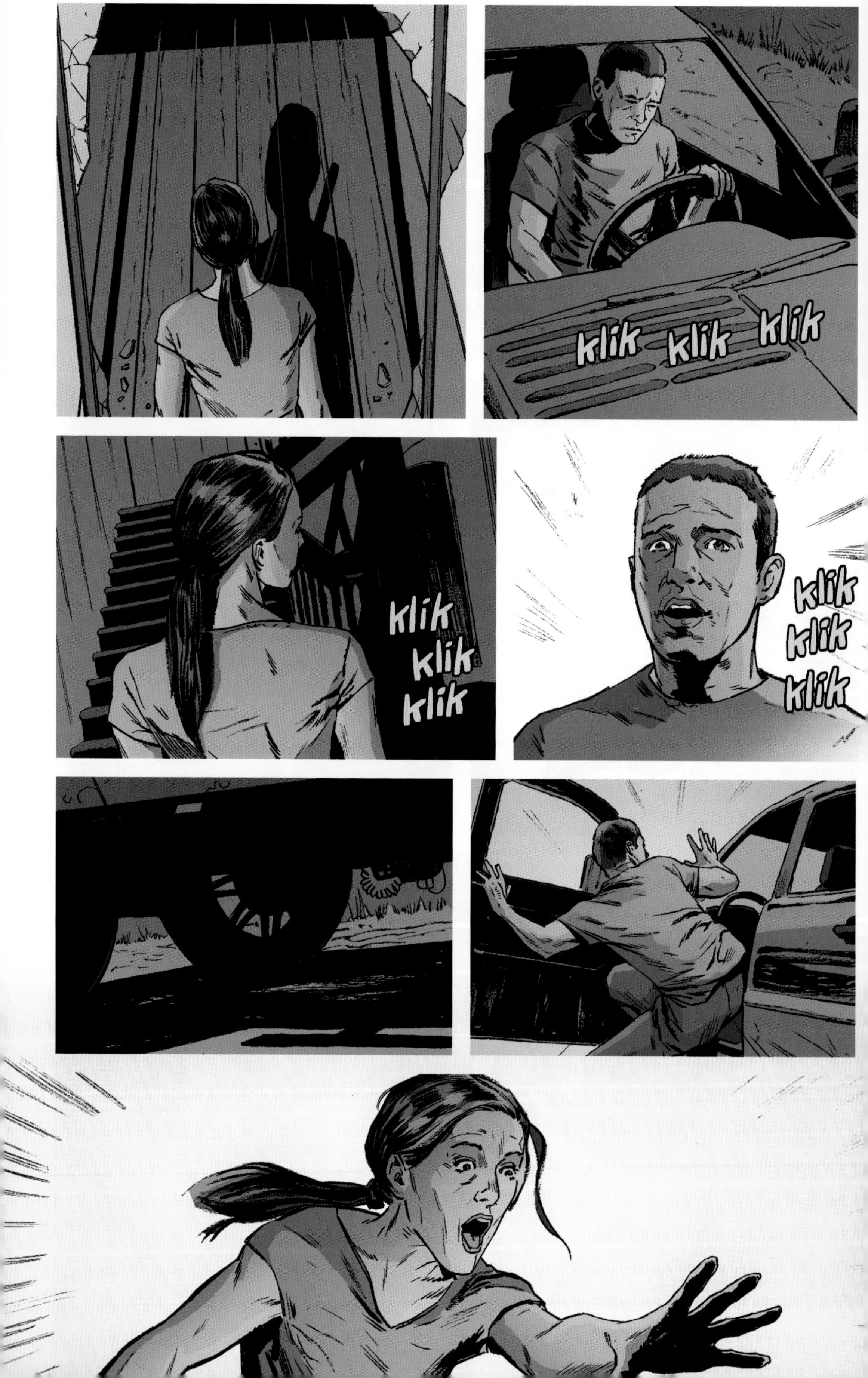
klik klik klik
klik
klik
klik
klik
klik
klik

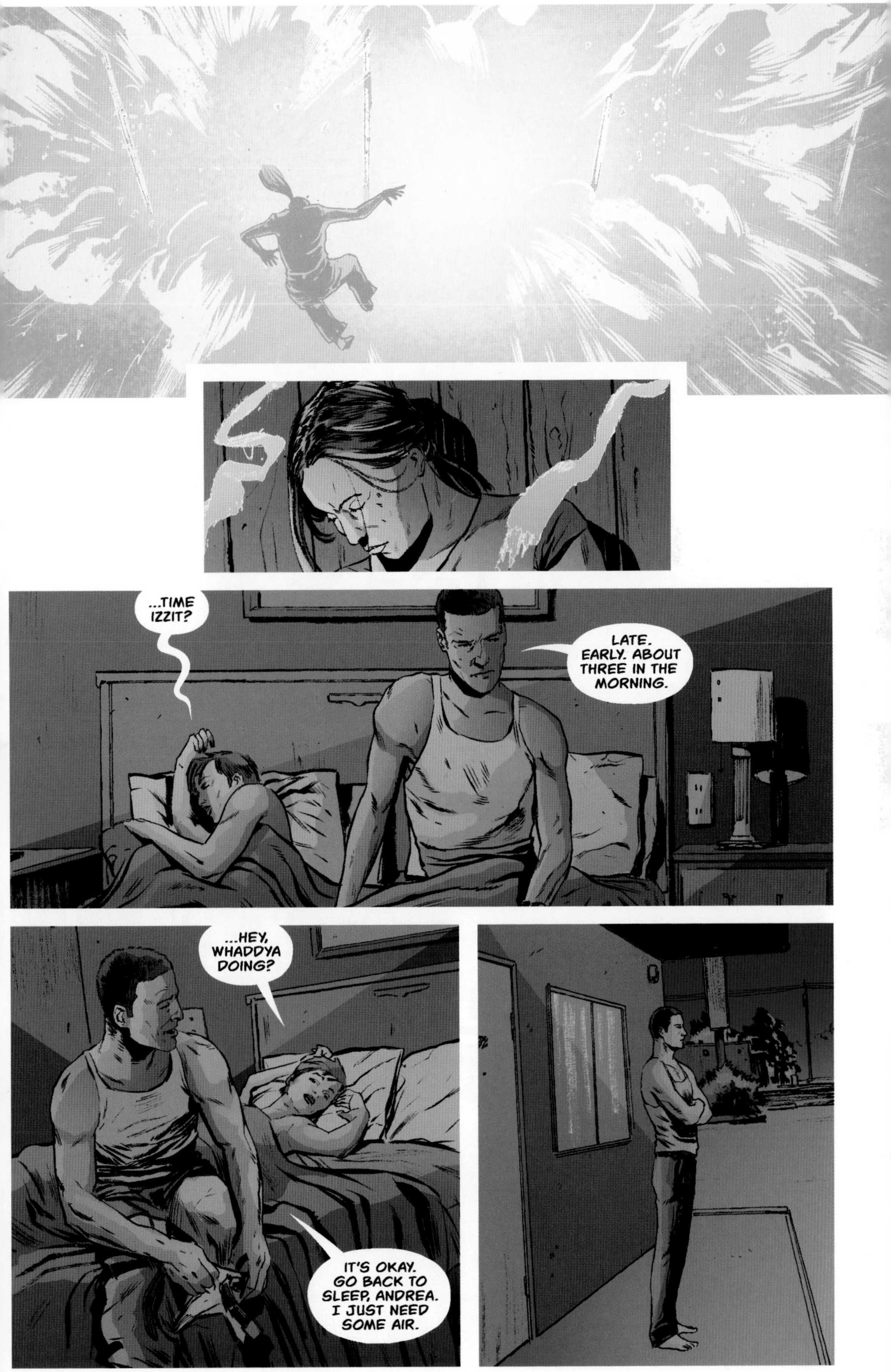
...TIME IZZIT?
LATE. EARLY. ABOUT THREE IN THE MORNING.
...HEY, WHADDYA DOING?
IT'S OKAY. GO BACK TO SLEEP, ANDREA. I JUST NEED SOME AIR.

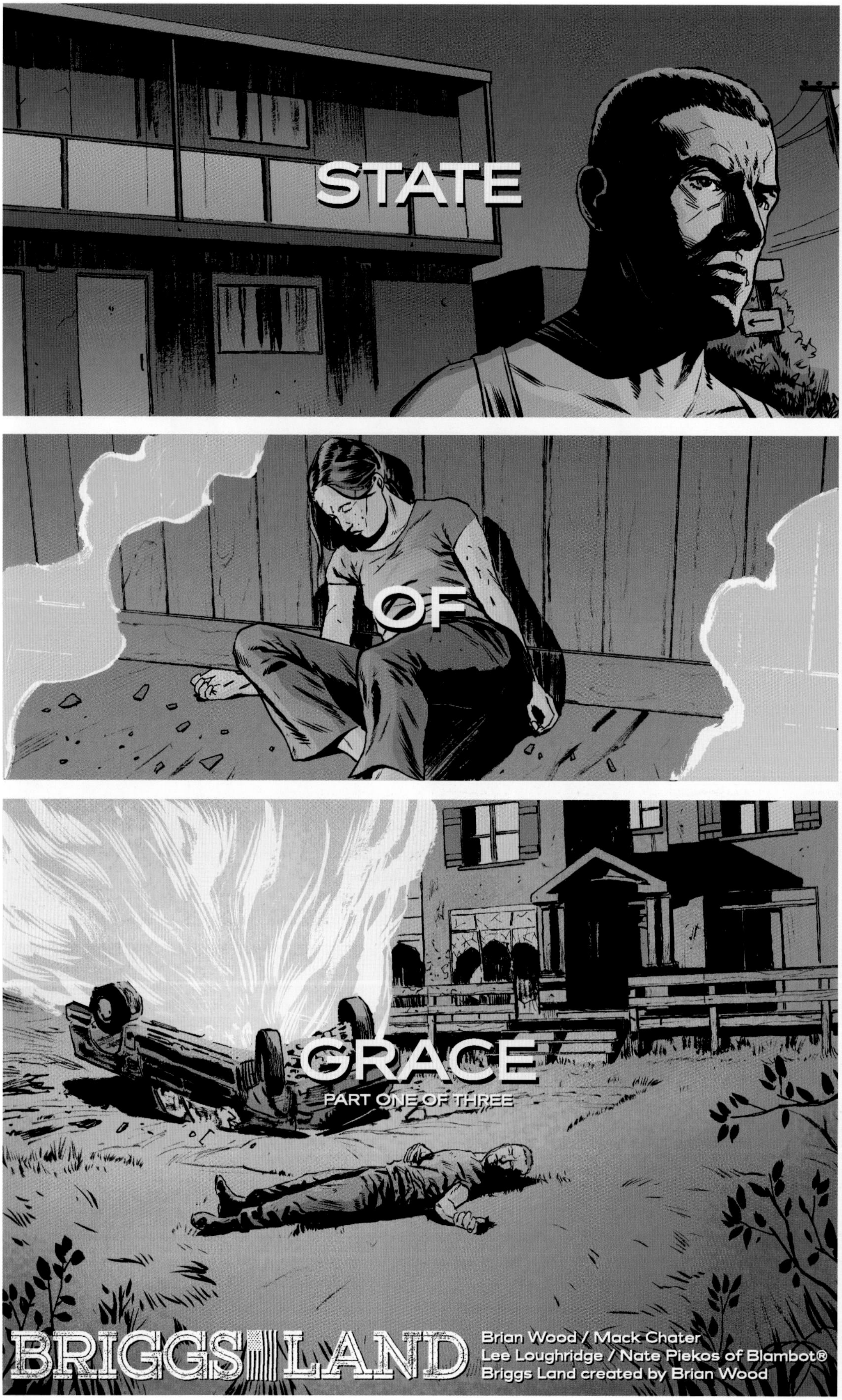

STATE
OF
GRACE
PART ONE OF THREE
BRIGGS LAND
Brian Wood / Mack Chater
Lee Loughridge / Nate Piekos of Blambot®
Briggs Land created by Brian Wood

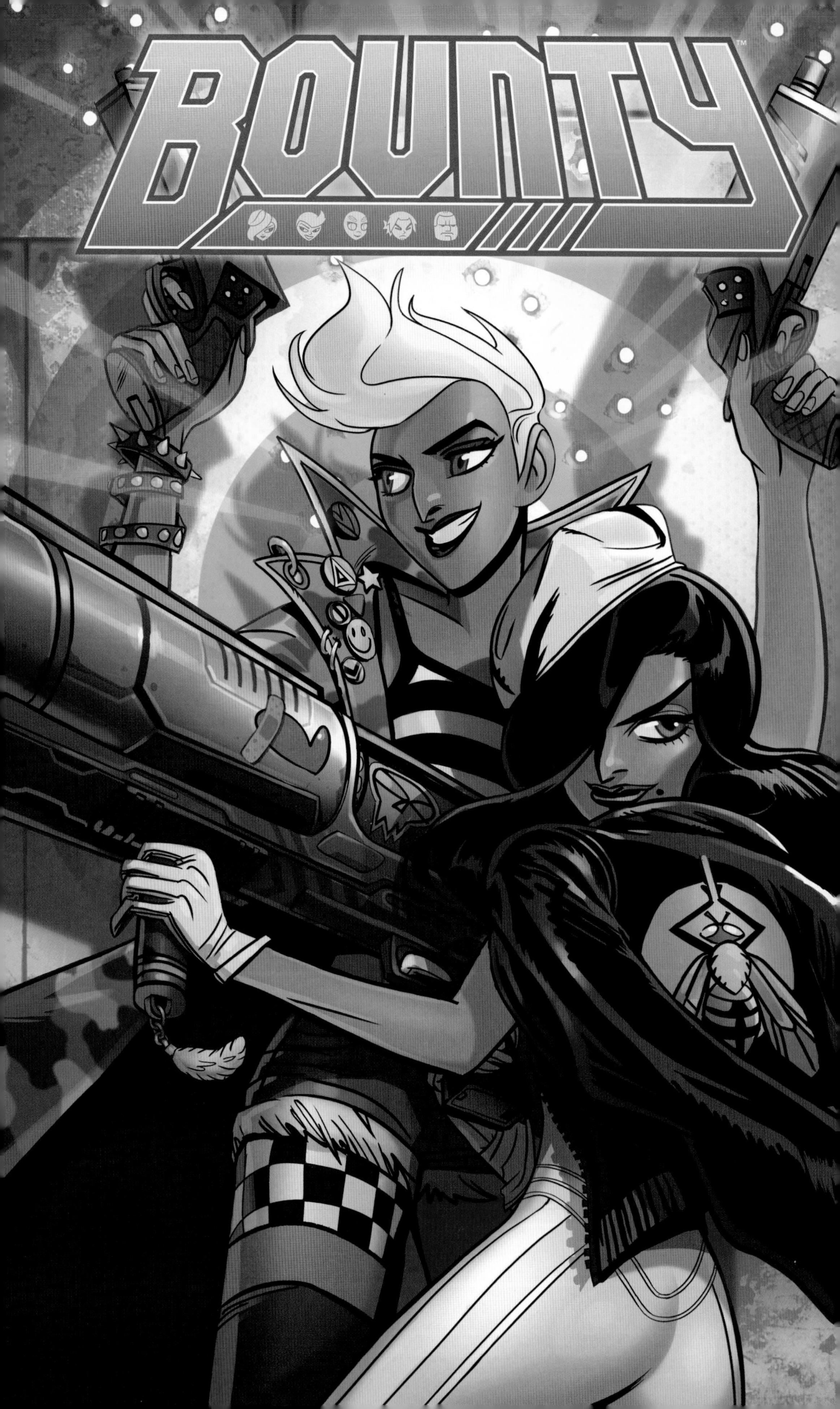

BOUNTY™

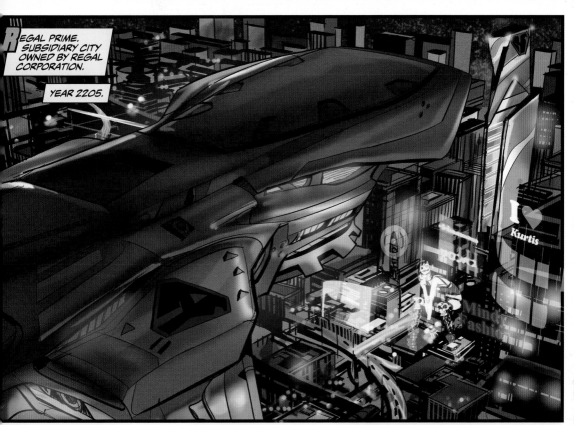

REGAL PRIME. SUBSIDIARY CITY OWNED BY REGAL CORPORATION.

YEAR 2205.

WITH SUCH AN IMPRESSIVE RÉSUMÉ, YOU WERE DISAPPOINTINGLY EASY TO NEUTRALIZE.

MUST BE A BITTER PILL TO SWALLOW FOR THE INFAMOUS *GADFLIES.*

PUT TEN OF YOURS IN THE HOSPITAL BEFORE THE REST TOOK US DOWN. *WE'RE* NOT THE ONES IN NEED OF MEDICATION.

HUMBLEBRAG ALL YOU WANT, CORP STOOGE. DIDN'T SEE YOU LIFT A FINGER. THIS ISN'T *YOUR* WIN.

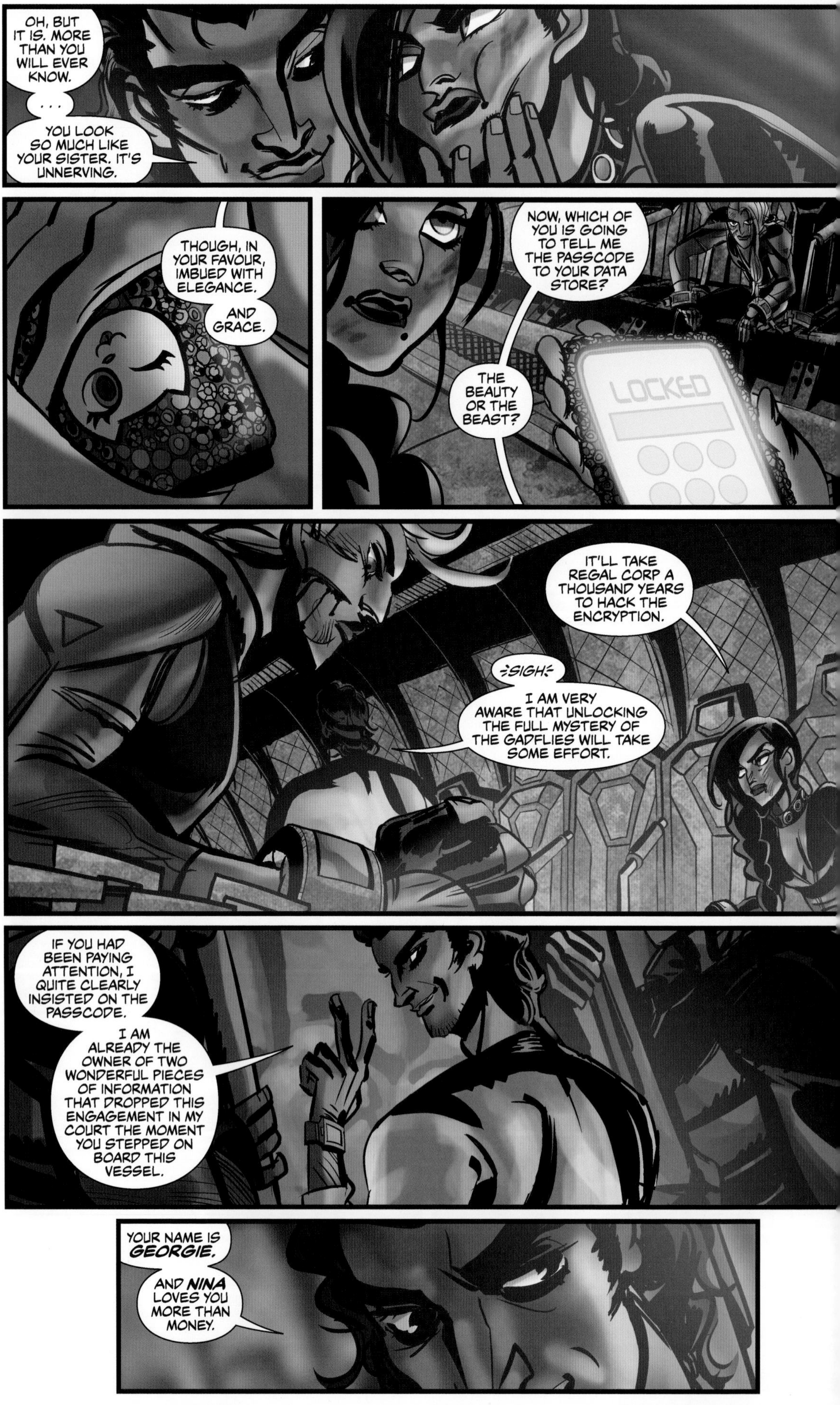
OH, BUT IT IS. MORE THAN YOU WILL EVER KNOW.
. . .
YOU LOOK SO MUCH LIKE YOUR SISTER. IT'S UNNERVING.
THOUGH, IN YOUR FAVOUR, IMBUED WITH ELEGANCE.
AND GRACE.
NOW, WHICH OF YOU IS GOING TO TELL ME THE PASSCODE TO YOUR DATA STORE?
THE BEAUTY OR THE BEAST?
LOCKED
IT'LL TAKE REGAL CORP A THOUSAND YEARS TO HACK THE ENCRYPTION.
SIGH
I AM VERY AWARE THAT UNLOCKING THE FULL MYSTERY OF THE GADFLIES WILL TAKE SOME EFFORT.
IF YOU HAD BEEN PAYING ATTENTION, I QUITE CLEARLY INSISTED ON THE PASSCODE.
I AM ALREADY THE OWNER OF TWO WONDERFUL PIECES OF INFORMATION THAT DROPPED THIS ENGAGEMENT IN MY COURT THE MOMENT YOU STEPPED ON BOARD THIS VESSEL.
YOUR NAME IS GEORGIE.
AND NINA LOVES YOU MORE THAN MONEY.

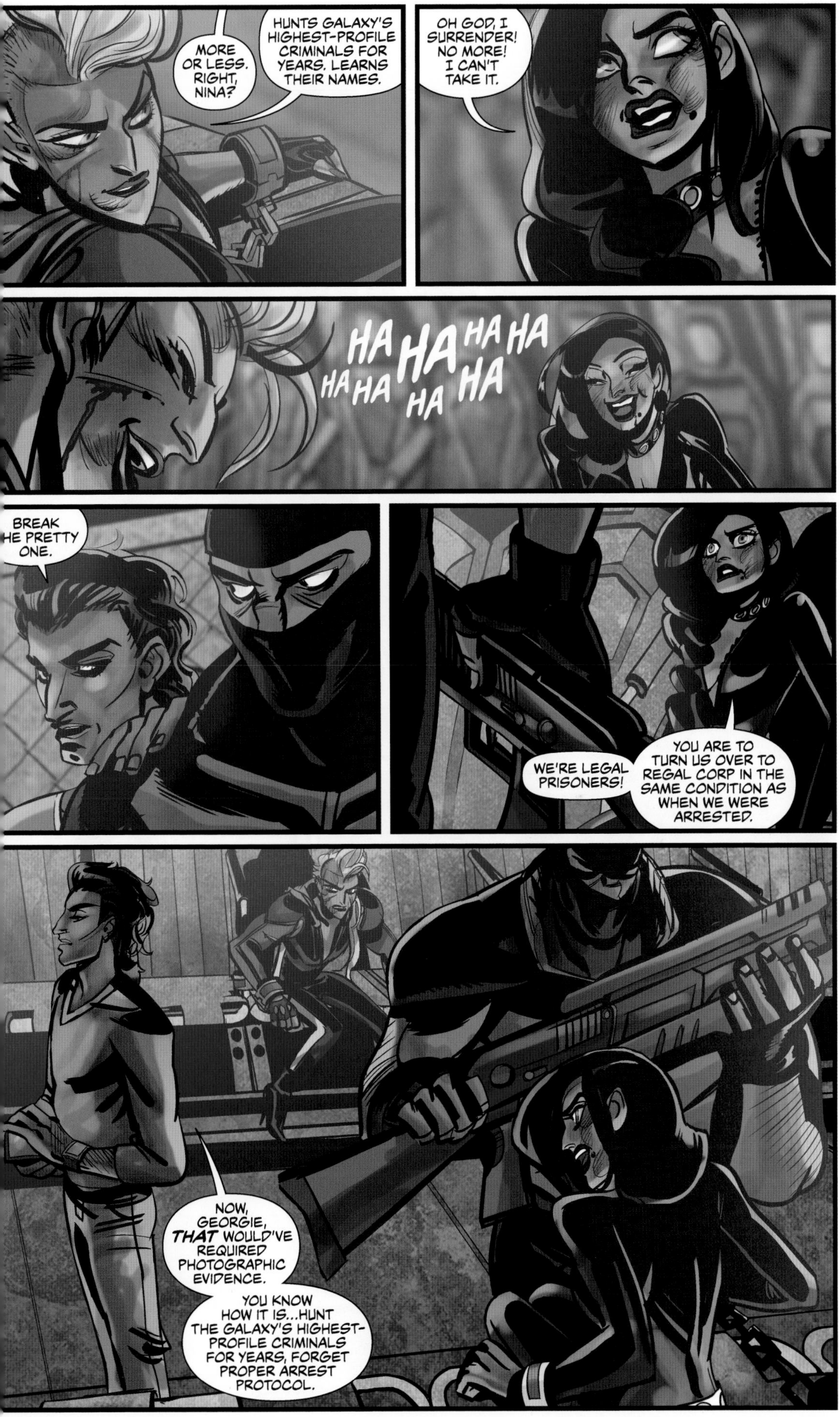
MORE OR LESS. RIGHT, NINA?
HUNTS GALAXY'S HIGHEST-PROFILE CRIMINALS FOR YEARS. LEARNS THEIR NAMES.
OH GOD, I SURRENDER! NO MORE! I CAN'T TAKE IT.
HA HA HA HA HA HA HA HA HA
BREAK HE PRETTY ONE.
WE'RE LEGAL PRISONERS!
YOU ARE TO TURN US OVER TO REGAL CORP IN THE SAME CONDITION AS WHEN WE WERE ARRESTED.
NOW, GEORGIE, THAT WOULD'VE REQUIRED PHOTOGRAPHIC EVIDENCE.
YOU KNOW HOW IT IS...HUNT THE GALAXY'S HIGHEST-PROFILE CRIMINALS FOR YEARS, FORGET PROPER ARREST PROTOCOL.

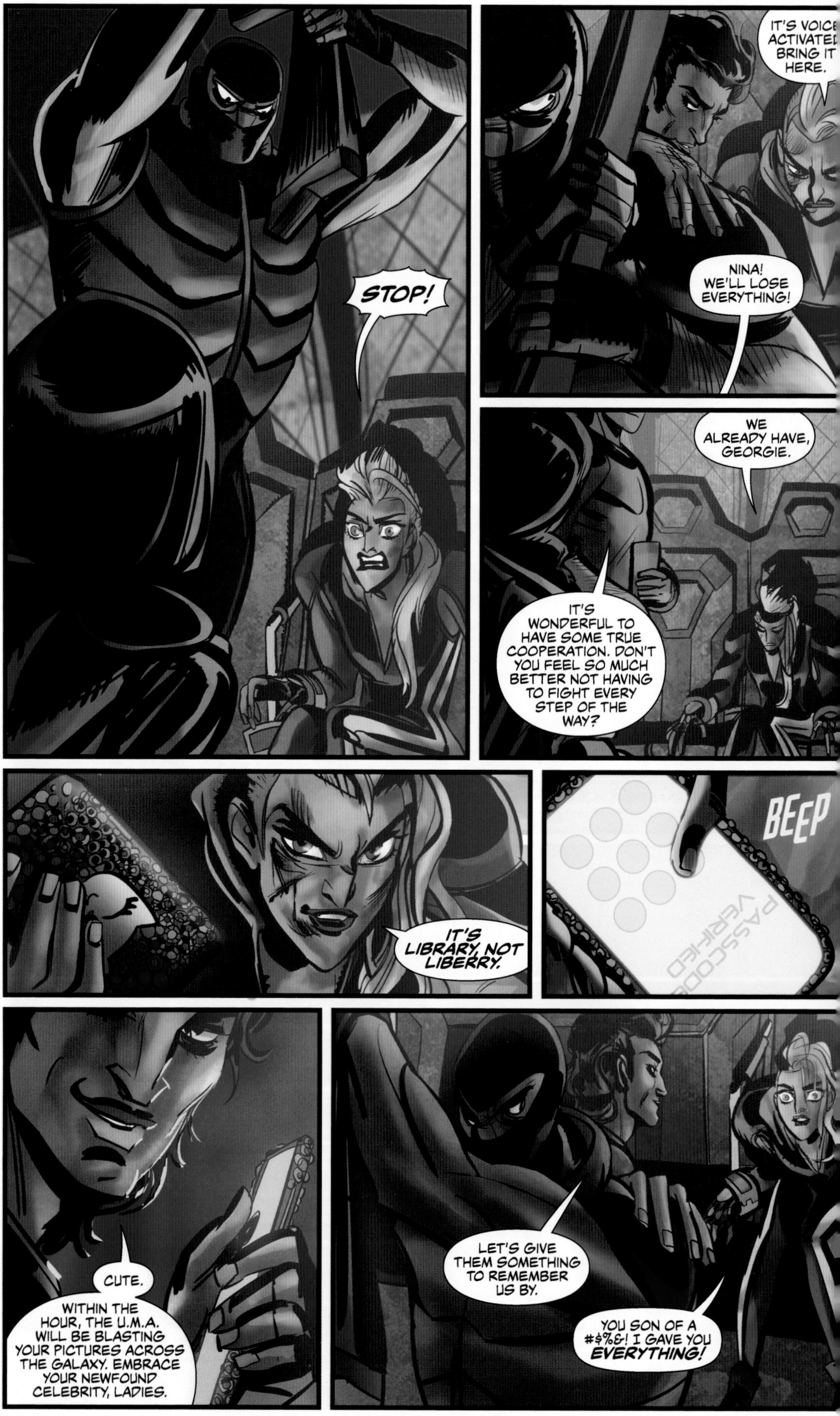
STOP!
IT'S VOICE ACTIVATED. BRING IT HERE.
NINA! WE'LL LOSE EVERYTHING!
WE ALREADY HAVE, GEORGIE.
IT'S WONDERFUL TO HAVE SOME TRUE COOPERATION. DON'T YOU FEEL SO MUCH BETTER NOT HAVING TO FIGHT EVERY STEP OF THE WAY?
IT'S LIBRARY, NOT LIBERRY.
BEEP
PASSCODE VERIFIED
CUTE.
WITHIN THE HOUR, THE U.M.A. WILL BE BLASTING YOUR PICTURES ACROSS THE GALAXY. EMBRACE YOUR NEWFOUND CELEBRITY, LADIES.
LET'S GIVE THEM SOMETHING TO REMEMBER US BY.
YOU SON OF A #$%&! I GAVE YOU EVERYTHING!

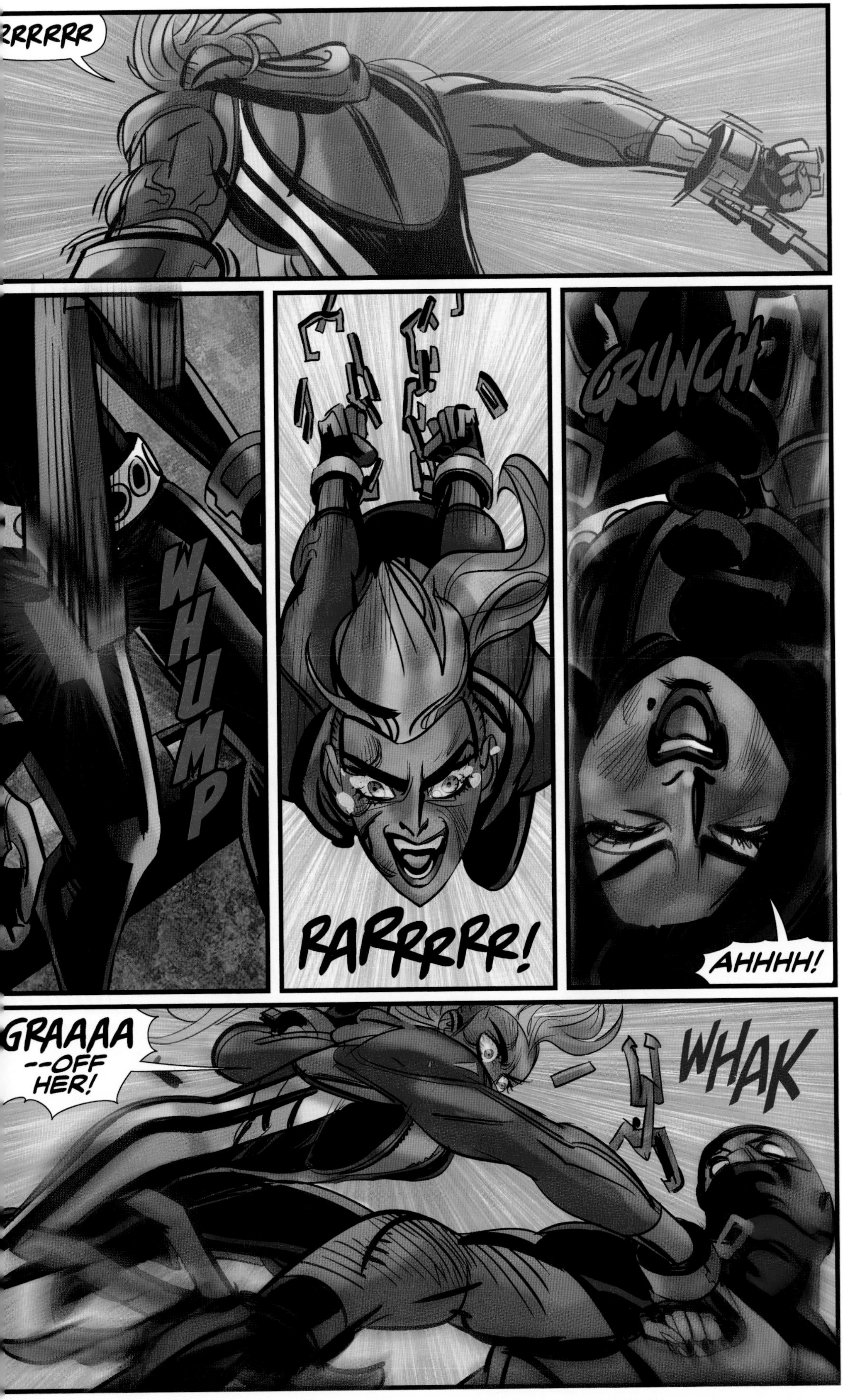
RRRRRR
WHUMP
RARRRRR!
CRUNCH
AHHHH!
GRAAAA
--OFF
HER!
WHAK

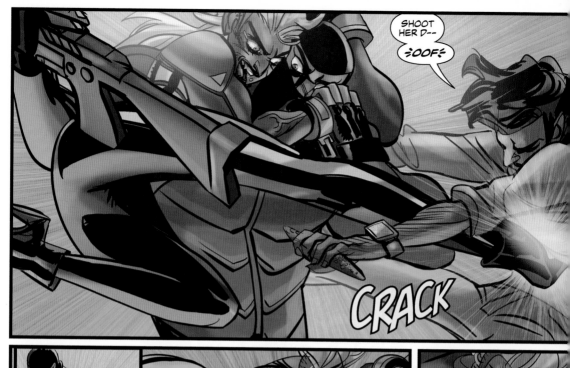

CRACK

KER-CHIK

AUGHH!

BUDDA BUDDA BUDDA BUDDA BUDDA RIIINN B

NINA... PLEASE... I--

RELEASE GEORGIE.

OF COURSE.

BEEP

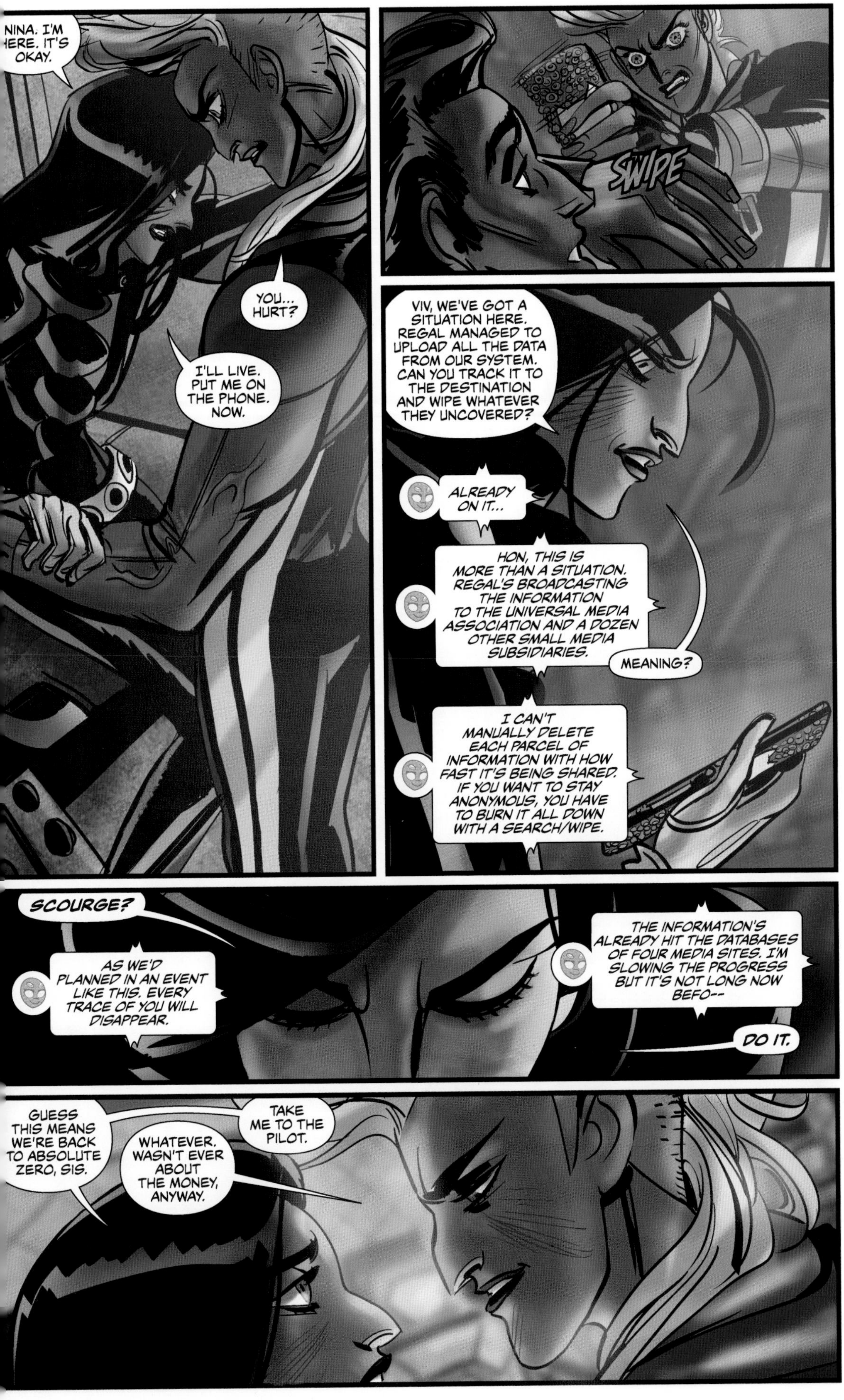
NINA. I'M HERE. IT'S OKAY.
SWIPE
YOU... HURT?
I'LL LIVE. PUT ME ON THE PHONE. NOW.
VIV, WE'VE GOT A SITUATION HERE. REGAL MANAGED TO UPLOAD ALL THE DATA FROM OUR SYSTEM. CAN YOU TRACK IT TO THE DESTINATION AND WIPE WHATEVER THEY UNCOVERED?
ALREADY ON IT...
HON, THIS IS MORE THAN A SITUATION. REGAL'S BROADCASTING THE INFORMATION TO THE UNIVERSAL MEDIA ASSOCIATION AND A DOZEN OTHER SMALL MEDIA SUBSIDIARIES.
MEANING?
I CAN'T MANUALLY DELETE EACH PARCEL OF INFORMATION WITH HOW FAST IT'S BEING SHARED. IF YOU WANT TO STAY ANONYMOUS, YOU HAVE TO BURN IT ALL DOWN WITH A SEARCH/WIPE.
SCOURGE?
AS WE'D PLANNED IN AN EVENT LIKE THIS. EVERY TRACE OF YOU WILL DISAPPEAR.
THE INFORMATION'S ALREADY HIT THE DATABASES OF FOUR MEDIA SITES. I'M SLOWING THE PROGRESS BUT IT'S NOT LONG NOW BEFO--
DO IT.
GUESS THIS MEANS WE'RE BACK TO ABSOLUTE ZERO, SIS.
WHATEVER. WASN'T EVER ABOUT THE MONEY, ANYWAY.
TAKE ME TO THE PILOT.

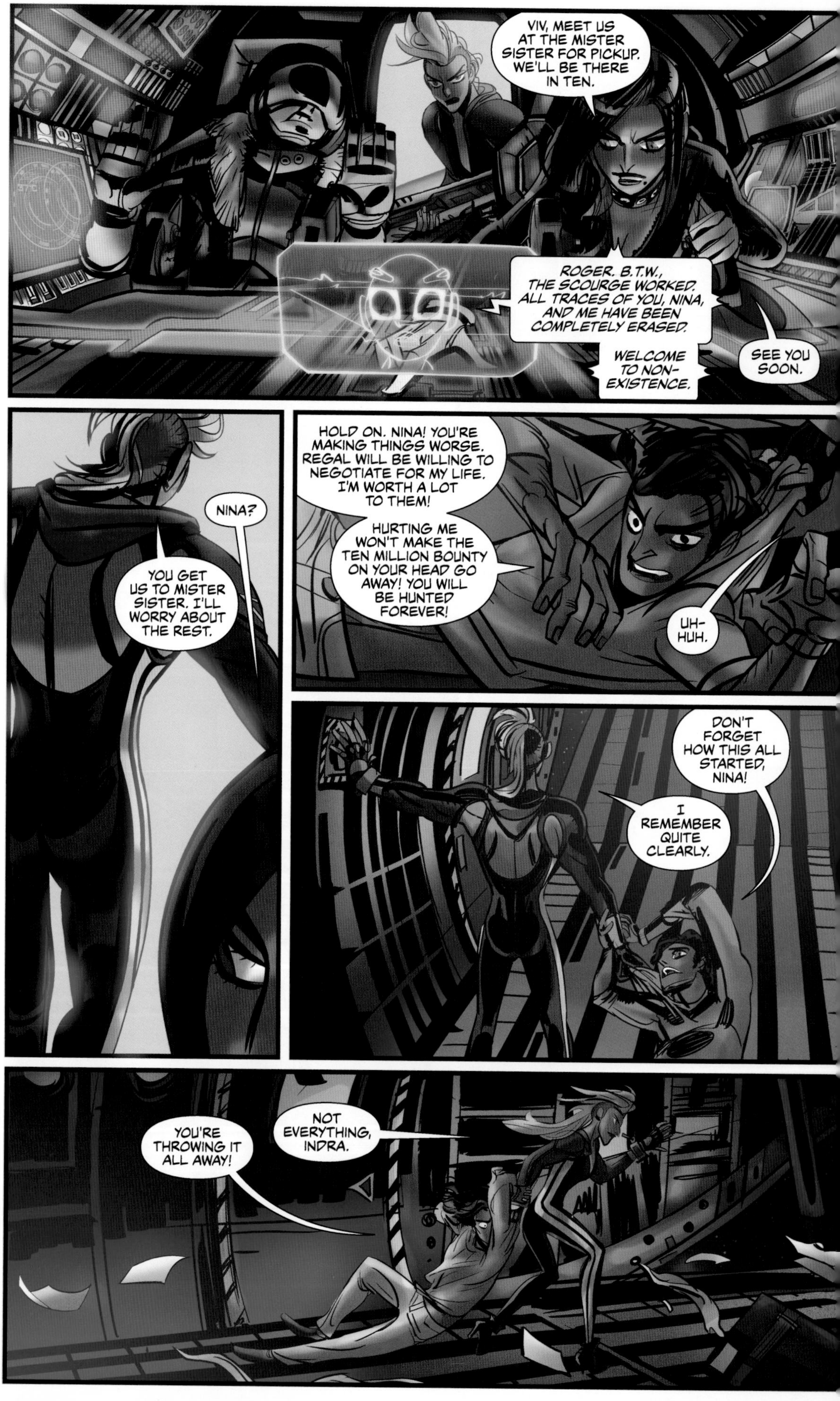
VIV, MEET US AT THE MISTER SISTER FOR PICKUP. WE'LL BE THERE IN TEN.
ROGER. B.T.W., THE SCOURGE WORKED. ALL TRACES OF YOU, NINA, AND ME HAVE BEEN COMPLETELY ERASED.
WELCOME TO NON-EXISTENCE.
SEE YOU SOON.
NINA?
YOU GET US TO MISTER SISTER. I'LL WORRY ABOUT THE REST.
HOLD ON. NINA! YOU'RE MAKING THINGS WORSE. REGAL WILL BE WILLING TO NEGOTIATE FOR MY LIFE. I'M WORTH A LOT TO THEM!
HURTING ME WON'T MAKE THE TEN MILLION BOUNTY ON YOUR HEAD GO AWAY! YOU WILL BE HUNTED FOREVER!
UH-HUH.
DON'T FORGET HOW THIS ALL STARTED, NINA!
I REMEMBER QUITE CLEARLY.
YOU'RE THROWING IT ALL AWAY!
NOT EVERYTHING, INDRA.

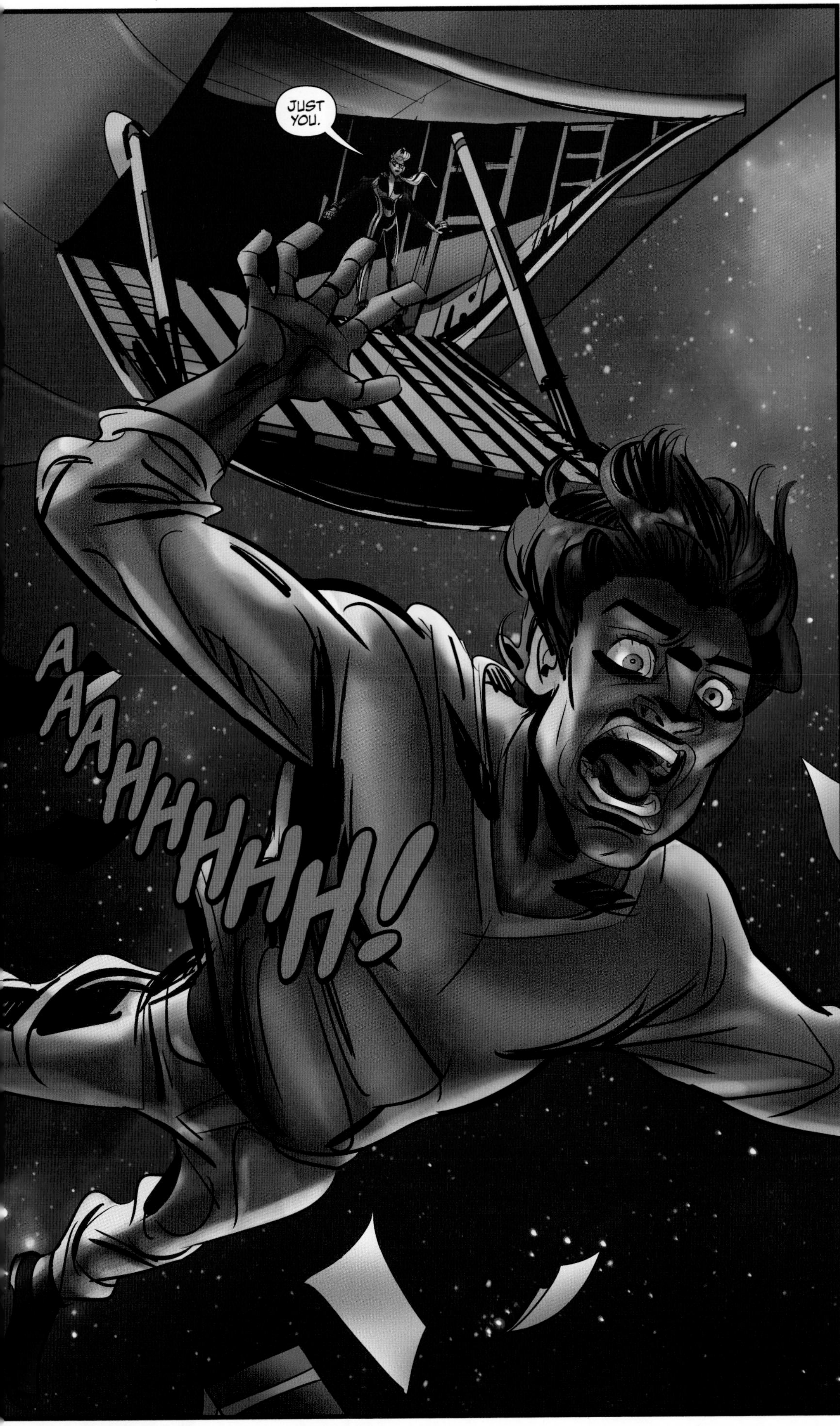
JUST YOU.
AAAHHHHHH!

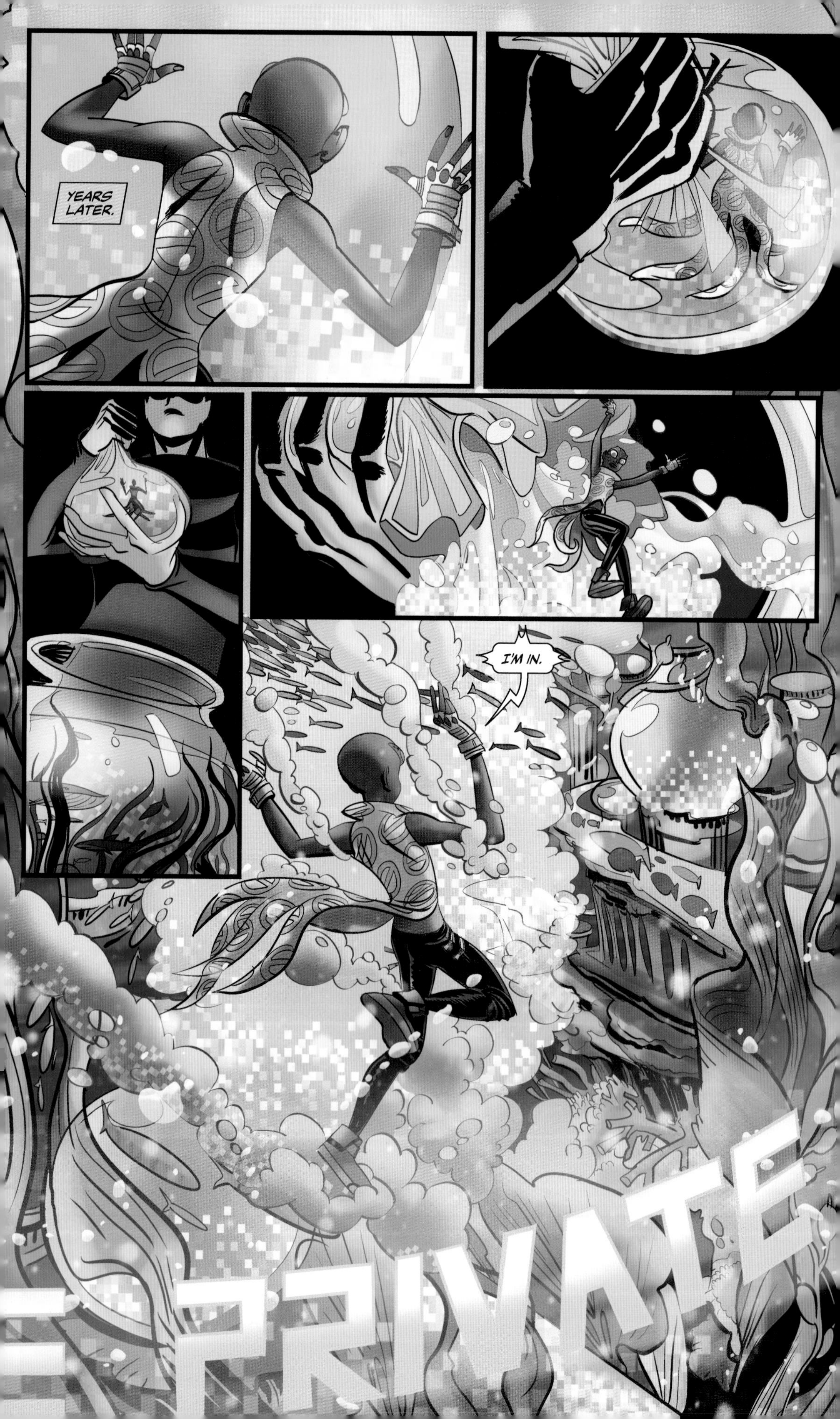
YEARS LATER.
I'M IN.
PRIVATE

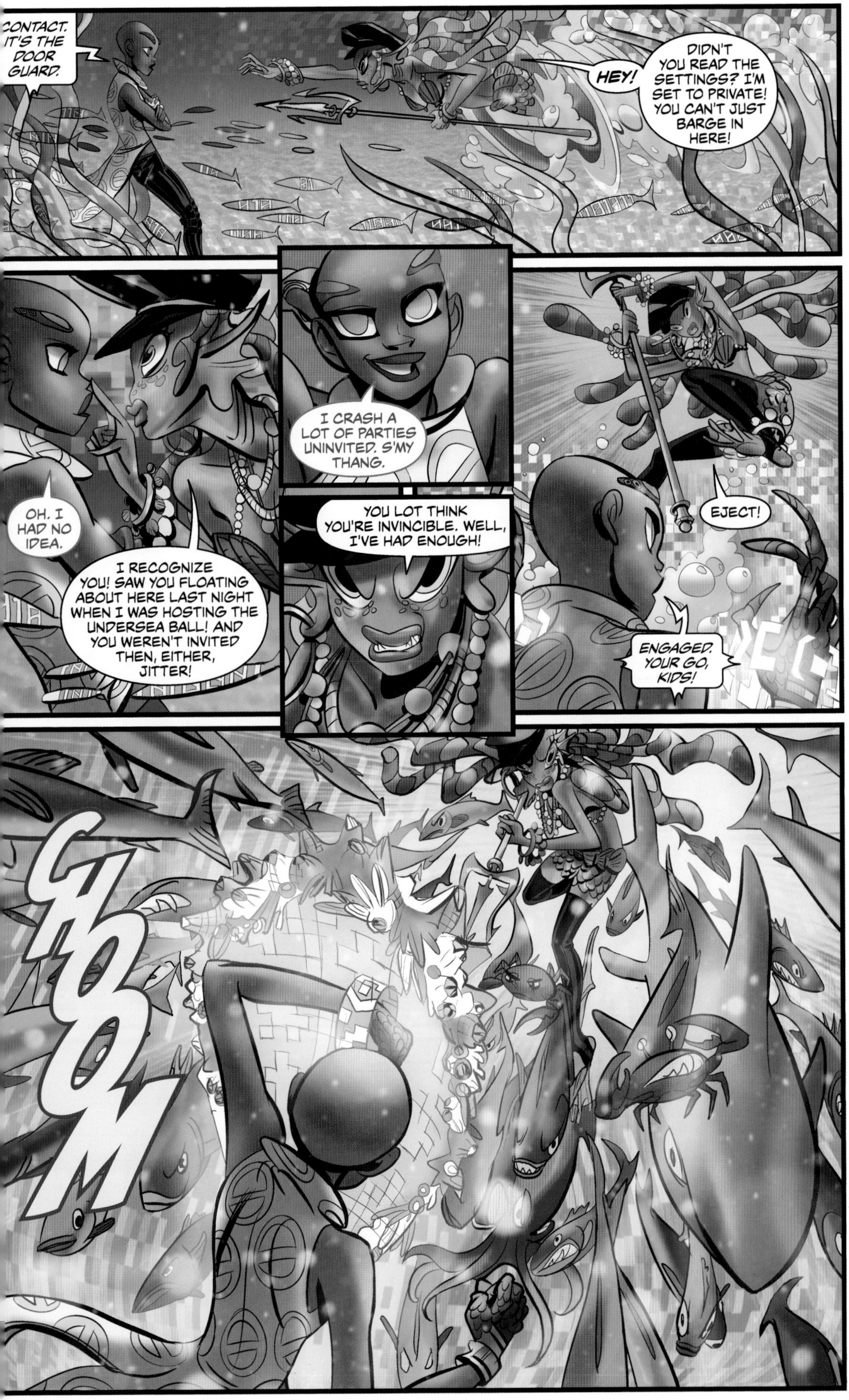
CONTACT. IT'S THE DOOR GUARD.
HEY!
DIDN'T YOU READ THE SETTINGS? I'M SET TO PRIVATE! YOU CAN'T JUST BARGE IN HERE!
OH. I HAD NO IDEA.
I RECOGNIZE YOU! SAW YOU FLOATING ABOUT HERE LAST NIGHT WHEN I WAS HOSTING THE UNDERSEA BALL! AND YOU WEREN'T INVITED THEN, EITHER, JITTER!
I CRASH A LOT OF PARTIES UNINVITED. S'MY THANG.
YOU LOT THINK YOU'RE INVINCIBLE. WELL, I'VE HAD ENOUGH!
EJECT!
ENGAGED. YOUR GO, KIDS!
CHOOM

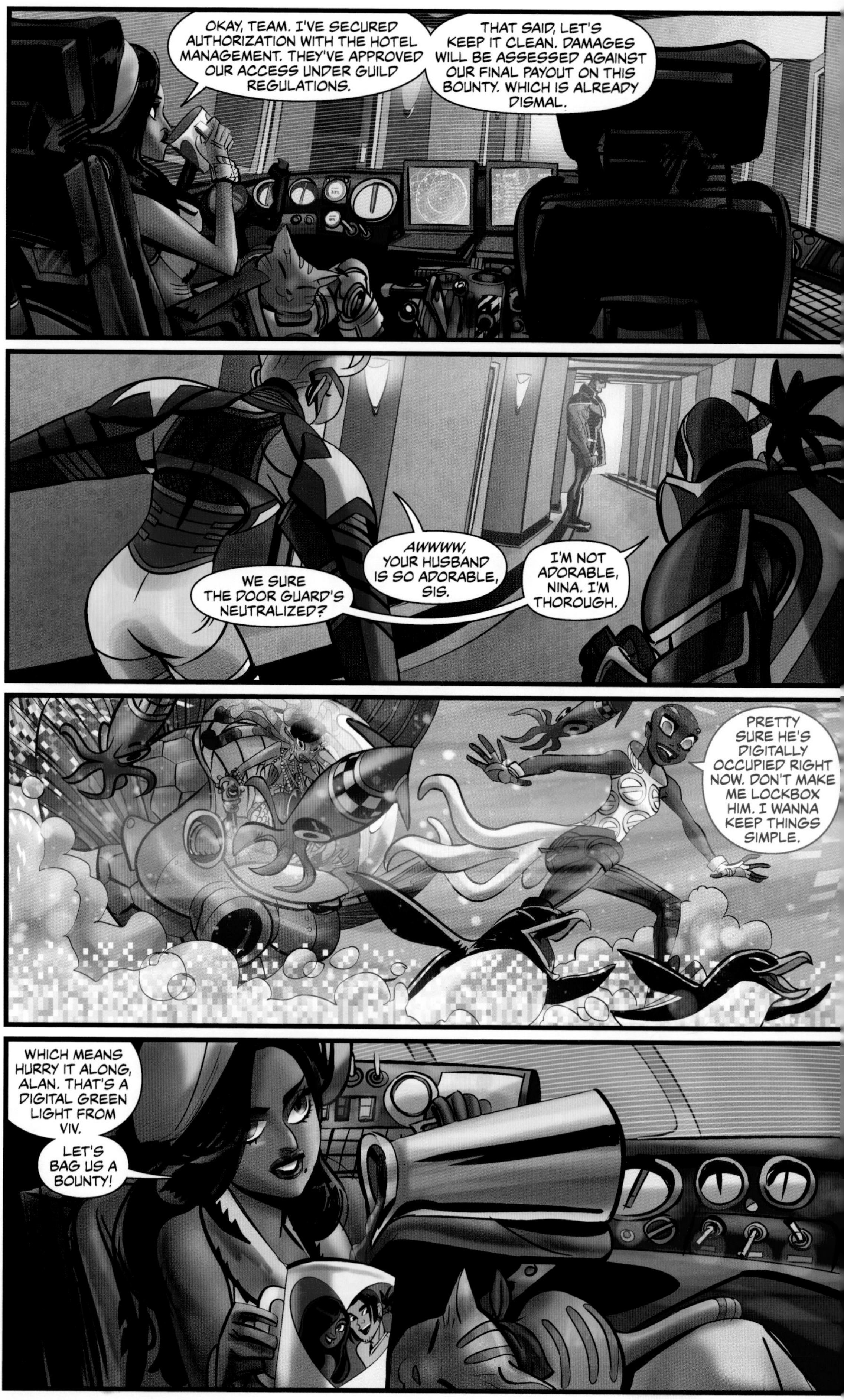
OKAY, TEAM. I'VE SECURED AUTHORIZATION WITH THE HOTEL MANAGEMENT. THEY'VE APPROVED OUR ACCESS UNDER GUILD REGULATIONS.
THAT SAID, LET'S KEEP IT CLEAN. DAMAGES WILL BE ASSESSED AGAINST OUR FINAL PAYOUT ON THIS BOUNTY. WHICH IS ALREADY DISMAL.
WE SURE THE DOOR GUARD'S NEUTRALIZED?
AWWWW, YOUR HUSBAND IS SO ADORABLE, SIS.
I'M NOT ADORABLE, NINA. I'M THOROUGH.
PRETTY SURE HE'S DIGITALLY OCCUPIED RIGHT NOW. DON'T MAKE ME LOCKBOX HIM. I WANNA KEEP THINGS SIMPLE.
WHICH MEANS HURRY IT ALONG, ALAN. THAT'S A DIGITAL GREEN LIGHT FROM VIV.
LET'S BAG US A BOUNTY!

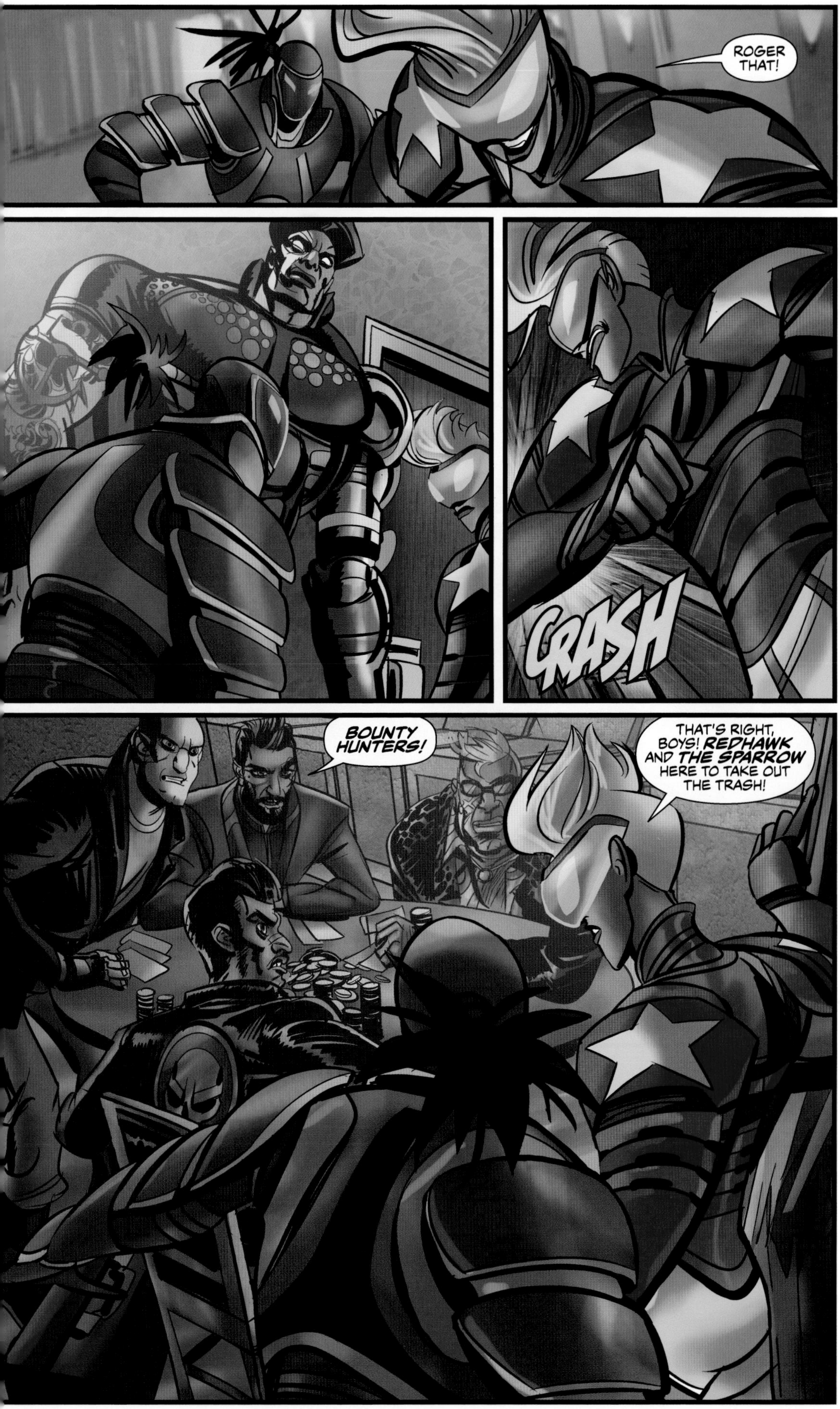
ROGER THAT!
CRASH
BOUNTY HUNTERS!
THAT'S RIGHT, BOYS! REDHAWK AND THE SPARROW HERE TO TAKE OUT THE TRASH!

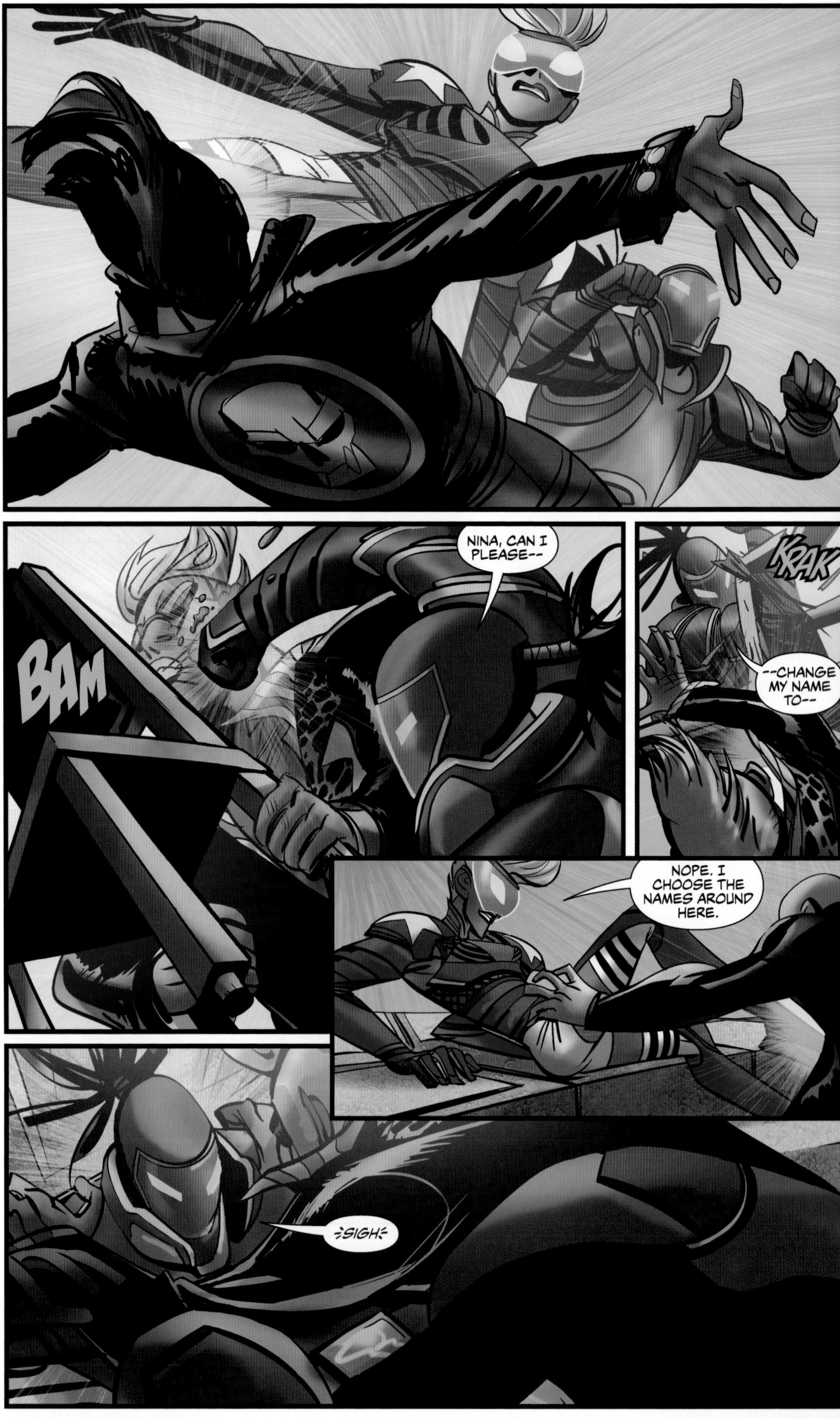
NINA, CAN I PLEASE--
BAM
KRAK
--CHANGE MY NAME TO--
NOPE. I CHOOSE THE NAMES AROUND HERE.
SIGH

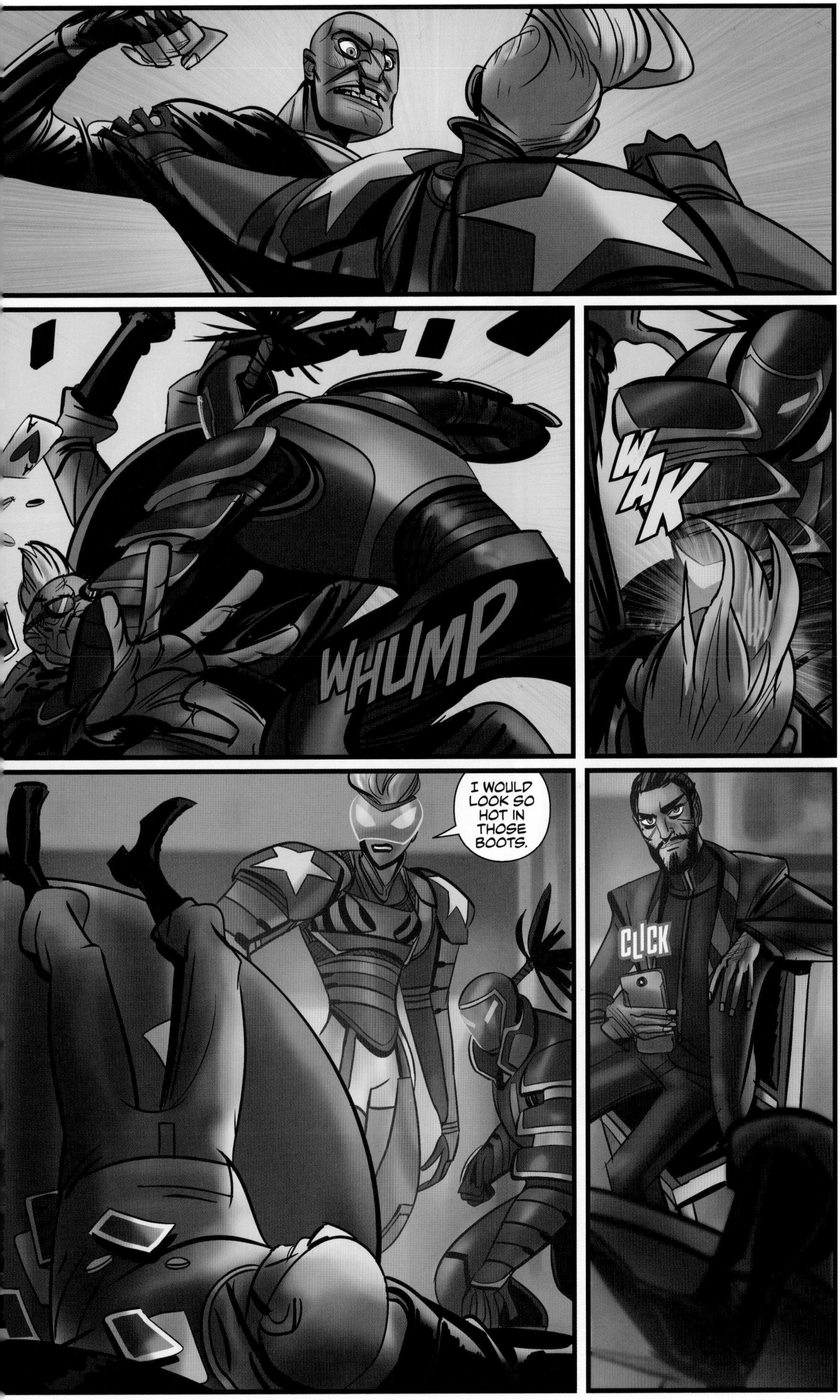
WHUMP
WAK
I WOULD LOOK SO HOT IN THOSE BOOTS.
CLICK

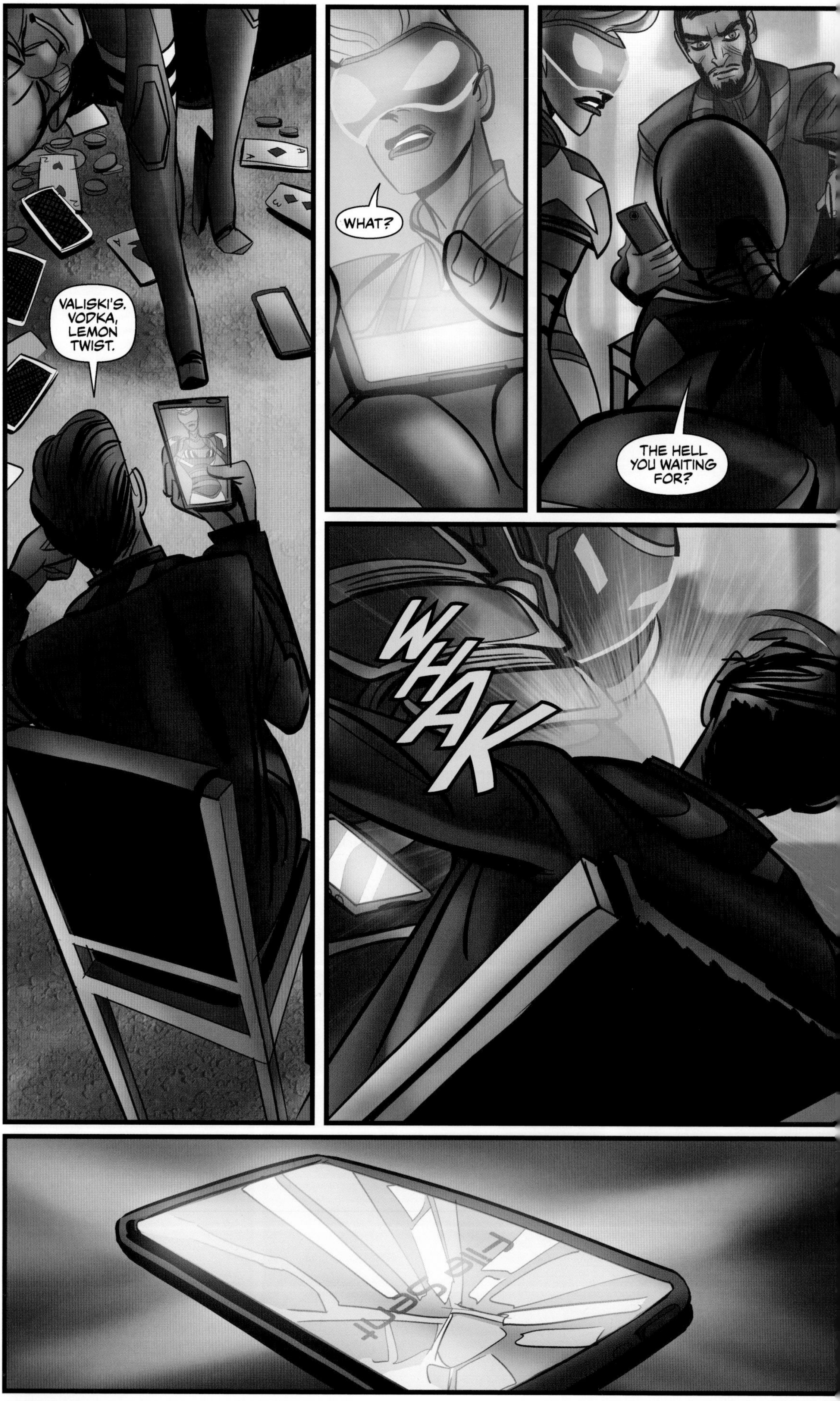
VALISKI'S. VODKA, LEMON TWIST.
WHAT?
THE HELL YOU WAITING FOR?
WHAK
File Sent

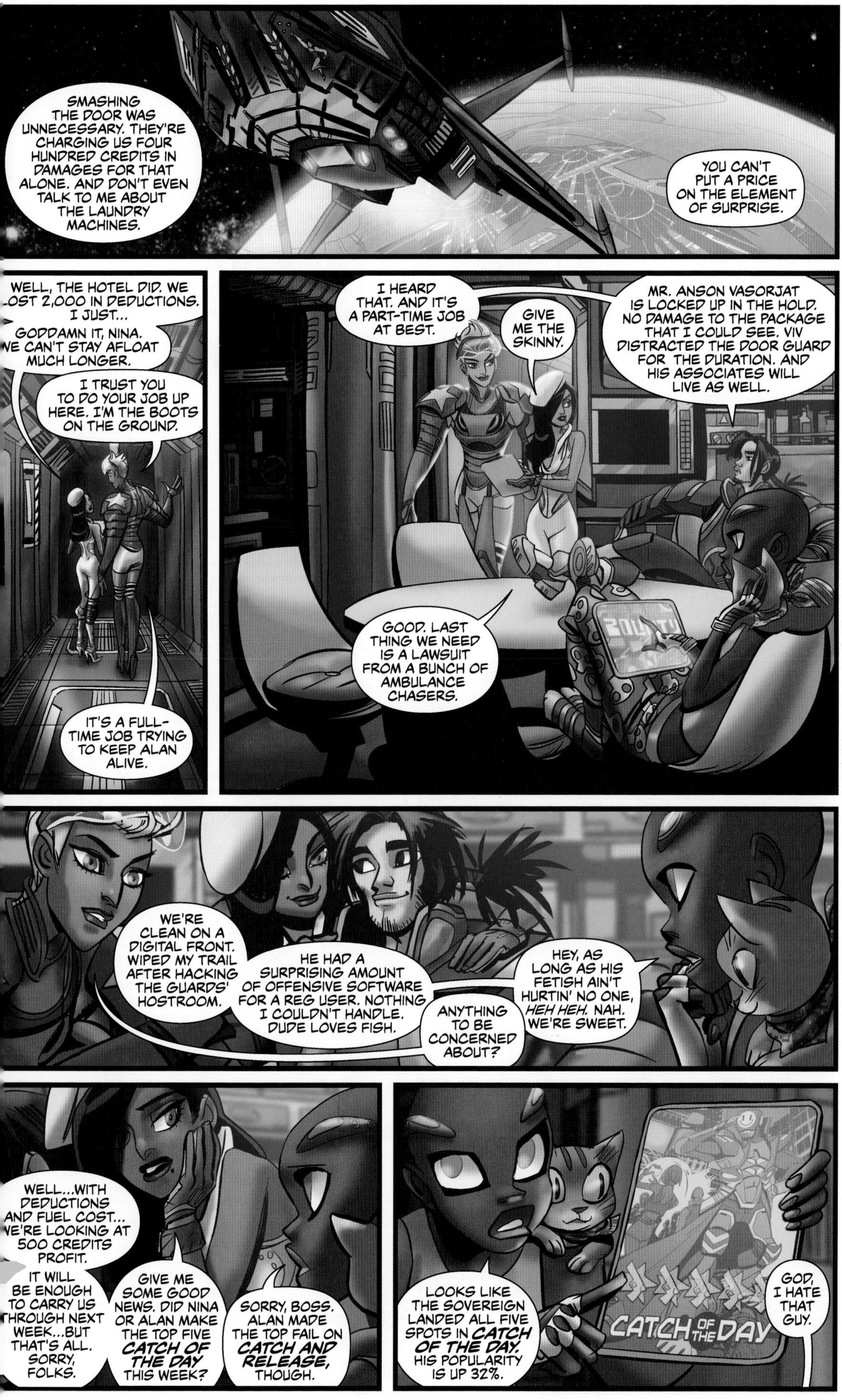

SMASHING THE DOOR WAS UNNECESSARY. THEY'RE CHARGING US FOUR HUNDRED CREDITS IN DAMAGES FOR THAT ALONE. AND DON'T EVEN TALK TO ME ABOUT THE LAUNDRY MACHINES.
YOU CAN'T PUT A PRICE ON THE ELEMENT OF SURPRISE.
WELL, THE HOTEL DID. WE LOST 2,000 IN DEDUCTIONS. I JUST...
GODDAMN IT, NINA. WE CAN'T STAY AFLOAT MUCH LONGER.
I TRUST YOU TO DO YOUR JOB UP HERE. I'M THE BOOTS ON THE GROUND.
IT'S A FULL-TIME JOB TRYING TO KEEP ALAN ALIVE.
I HEARD THAT. AND IT'S A PART-TIME JOB AT BEST.
GIVE ME THE SKINNY.
MR. ANSON VASORJAT IS LOCKED UP IN THE HOLD. NO DAMAGE TO THE PACKAGE THAT I COULD SEE. VIV DISTRACTED THE DOOR GUARD FOR THE DURATION. AND HIS ASSOCIATES WILL LIVE AS WELL.
GOOD. LAST THING WE NEED IS A LAWSUIT FROM A BUNCH OF AMBULANCE CHASERS.
WE'RE CLEAN ON A DIGITAL FRONT. WIPED MY TRAIL AFTER HACKING THE GUARDS' HOSTROOM.
ANYTHING TO BE CONCERNED ABOUT?
HE HAD A SURPRISING AMOUNT OF OFFENSIVE SOFTWARE FOR A REG USER. NOTHING I COULDN'T HANDLE. DUDE LOVES FISH.
HEY, AS LONG AS HIS FETISH AIN'T HURTIN' NO ONE, *HEH HEH.* NAH. WE'RE SWEET.
WELL...WITH DEDUCTIONS AND FUEL COST... WE'RE LOOKING AT 500 CREDITS PROFIT.
IT WILL BE ENOUGH TO CARRY US THROUGH NEXT WEEK...BUT THAT'S ALL. SORRY, FOLKS.
GIVE ME SOME GOOD NEWS. DID NINA OR ALAN MAKE THE TOP FIVE ***CATCH OF THE DAY*** THIS WEEK?
SORRY, BOSS. ALAN MADE THE TOP FAIL ON ***CATCH AND RELEASE,*** THOUGH.
LOOKS LIKE THE SOVEREIGN LANDED ALL FIVE SPOTS IN ***CATCH OF THE DAY.*** HIS POPULARITY IS UP 32%.
CATCH OF THE DAY
GOD, I HATE THAT GUY.

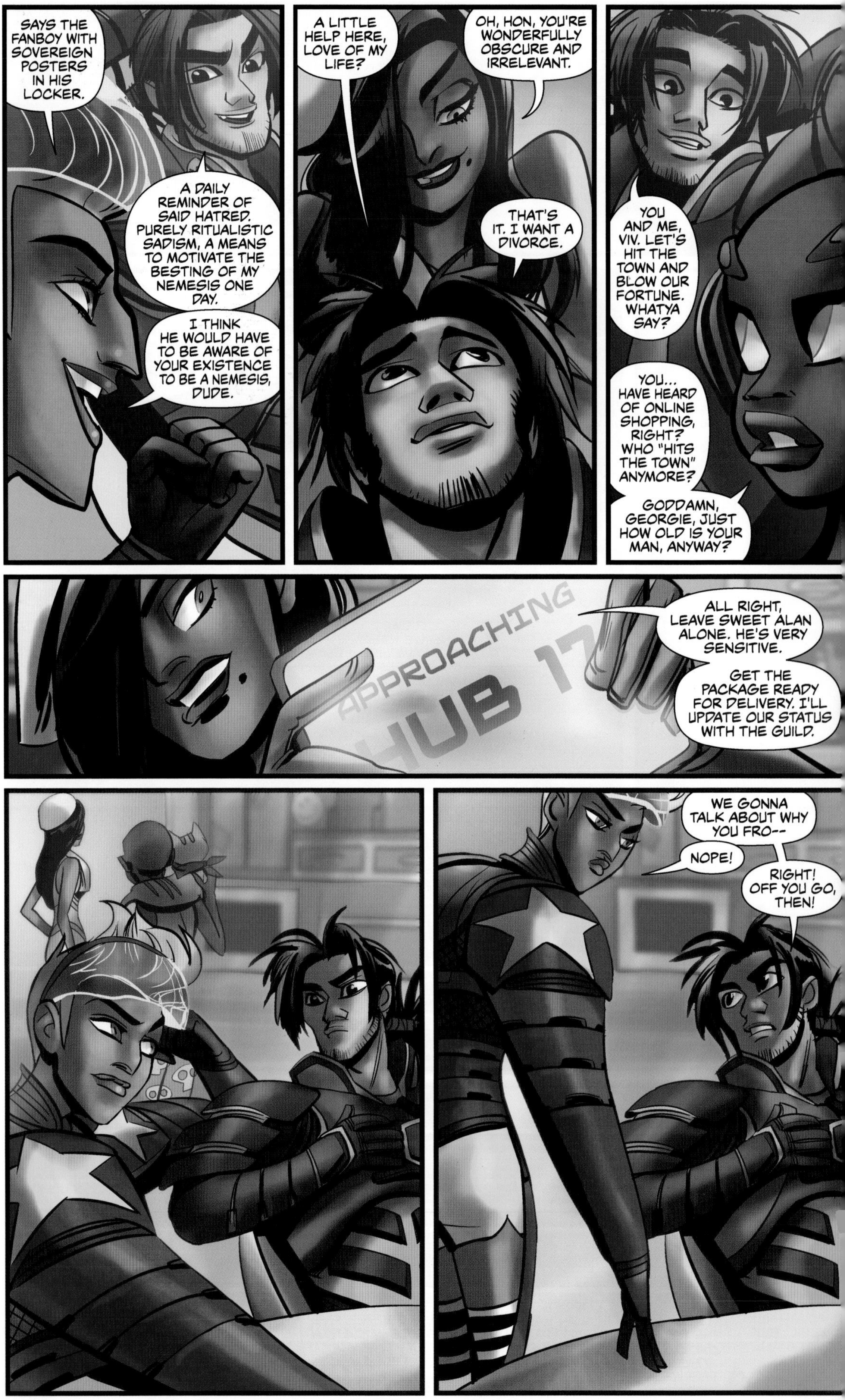

SAYS THE FANBOY WITH SOVEREIGN POSTERS IN HIS LOCKER.
A DAILY REMINDER OF SAID HATRED. PURELY RITUALISTIC SADISM, A MEANS TO MOTIVATE THE BESTING OF MY NEMESIS ONE DAY.
I THINK HE WOULD HAVE TO BE AWARE OF YOUR EXISTENCE TO BE A NEMESIS, DUDE.
A LITTLE HELP HERE, LOVE OF MY LIFE?
OH, HON, YOU'RE WONDERFULLY OBSCURE AND IRRELEVANT.
THAT'S IT. I WANT A DIVORCE.
YOU AND ME, VIV. LET'S HIT THE TOWN AND BLOW OUR FORTUNE. WHATYA SAY?
YOU... HAVE HEARD OF ONLINE SHOPPING, RIGHT? WHO "HITS THE TOWN" ANYMORE?
GODDAMN, GEORGIE, JUST HOW OLD IS YOUR MAN, ANYWAY?
APPROACHING HUB 17
ALL RIGHT, LEAVE SWEET ALAN ALONE. HE'S VERY SENSITIVE.
GET THE PACKAGE READY FOR DELIVERY. I'LL UPDATE OUR STATUS WITH THE GUILD.
WE GONNA TALK ABOUT WHY YOU FRO--
NOPE!
RIGHT! OFF YOU GO, THEN!

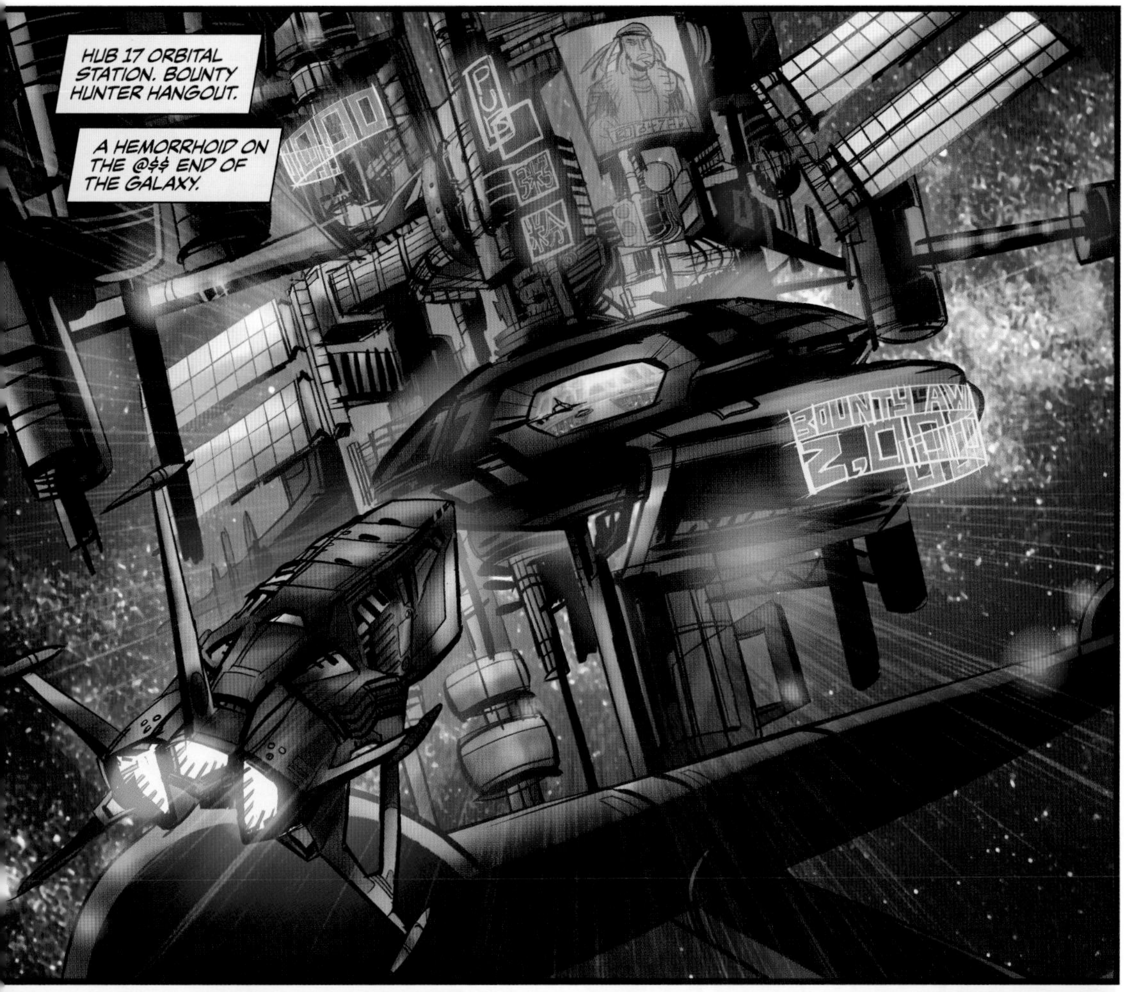
HUB 17 ORBITAL STATION. BOUNTY HUNTER HANGOUT.
A HEMORRHOID ON THE @$$ END OF THE GALAXY.
PUB
BOUNTY AWD 2,000

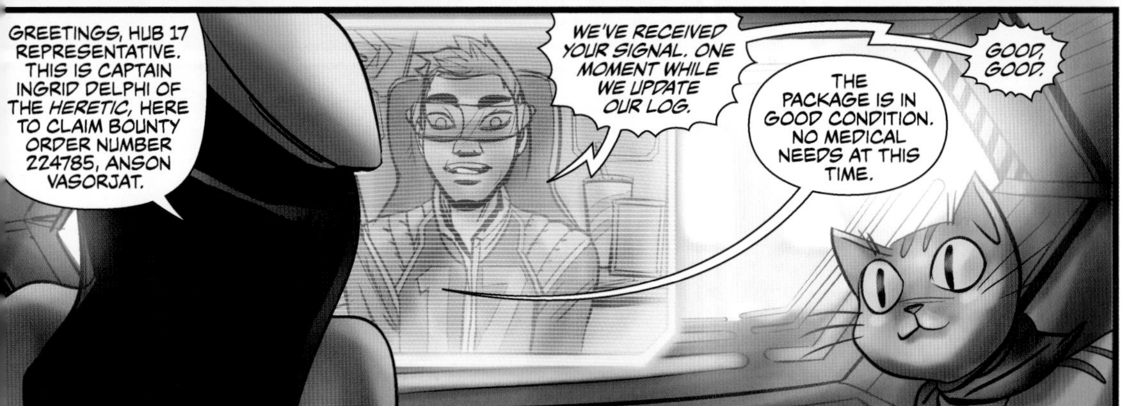
GREETINGS, HUB 17 REPRESENTATIVE. THIS IS CAPTAIN INGRID DELPHI OF THE *HERETIC*, HERE TO CLAIM BOUNTY ORDER NUMBER 224785, ANSON VASORJAT.
WE'VE RECEIVED YOUR SIGNAL. ONE MOMENT WHILE WE UPDATE OUR LOG.
GOOD, GOOD.
THE PACKAGE IS IN GOOD CONDITION. NO MEDICAL NEEDS AT THIS TIME.

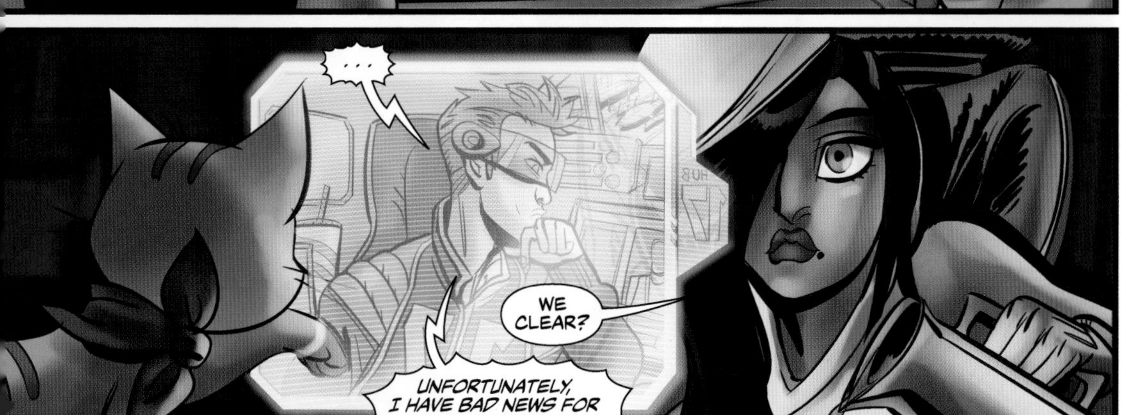
. . .
WE CLEAR?
UNFORTUNATELY, I HAVE BAD NEWS FOR YOU, CAPTAIN...

I'M IN THE HEAT OF THE MOMENT. ADRENALINE. RAGE. THE GOOD STUFF. THEN OUT OF NOWHERE THE TARGET YELLS A DRINK RECIPE AT ME.

LOOK, I GET IT. IT'S WEIRD. JUST HAVEN'T SEEN YOU CLAM UP LIKE THAT BEFORE.

ALTHOUGH THERE WAS THAT INCIDENT WITH THE BACON...

MY GOOD MAN, WE HAVE A--

HAND HIM OVER AND LET'S BE ON OUR WAY.

WHAT? BUT WE HAVEN'T EVEN BEEN P--

CONTRACTOR DROPPED THE BOUNTY CLAIM TWO HOURS AGO.

SORRY FOR THE INCONVENIENCE, SIR.

NO TROUBLE AT ALL, MY FRIEND. I UNDERSTAND THESE FINE PEOPLE WERE SIMPLY DOING THEIR JOBS. CAN'T FAULT THEM FOR SOMEONE ELSE'S CHANGE OF HEART. WOULDN'T YOU AGREE?

SO, WHAT'S THIS GUY WORTH, THEN?

AS I SAID, THE BOUNTY IS VOID. HE IS OF NO FINANCIAL VALUE AT THIS TIME.

GOOD.

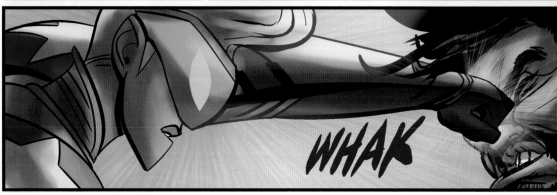

WHAK

Finn Larmer
Runaway, Loc[...]
Return, [...]

June Park
Embezzler, Locate
and Return, Recover
data, 1,500 credits

Oscar Del Rada
Terrorist, Locate and
Return, Alive Only,
5,000 credits

*Warning! ARMED AND
DANGEROUS, RESPONSIBLE
FOR TWO HUNTER
DEATHS TO DATE*

⸗SIGH⸗
WHAT THE HELL HAPPENED TO MY LIFE?

[...]a Larmer
[...]ocate and
[...]00 Credits

June Park
Embezzler, Locate
and Return, Recover
data, 1,500 credits

Oscar Del Rad[...]
Terrorist, Locate [...]
Return, Alive O[...]
5,000 credit[...]

*Warning! AR[...]
DANGEROUS, RESPO[...]SIBLE
FOR TWO HUNT[...]R
DEATHS T[...]

RAMP'S RAISED. HOLD IS LOCKED UP TIGHT.

HATE MY LIFE AND JOB. READY TO ROLL WHEN YOU ARE.

Oscar Del Rada
Terrorist, L[...]ate and
Return, A[...] Only,
5,000 c[...]dits

HEY, NINA? CAN WE STILL GO FOR BROKE WHEN WE'RE ALREADY BROKE?

REMEMBER THAT TIME WHEN WE WERE THE WEALTHIEST CRIMINALS IN THE UNIVERSE?

NOPE.

[...]Wa[...]
[...]NGEROU[...]
FOR TWO HUN[...]
DEATHS TO DA[...]

Accept Bounty on
Oscar Del Rada?

ACCEPT   DENY

Warning! ARME[...]
[...]GEROUS, RESP[...]
FOR TWO HUN[...]
DEATHS TO D[...]

ME EITHER.

BEEP

A[...]EPT

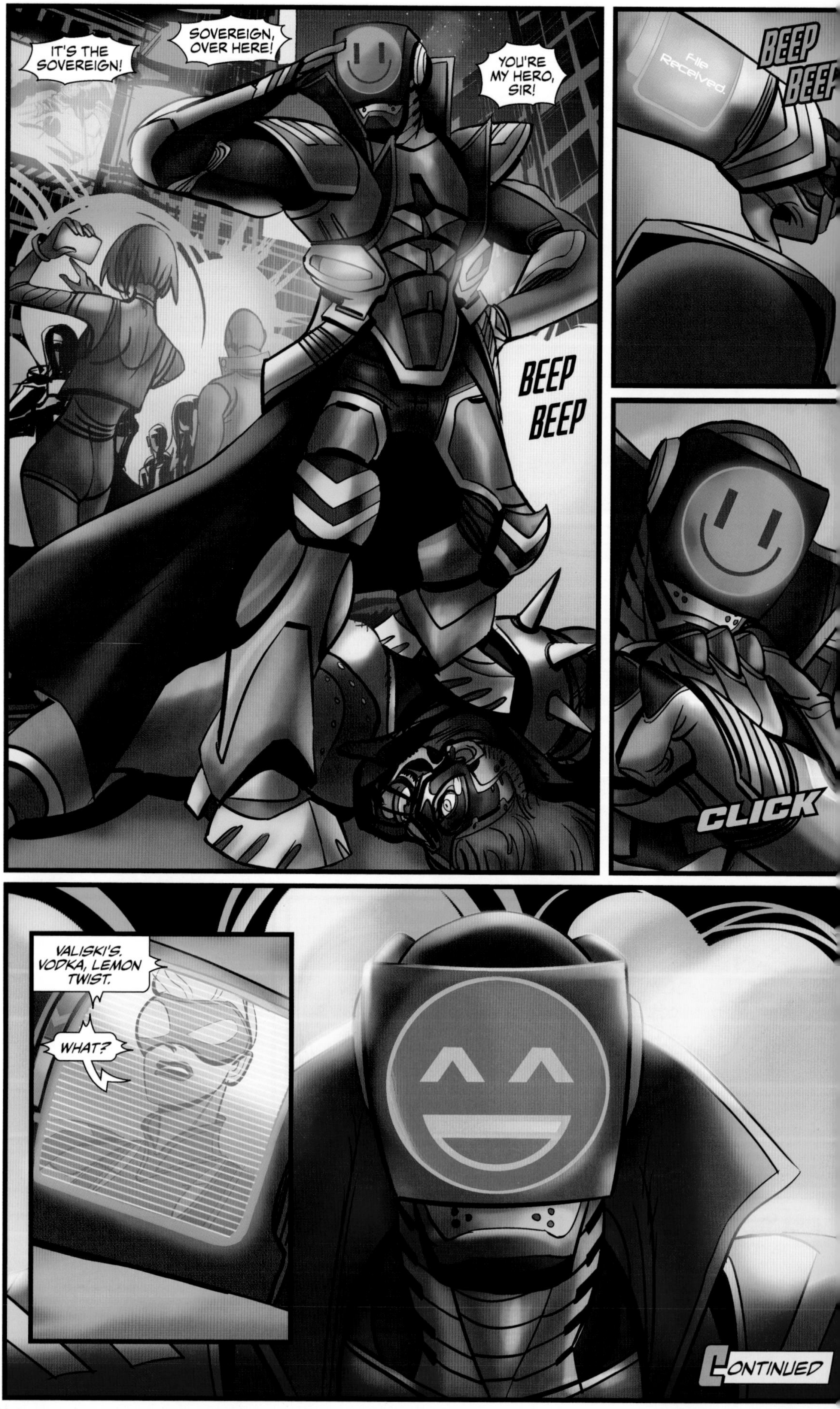
IT'S THE SOVEREIGN!
SOVEREIGN, OVER HERE!
YOU'RE MY HERO, SIR!
BEEP BEEP
File Received.
BEEP BEEP
CLICK
VALISKI'S. VODKA, LEMON TWIST.
WHAT?
CONTINUED

DARK HORSE BOOKS BRINGS YOU

THE BEST IN SCIENCE FICTION!

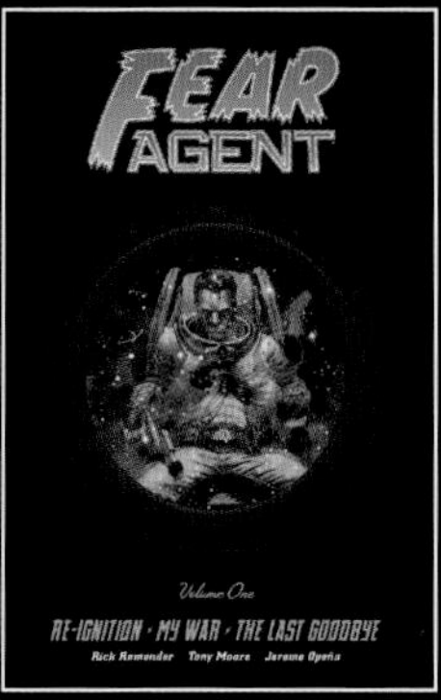
FEAR AGENT
Volume One
RE-IGNITION · MY WAR · THE LAST GOODBYE
Rick Remender Tony Moore Jerome Opeña

FEAR AGENT LIBRARY EDITION VOLUME 1

Rick Remender, Tony Moore, and others

Down-and-out alien exterminator Heath Huston stumbles upon a genocidal extraterrestrial plot against the human race. Now he must resume his role as the last Fear Agent.

ISBN 978-1-61655-005-9 | $49.99

FALLING SKIES

Paul Tobin and Juan Ferreyra

Following the devastating events of an alien invasion, professor Tom Mason and his sons combine forces with a militia group determined to wipe out the aliens and ensure the survival of the human race!

VOLUME 1 ISBN 978-1-59582-737-1 | $9.99
VOLUME 2: THE BATTLE OF FITCHBURG TPB ISBN 978-1-61655-014-1 | $9.99

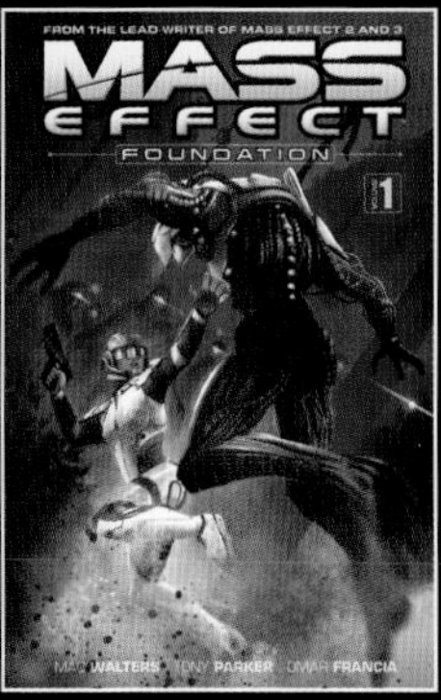
FROM THE LEAD WRITER OF MASS EFFECT 2 AND 3
MASS EFFECT
FOUNDATION
1

MASS EFFECT: FOUNDATION

Mac Walters, Jeremy Barlow, Tony Parker, and others

Continuing and expanding the story from the smash-hit video game series! From Mac Walters, lead writer of *Mass Effect 2* and *3*.

VOLUME 1 ISBN 978-1-61655-270-1 | $16.99
VOLUME 2 ISBN 978-1-61655-349-4 | $16.99
VOLUME 3 ISBN 978-1-61655-488-0 | $16.99

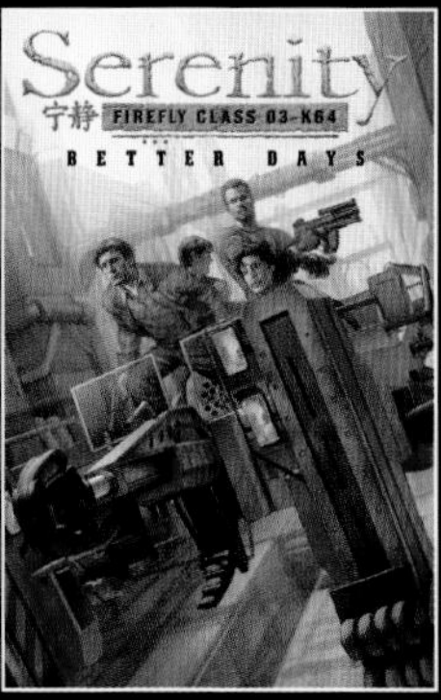
Serenity
宁静 FIREFLY CLASS 03-K64
BETTER DAYS

SERENITY VOLUME 1: THOSE LEFT BEHIND

Joss Whedon, Brett Mathews, Will Conrad, Adam Hughes, and Laura Martin

A previously unknown chapter in the lives of this favorite band of space brigands is told in this comics prequel of the *Serenity* feature film.

ISBN 978-1-59307-449-4 | $19.99

SERENITY VOLUME 2: BETTER DAYS AND OTHER STORIES

Joss Whedon, Will Conrad, Patton Oswalt, and others

The crew takes on a heist that promises a big payoff. But when someone is taken captive, the gang must put aside their enduring differences and work together, at the risk of losing their cash prize.

ISBN 978-1-59582-739-5 | $14.99

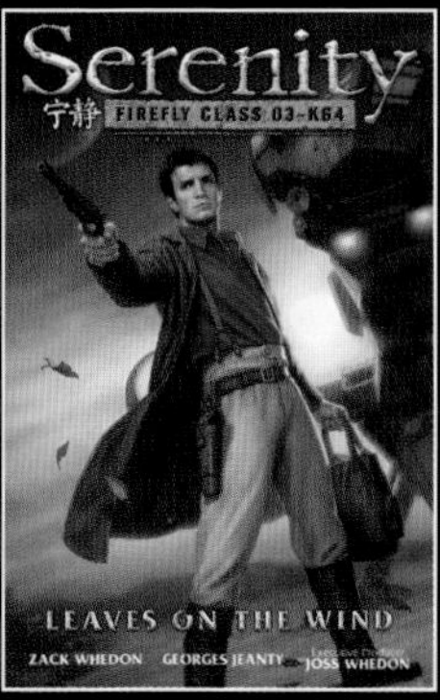
Serenity
宁静 FIREFLY CLASS 03-K64
LEAVES ON THE WIND
ZACK WHEDON GEORGES JEANTY JOSS WHEDON

SERENITY VOLUME 3: THE SHEPHERD'S TALE

Joss Whedon, Zack Whedon, and Chris Samnee

Who was Book before meeting Mal and the rest of the *Serenity* crew, how did he become one of their most trusted allies, and how did he find God in a bowl of soup?

ISBN 978-1-ISBN 59582-561-2 | $14.99

SERENITY VOLUME 4: LEAVES ON THE WIND

Zack Whedon, Georges Jeanty, Fábio Moon, and Karl Story

In the film *Serenity*, outlaw Malcolm Reynolds and his crew revealed the crimes against humanity undertaken by the sinister Alliance government. In this official follow-up, circumstances force the crew to come out of hiding, and one of their own is captured, setting them on another mission of rescue and resistance.

ISBN 978-1-61655-489-7 | $19.99

DARK HORSE BOOKS

AVAILABLE AT YOUR LOCAL COMICS SHOP OR BOOKSTORE! • To find a comics shop in your area, call 1-888-266-4226.
For more information or to order direct visit DarkHorse.com or call 1-800-862-0052 Mon.–Fri. 9 AM to 5 PM Pacific Time. Prices and availability subject to change without notice.

HARROW COUNTY™

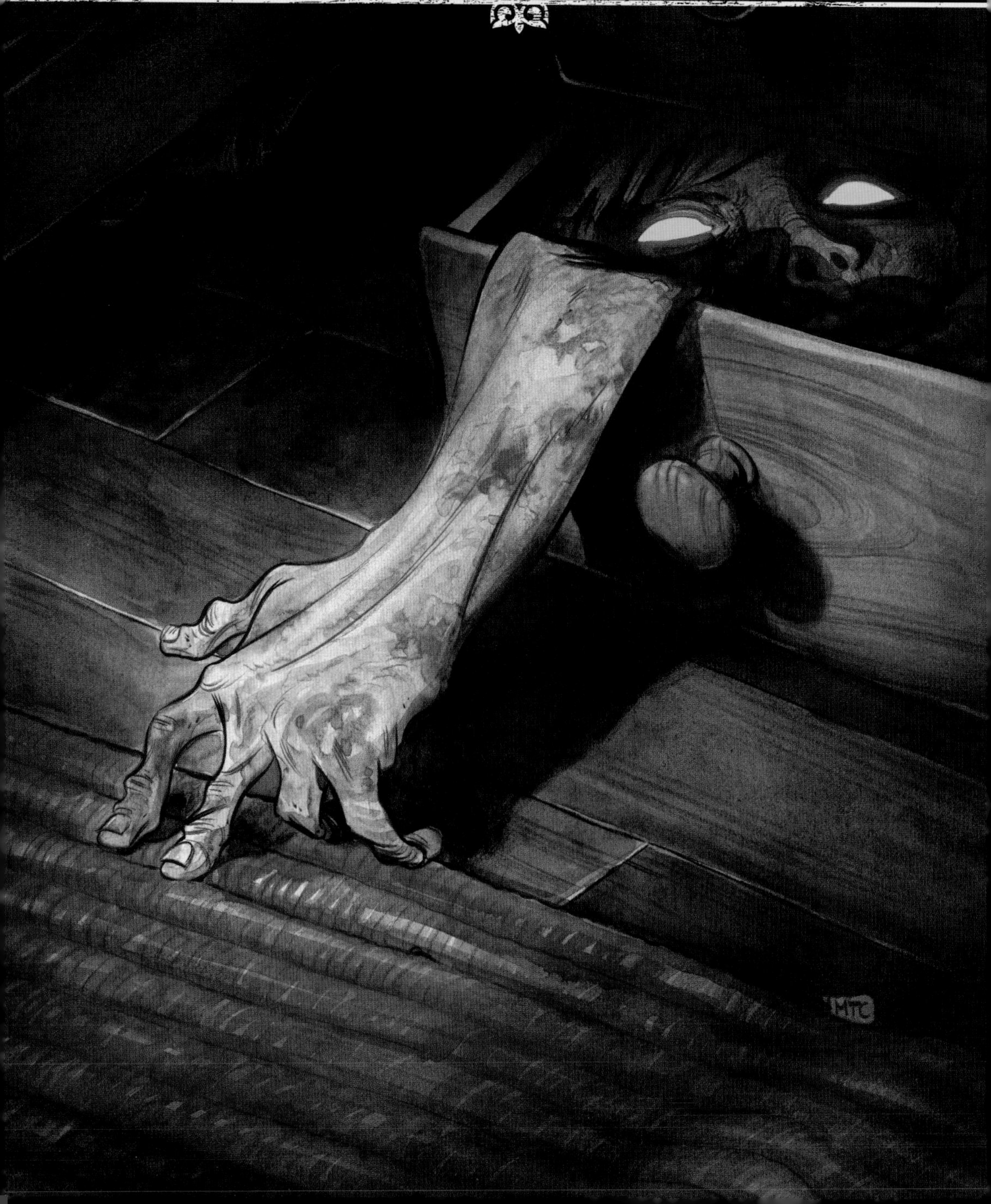
MTC

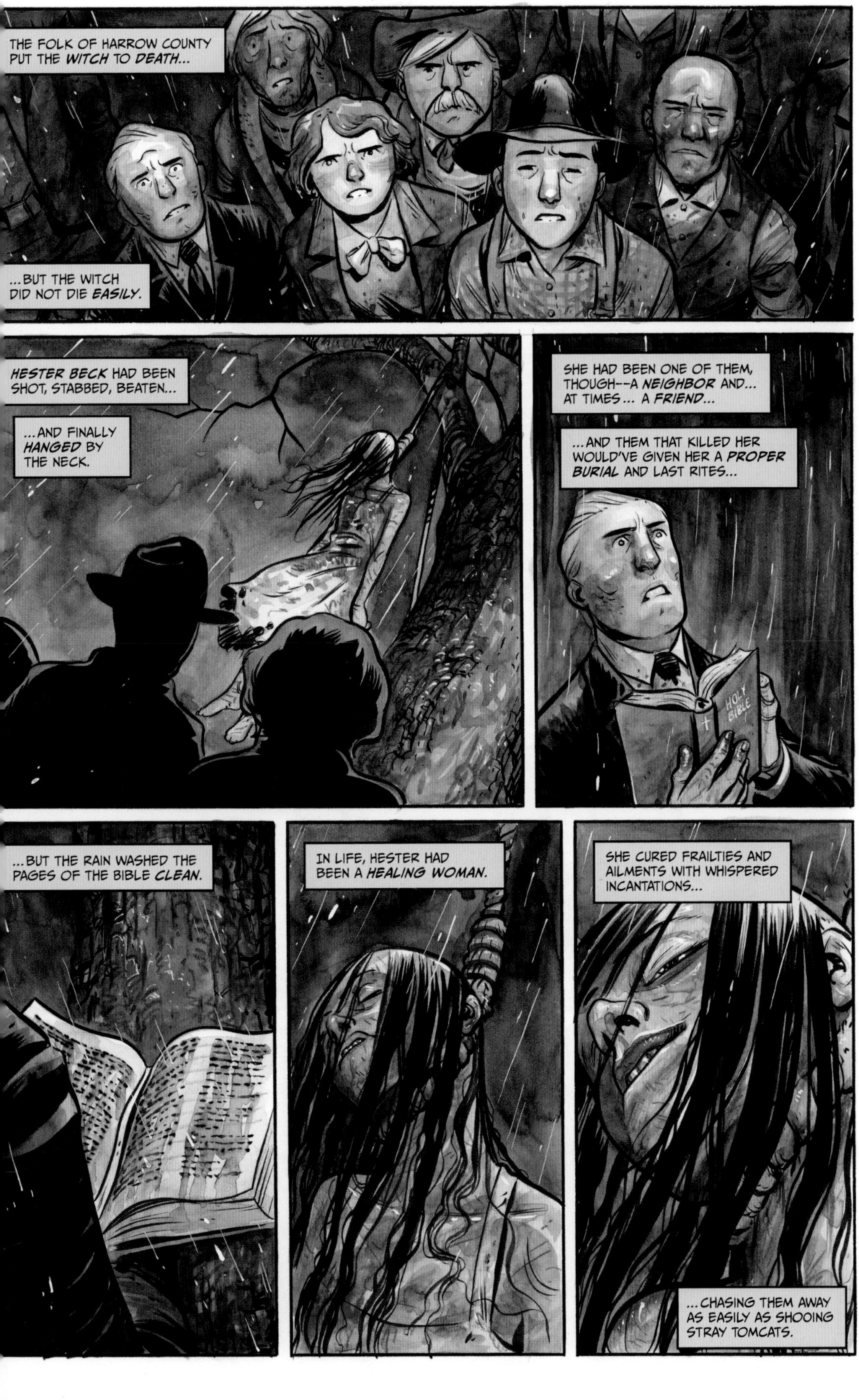
THE FOLK OF HARROW COUNTY PUT THE WITCH TO DEATH...
...BUT THE WITCH DID NOT DIE EASILY.
HESTER BECK HAD BEEN SHOT, STABBED, BEATEN...
...AND FINALLY HANGED BY THE NECK.
SHE HAD BEEN ONE OF THEM, THOUGH--A NEIGHBOR AND... AT TIMES... A FRIEND...
...AND THEM THAT KILLED HER WOULD'VE GIVEN HER A PROPER BURIAL AND LAST RITES...
HOLY BIBLE
...BUT THE RAIN WASHED THE PAGES OF THE BIBLE CLEAN.
IN LIFE, HESTER HAD BEEN A HEALING WOMAN.
SHE CURED FRAILTIES AND AILMENTS WITH WHISPERED INCANTATIONS...
...CHASING THEM AWAY AS EASILY AS SHOOING STRAY TOMCATS.

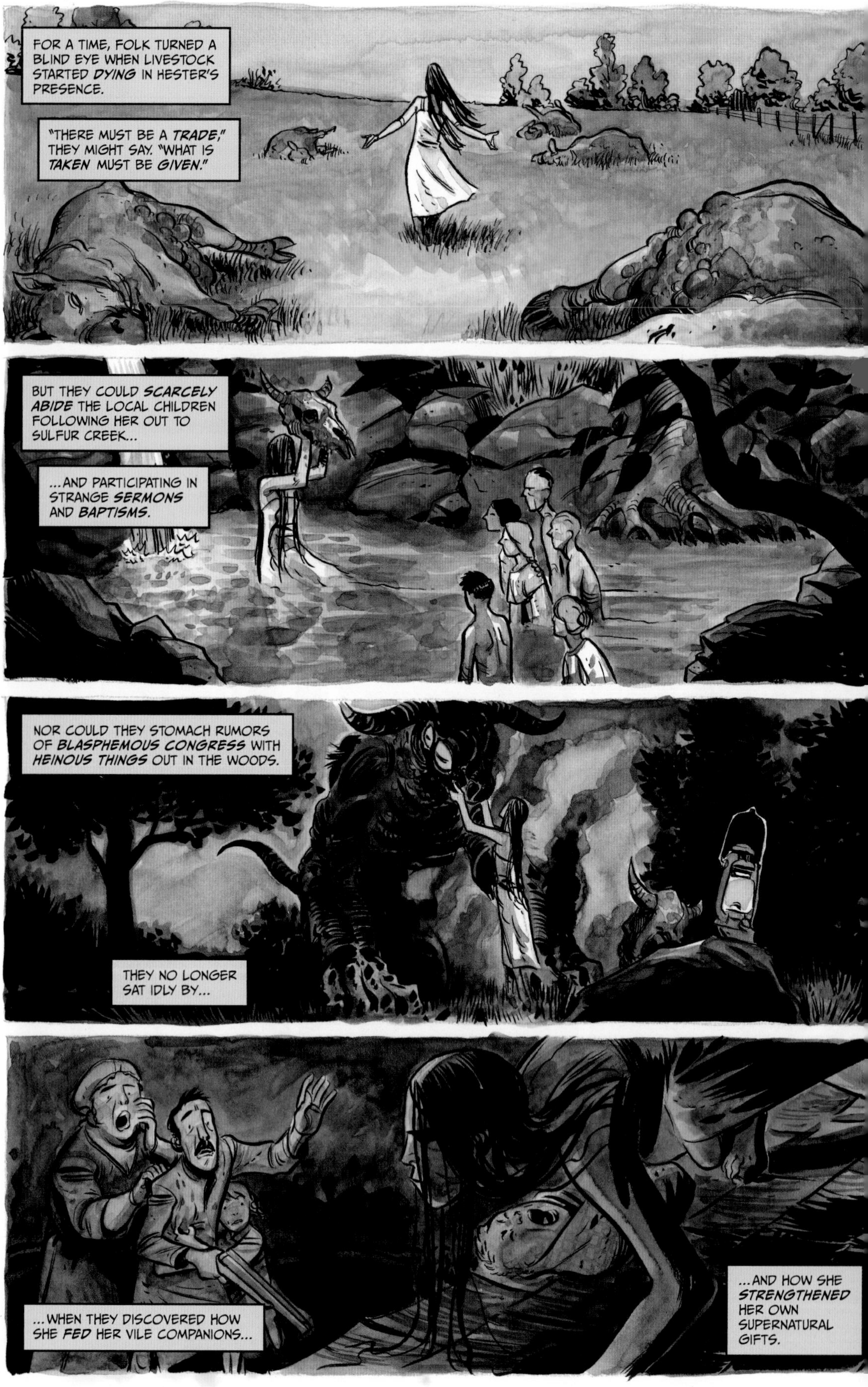
FOR A TIME, FOLK TURNED A BLIND EYE WHEN LIVESTOCK STARTED *DYING* IN HESTER'S PRESENCE.
"THERE MUST BE A *TRADE,*" THEY MIGHT SAY. "WHAT IS *TAKEN* MUST BE *GIVEN.*"
BUT THEY COULD *SCARCELY ABIDE* THE LOCAL CHILDREN FOLLOWING HER OUT TO SULFUR CREEK...
...AND PARTICIPATING IN STRANGE *SERMONS* AND *BAPTISMS.*
NOR COULD THEY STOMACH RUMORS OF *BLASPHEMOUS CONGRESS* WITH *HEINOUS THINGS* OUT IN THE WOODS.
THEY NO LONGER SAT IDLY BY...
...WHEN THEY DISCOVERED HOW SHE *FED* HER VILE COMPANIONS...
...AND HOW SHE *STRENGTHENED* HER OWN SUPERNATURAL GIFTS.

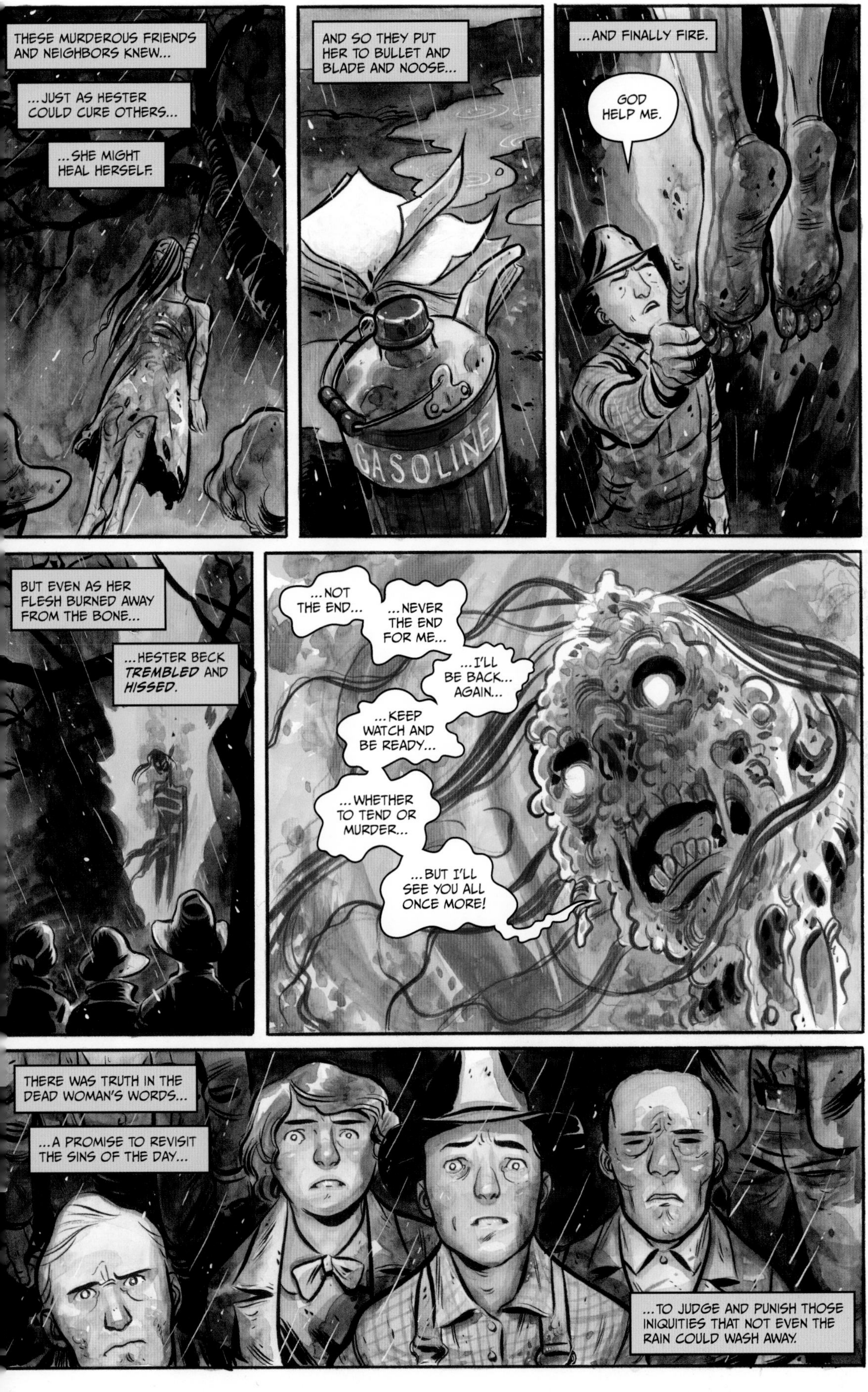
THESE MURDEROUS FRIENDS AND NEIGHBORS KNEW...
...JUST AS HESTER COULD CURE OTHERS...
...SHE MIGHT HEAL HERSELF.
AND SO THEY PUT HER TO BULLET AND BLADE AND NOOSE...
GASOLINE
...AND FINALLY FIRE.
GOD HELP ME.
BUT EVEN AS HER FLESH BURNED AWAY FROM THE BONE...
...HESTER BECK *TREMBLED* AND *HISSED*.
...NOT THE END...
...NEVER THE END FOR ME...
...I'LL BE BACK... AGAIN...
...KEEP WATCH AND BE READY...
...WHETHER TO TEND OR MURDER...
...BUT I'LL SEE YOU ALL ONCE MORE!
THERE WAS TRUTH IN THE DEAD WOMAN'S WORDS...
...A PROMISE TO REVISIT THE SINS OF THE DAY...
...TO JUDGE AND PUNISH THOSE INIQUITIES THAT NOT EVEN THE RAIN COULD WASH AWAY.

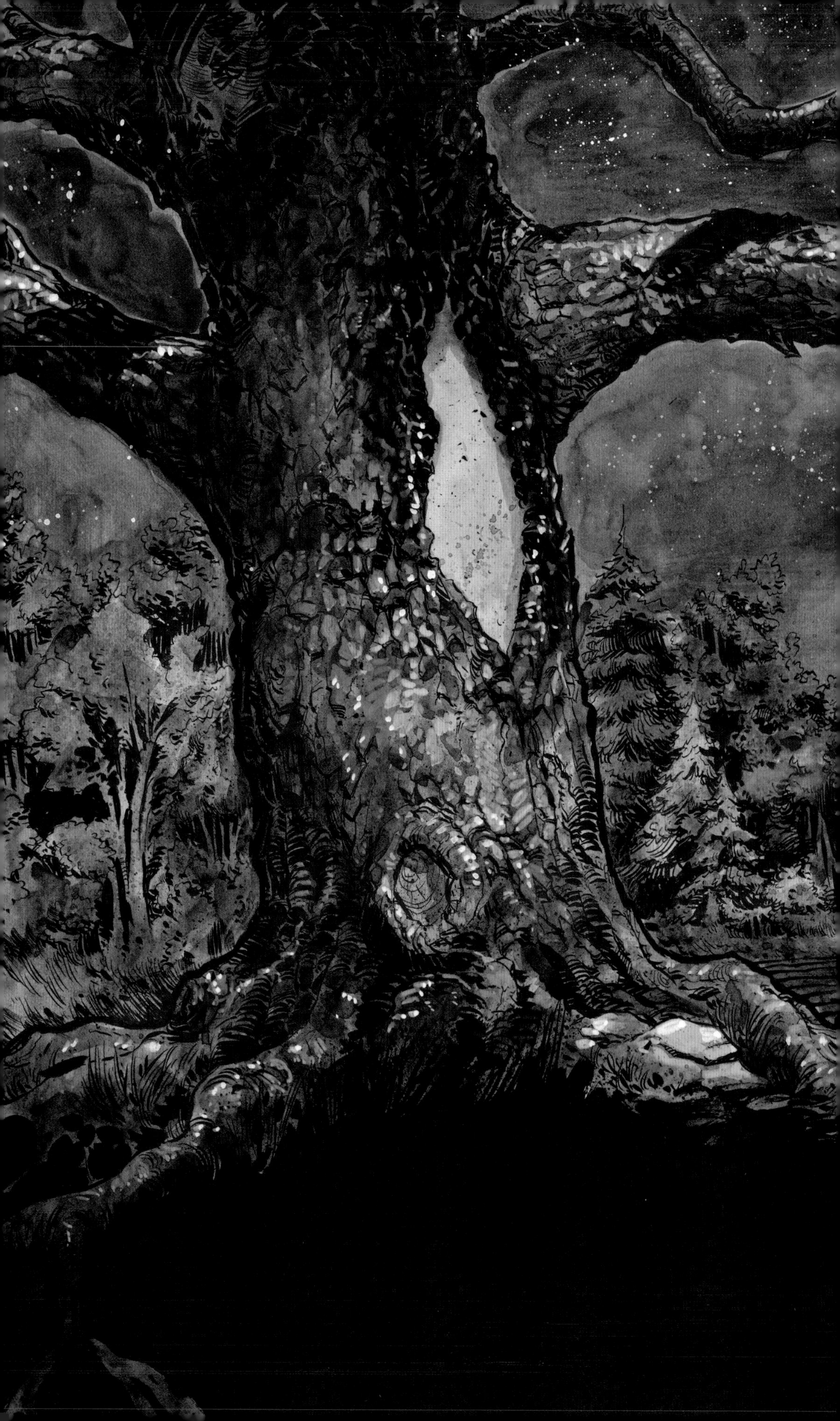

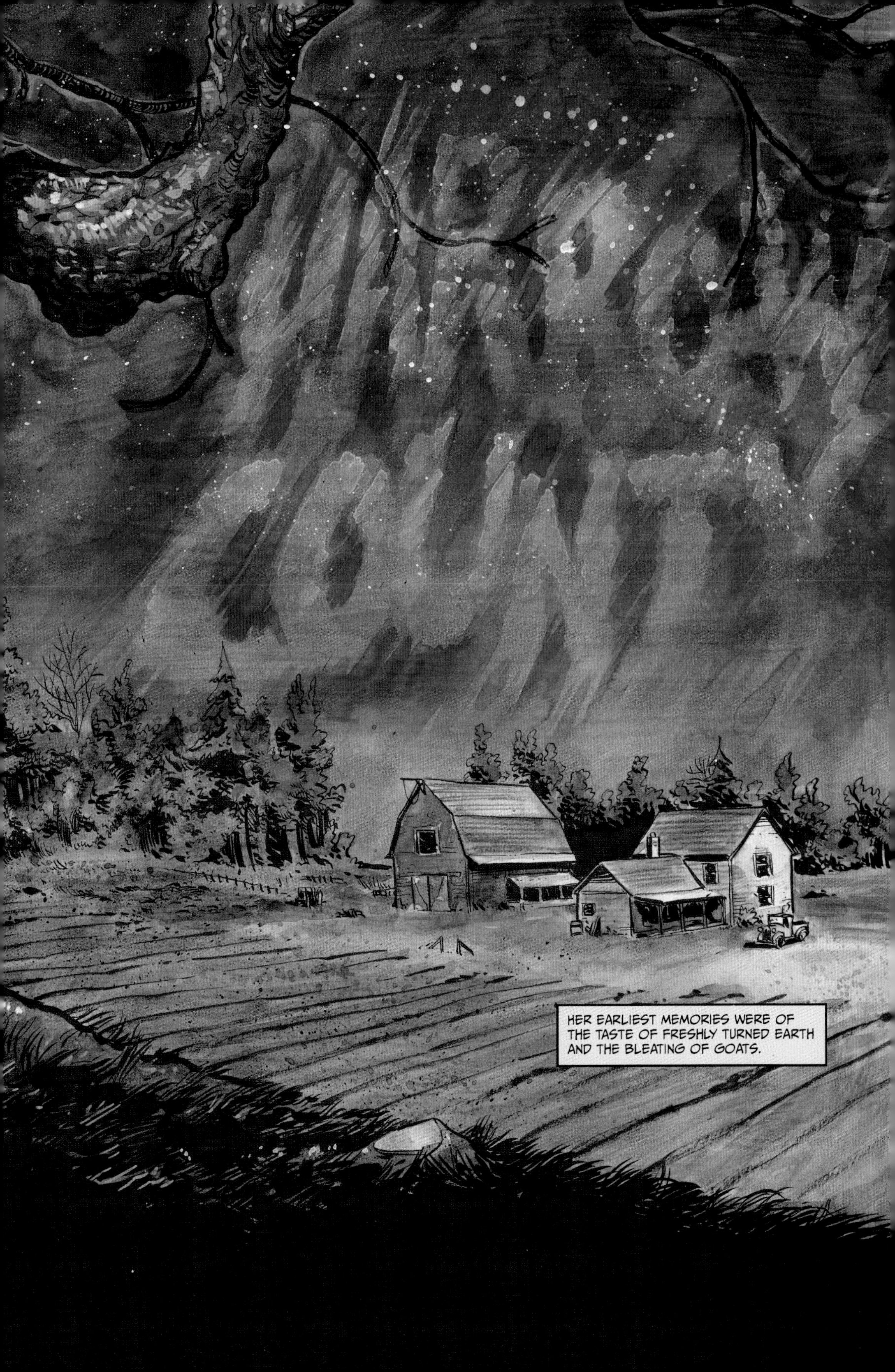
HER EARLIEST MEMORIES WERE OF THE TASTE OF FRESHLY TURNED EARTH AND THE BLEATING OF GOATS.

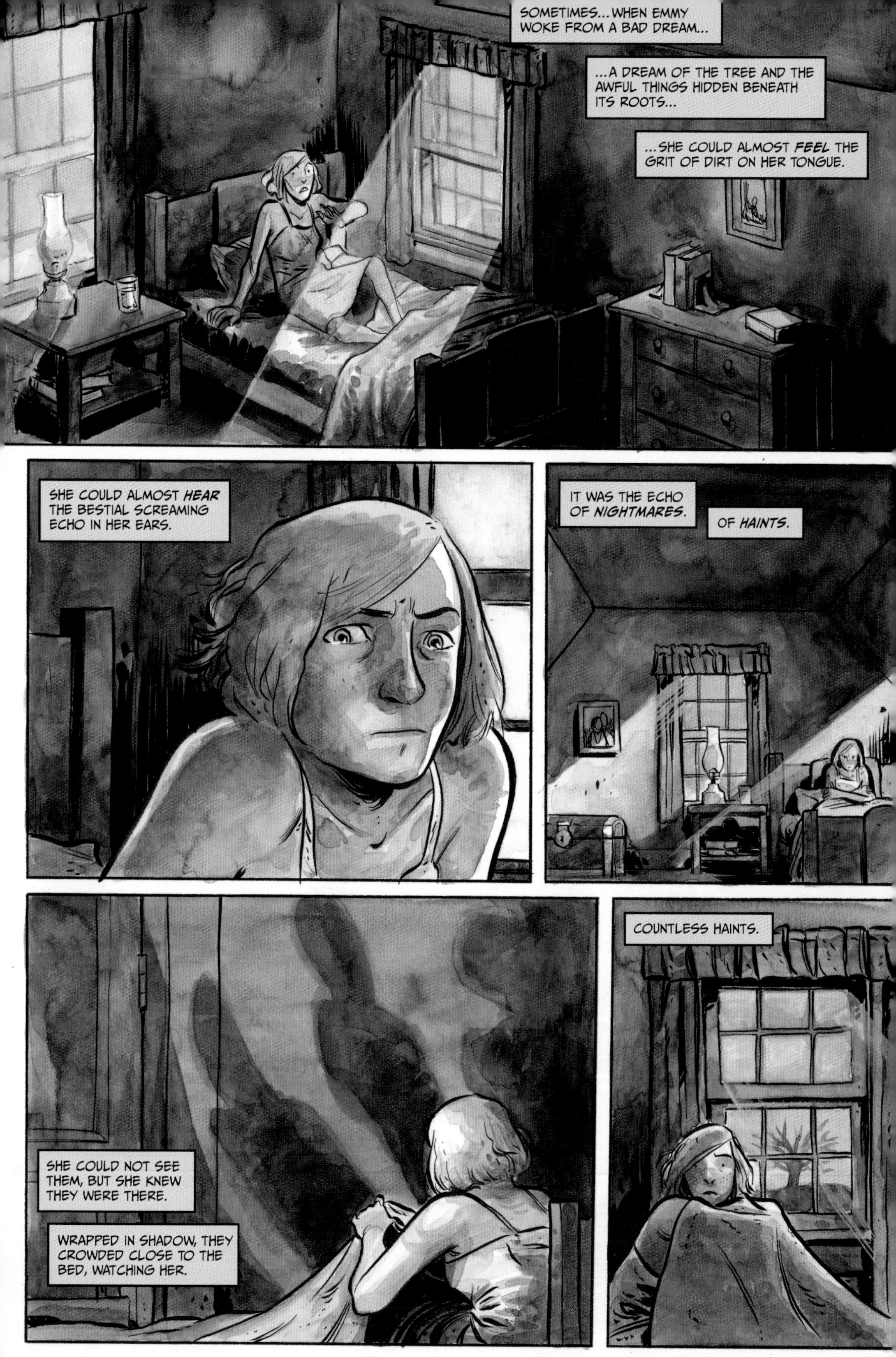
SOMETIMES... WHEN EMMY WOKE FROM A BAD DREAM...
...A DREAM OF THE TREE AND THE AWFUL THINGS HIDDEN BENEATH ITS ROOTS...
...SHE COULD ALMOST FEEL THE GRIT OF DIRT ON HER TONGUE.
SHE COULD ALMOST HEAR THE BESTIAL SCREAMING ECHO IN HER EARS.
IT WAS THE ECHO OF NIGHTMARES.
OF HAINTS.
SHE COULD NOT SEE THEM, BUT SHE KNEW THEY WERE THERE.
WRAPPED IN SHADOW, THEY CROWDED CLOSE TO THE BED, WATCHING HER.
COUNTLESS HAINTS.

AND THE TREE WATCHED OVER THEM ALL.

AT THE HILL'S SUMMIT, THE CROOKED OAK STOOD IN STARK SILHOUETTE.

SHROUDED IN SCUPPERNONG VINES, ITS BLACK BRANCHES VANISHED INTO THE DARKNESS, ALMOST AS IF *GROWING* INTO THE NIGHT ITSELF.

YEARS AGO, OR SO EMMY HAD BEEN TOLD, THE OAK HAD BEEN STRUCK BY LIGHTNING.

THE TREE HAD NOT GROWN SINCE, AND A ROTTING HOLLOW NOW YAWNED IN THE TRUNK.

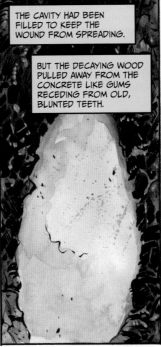

THE CAVITY HAD BEEN FILLED TO KEEP THE WOUND FROM SPREADING.

BUT THE DECAYING WOOD PULLED AWAY FROM THE CONCRETE LIKE GUMS RECEDING FROM OLD, BLUNTED TEETH.

EMMY *HATED* THAT TREE, AND SHE *FEARED* IT, TOO.

FEARED ITS *SECRETS*.

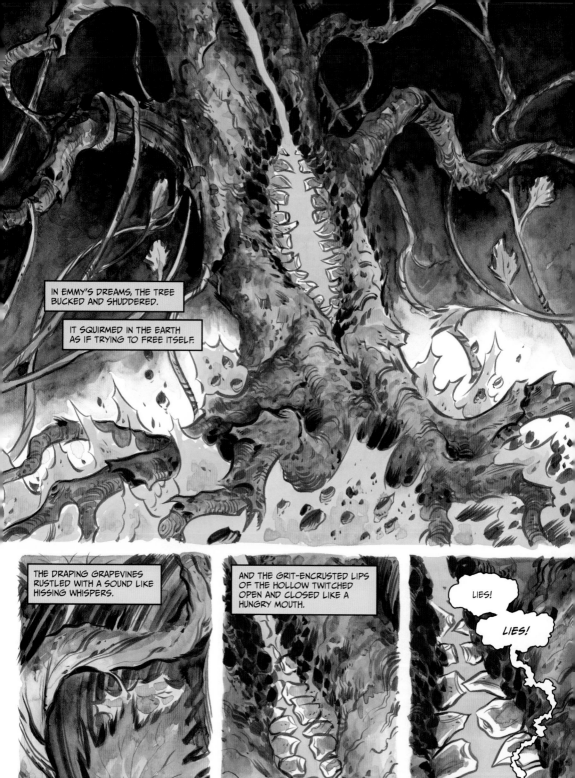

IN EMMY'S DREAMS, THE TREE BUCKED AND SHUDDERED.

IT SQUIRMED IN THE EARTH AS IF TRYING TO FREE ITSELF.

THE DRAPING GRAPEVINES RUSTLED WITH A SOUND LIKE HISSING WHISPERS.

AND THE GRIT-ENCRUSTED LIPS OF THE HOLLOW TWITCHED OPEN AND CLOSED LIKE A HUNGRY MOUTH.

LIES!

LIES!

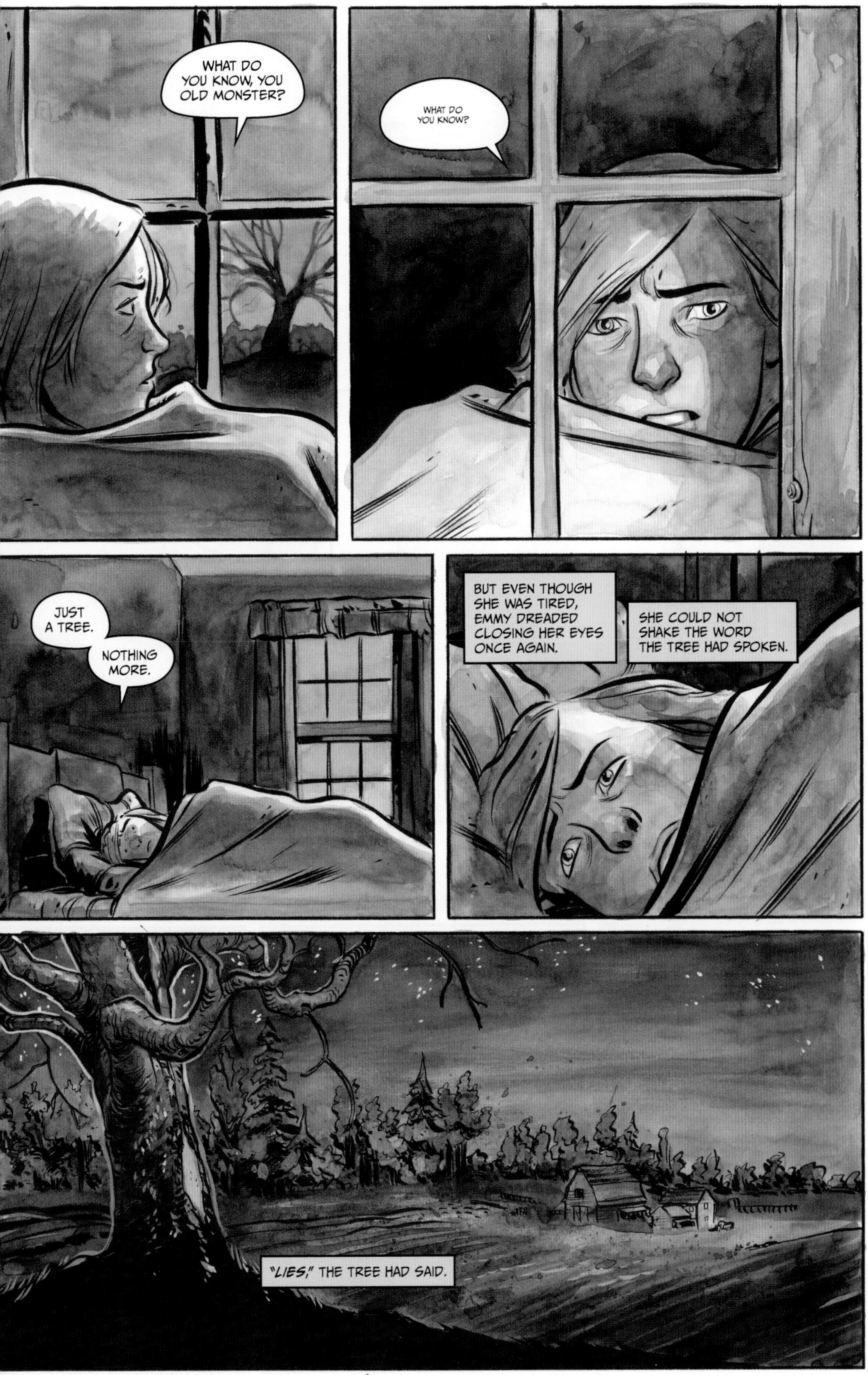
WHAT DO YOU KNOW, YOU OLD MONSTER?
WHAT DO YOU KNOW?
JUST A TREE.
NOTHING MORE.
BUT EVEN THOUGH SHE WAS TIRED, EMMY DREADED CLOSING HER EYES ONCE AGAIN.
SHE COULD NOT SHAKE THE WORD THE TREE HAD SPOKEN.
"LIES," THE TREE HAD SAID.

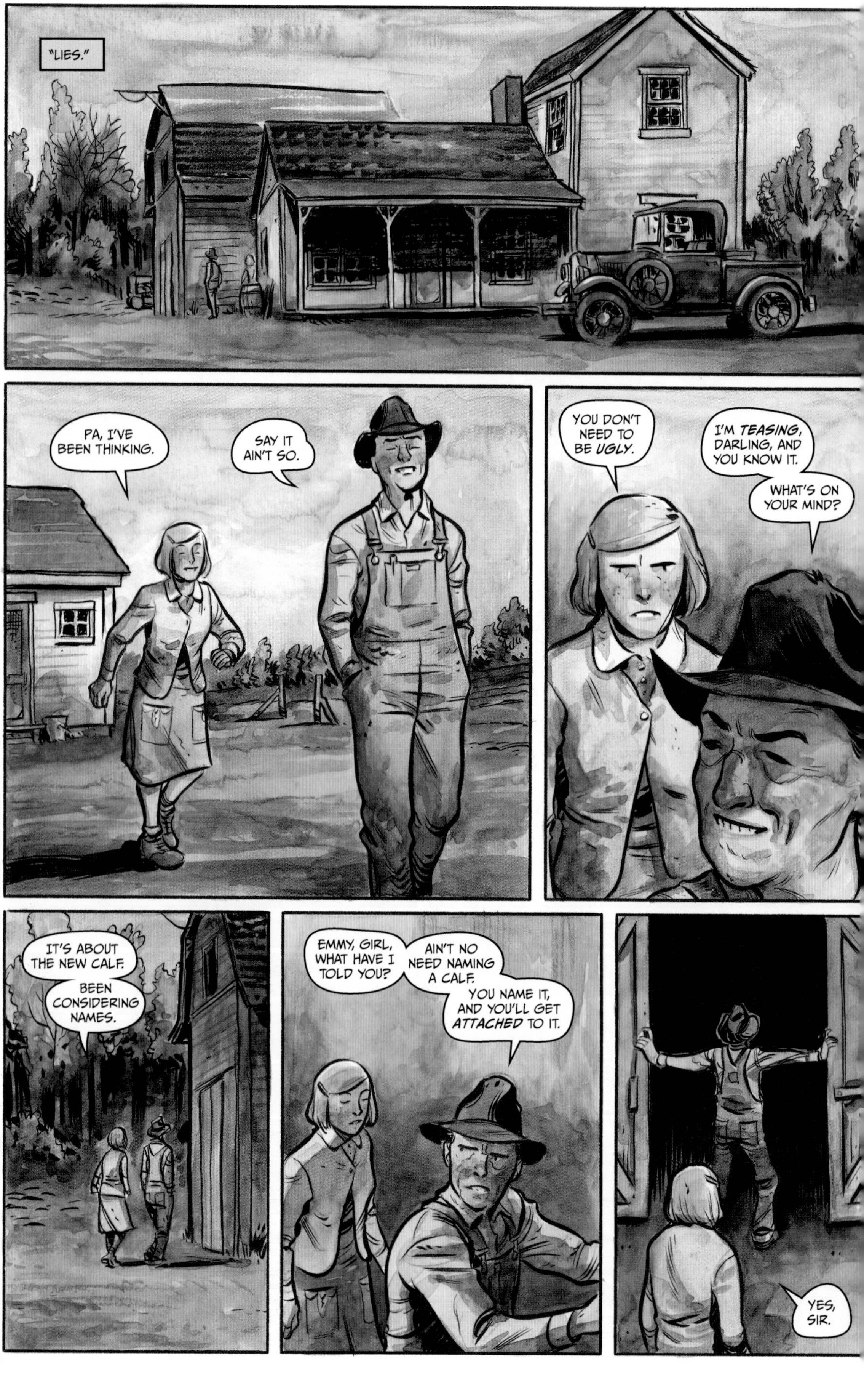
"LIES."
PA, I'VE BEEN THINKING.
SAY IT AIN'T SO.
YOU DON'T NEED TO BE *UGLY*.
I'M *TEASING*, DARLING, AND YOU KNOW IT.
WHAT'S ON YOUR MIND?
IT'S ABOUT THE NEW CALF.
BEEN CONSIDERING NAMES.
EMMY, GIRL, WHAT HAVE I TOLD YOU?
AIN'T NO NEED NAMING A CALF.
YOU NAME IT, AND YOU'LL GET *ATTACHED* TO IT.
YES, SIR.

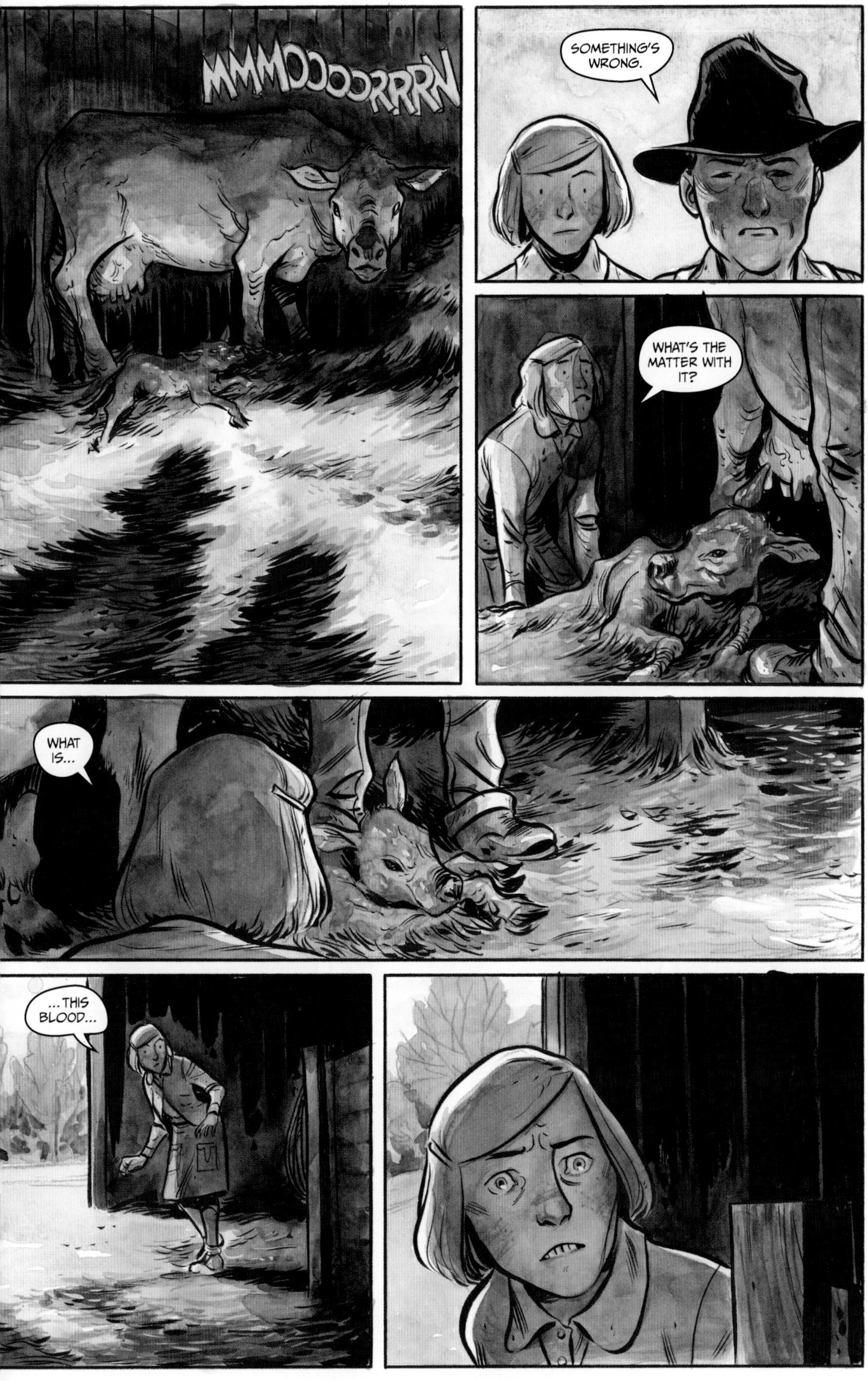
MMMOOOORRRRN
SOMETHING'S WRONG.
WHAT'S THE MATTER WITH IT?
WHAT IS...
...THIS BLOOD...

THERE'S ANOTHER ONE. IT'S...

...DEAD, I THINK.

AND THIS ONE'S NOT FAR BEHIND. BUT THERE'S NO SENSE IN LETTING HIM SUFFER.

NO SENSE NAMING A CALF.

I'LL FETCH MY GUN.

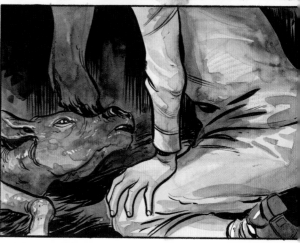

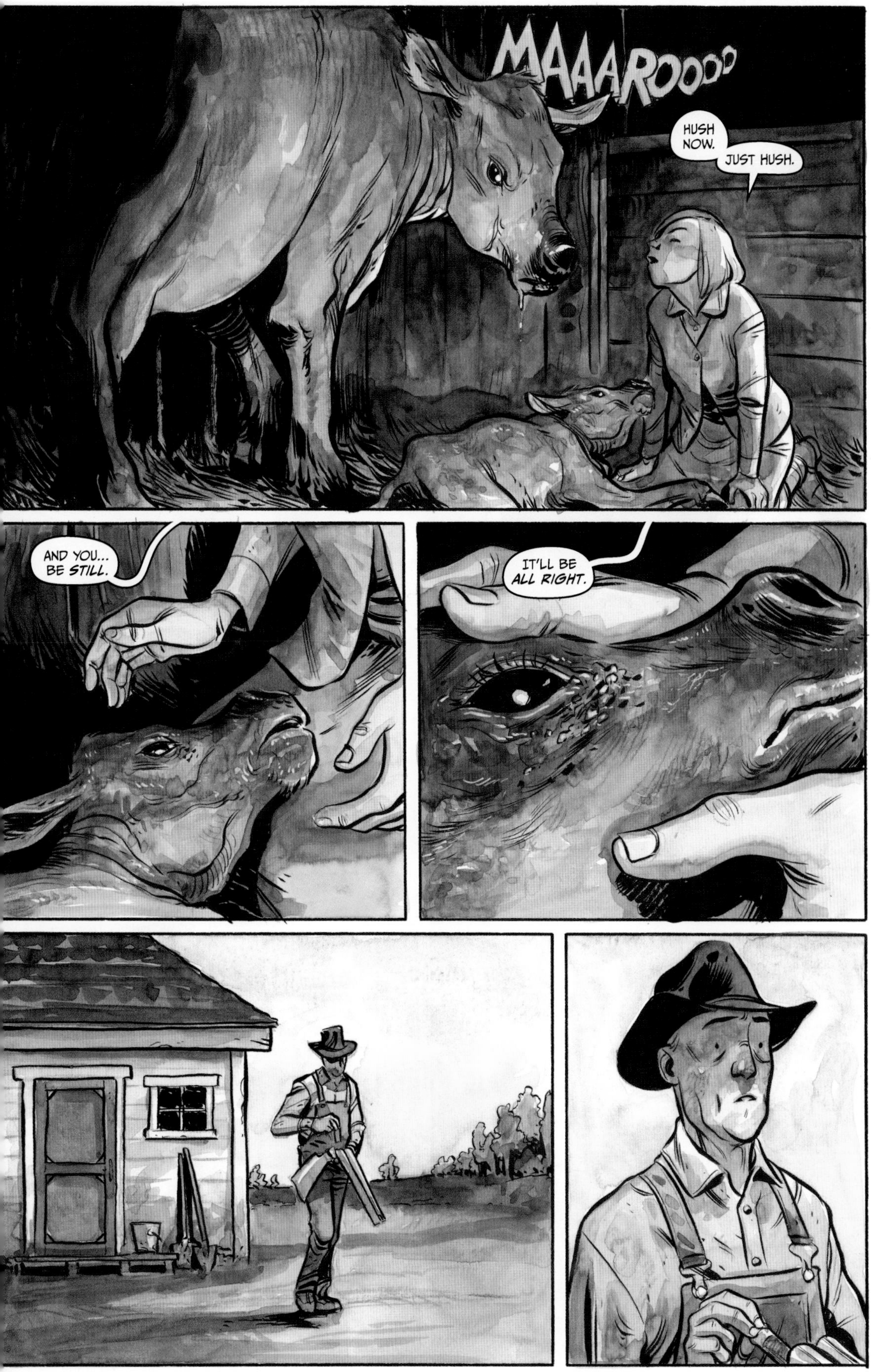
MAAAROOOO
HUSH NOW.
JUST HUSH.
AND YOU... BE STILL.
IT'LL BE ALL RIGHT.

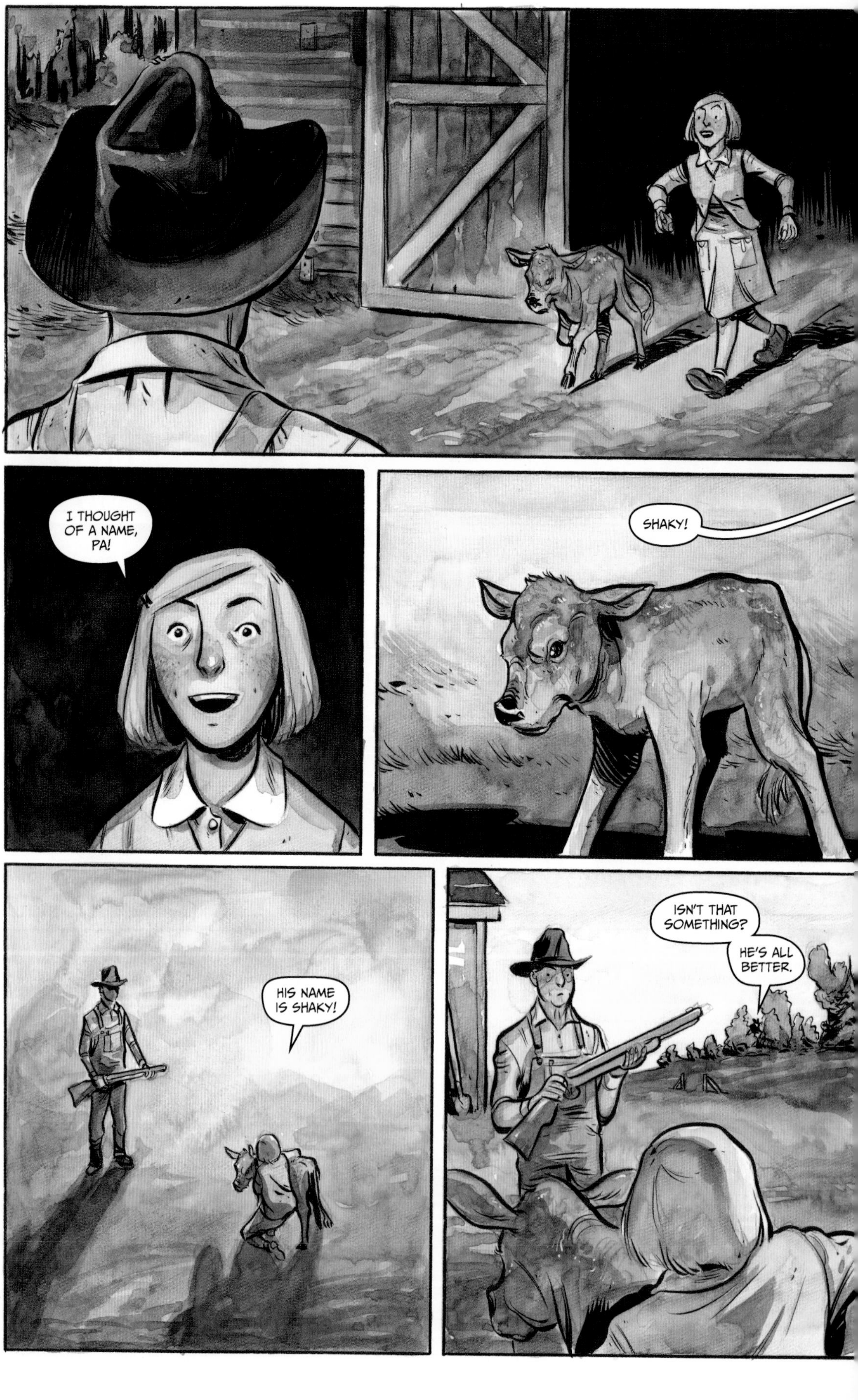
I THOUGHT OF A NAME, PA!
SHAKY!
HIS NAME IS SHAKY!
ISN'T THAT SOMETHING?
HE'S ALL BETTER.

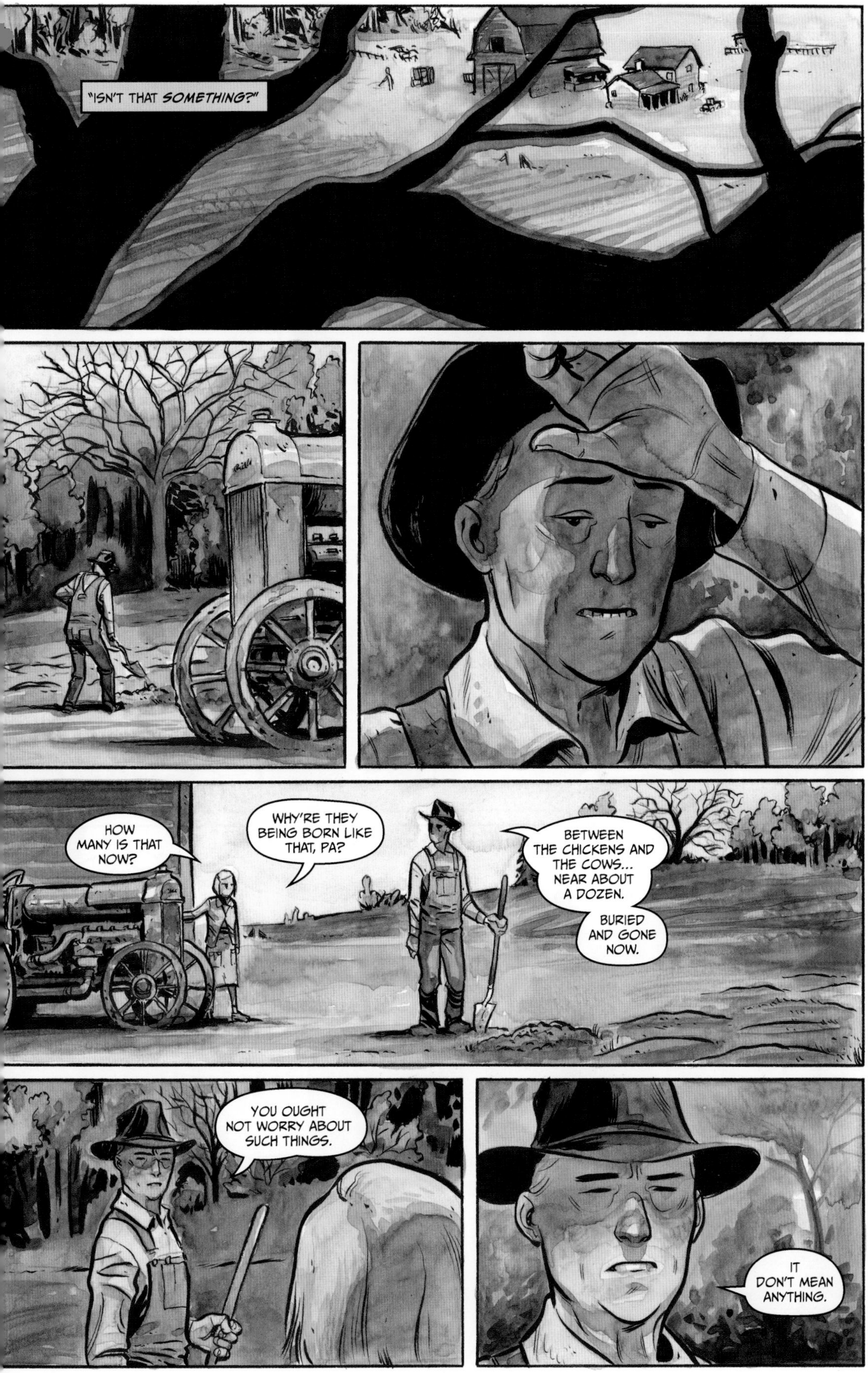
"ISN'T THAT SOMETHING?"
HOW MANY IS THAT NOW?
WHY'RE THEY BEING BORN LIKE THAT, PA?
BETWEEN THE CHICKENS AND THE COWS... NEAR ABOUT A DOZEN.
BURIED AND GONE NOW.
YOU OUGHT NOT WORRY ABOUT SUCH THINGS.
IT DON'T MEAN ANYTHING.

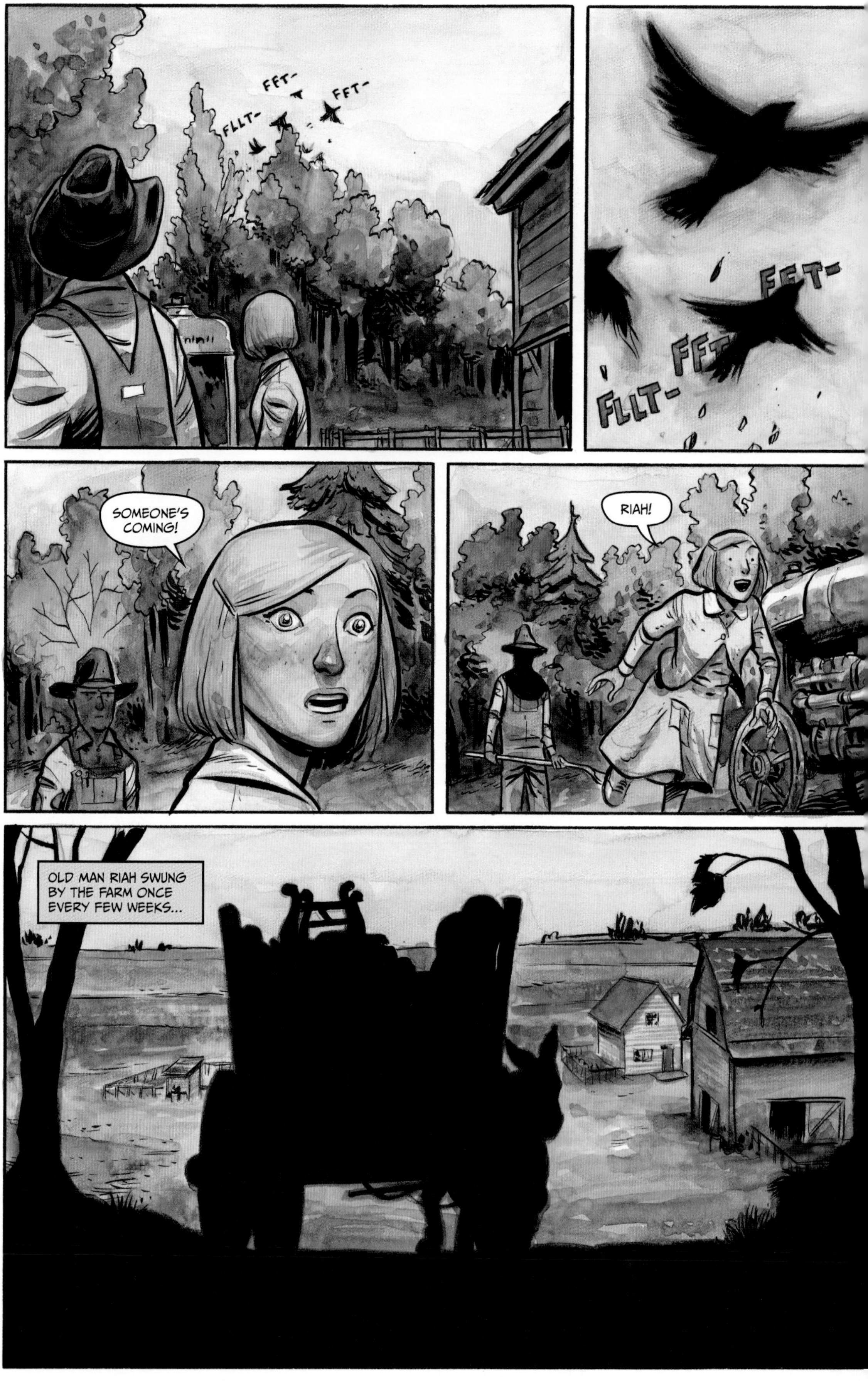
FLLT-
FFT-
FFT-
FFT-
FFT-
FLLT-
SOMEONE'S COMING!
RIAH!
OLD MAN RIAH SWUNG BY THE FARM ONCE EVERY FEW WEEKS...

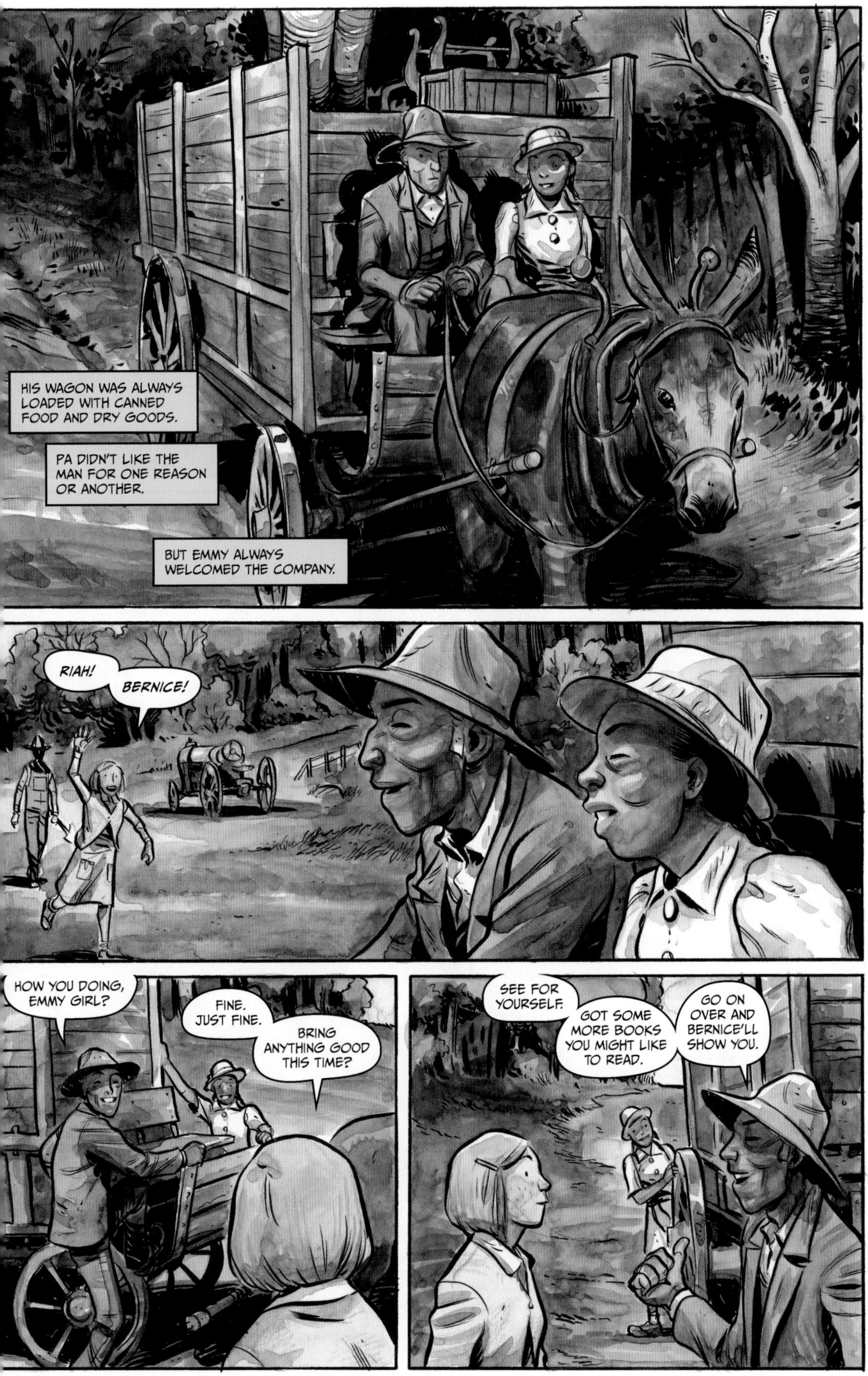
HIS WAGON WAS ALWAYS LOADED WITH CANNED FOOD AND DRY GOODS.
PA DIDN'T LIKE THE MAN FOR ONE REASON OR ANOTHER.
BUT EMMY ALWAYS WELCOMED THE COMPANY.
RIAH!
BERNICE!
HOW YOU DOING, EMMY GIRL?
FINE. JUST FINE.
BRING ANYTHING GOOD THIS TIME?
SEE FOR YOURSELF.
GOT SOME MORE BOOKS YOU MIGHT LIKE TO READ.
GO ON OVER AND BERNICE'LL SHOW YOU.

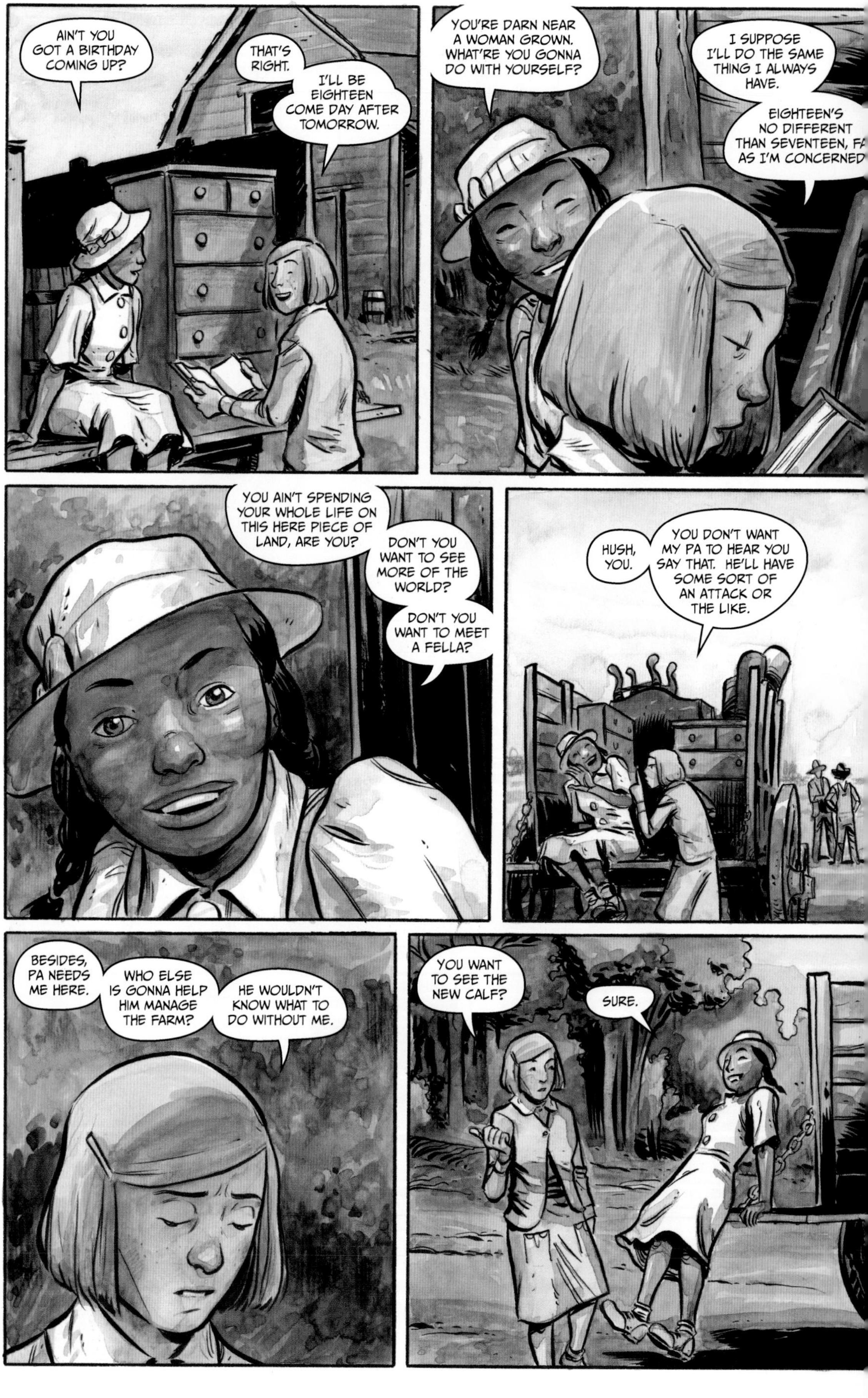
AIN'T YOU GOT A BIRTHDAY COMING UP?
THAT'S RIGHT.
I'LL BE EIGHTEEN COME DAY AFTER TOMORROW.
YOU'RE DARN NEAR A WOMAN GROWN. WHAT'RE YOU GONNA DO WITH YOURSELF?
I SUPPOSE I'LL DO THE SAME THING I ALWAYS HAVE.
EIGHTEEN'S NO DIFFERENT THAN SEVENTEEN, FA
AS I'M CONCERNED
YOU AIN'T SPENDING YOUR WHOLE LIFE ON THIS HERE PIECE OF LAND, ARE YOU?
DON'T YOU WANT TO SEE MORE OF THE WORLD?
DON'T YOU WANT TO MEET A FELLA?
HUSH, YOU.
YOU DON'T WANT MY PA TO HEAR YOU SAY THAT. HE'LL HAVE SOME SORT OF AN ATTACK OR THE LIKE.
BESIDES, PA NEEDS ME HERE.
WHO ELSE IS GONNA HELP HIM MANAGE THE FARM?
HE WOULDN'T KNOW WHAT TO DO WITHOUT ME.
YOU WANT TO SEE THE NEW CALF?
SURE.

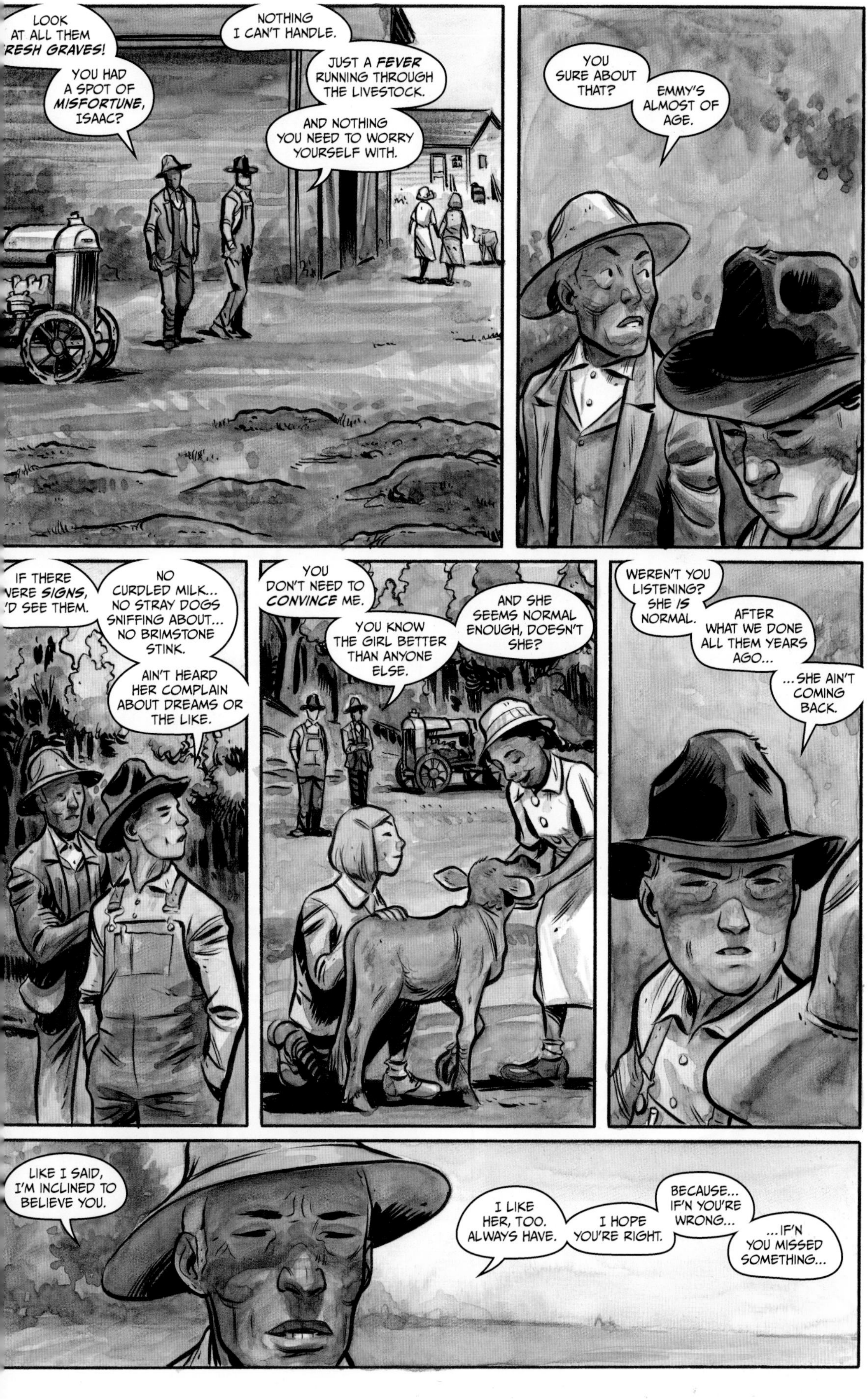
LOOK AT ALL THEM FRESH GRAVES!
YOU HAD A SPOT OF MISFORTUNE, ISAAC?
NOTHING I CAN'T HANDLE.
JUST A FEVER RUNNING THROUGH THE LIVESTOCK.
AND NOTHING YOU NEED TO WORRY YOURSELF WITH.
YOU SURE ABOUT THAT?
EMMY'S ALMOST OF AGE.
IF THERE WERE SIGNS, I'D SEE THEM.
NO CURDLED MILK... NO STRAY DOGS SNIFFING ABOUT... NO BRIMSTONE STINK.
AIN'T HEARD HER COMPLAIN ABOUT DREAMS OR THE LIKE.
YOU DON'T NEED TO CONVINCE ME.
YOU KNOW THE GIRL BETTER THAN ANYONE ELSE.
AND SHE SEEMS NORMAL ENOUGH, DOESN'T SHE?
WEREN'T YOU LISTENING? SHE IS NORMAL.
AFTER WHAT WE DONE ALL THEM YEARS AGO...
...SHE AIN'T COMING BACK.
LIKE I SAID, I'M INCLINED TO BELIEVE YOU.
I LIKE HER, TOO. ALWAYS HAVE.
I HOPE YOU'RE RIGHT.
BECAUSE... IF'N YOU'RE WRONG...
...IF'N YOU MISSED SOMETHING...

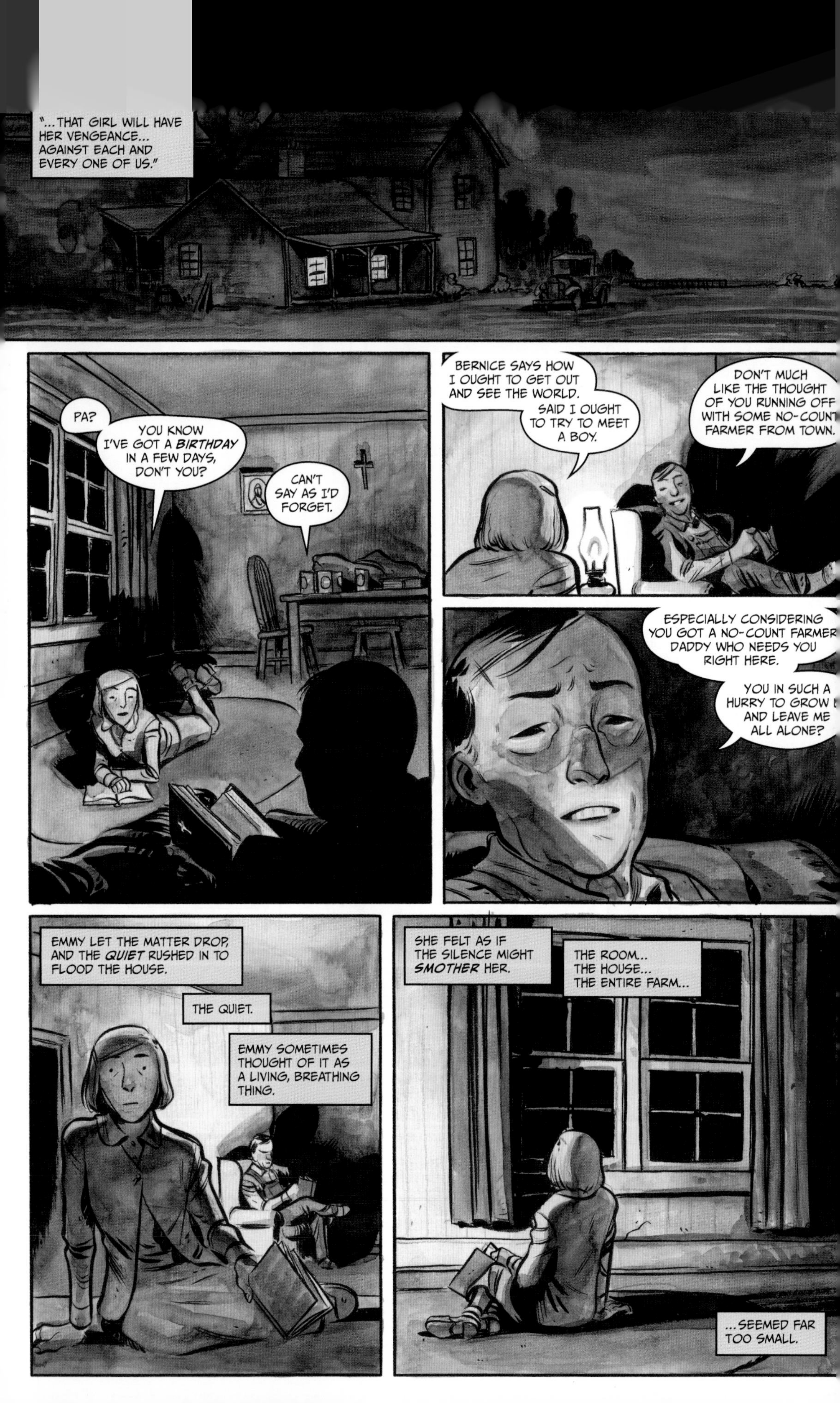
"...THAT GIRL WILL HAVE HER VENGEANCE... AGAINST EACH AND EVERY ONE OF US."
PA?
YOU KNOW I'VE GOT A *BIRTHDAY* IN A FEW DAYS, DON'T YOU?
CAN'T SAY AS I'D FORGET.
BERNICE SAYS HOW I OUGHT TO GET OUT AND SEE THE WORLD.
SAID I OUGHT TO TRY TO MEET A BOY.
DON'T MUCH LIKE THE THOUGHT OF YOU RUNNING OFF WITH SOME NO-COUNT FARMER FROM TOWN.
ESPECIALLY CONSIDERING YOU GOT A NO-COUNT FARMER DADDY WHO NEEDS YOU RIGHT HERE.
YOU IN SUCH A HURRY TO GROW AND LEAVE ME ALL ALONE?
EMMY LET THE MATTER DROP, AND THE *QUIET* RUSHED IN TO FLOOD THE HOUSE.
THE QUIET.
EMMY SOMETIMES THOUGHT OF IT AS A LIVING, BREATHING THING.
SHE FELT AS IF THE SILENCE MIGHT *SMOTHER* HER.
THE ROOM... THE HOUSE... THE ENTIRE FARM...
...SEEMED FAR TOO SMALL.

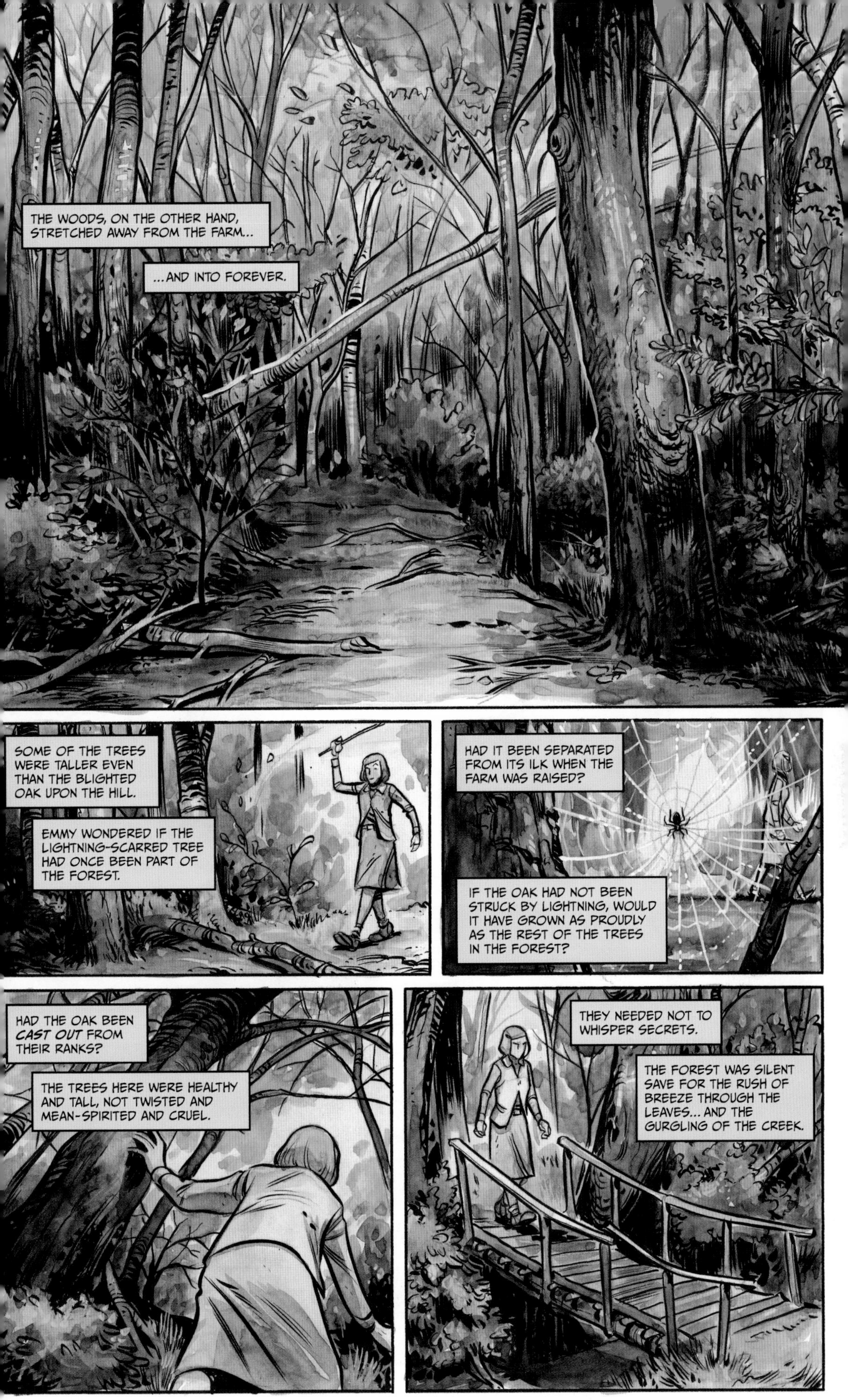
THE WOODS, ON THE OTHER HAND, STRETCHED AWAY FROM THE FARM...
...AND INTO FOREVER.
SOME OF THE TREES WERE TALLER EVEN THAN THE BLIGHTED OAK UPON THE HILL.
EMMY WONDERED IF THE LIGHTNING-SCARRED TREE HAD ONCE BEEN PART OF THE FOREST.
HAD IT BEEN SEPARATED FROM ITS ILK WHEN THE FARM WAS RAISED?
IF THE OAK HAD NOT BEEN STRUCK BY LIGHTNING, WOULD IT HAVE GROWN AS PROUDLY AS THE REST OF THE TREES IN THE FOREST?
HAD THE OAK BEEN *CAST OUT* FROM THEIR RANKS?
THE TREES HERE WERE HEALTHY AND TALL, NOT TWISTED AND MEAN-SPIRITED AND CRUEL.
THEY NEEDED NOT TO WHISPER SECRETS.
THE FOREST WAS SILENT SAVE FOR THE RUSH OF BREEZE THROUGH THE LEAVES... AND THE GURGLING OF THE CREEK.

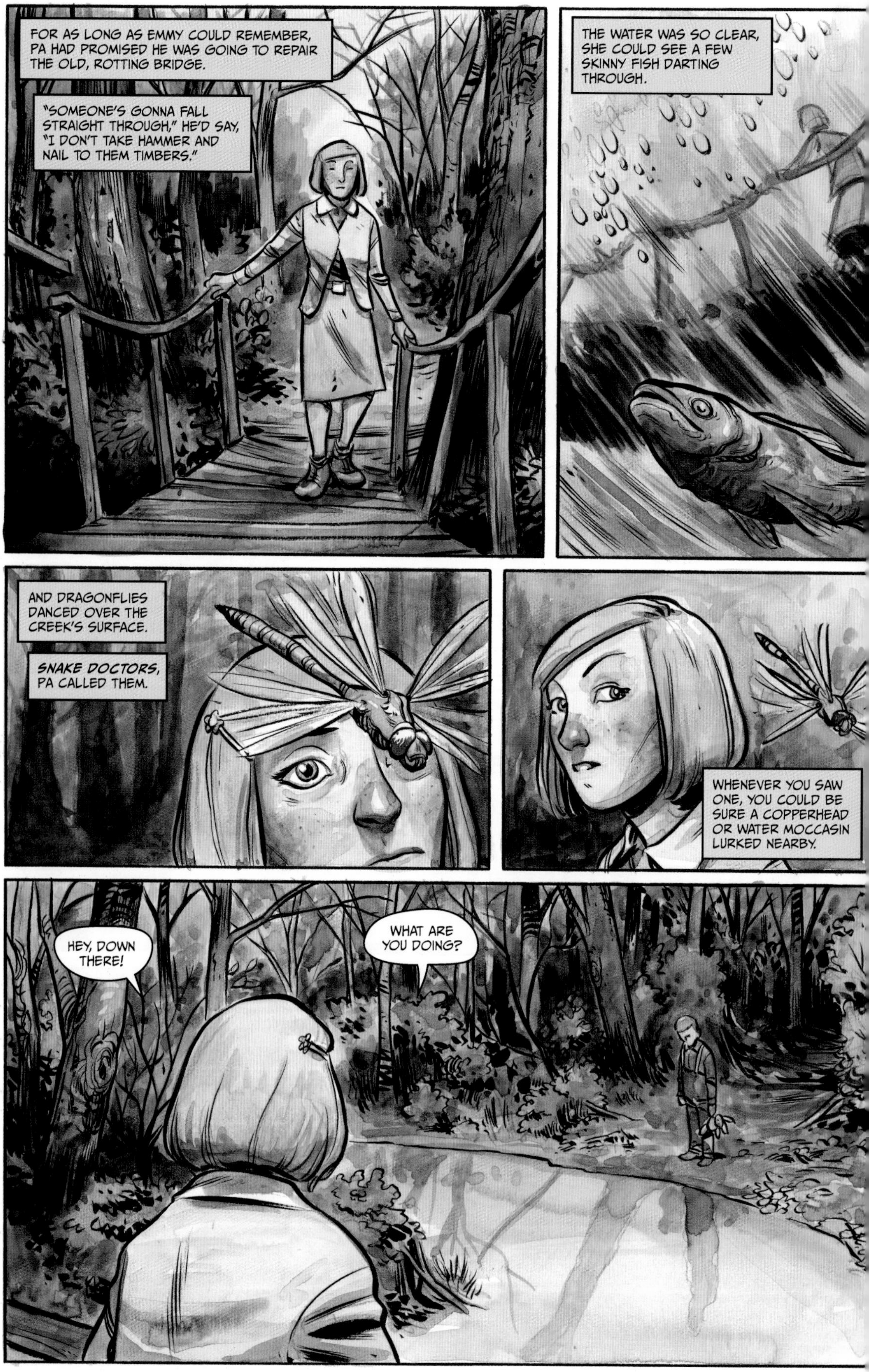
FOR AS LONG AS EMMY COULD REMEMBER, PA HAD PROMISED HE WAS GOING TO REPAIR THE OLD, ROTTING BRIDGE.
"SOMEONE'S GONNA FALL STRAIGHT THROUGH," HE'D SAY, "I DON'T TAKE HAMMER AND NAIL TO THEM TIMBERS."
THE WATER WAS SO CLEAR, SHE COULD SEE A FEW SKINNY FISH DARTING THROUGH.
AND DRAGONFLIES DANCED OVER THE CREEK'S SURFACE.
SNAKE DOCTORS, PA CALLED THEM.
WHENEVER YOU SAW ONE, YOU COULD BE SURE A COPPERHEAD OR WATER MOCCASIN LURKED NEARBY.
HEY, DOWN THERE!
WHAT ARE YOU DOING?

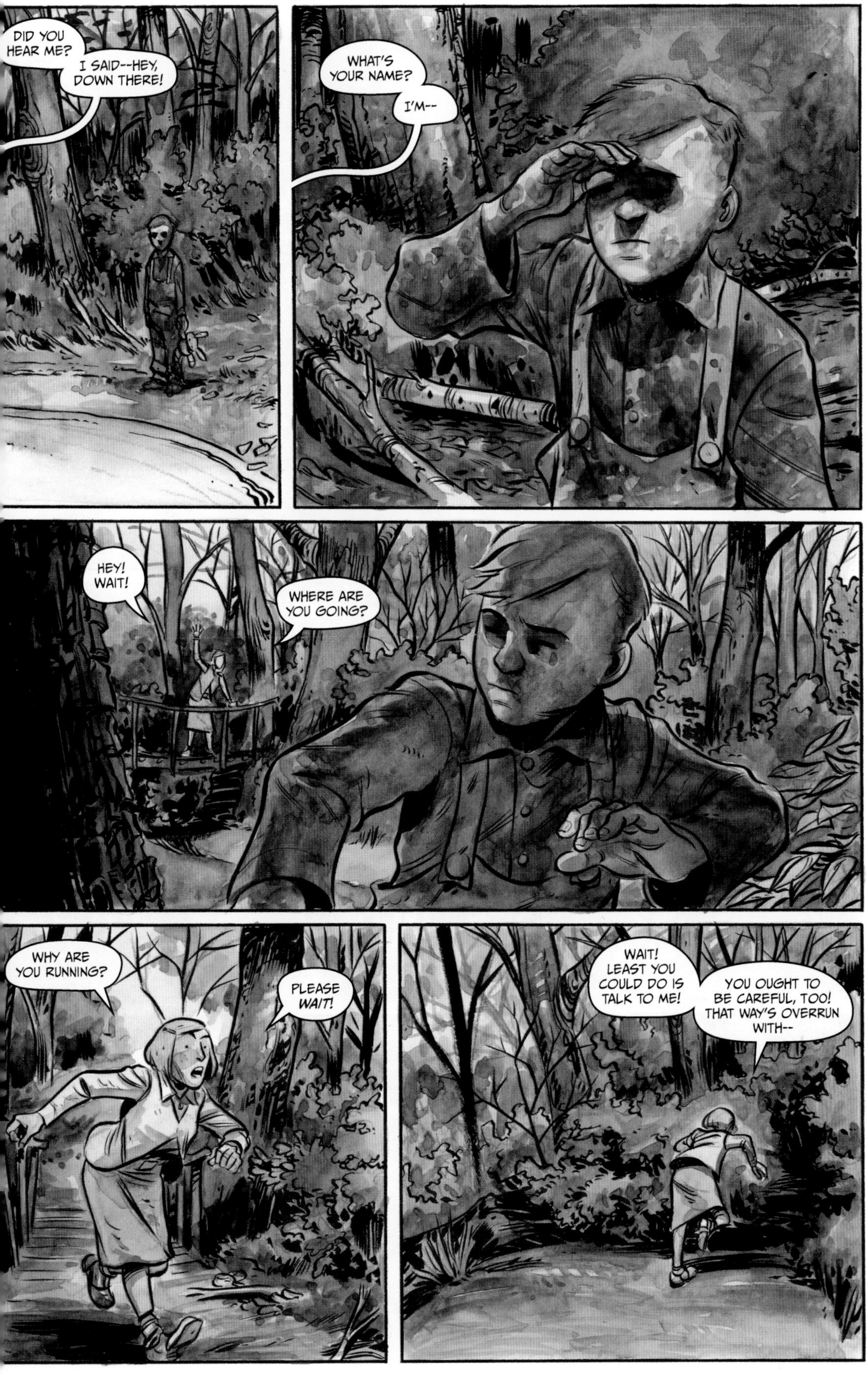
DID YOU HEAR ME?
I SAID--HEY, DOWN THERE!
WHAT'S YOUR NAME?
I'M--
HEY! WAIT!
WHERE ARE YOU GOING?
WHY ARE YOU RUNNING?
PLEASE *WAIT!*
WAIT! LEAST YOU COULD DO IS TALK TO ME!
YOU OUGHT TO BE CAREFUL, TOO! THAT WAY'S OVERRUN WITH--

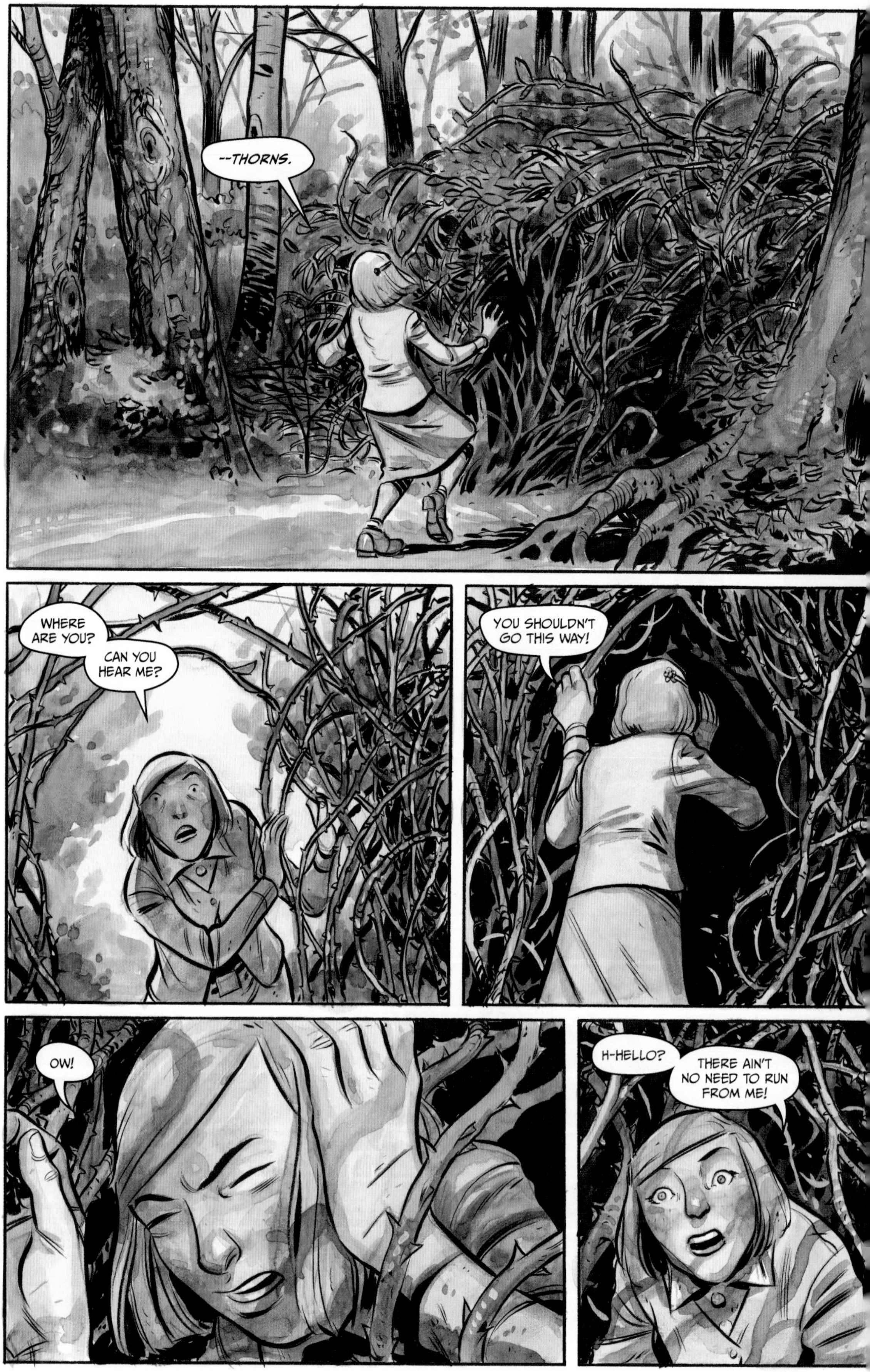
--THORNS.
WHERE ARE YOU?
CAN YOU HEAR ME?
YOU SHOULDN'T GO THIS WAY!
OW!
H-HELLO?
THERE AIN'T NO NEED TO RUN FROM ME!

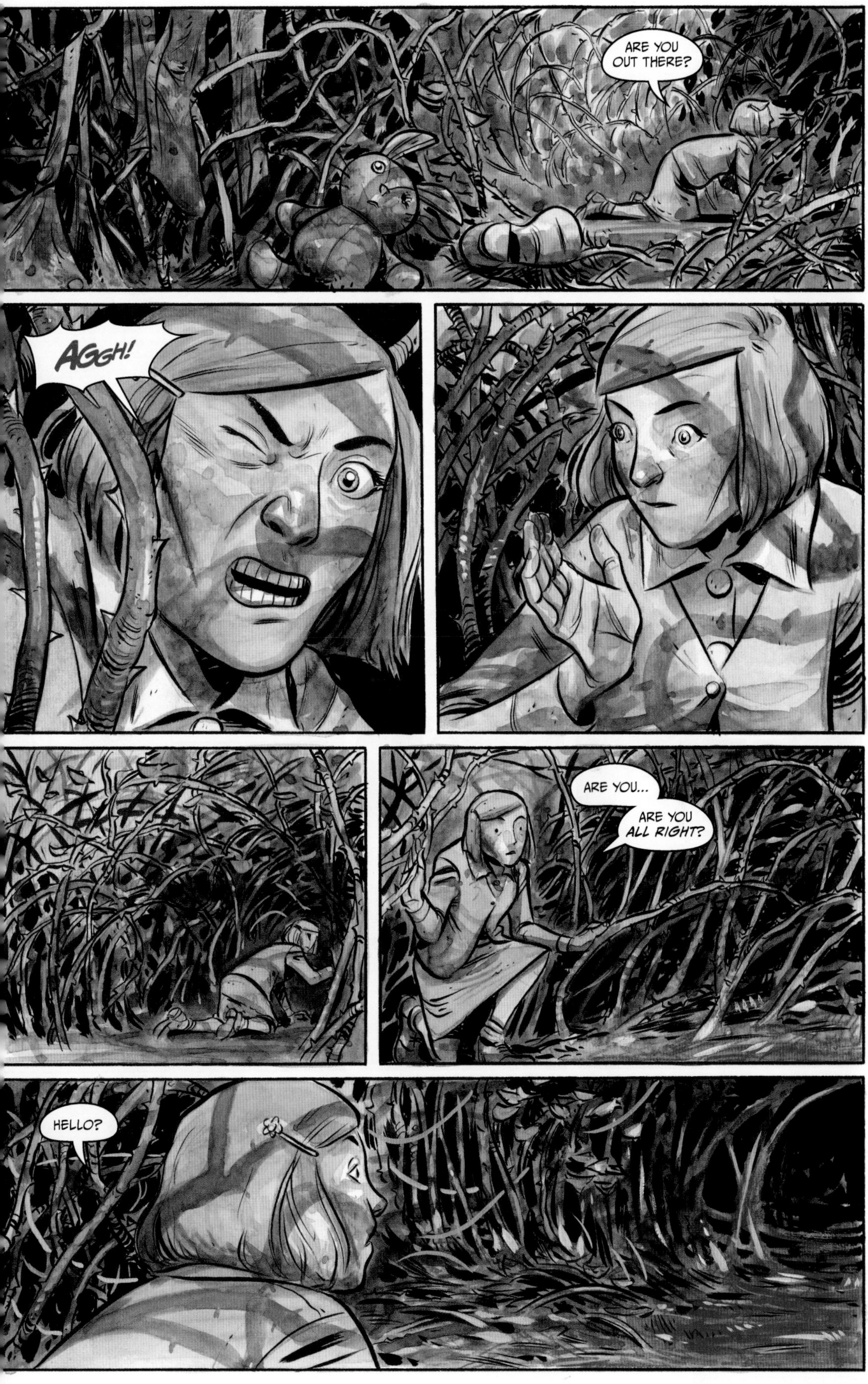
ARE YOU OUT THERE?
AGGH!
ARE YOU...
ARE YOU *ALL RIGHT?*
HELLO?

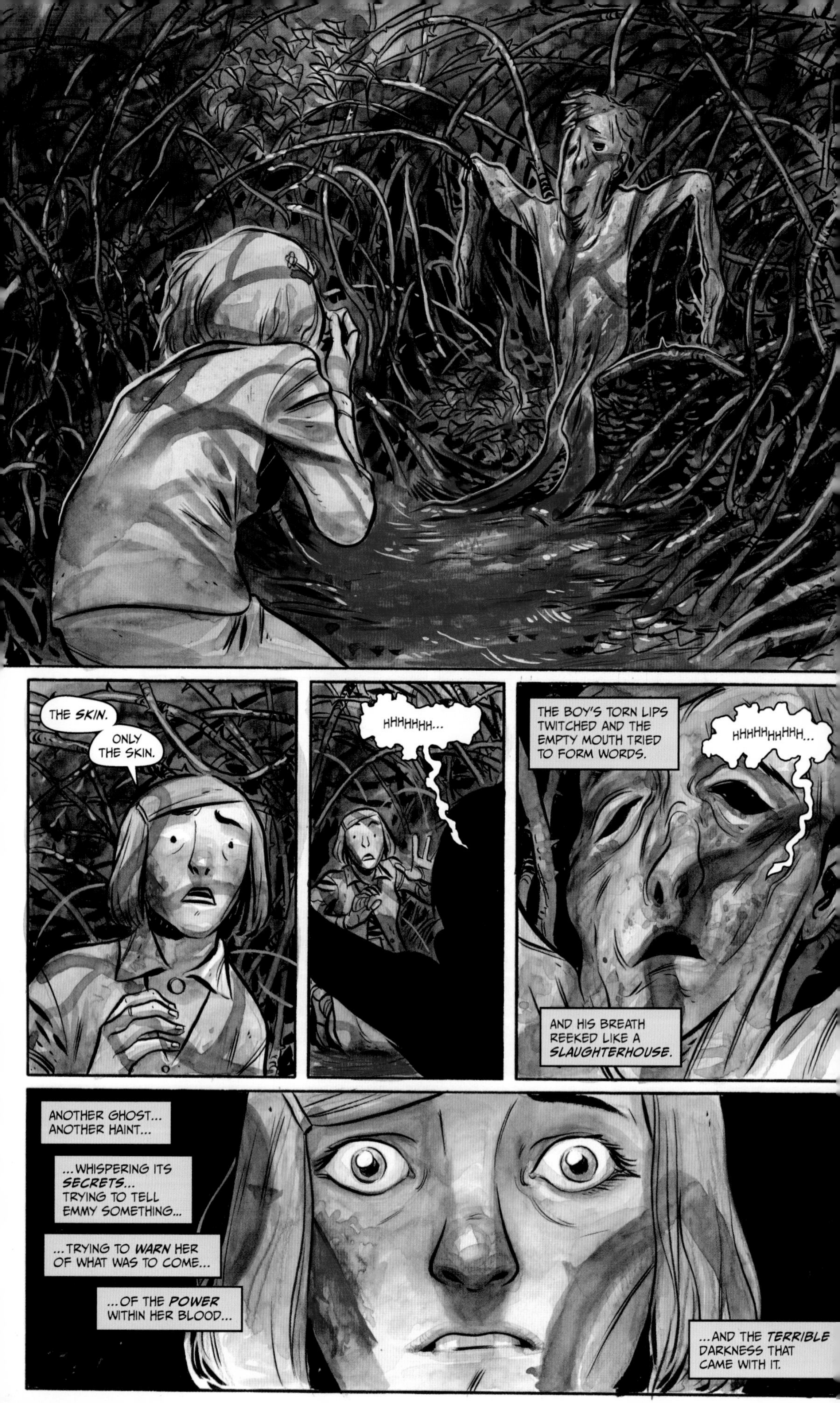
THE SKIN.
ONLY THE SKIN.
HHHHHHH...
THE BOY'S TORN LIPS TWITCHED AND THE EMPTY MOUTH TRIED TO FORM WORDS.
HHHHHHHHHH...
AND HIS BREATH REEKED LIKE A SLAUGHTERHOUSE.
ANOTHER GHOST... ANOTHER HAINT...
...WHISPERING ITS SECRETS... TRYING TO TELL EMMY SOMETHING...
...TRYING TO WARN HER OF WHAT WAS TO COME...
...OF THE POWER WITHIN HER BLOOD...
...AND THE TERRIBLE DARKNESS THAT CAME WITH IT.

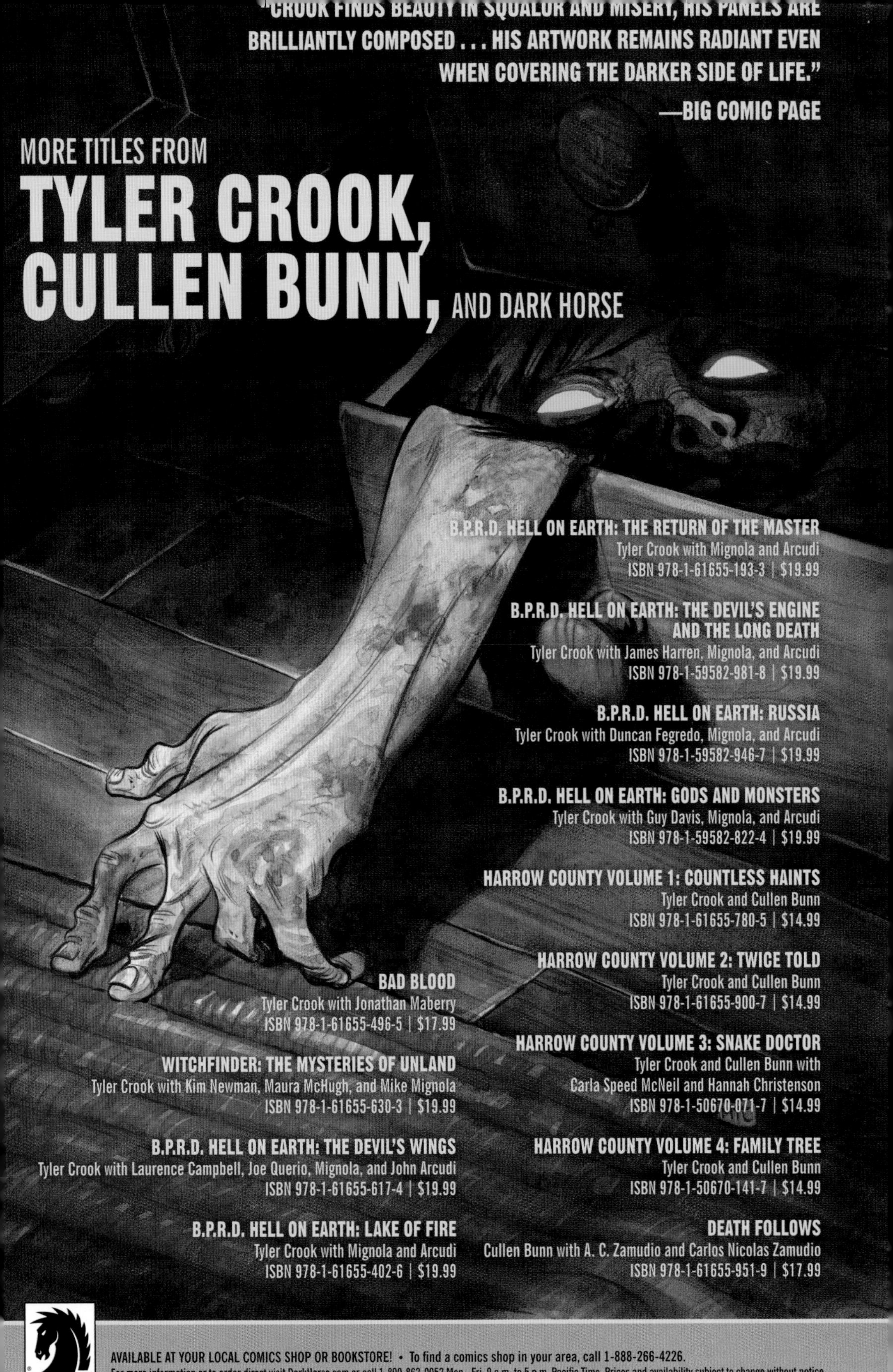

HELLBOY

IN HELL

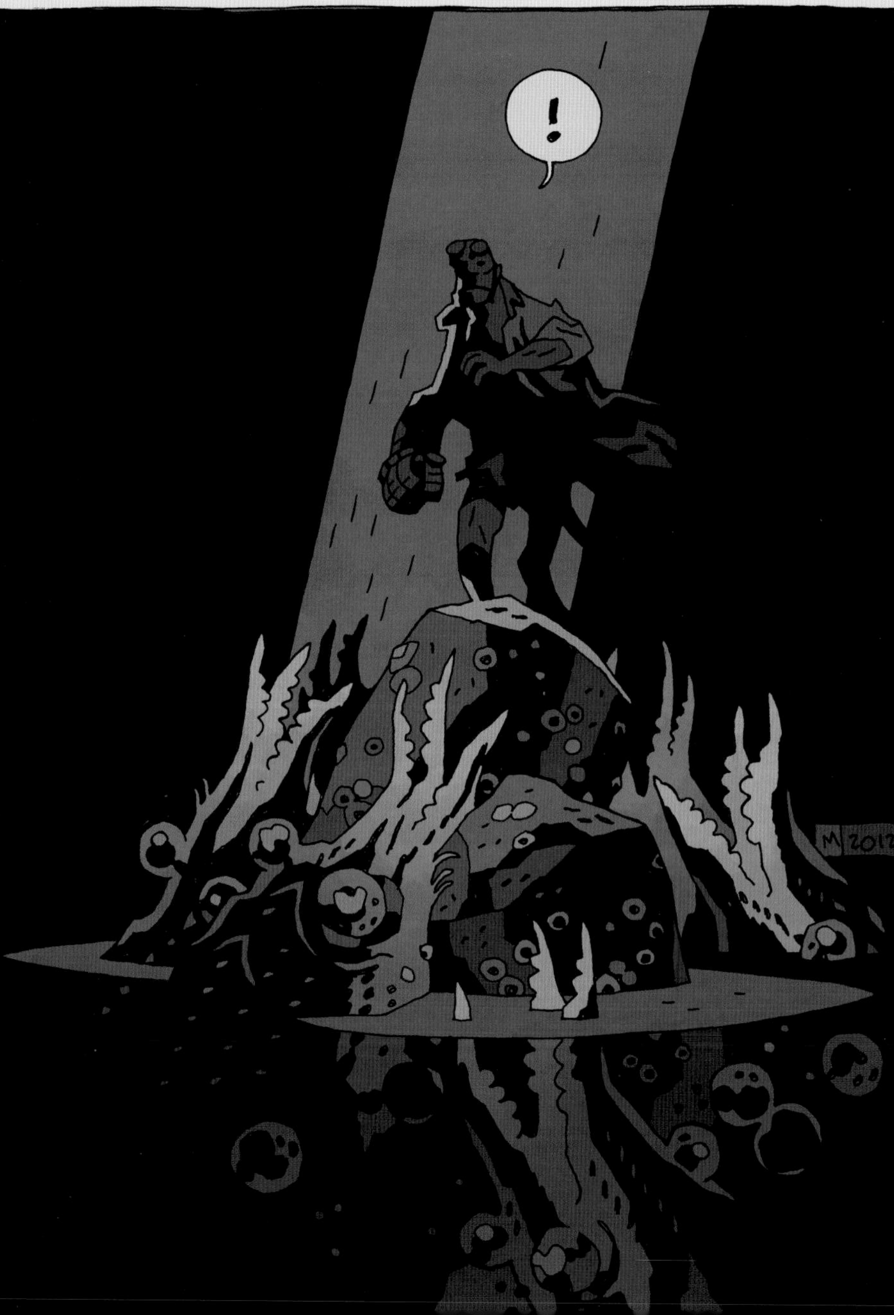
!
M 2012

HELLBOY
A Brief History

On December 23, 1944, Hellboy appeared in a fireball in the ruins of a church near East Bromwich, England. In 1952 he was granted honorary human status by a special act of the United Nations and began working as a field agent for the Bureau for Paranormal Research and Defense. He quit the B.P.R.D. in 2001 and traveled to Africa, where he was abducted by mermaids. After several years lost at sea, he returned to England, fought some giants, fell in love, and learned that he was a direct descendant of King Arthur and therefore the rightful King of all Britain.

Shortly thereafter he fought a dragon and was killed.

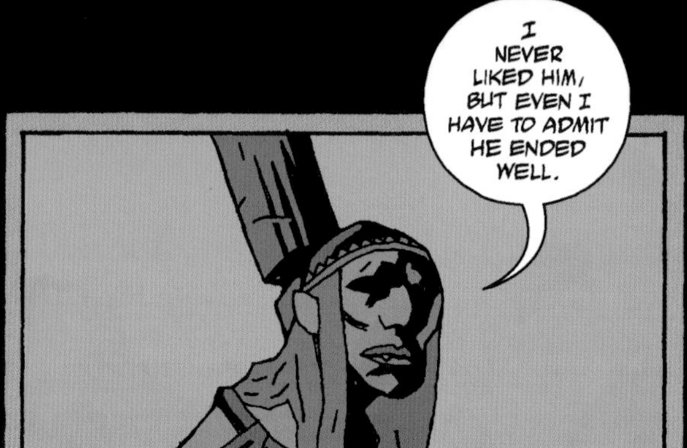
I NEVER LIKED HIM, BUT EVEN I HAVE TO ADMIT HE ENDED WELL.

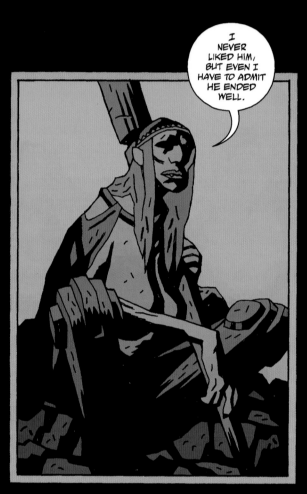

The Baba Yaga

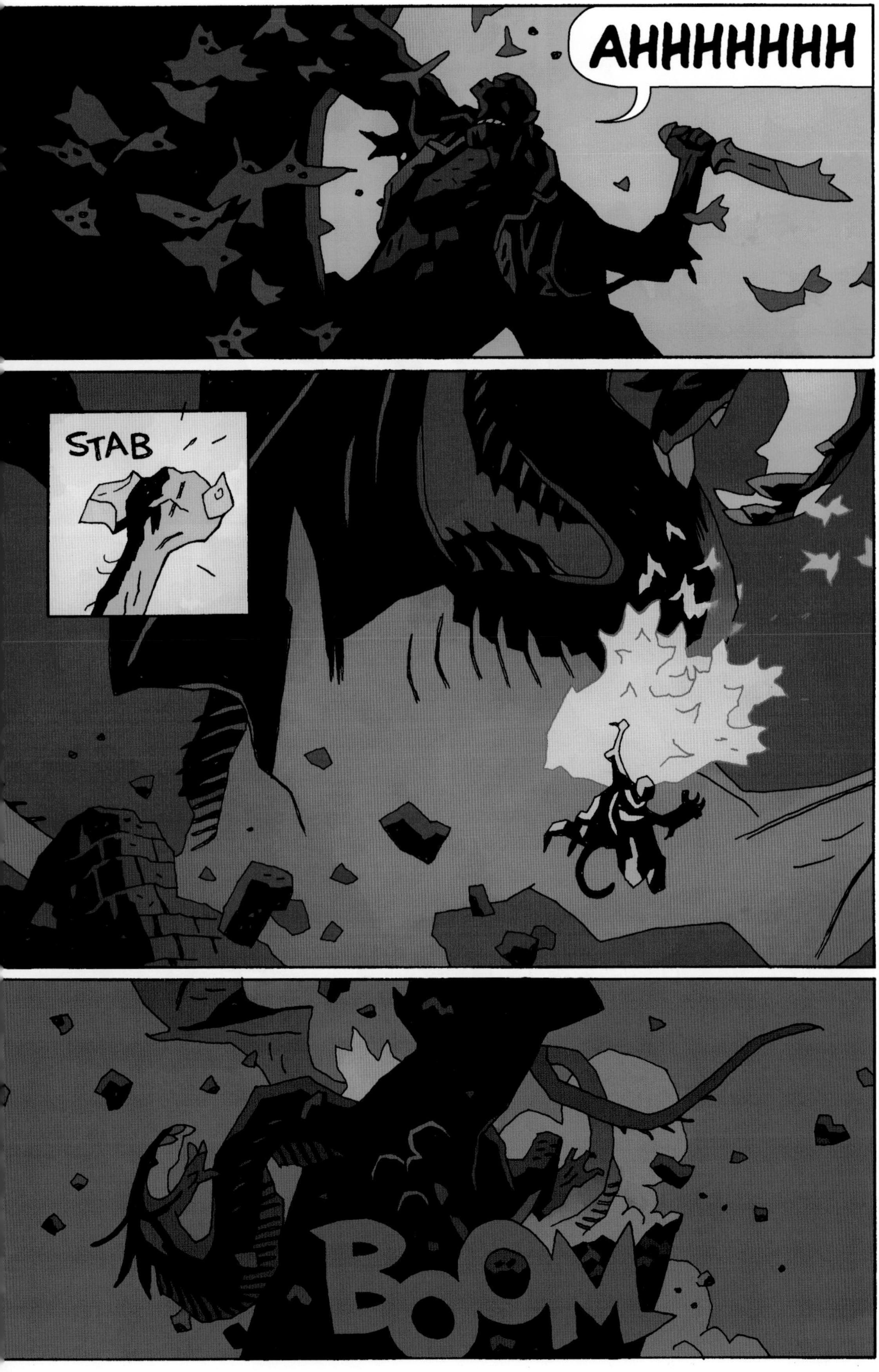
AHHHHHHH
STAB
BOOM

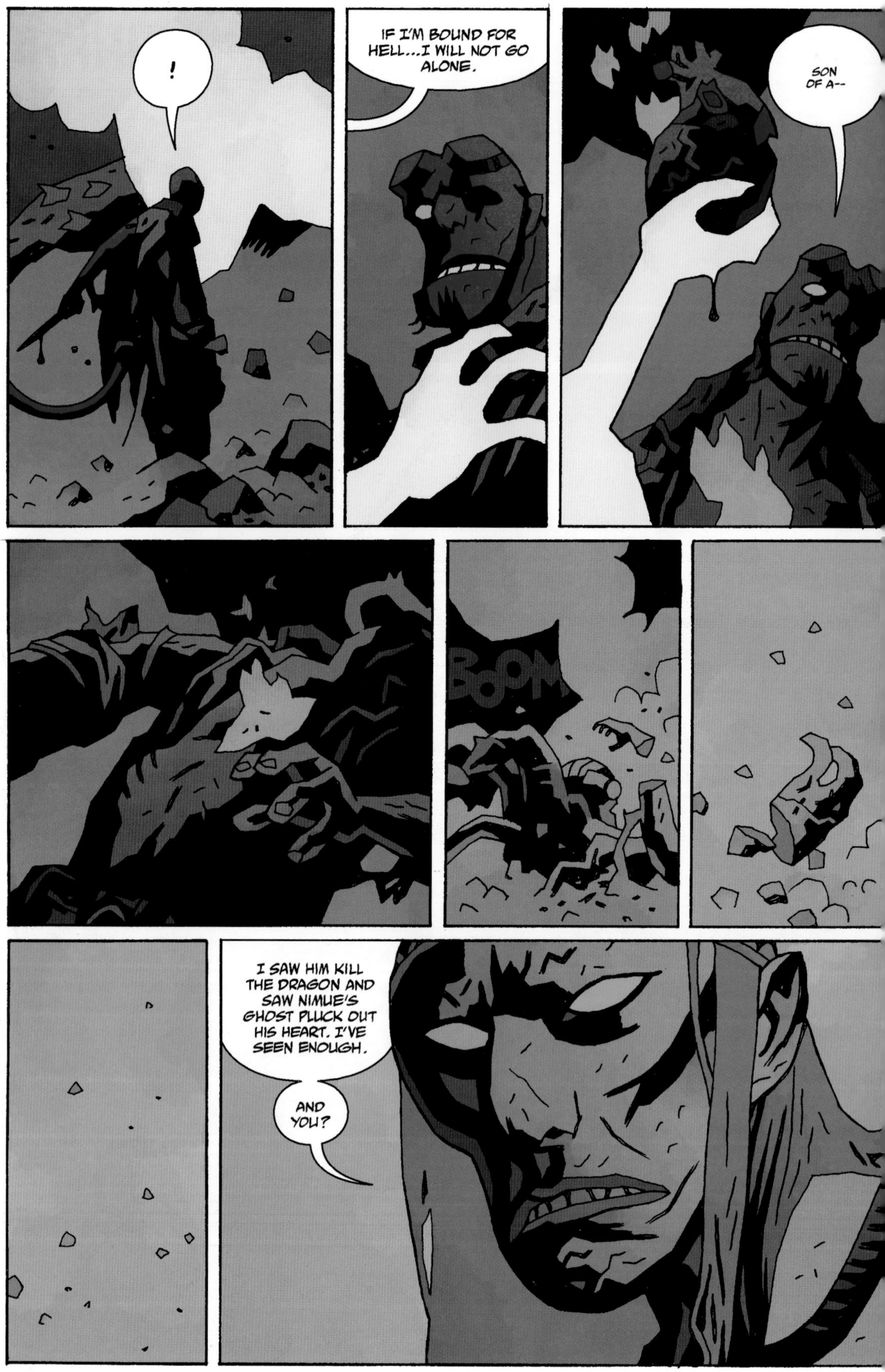
!
IF I'M BOUND FOR HELL...I WILL NOT GO ALONE.
SON OF A--
BOOM
I SAW HIM KILL THE DRAGON AND SAW NIMUE'S GHOST PLUCK OUT HIS HEART. I'VE SEEN ENOUGH.
AND YOU?

YOU WANT TO GO AFTER HIM. YOU THINK YOU CAN **SAVE** HIM.

HIS STORY IS NOT FINISHED.

BUT IT'S **HIS** STORY, SIR EDWARD. NOT YOURS...

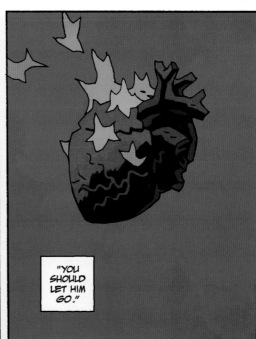

"YOU SHOULD LET HIM GO."

THERE ARE THINGS HE HAS YET TO DO. HORRIBLE THINGS. YOU GO NOW AND DRAG HIM OUT OF THE PIT--YOU MAY FIND THAT YOU TAKE SOME OF HIS BURDEN UPON YOURSELF.

ARE YOU PREPARED TO DO THAT?

I AM.

SHOW ME WHERE HE IS.

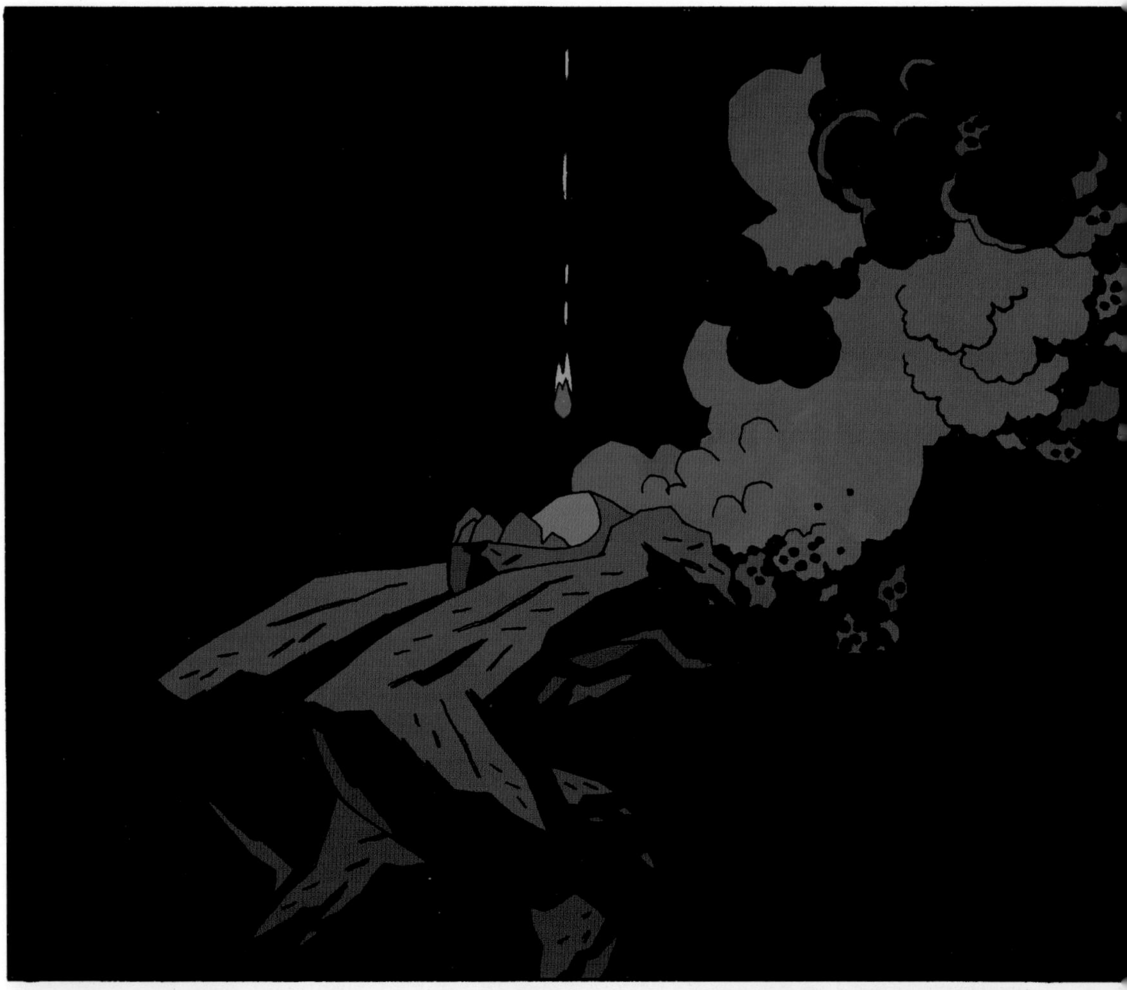
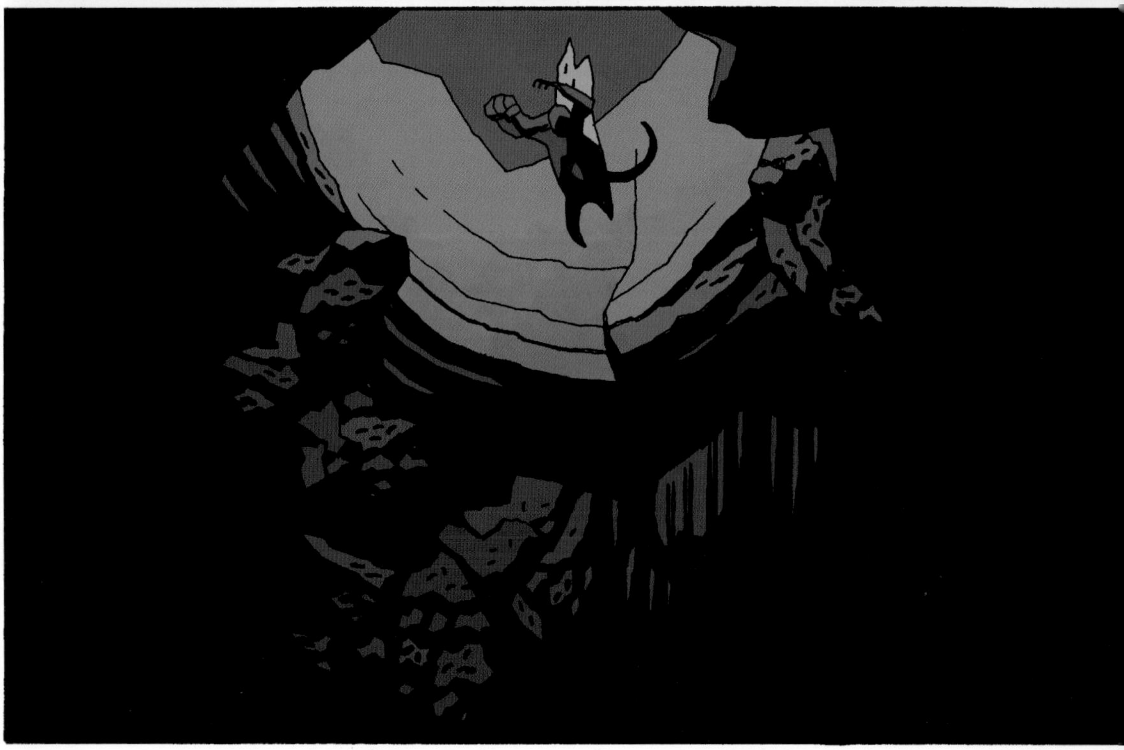

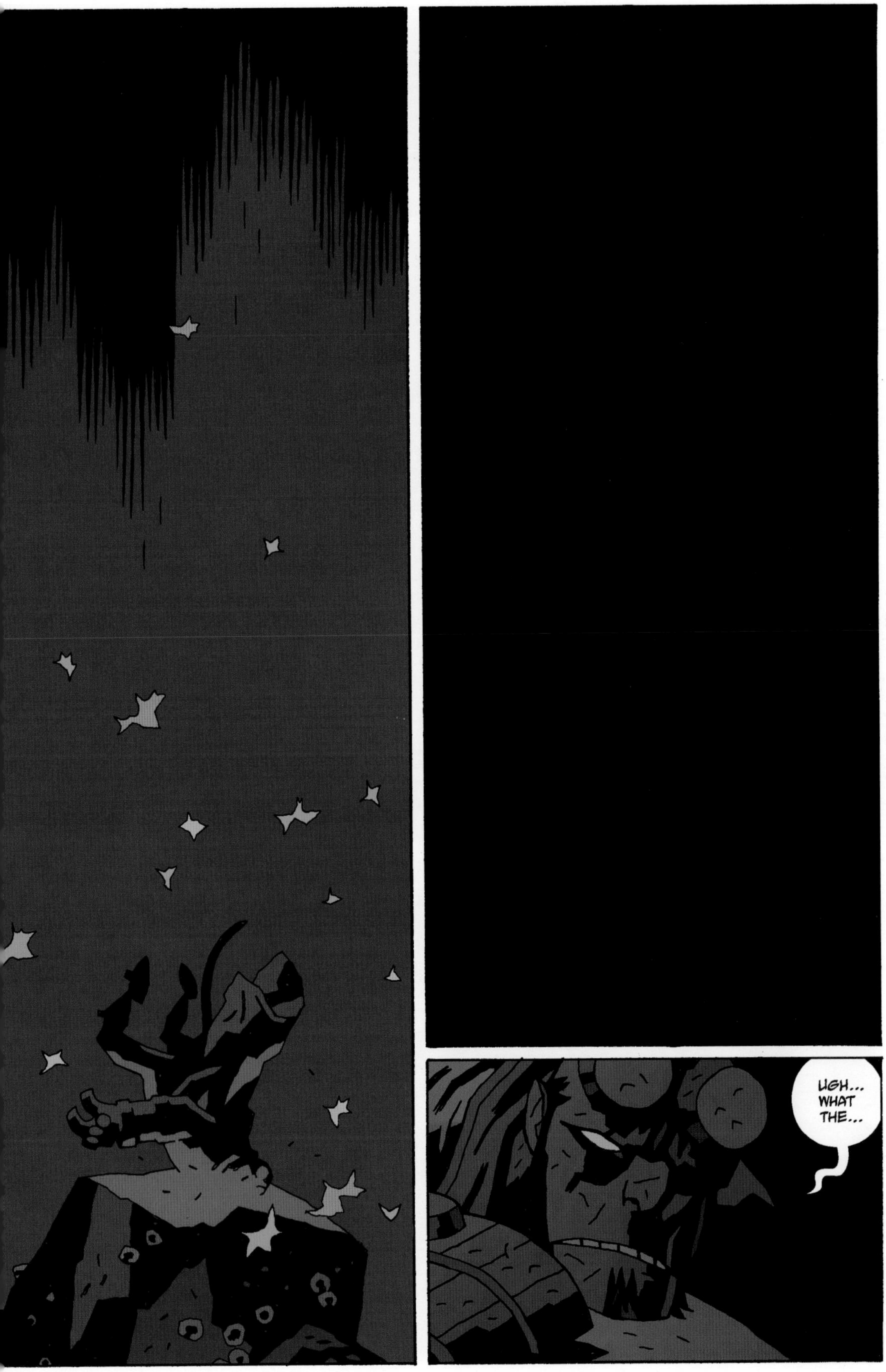
UGH... WHAT THE...

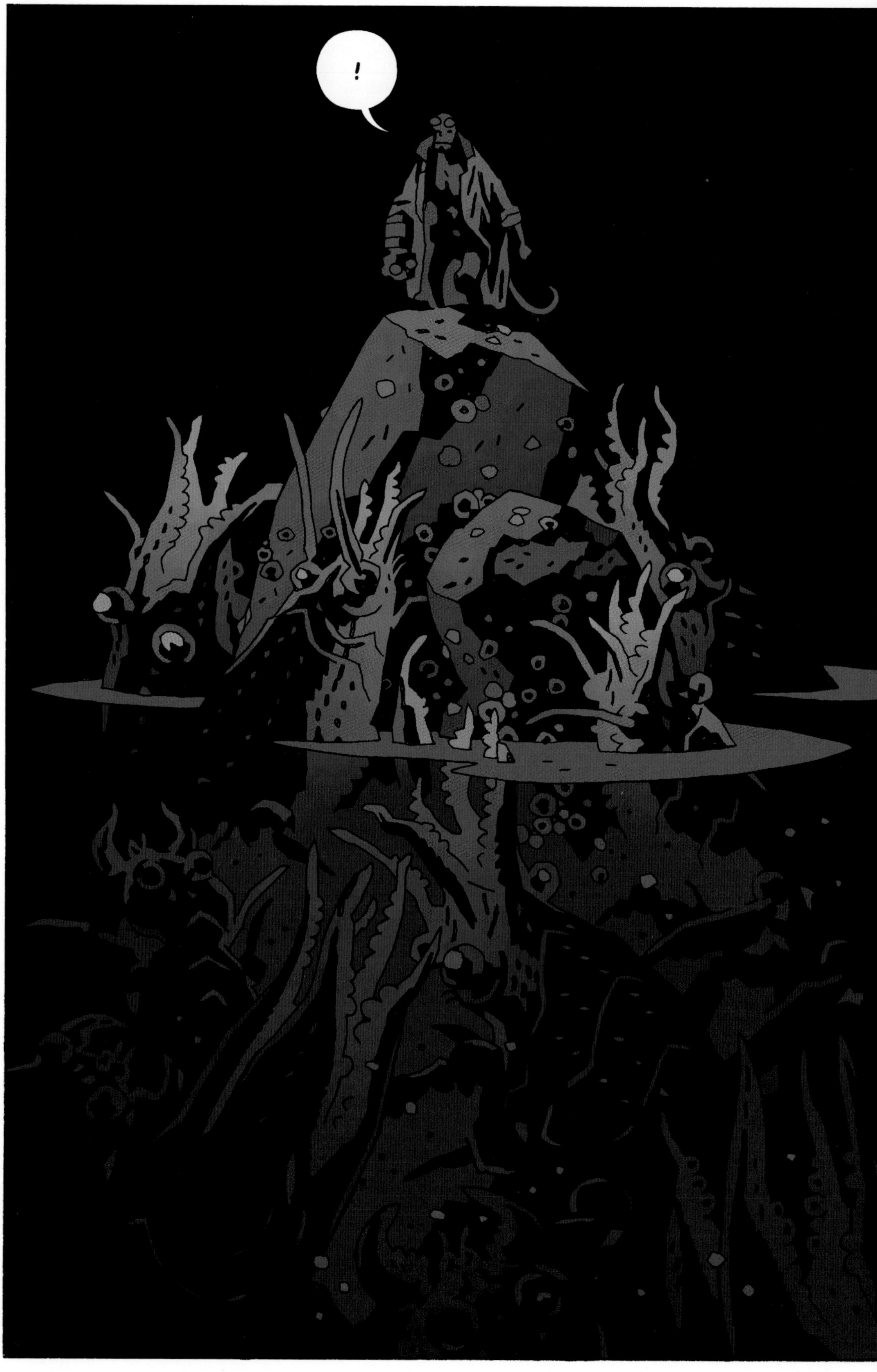
!

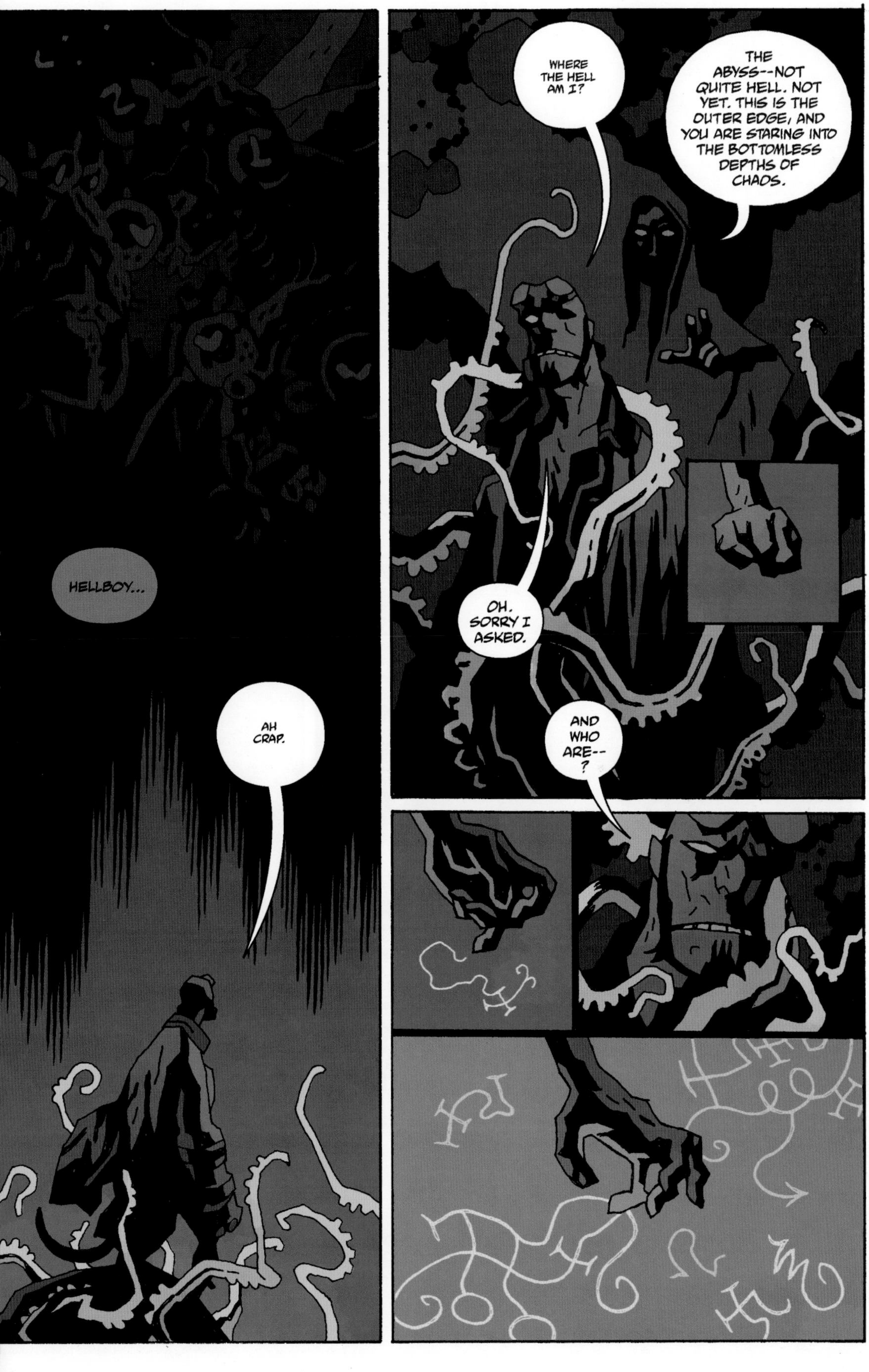
HELLBOY...
AH CRAP.
WHERE THE HELL AM I?
THE ABYSS--NOT QUITE HELL. NOT YET. THIS IS THE OUTER EDGE, AND YOU ARE STARING INTO THE BOTTOMLESS DEPTHS OF CHAOS.
OH. SORRY I ASKED.
AND WHO ARE-- ?

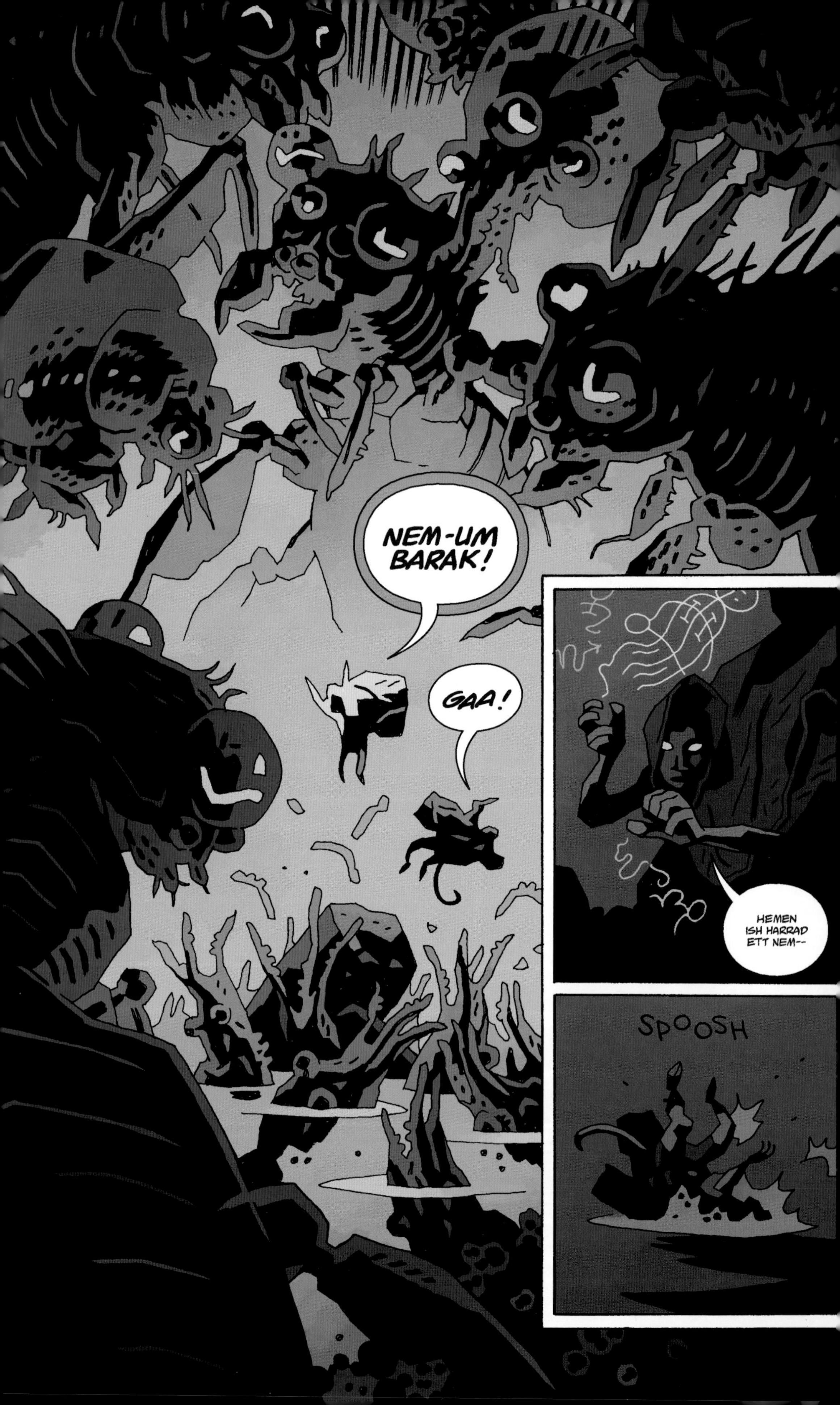
NEM-UM BARAK!
GAA!
HEMEN ISH HARRAD ETT NEM--
SPOOSH

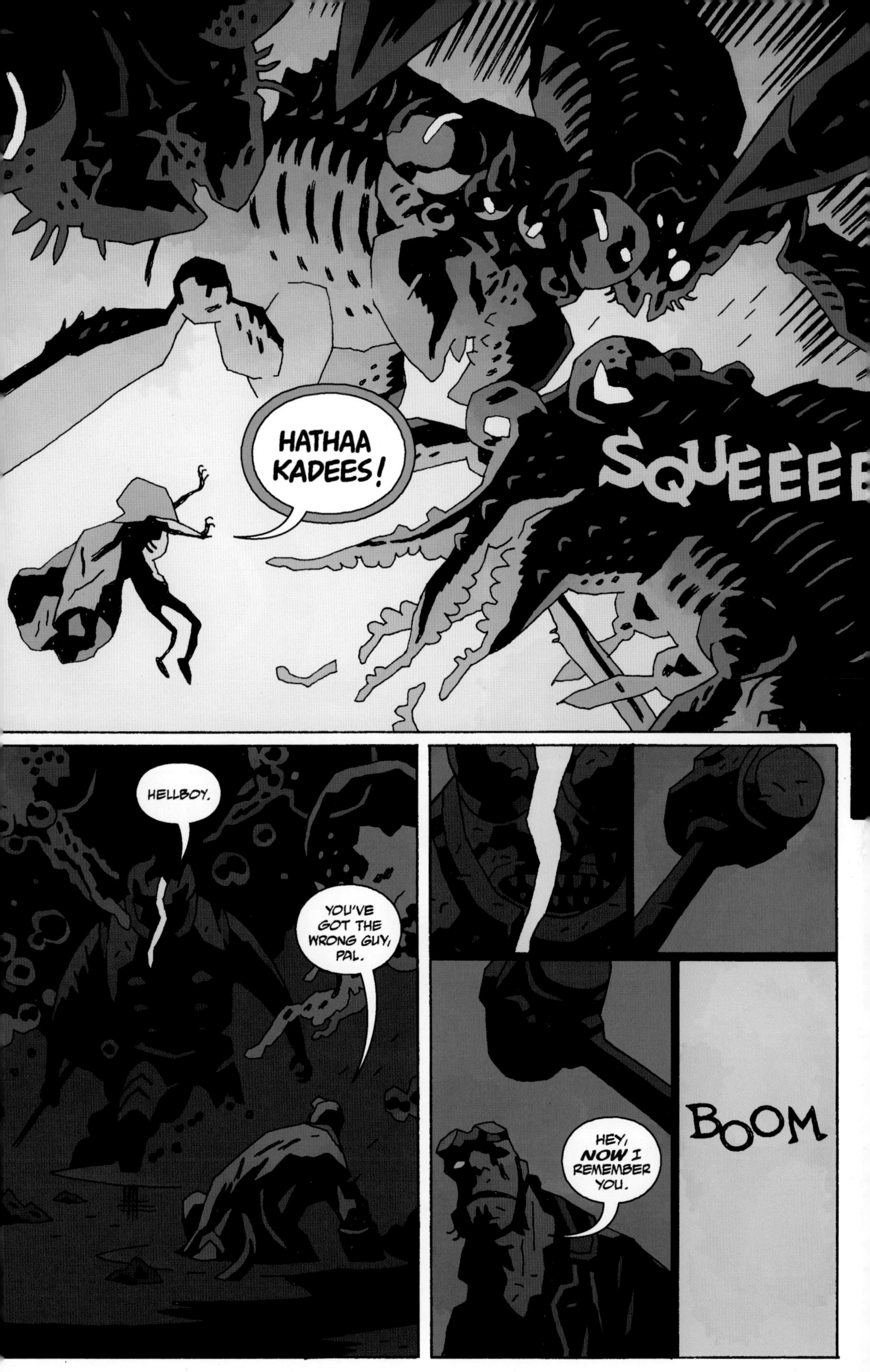
HATHAA KADEES!
SQUEEEEE
HELLBOY.
YOU'VE GOT THE WRONG GUY, PAL.
BOOM
HEY, **NOW** I REMEMBER YOU.

AHH! JEEZ!

WHAT THE HELL?!

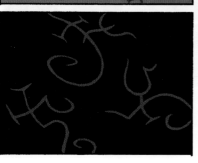

BOOM BOOM

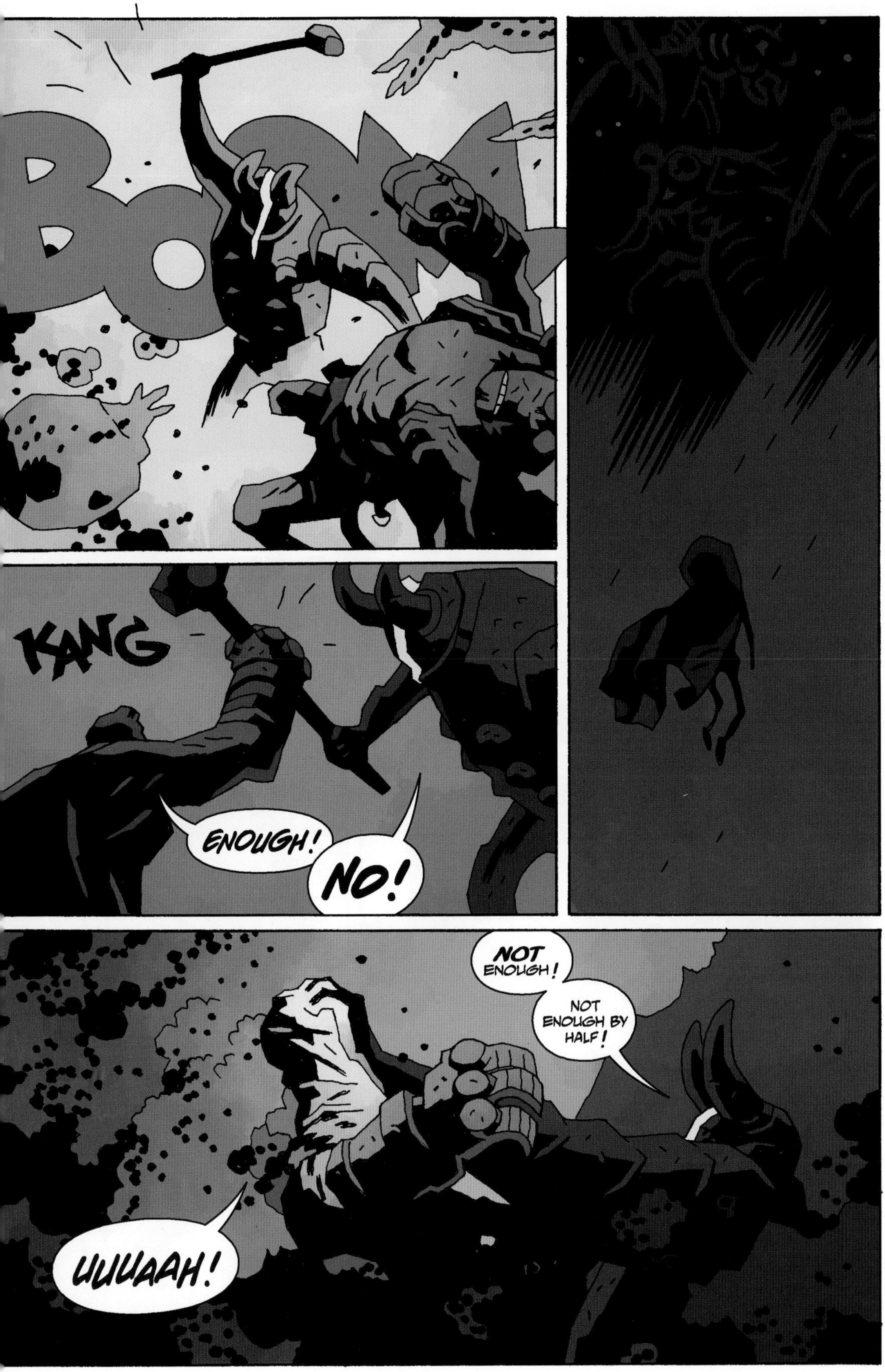
BOOM
KANG
ENOUGH!
NO!
NOT ENOUGH!
NOT ENOUGH BY HALF!
UUUAAH!

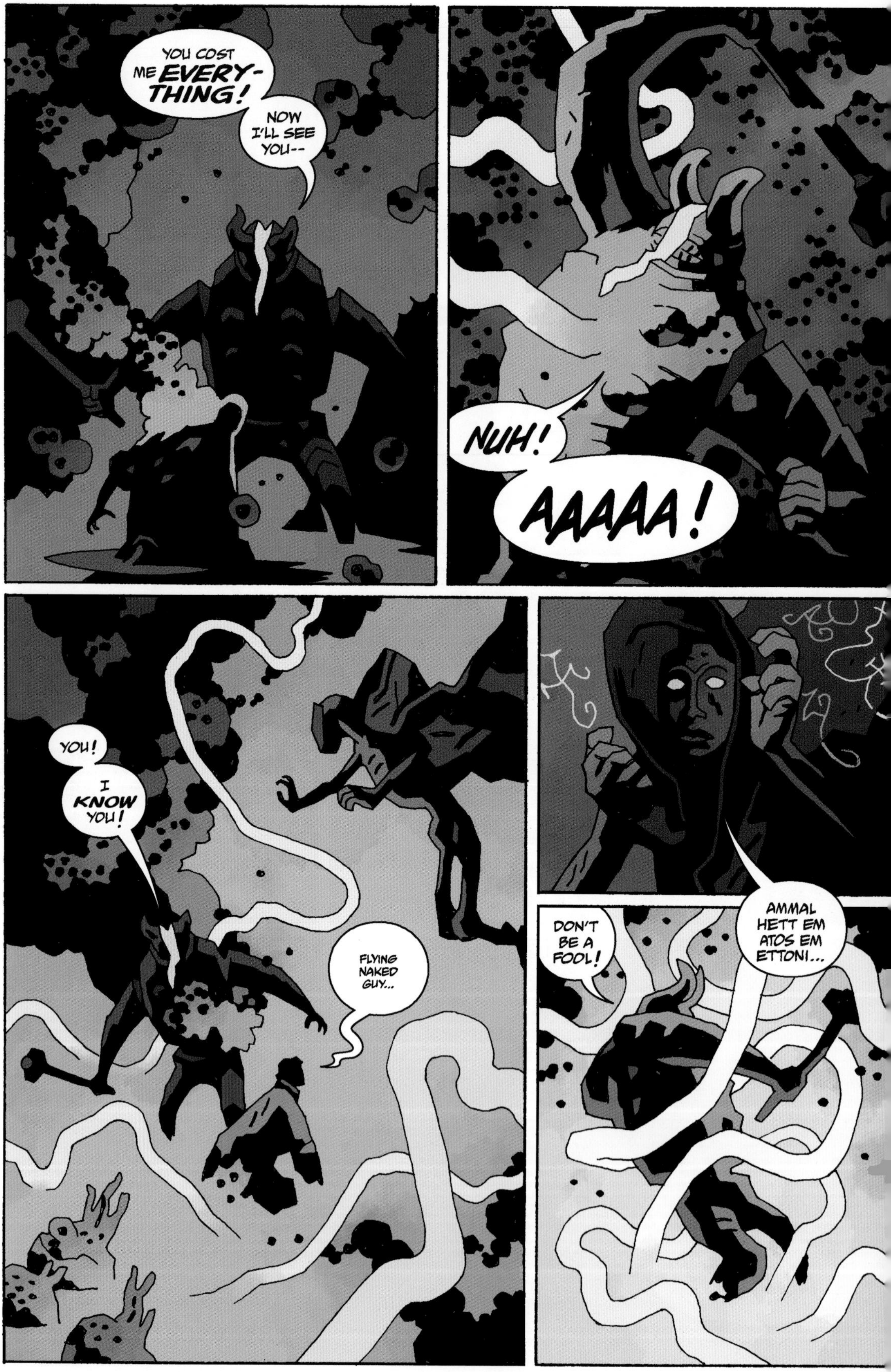
YOU COST ME EVERY-THING!
NOW I'LL SEE YOU--
NUH!
AAAAA!
YOU!
I KNOW YOU!
FLYING NAKED GUY...
AMMAL HETT EM ATOS EM ETTONI...
DON'T BE A FOOL!

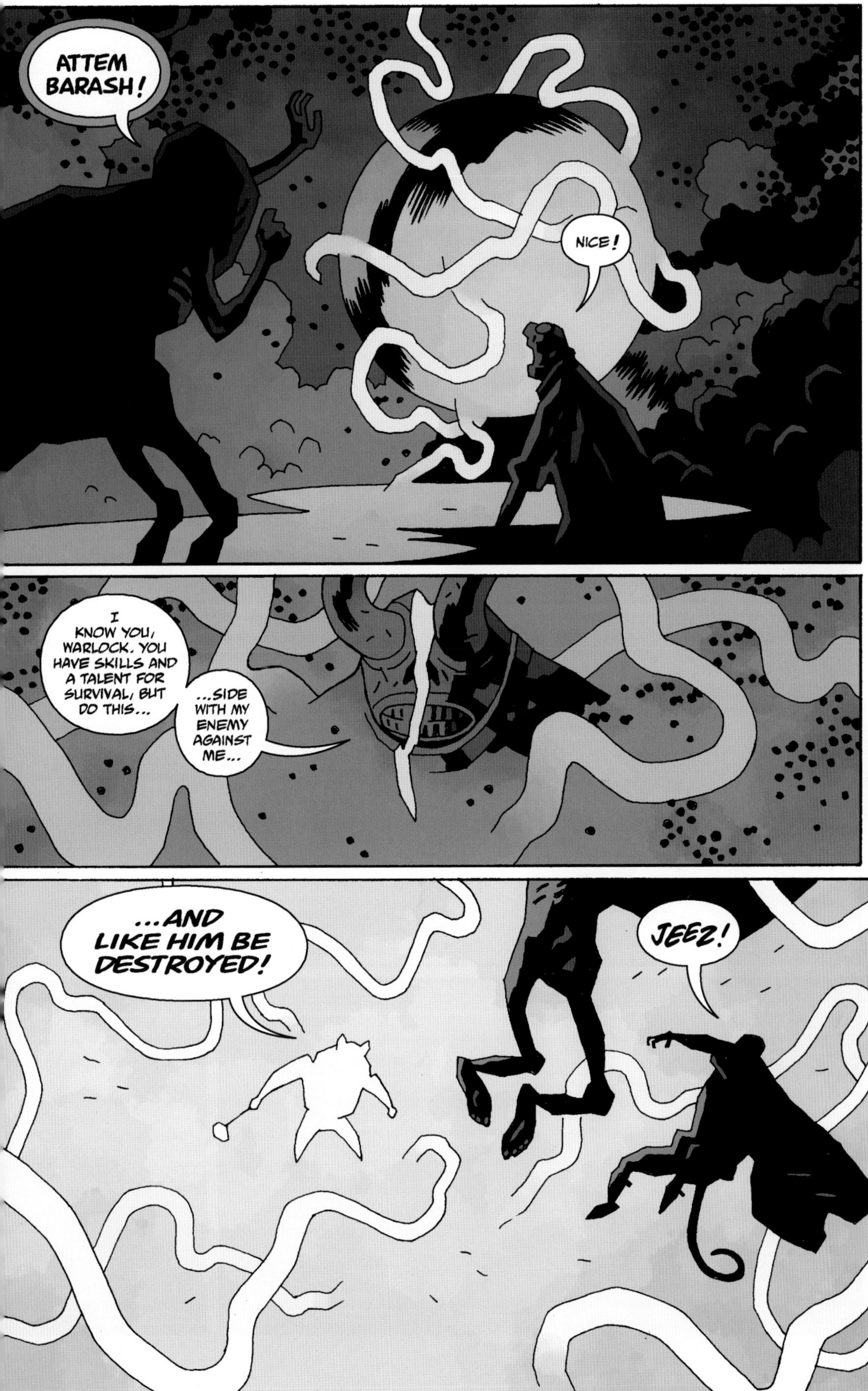
ATTEM BARASH!
NICE!
I KNOW YOU, WARLOCK. YOU HAVE SKILLS AND A TALENT FOR SURVIVAL, BUT DO THIS...
...SIDE WITH MY ENEMY AGAINST ME...
...AND LIKE HIM BE DESTROYED!
JEEZ!

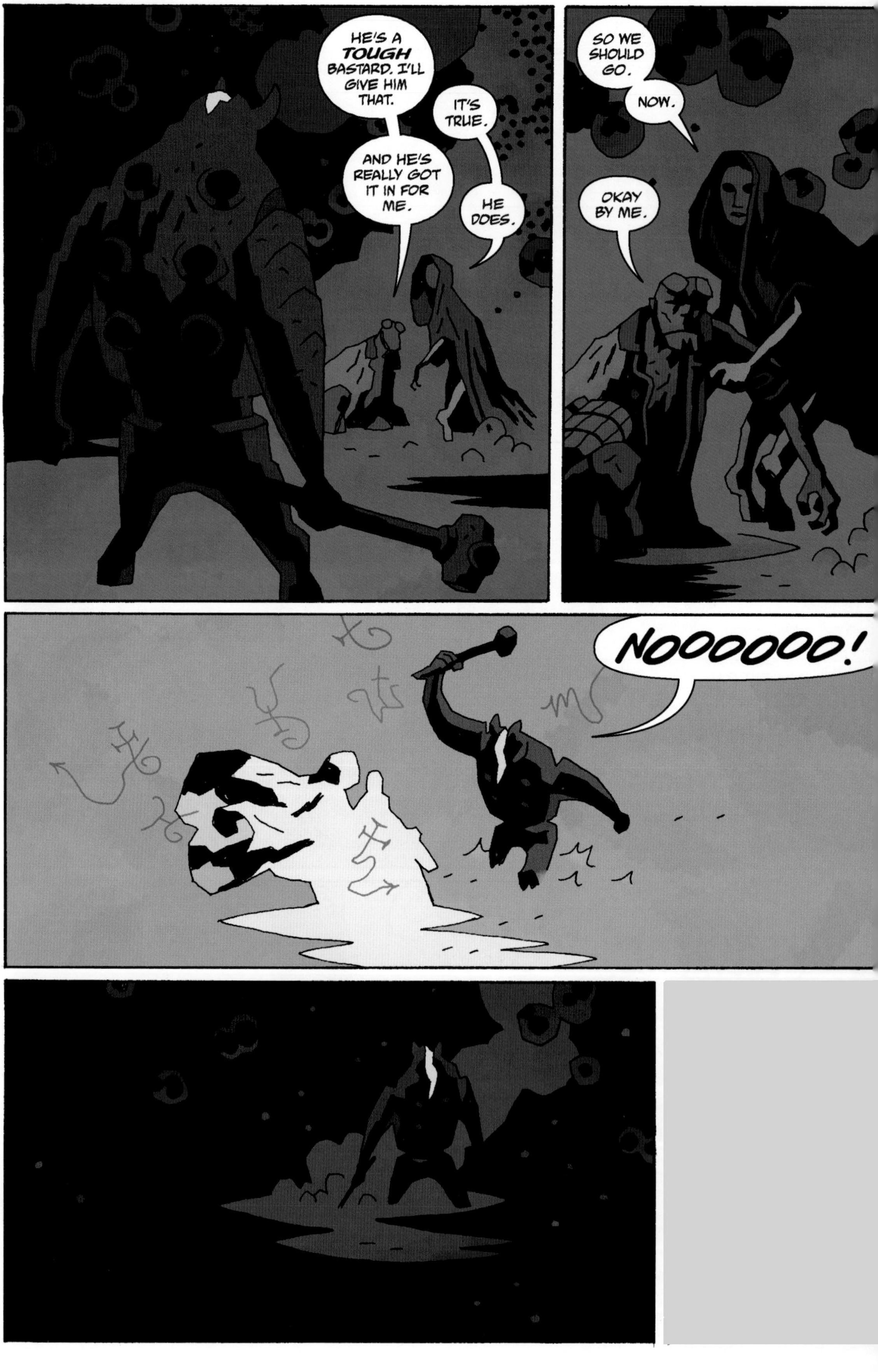
HE'S A TOUGH BASTARD. I'LL GIVE HIM THAT.
IT'S TRUE.
AND HE'S REALLY GOT IT IN FOR ME.
HE DOES.
SO WE SHOULD GO.
NOW.
OKAY BY ME.
NOOOOOO!

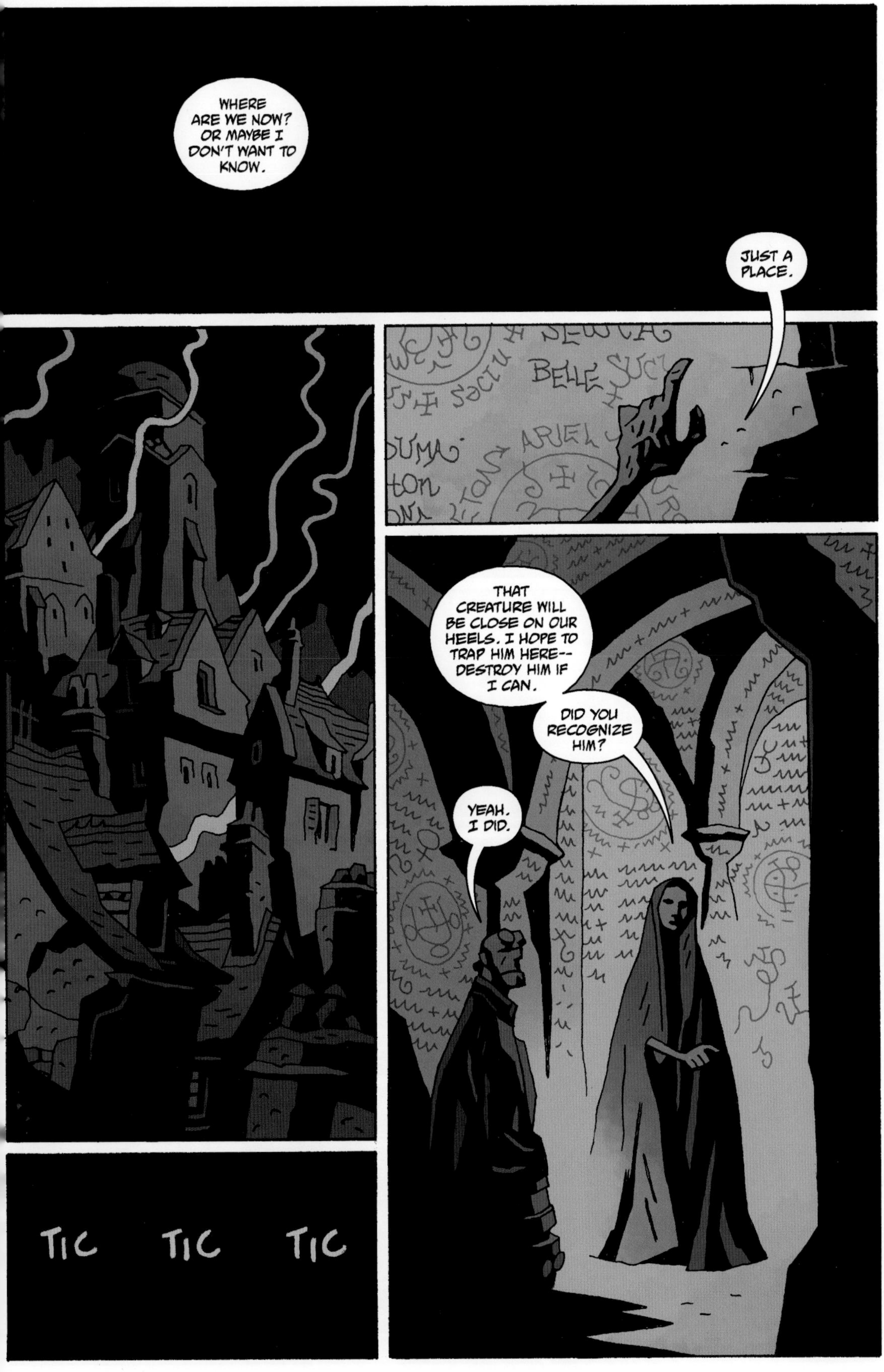
WHERE ARE WE NOW? OR MAYBE I DON'T WANT TO KNOW.
JUST A PLACE.
THAT CREATURE WILL BE CLOSE ON OUR HEELS. I HOPE TO TRAP HIM HERE-- DESTROY HIM IF I CAN.
DID YOU RECOGNIZE HIM?
YEAH. I DID.
TIC TIC TIC

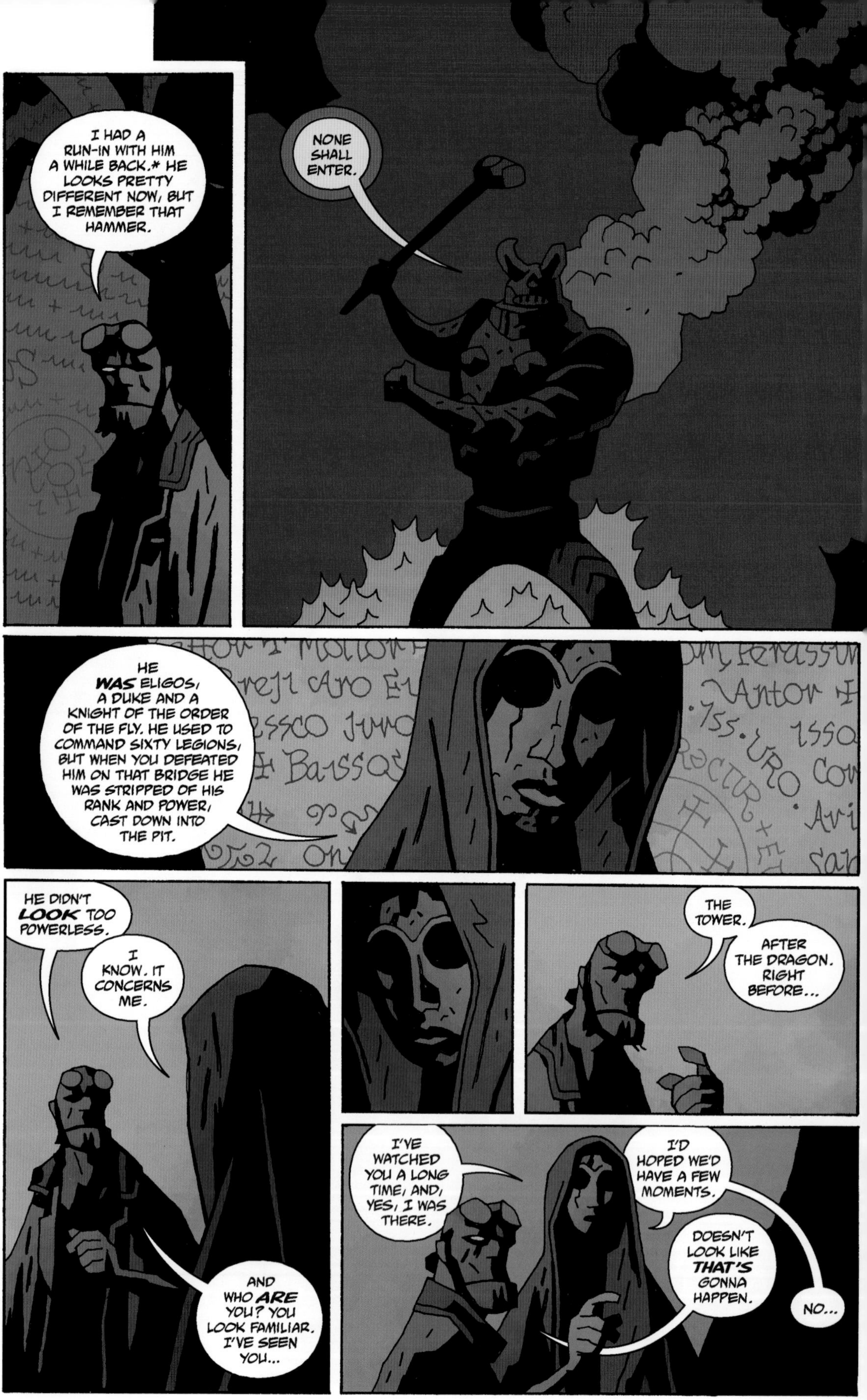

I HAD A RUN-IN WITH HIM A WHILE BACK.* HE LOOKS PRETTY DIFFERENT NOW, BUT I REMEMBER THAT HAMMER.
NONE SHALL ENTER.
HE **WAS** ELIGOS, A DUKE AND A KNIGHT OF THE ORDER OF THE FLY. HE USED TO COMMAND SIXTY LEGIONS, BUT WHEN YOU DEFEATED HIM ON THAT BRIDGE HE WAS STRIPPED OF HIS RANK AND POWER, CAST DOWN INTO THE PIT.
HE DIDN'T **LOOK** TOO POWERLESS.
I KNOW. IT CONCERNS ME.
AND WHO **ARE** YOU? YOU LOOK FAMILIAR. I'VE SEEN YOU...
THE TOWER.
AFTER THE DRAGON. RIGHT BEFORE...
I'VE WATCHED YOU A LONG TIME, AND, YES, I WAS THERE.
I'D HOPED WE'D HAVE A FEW MOMENTS.
DOESN'T LOOK LIKE **THAT'S** GONNA HAPPEN.
NO...

*HELLBOY: THE WILD HUNT

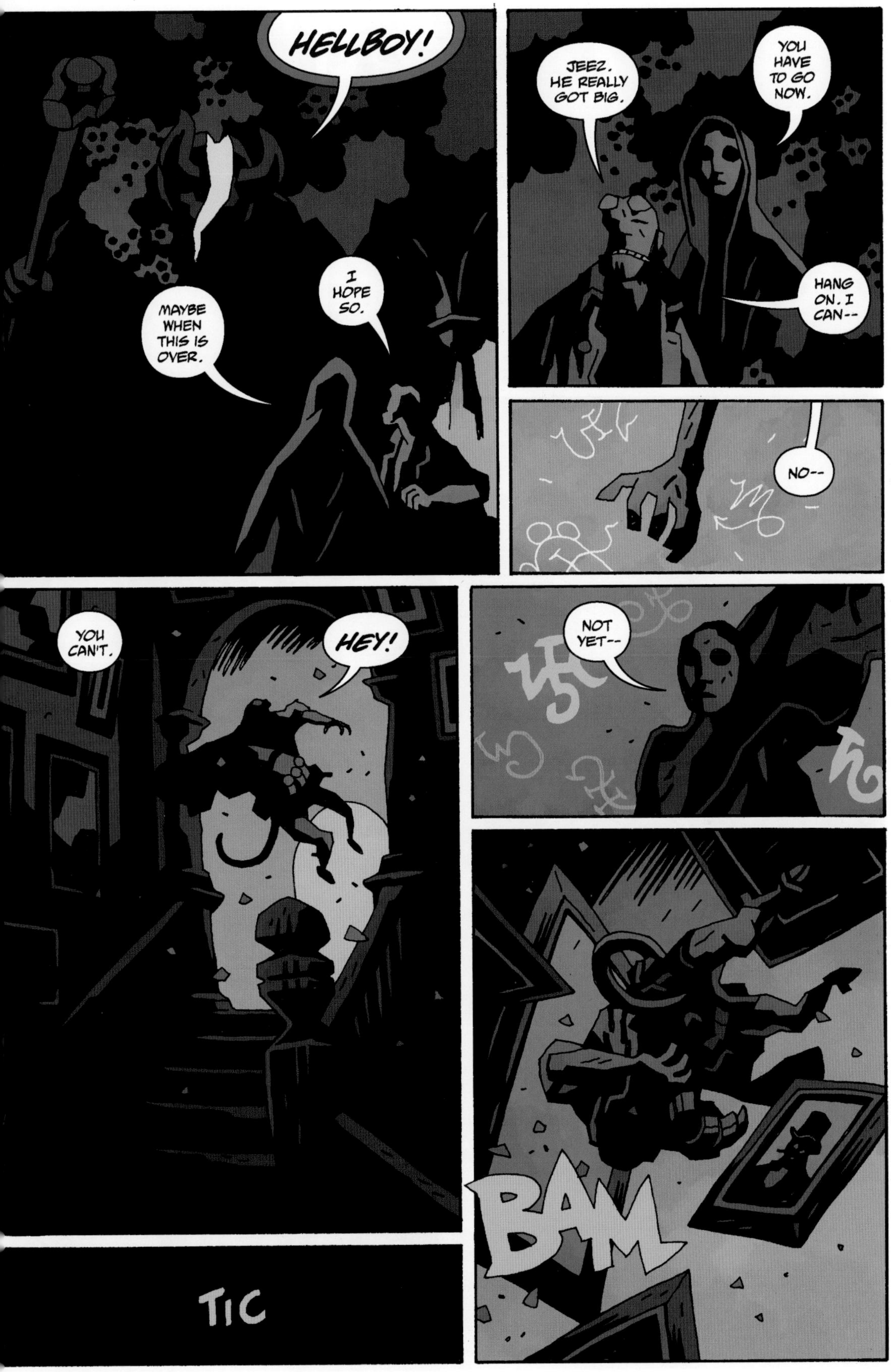
HELLBOY!
MAYBE WHEN THIS IS OVER.
I HOPE SO.
JEEZ. HE REALLY GOT BIG.
YOU HAVE TO GO NOW.
HANG ON. I CAN--
NO--
YOU CAN'T.
HEY!
NOT YET--
TIC
BAM

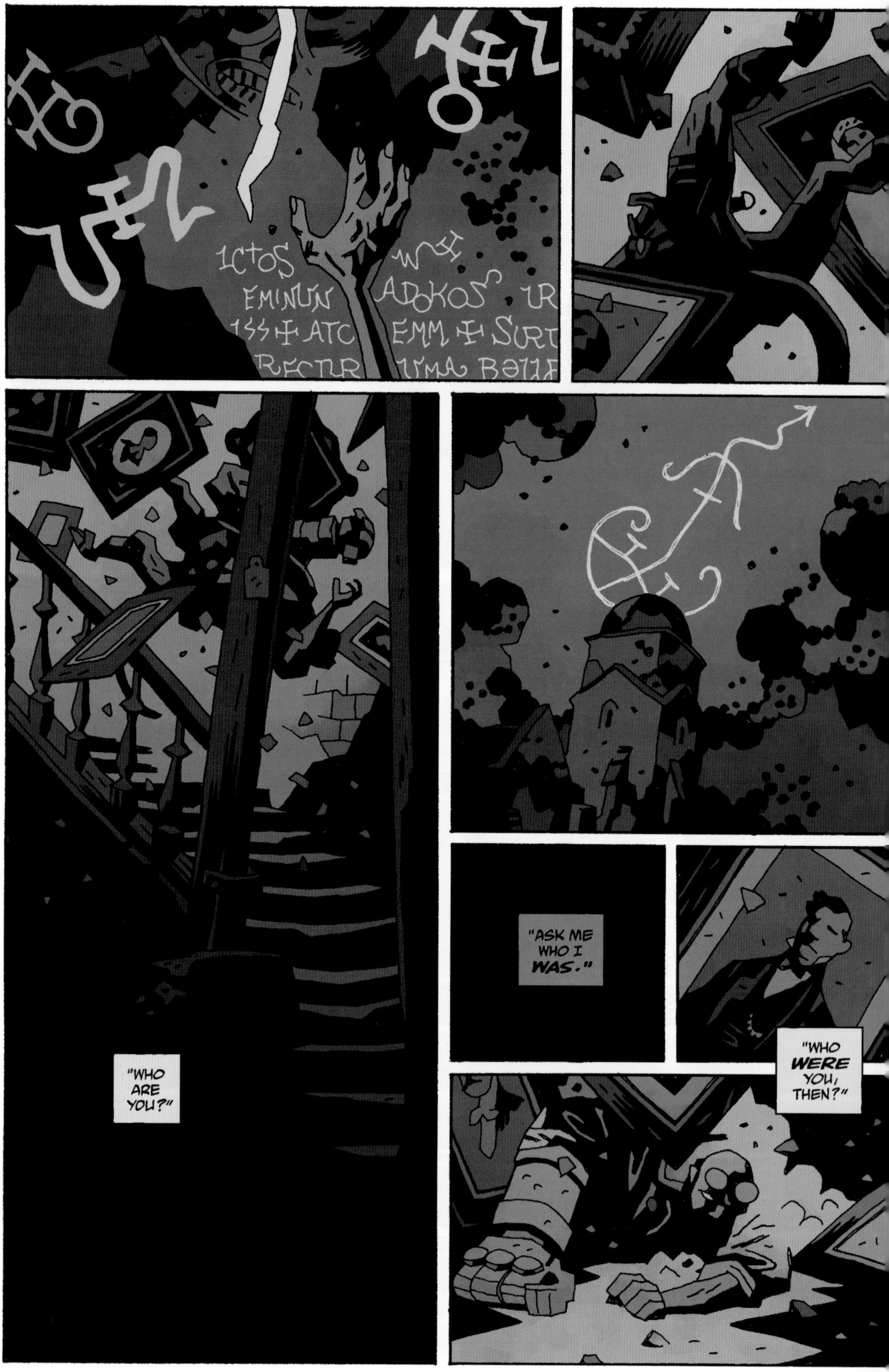
"WHO ARE YOU?"
"ASK ME WHO I WAS."
"WHO WERE YOU, THEN?"

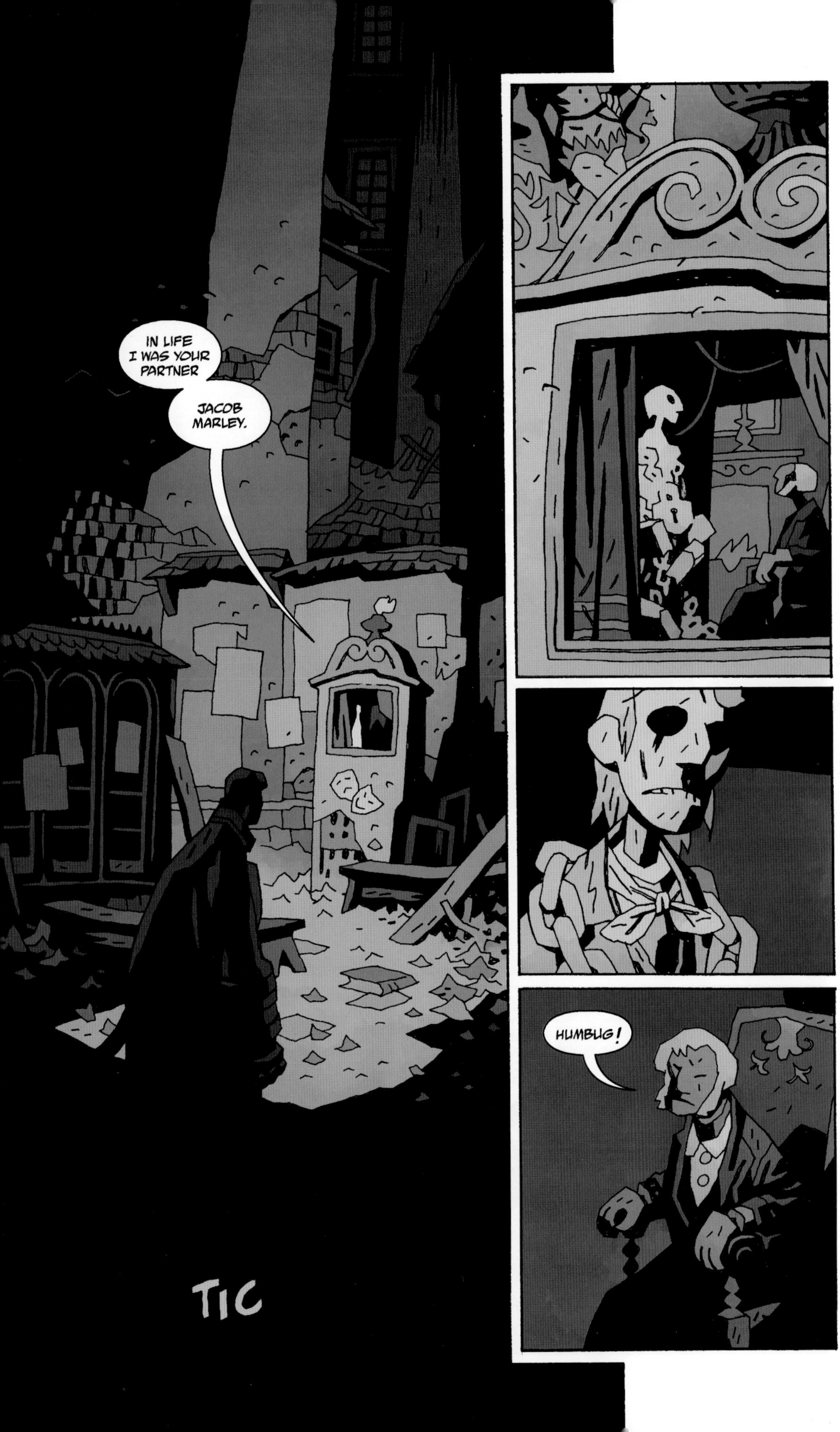

IN LIFE I WAS YOUR PARTNER
JACOB MARLEY.
TIC
HUMBUG!

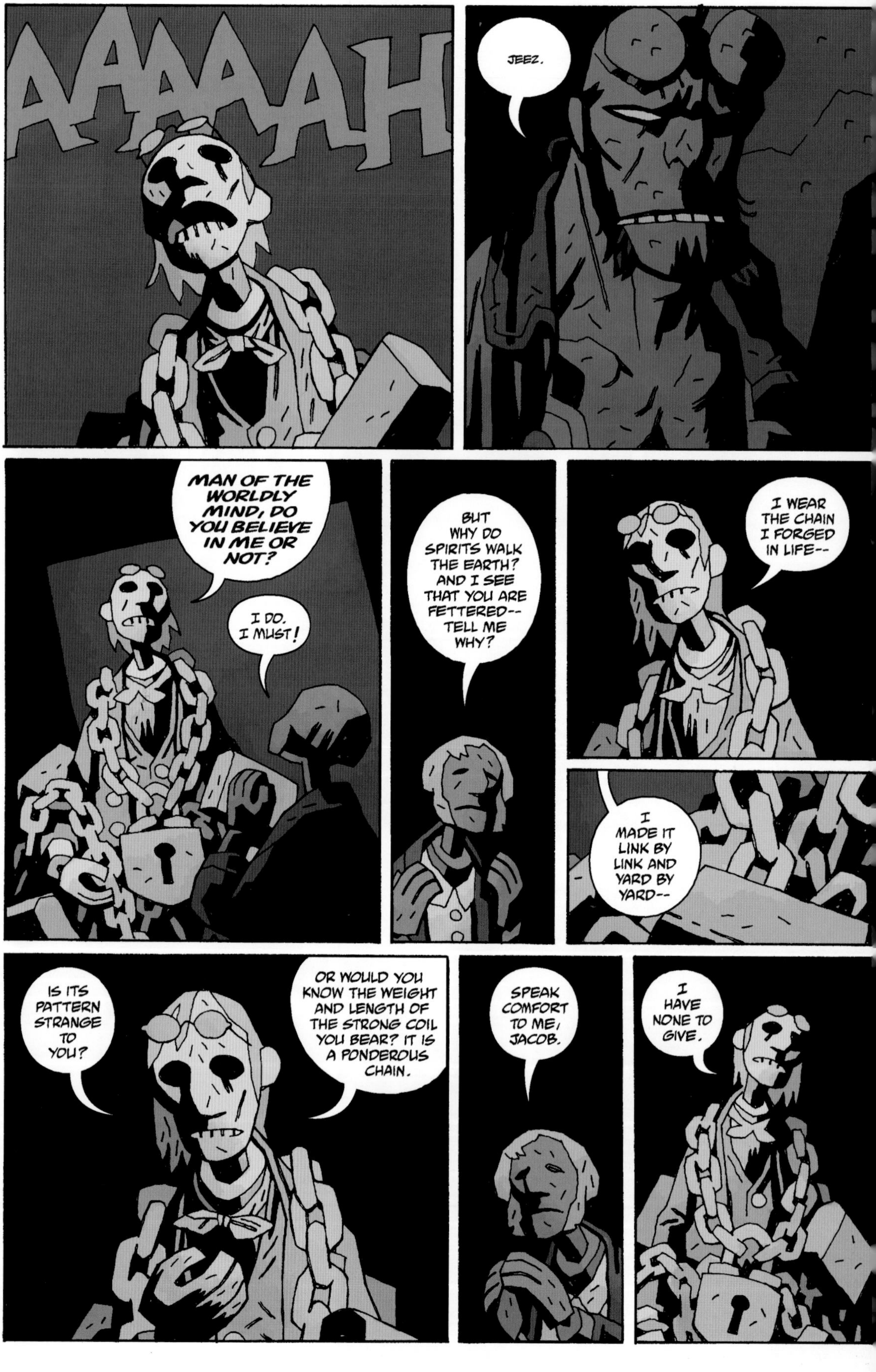
AAAAAH
JEEZ.
MAN OF THE WORLDLY MIND, DO YOU BELIEVE IN ME OR NOT?
I DO. I MUST!
BUT WHY DO SPIRITS WALK THE EARTH? AND I SEE THAT YOU ARE FETTERED-- TELL ME WHY?
I WEAR THE CHAIN I FORGED IN LIFE--
I MADE IT LINK BY LINK AND YARD BY YARD--
IS ITS PATTERN STRANGE TO YOU?
OR WOULD YOU KNOW THE WEIGHT AND LENGTH OF THE STRONG COIL YOU BEAR? IT IS A PONDEROUS CHAIN.
SPEAK COMFORT TO ME, JACOB.
I HAVE NONE TO GIVE.

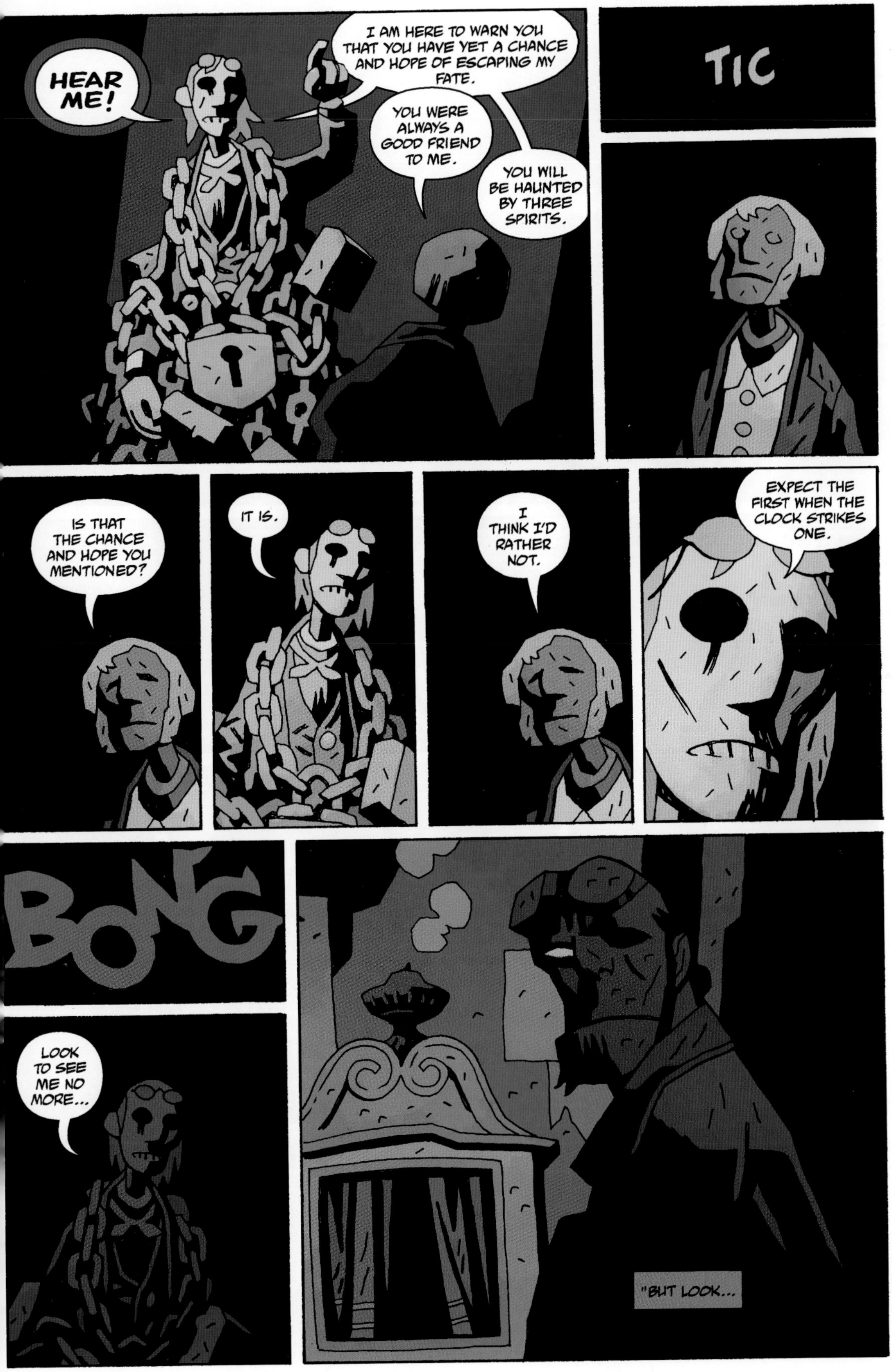
HEAR ME!
I AM HERE TO WARN YOU THAT YOU HAVE YET A CHANCE AND HOPE OF ESCAPING MY FATE.
YOU WERE ALWAYS A GOOD FRIEND TO ME.
YOU WILL BE HAUNTED BY THREE SPIRITS.
TIC
IS THAT THE CHANCE AND HOPE YOU MENTIONED?
IT IS.
I THINK I'D RATHER NOT.
EXPECT THE FIRST WHEN THE CLOCK STRIKES ONE.
BONG
LOOK TO SEE ME NO MORE...
"BUT LOOK...

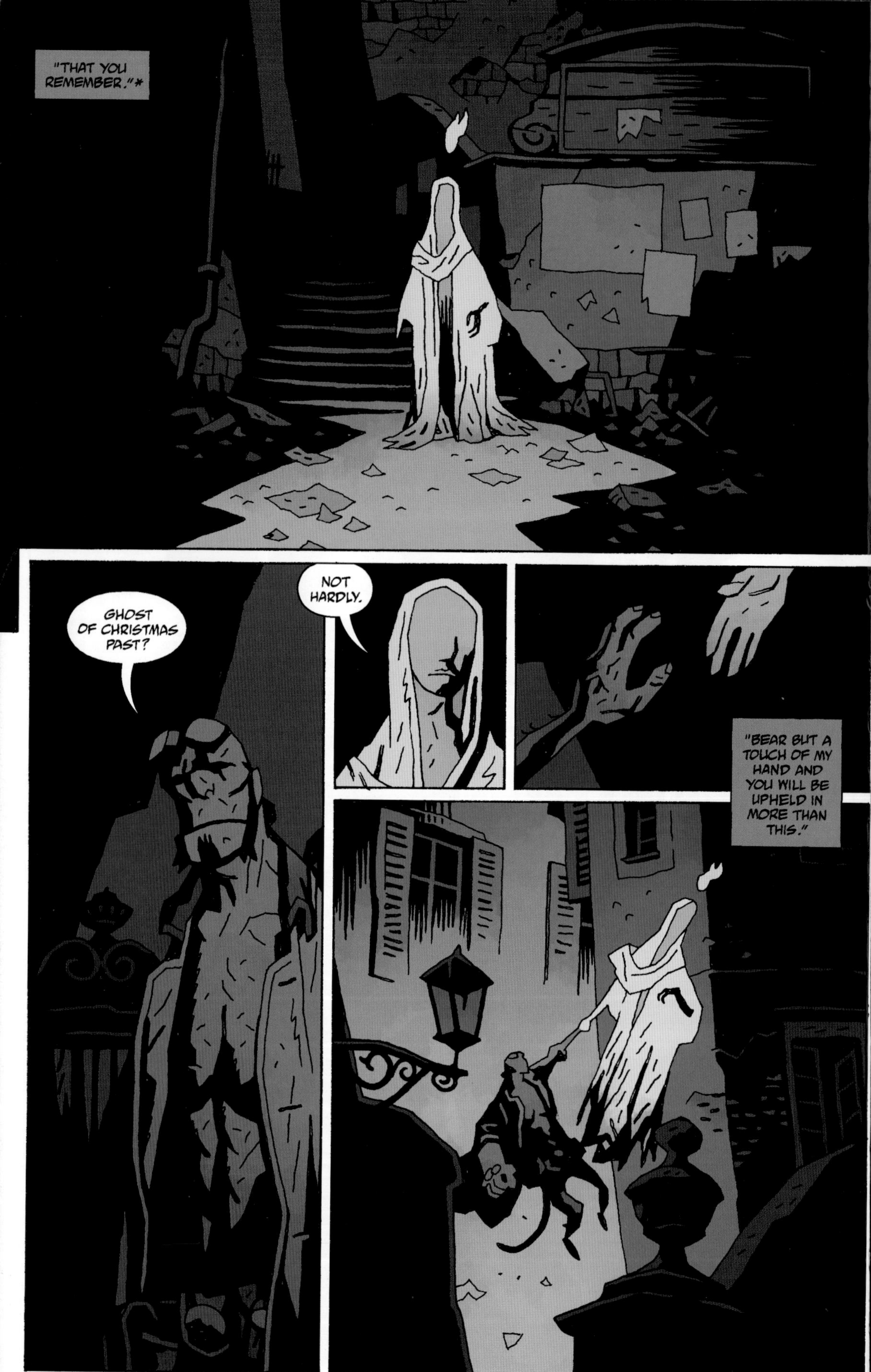
"THAT YOU REMEMBER."*
GHOST OF CHRISTMAS PAST?
NOT HARDLY.
"BEAR BUT A TOUCH OF MY HAND AND YOU WILL BE UPHELD IN MORE THAN THIS."

*PUPPET SHOW FREELY ADAPTED FROM
A CHRISTMAS CAROL BY CHARLES DICKENS

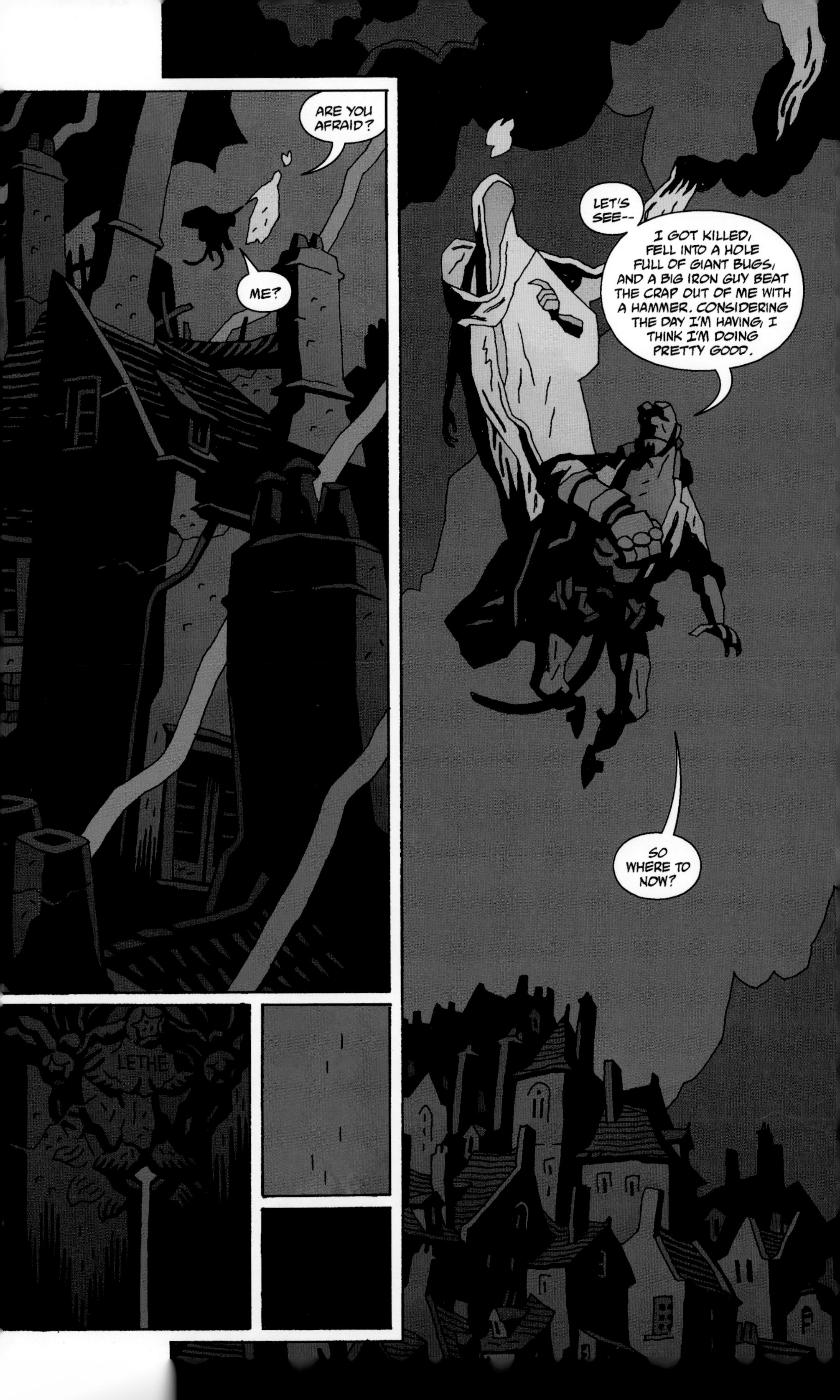
ARE YOU AFRAID?
ME?
LET'S SEE--
I GOT KILLED, FELL INTO A HOLE FULL OF GIANT BUGS, AND A BIG IRON GUY BEAT THE CRAP OUT OF ME WITH A HAMMER. CONSIDERING THE DAY I'M HAVING, I THINK I'M DOING PRETTY GOOD.
SO WHERE TO NOW?
LETHE

Next Issue

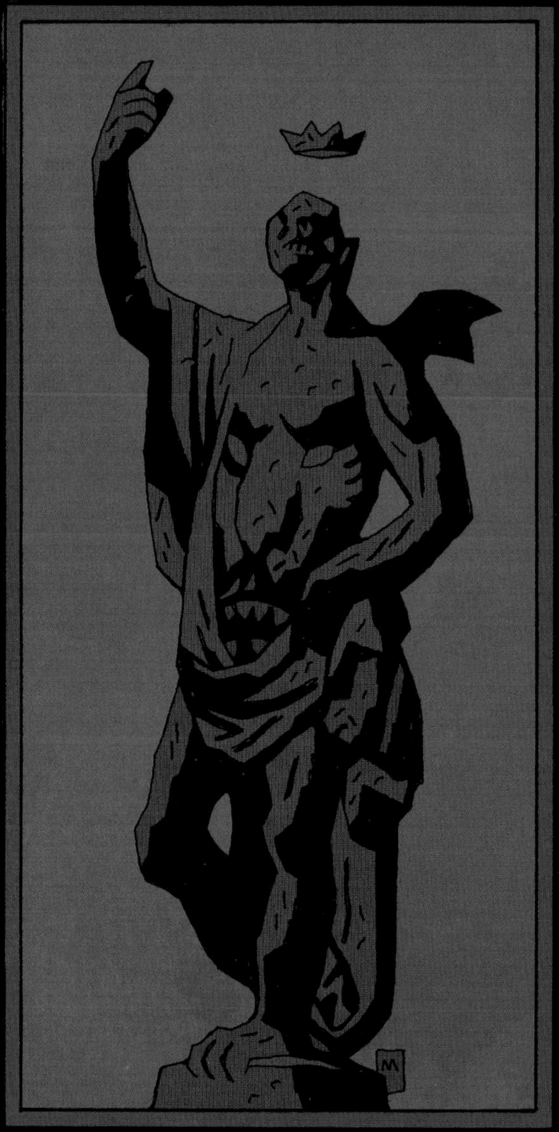

PANDEMONIUM

HELLBOY™

by MIKE MIGNOLA

HELLBOY LIBRARY EDITION VOLUME 1:
Seed of Destruction and Wake the Devil
ISBN 978-1-59307-910-9 | $49.99

HELLBOY LIBRARY EDITION VOLUME 2:
The Chained Coffin and The Right Hand of Doom
ISBN 978-1-59307-989-5 | $49.99

HELLBOY LIBRARY EDITION VOLUME 3:
Conqueror Worm and Strange Places
ISBN 978-1-59582-352-6 | $49.99

HELLBOY LIBRARY EDITION VOLUME 4:
The Crooked Man and the Troll Witch
with Richard Corben and others
ISBN 978-1-59582-658-9 | $49.99

HELLBOY LIBRARY EDITION VOLUME 5:
Darkness Calls and the Wild Hunt
with Duncan Fegredo
ISBN 978-1-59582-886-6 | $49.99

HELLBOY LIBRARY EDITION VOLUME 6:
The Storm and the Fury and The Bride of Hell
with Duncan Fegredo, Richard Corben, Kevin Nowlan, and Scott Hampton
ISBN 978-1-61655-133-9 | $49.99

SEED OF DESTRUCTION
with John Byrne
ISBN 978-1-59307-094-6 | $17.99

WAKE THE DEVIL
ISBN 978-1-59307-095-3 | $17.99

THE CHAINED COFFIN AND OTHERS
ISBN 978-1-59307-091-5 | $17.99

THE RIGHT HAND OF DOOM
ISBN 978-1-59307-093-9 | $17.99

CONQUEROR WORM
ISBN 978-1-59307-092-2 | $17.99

STRANGE PLACES
ISBN 978-1-59307-475-3 | $17.99

THE TROLL WITCH AND OTHERS
with Richard Corben and others
ISBN 978-1-59307-860-7 | $17.99

DARKNESS CALLS
with Duncan Fegredo
ISBN 978-1-59307-896-6 | $19.99

THE WILD HUNT
with Duncan Fegredo
ISBN 978-1-59582-431-8 | $19.99

THE CROOKED MAN AND OTHERS
with Richard Corben
ISBN 978-1-59582-477-6 | $17.99

THE BRIDE OF HELL AND OTHERS
with Richard Corben, Kevin Nowlan, and Scott Hampton
ISBN 978-1-59582-740-1 | $19.99

THE STORM AND THE FURY
with Duncan Fegredo
ISBN 978-1-59582-827-9 | $19.99

HOUSE OF THE LIVING DEAD
with Richard Corben
ISBN 978-1-59582-757-9 | $14.99

THE MIDNIGHT CIRCUS
with Duncan Fegredo
ISBN 978-1-61655-238-1 | $14.99

INTO THE SILENT SEA
with Gary Gianni
ISBN 978-1-50670-143-1 | $14.99

HELLBOY IN MEXICO
with Richard Corben, Fábio Moon, Gabriel Bá, and others
ISBN 978-1-61655-897-0 | $19.99

HELLBOY IN HELL VOLUME 1: THE DESCENT
ISBN 978-1-61655-444-6 | $17.99

HELLBOY IN HELL VOLUME 2: THE DEATH CARD
ISBN 978-1-50670-113-4 | $17.99

HELLBOY: THE FIRST 20 YEARS
ISBN 978-1-61655-353-1 | $19.99

THE ART OF HELLBOY
ISBN 978-1-59307-089-2 | $29.99

HELLBOY II: THE ART OF THE MOVIE
ISBN 978-1-59307-964-2 | $24.99

HELLBOY: THE COMPANION
ISBN 978-1-59307-655-9 | $14.99

HELLBOY: WEIRD TALES
ISBN 978-1-61655-510-8 | $24.99

HELLBOY: MASKS AND MONSTERS
with James Robinson and Scott Benefiel
ISBN 978-1-59582-567-4 | $17.99

HELLBOY AND THE B.P.R.D: 1952
with John Arcudi and Alex Maleev
ISBN 978-1-61655-660-0 | $19.99

HELLBOY AND THE B.P.R.D: 1953
with Chris Roberson, Ben Stenbeck, Paolo Rivera, and Joe Rivera
ISBN 978-1-61655-967-0 | $19.99

THE HELLBOY 100 PROJECT
TPB: ISBN 978-1-61655-932-8 | $12.99
HC: ISBN 978-1-61655-933-5 | $24.99

NOVELS

HELLBOY: EMERALD HELL
By Tom Piccirilli
ISBN 978-1-59582-141-6 | $12.99

HELLBOY: THE ALL-SEEING EYE
By Mark Morris
ISBN 978-1-59582-142-3 | $12.99

HELLBOY: THE FIRE WOLVES
By Tim Lebbon
ISBN 978-1-59582-204-8 | $12.99

HELLBOY: THE ICE WOLVES
By Mark Chadbourn
ISBN 978-1-59582-205-5 | $12.99

SHORT STORIES

Illustrated by Mike Mignola

HELLBOY: ODDER JOBS
By Frank Darabont, Charles de Lint, Guillermo del Toro, and others
ISBN 978-1-59307-226-1 | $14.99

HELLBOY: ODDEST JOBS
By Joe R. Lansdale, China Miéville, and others
ISBN 978-1-59307-944-4 | $14.99

AVAILABLE AT YOUR LOCAL COMICS SHOP OR BOOKSTORE! • To find a comics shop in your area, call 1-888-266-4226.
For more information or to order direct visit DarkHorse.com or call 1-800-862-0052 Mon.–Fri. 9 AM to 5 PM Pacific Time.
Prices and availability subject to change without notice.

DarkHorse.com

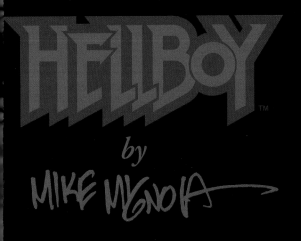

Also by MIKE MIGNOLA

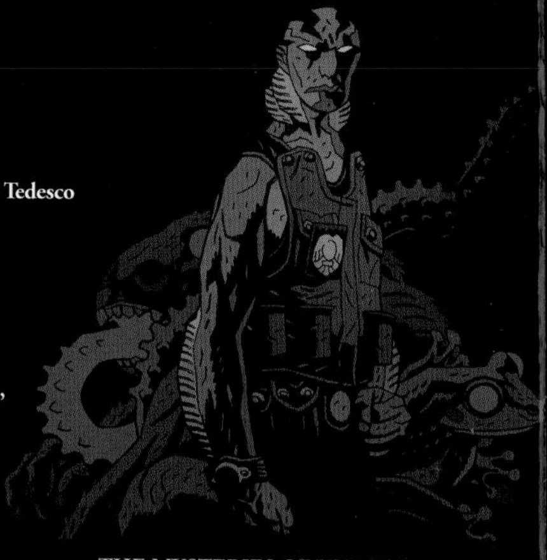

B.P.R.D.
PLAGUE OF FROGS
Volume 1
with Chris Golden, Guy Davis, and others
TPB: ISBN 978-1-59582-675-6 | $19.99

Volume 2
with John Arcudi, Davis, and others
TPB: ISBN 978-1-59582-676-3 | $24.99

Volume 3
with Arcudi and Davis
TPB: ISBN 978-1-61655-622-8 | $24.99

Volume 4
with Arcudi and Davis
TPB: ISBN 978-1-61655-641-9 | $24.99

1946–1948
with Joshua Dysart, Paul Azaceta, Fábio Moon, Gabriel Bá, Max Fiumara, and Arcudi
ISBN 978-1-61655-646-4 | $34.99

BEING HUMAN
with Scott Allie, Arcudi, Davis, and others
ISBN 978-1-59582-756-2 | $17.99

VAMPIRE
with Moon and Bá
ISBN 978-1-61655-196-4 | $19.99

B.P.R.D. HELL ON EARTH
NEW WORLD
with Arcudi and Davis
ISBN 978-1-59582-707-4 | $19.99

GODS AND MONSTERS
with Arcudi, Davis, and Tyler Crook
ISBN 978-1-59582-822-4 | $19.99

RUSSIA
with Arcudi, Crook, and Duncan Fegredo
ISBN 978-1-59582-946-7 | $19.99

THE DEVIL'S ENGINE AND THE LONG DEATH
with Arcudi, Crook, and James Harren
ISBN 978-1-59582-981-8 | $19.99

THE PICKENS COUNTY HORROR AND OTHERS
with Allie, Jason Latour, Harren, and Max Fiumara
ISBN 978-1-61655-140-7 | $19.99

THE RETURN OF THE MASTER
with Arcudi and Crook
ISBN 978-1-61655-193-3 | $19.99

A COLD DAY IN HELL
with Arcudi, Peter Snejbjerg, and Laurence Campbell
ISBN 978-1-61655-199-5 | $19.99

THE REIGN OF THE BLACK FLAME
with Arcudi and Harren
ISBN 978-1-61655-471-2 | $19.99

THE DEVIL'S WINGS
with Arcudi, Campbell, Joe Querio, and Crook
ISBN 978-1-61655-617-4 | $19.99

LAKE OF FIRE
with Arcudi and Crook
ISBN 978-1-61655-402-6 | $19.99

FLESH AND STONE
with Arcudi and Harren
ISBN 978-1-61655-762-1 | $19.99

METAMORPHOSIS
with Arcudi, Snejbjerg, and Julián Totino Tedesco
ISBN 978-1-61655-794-2 | $19.99

END OF DAYS
with Arcudi and Campbell
ISBN 978-1-61655-910-6 | $19.99

THE EXORCIST
with Cameron Stewart, Chris Roberson, and Mike Norton
ISBN 978-1-50670-011-3 | $19.99

COMETH THE HOUR
with Arcudi and Campbell
ISBN 978-1-50670-131-8 | $19.99

ABE SAPIEN
THE DROWNING
with Jason Shawn Alexander
ISBN 978-1-59582-185-0 | $17.99

THE DEVIL DOES NOT JEST AND OTHER STORIES
with Arcudi, Harren, and others
ISBN 978-1-59582-925-2 | $17.99

DARK AND TERRIBLE AND THE NEW RACE OF MAN
with Allie, Arcudi, Sebastián Fiumara, and Max Fiumara
ISBN 978-1-61655-284-8 | $19.99

THE SHAPE OF THINGS TO COME
with Allie, S. Fiumara, and M. Fiumara
ISBN 978-1-61655-443-9 | $19.99

SACRED PLACES
with Allie, S. Fiumara, and M. Fiumara
ISBN 978-1-61655-515-3 | $19.99

A DARKNESS SO GREAT
with Allie, S. Fiumara, and M. Fiumara
ISBN 978-1-61655-656-3 | $19.99

THE SECRET FIRE
with Allie, S. Fiumara, and M. Fiumara
ISBN 978-1-61655-891-8 | $19.99

THE DESOLATE SHORE
with Allie, S. Fiumara, and M. Fiumara
ISBN 978-1-50670-031-1 | $19.99

LOBSTER JOHNSON
THE IRON PROMETHEUS
with Jason Armstrong
ISBN 978-1-59307-975-8 | $17.99

THE BURNING HAND
with Arcudi and Tonci Zonjic
ISBN 978-1-61655-031-8 | $17.99

SATAN SMELLS A RAT
with Arcudi, Fiumara, Querio, Wilfredo Torres, and Kevin Nowlan
ISBN 978-1-61655-203-9 | $18.99

GET THE LOBSTER
with Arcudi and Zonjic
ISBN 978-1-61655-505-4 | $19.99

WITCHFINDER
IN THE SERVICE OF ANGELS
with Ben Stenbeck
ISBN 978-1-59582-483-7 | $17.99

LOST AND GONE FOREVER
with Arcudi and John Severin
ISBN 978-1-59582-794-4 | $17.99

THE MYSTERIES OF UNLAND
with Kim Newman, Maura McHugh, and Crook
ISBN 978-1-61655-630-3 | $19.99

CITY OF THE DEAD
with Roberson and Stenbeck
ISBN 978-1-50670-166-0 | $19.99

FRANKENSTEIN UNDERGROUND
with Stenbeck
ISBN 978-1-61655-782-9 | $19.99

JOE GOLEM: OCCULT DETECTIVE—
THE RAT CATCHER & THE SUNKEN DEAD
with Golden and Patric Reynolds
ISBN 978-1-61655-964-9 | $24.99

BALTIMORE
THE PLAGUE SHIPS
with Golden and Stenbeck
ISBN 978-1-59582-677-0 | $24.99

THE CURSE BELLS
with Golden and Stenbeck
ISBN 978-1-59582-674-9 | $24.99

A PASSING STRANGER AND OTHER STORIES
with Golden and Stenbeck
ISBN 978-1-61655-182-7 | $24.99

CHAPEL OF BONES
with Golden and Stenbeck
ISBN 978-1-61655-328-9 | $24.99

EMPTY GRAVES
with Golden and Bergting
ISBN 978-1-50670-042-7 | $24.99

THE APOSTLE AND THE WITCH OF HARJU
with Golden, Stenbeck, and Peter Bergting
ISBN 978-1-61655-618-1 | $24.99

THE CULT OF THE RED KING
with Golden and Bergting
ISBN 978-1-61655-821-5 | $24.99

NOVELS
LOBSTER JOHNSON: THE SATAN FACTORY
with Thomas E. Sniegoski
ISBN 978-1-59582-203-1 | $12.95

JOE GOLEM AND THE DROWNING CITY
with Golden
ISBN 978-1-59582-971-9 | $99.99

BALTIMORE; OR, THE STEADFAST TIN SOLDIER & THE VAMPIRE
with Golden
ISBN 978-1-61655-803-1 | $12.99

AVAILABLE AT YOUR LOCAL COMICS SHOP OR BOOKSTORE! • To find a comics shop in your area, call 1-888-266-4226.
For more information or to order direct visit DarkHorse.com or call 1-800-862-0052 Mon.–Fri. 9 AM to 5 PM Pacific Time.
Prices and availability subject to change without notice.

DARK HORSE BOOKS
DarkHorse.com